First Workshop on Language Technology for Equality, Diversity and Inclusion (LT-EDI-2021)

Online
19 April 2021

ISBN: 978-1-7138-2970-6

Printed from e-media with permission by:

Curran Associates, Inc.
57 Morehouse Lane
Red Hook, NY 12571

Some format issues inherent in the e-media version may also appear in this print version.

Association for Computational Linguistics
209 N. Eighth Street
Stroudsburg, Pennsylvania 18360

Phone: 1-570-476-8006
Fax: 1-570-476-0860

acl@aclweb.org

Additional copies of this publication are available from:

Curran Associates, Inc.
57 Morehouse Lane
Red Hook, NY 12571 USA
Phone: 845-758-0400
Fax: 845-758-2633
Email: curran@proceedings.com
Web: www.proceedings.com

LT-EDI EACL 2021

First Workshop on Language Technology for Equality, Diversity and Inclusion (LT-EDI-2021)

Proceedings of the Workshop

April 19, 2021
Online

Preface

Equality, Diversity and Inclusion (EDI) is an important agenda across every field in the world. Language as a major part of communication should be inclusive and treat everyone equally. The internet community that uses language technology has a direct impact on people across the globe. EDI is crucial to make everyone valued and included, so it is necessary to build language technology that serves this purpose. Our workshop brings together researchers to research into inclusivity of gender, racial, sexual orientation, persons with disability, and other minorities in language technologies with the aim to build and use datasets addressing the concerns of EDI.

Organizing Committee

Bharathi Raja Chakravarthi, National University of Ireland Galway
John P. McCrae, National University of Ireland Galway
Manel Zarrouk, Institut Galilee Universite Paris 13
Kalika Bali, Microsoft Research India
Paul Buitelaar, National University of Ireland Galway

Programme Committee

Adeep Hande, Indian Institute of Information Technology Tiruchirappalli
Aline Villavicencio, University of Sheffield, United Kingdom
Alla Rozovskaya, Queens College (CUNY), United States of America
Bianca Pereira, National University of Ireland Galway, Ireland
Christiane D. Fellbaum, Princeton University, United States of America
Dhivya Chinnappa, Thomson Reuters, United States of America
Emily Bender, University of Washington, United States of America
Emily Prudhommeaux, Boston College, United States of America
Eswari Rajagopal, National Institute of Technology Tiruchirappalli, India
Eva Schaeffer-Lacroix, Universite INSPE de lacademie de Paris
Hung-Yu Kao, National Cheng Kung University, Taiwan
Jamin Shin, Hong Kong University of Science and Technology, China
Kathleen McKeown, Columbia University, United States of America
Kevin Patrick Scannell, Saint Louis University, Missouri, United States of America
Marissa Griesel, University of South Africa, South Africa
Mathieu dAquin, National University of Ireland Galway, Ireland
Manikandan Ravikiran, Hitachi Research and Development, India
Marta R. Costajussa, Universitat Politecnica de Catalunya
Menno Van Zaanen, North-West University, South Africa
Monojit Choudhury, Microsoft Research, India
Pascale Fung, Hong Kong University of Science Technology, Hong Kong
Rachael Tatmam, Kaggle, United States of America
Ruba Priyadharshini, ULTRA Arts and Science College, Madurai, India
Sajeetha Thavareesan, Eastern University, Sri Lanka
Senthil Kumar B, SSN College of Engineering, India
Shubhanker Banerjee, National University of Ireland Galway
Thenmozhi D. Sri Sivasubramaniya Nadar College of Engineering, India
Thomas Mandl, Universitat Hildesheim, Germany
Viktor Hangya, Ludwig Maximilian University of Munich, Germany

Table of Contents

Conference Program

Monday, April 19, 2021

9:00–10:00 Invited Talk

10:00–11:00 Paper Session-I

10:00–10:20 *Impact of COVID-19 in Natural Language Processing Publications: a Disaggregated Study in Gender, Contribution and Experience*
Christine Basta and Marta R. Costa-jussa

10:20–10:40 *Adapting the Portuguese Braille System to Formal Semantics*
Luís Filipe Cunha

10:40–11:00 *Cross-Lingual Transfer Learning for Hate Speech Detection*
Irina Bigoulaeva, Viktor Hangya and Alexander Fraser

11:00–11:30 Coffee Break

11:30–13:00 Paper Session II

11:30–11:50 *hBERT + BiasCorp - Fighting Racism on the Web*
Olawale Onabola, Zhuang Ma, Xie Yang, Benjamin Akera, Ibraheem Abdulrahman, Jia Xue, Dianbo Liu and Yoshua Bengio

11:50–12:10 *An Overview of Fairness in Data – Illuminating the Bias in Data Pipeline*
Senthil Kumar B, Aravindan Chandrabose and Bharathi Raja Chakravarthi

12:10–12:30 *GEPSA, a tool for monitoring social challenges in digital press*
Iñaki San Vicente, Xabier Saralegi and Nerea Zubia

12:30–12:50 *Finding Spoiler Bias in Tweets by Zero-shot Learning and Knowledge Distilling from Neural Text Simplification*
Avi Bleiweiss

13:00–14:00 Lunch Break

14:00–16:00 Poster Session

14:00–16:00 *Findings of the Shared Task on Hope Speech Detection for Equality, Diversity, and Inclusion*
Bharathi Raja Chakravarthi and Vigneshwaran Muralidaran

14:00–16:00 *dhivya-hope-detection@LT-EDI-EACL2021: Multilingual Hope Speech Detection for Code-mixed and Transliterated Texts*
Dhivya Chinnappa

14:00–16:00 *KU_NLP@LT-EDI-EACL2021: A Multilingual Hope Speech Detection for Equality, Diversity, and Inclusion using Context Aware Embeddings*
Junaida M K and Ajees A P

14:00–16:00 *EDIOne@LT-EDI-EACL2021: Pre-trained Transformers with Convolutional Neural Networks for Hope Speech Detection.*
Suman Dowlagar and Radhika Mamidi

14:00–16:00 *ssn_diBERTsity@LT-EDI-EACL2021:Hope Speech Detection on multilingual YouTube comments via transformer based approach*
Arunima S, Akshay Ramakrishnan, Avantika Balaji, Thenmozhi D. and Senthil Kumar B

14:00–16:00 *IIITT@LT-EDI-EACL2021-Hope Speech Detection: There is always hope in Transformers*
Karthik Puranik, Adeep Hande, Ruba Priyadharshini, Sajeetha Thavareesan and Bharathi Raja Chakravarthi

14:00–16:00 *IIIT_DWD@LT-EDI-EACL2021: Hope Speech Detection in YouTube multilingual comments*
SUNIL SAUMYA and ANKIT KUMAR MISHRA

14:00–16:00 *IRNLP_DAIICT@LT-EDI-EACL2021: Hope Speech detection in Code Mixed text using TF-IDF Char N-grams and MuRIL*
Bhargav Dave, Shripad Bhat and Prasenjit Majumder

14:00–16:00 *ZYJ@LT-EDI-EACL2021:XLM-RoBERTa-Based Model with Attention for Hope Speech Detection*
Yingjia Zhao and Xin Tao

14:00–16:00 *TEAM HUB@LT-EDI-EACL2021: Hope Speech Detection Based On Pre-trained Language Model*
Bo Huang and Yang Bai

Monday, April 19, 2021 (continued)

14:00–16:00 *cs_english@LT-EDI-EACL2021: Hope Speech Detection Based On Fine-tuning ALBERT Model*
shi chen and bing kong

14:00–16:00 *GCDH@LT-EDI-EACL2021: XLM-RoBERTa for Hope Speech Detection in English, Malayalam, and Tamil*
Stefan Ziehe, Franziska Pannach and Aravind Krishnan

14:00–16:00 *TeamUNCC@LT-EDI-EACL2021: Hope Speech Detection using Transfer Learning with Transformers*
Khyati Mahajan, Erfan Al-Hossami and Samira Shaikh

14:00–16:00 *Autobots@LT-EDI-EACL2021: One World, One Family: Hope Speech Detection with BERT Transformer Model*
Sunil Gundapu and Radhika Mamidi

14:00–16:00 *Amrita@LT-EDI-EACL2021: Hope Speech Detection on Multilingual Text*
Thara S, Ravi teja Tasubilli and Kothamasu Sai rahul

14:00–16:00 *Hopeful Men@LT-EDI-EACL2021: Hope Speech Detection Using Indic Transliteration and Transformers*
Ishan Sanjeev Upadhyay, Nikhil E, Anshul Wadhawan and Radhika Mamidi

14:00–16:00 *Hopeful NLP@LT-EDI-EACL2021: Finding Hope in YouTube Comment Section*
Vasudev Awatramani

14:00–16:00 *NLP-CUET@LT-EDI-EACL2021: Multilingual Code-Mixed Hope Speech Detection using Cross-lingual Representation Learner*
Eftekhar Hossain, Omar Sharif and Mohammed Moshiul Hoque

14:00–16:00 *Simon @ LT-EDI-EACL2021: Detecting Hope Speech with BERT*
Qinyu Que

14:00–16:00 *MUCS@LT-EDI-EACL2021:CoHope-Hope Speech Detection for Equality, Diversity, and Inclusion in Code-Mixed Texts*
Fazlourrahman Balouchzahi, Aparna B K and H L Shashirekha

14:00–16:00 *Spartans@LT-EDI-EACL2021: Inclusive Speech Detection using Pretrained Language Models*
Megha Sharma and Gaurav Arora

14:00–16:00 *CFILT IIT Bombay@LT-EDI-EACL2021: Hope Speech Detection for Equality, Diversity, and Inclusion using Multilingual Representation fromTransformers*
Pankaj Singh, Prince Kumar and Pushpak Bhattacharyya

Monday, April 19, 2021 (continued)

14:00–16:00 *IIITK@LT-EDI-EACL2021: Hope Speech Detection for Equality, Diversity, and Inclusion in Tamil , Malayalam and English*
Nikhil Ghanghor, Rahul Ponnusamy, Prasanna Kumar Kumaresan, Ruba Priyadharshini, Sajeetha Thavareesan and Bharathi Raja Chakravarthi

16:00–17:00 Closing Remarks

Impact of COVID-19 in Natural Language Processing Publications: a Disaggregated Study in Gender, Contribution and Experience

Christine Basta and Marta R. Costa-jussà
TALP Research Center, Universitat Politècnica de Catalunya, 08034 Barcelona
{christine.raouf.saad.basta,marta.ruiz}@upc.edu

Abstract

This study sheds light on the effects of COVID-19 in the particular field of Computational Linguistics and Natural Language Processing within Artificial Intelligence. We provide an inter-sectional study on gender, contribution, and experience that considers one school year (from August 2019 to August 2020) as a pandemic year. August is included twice for the purpose of an inter-annual comparison.

While there has been an increasing trend in publications during the crisis, the results show that the ratio between female authors' publications and male authors' publications decreased. This only reduces the importance of the female role in the scientific contributions of computational linguistics (it is now far below its peak of 0.24). The pandemic has a significantly negative effect on female senior researchers' production in the first position of authors (maximum work), followed by the female junior researchers in the last position of authors (supervision or collaborative work).

1 Introduction

The pandemic situation is a burden for everyone. Given the uncertainty and pressure of the situation, it is expected to have a significant impact on the lives of researchers. However, it appears that women are bearing considerable burdens due to the social impact of the virus. According to the Scientist article [1], the pandemic exacerbates existing inequalities, with female researchers' output increasing less during the pandemic. This is due to several factors: housework, children staying at home, and many other factors. In our paper, we aim to investigate the effects on the productivity of female researchers during the pandemic in Natural Processing Field (NLP). Women have long been underrepresented in NLP research. This fact leads to the question of whether the pandemic affects female NLP researchers more. We focus on testing the following hypothesis:

1. Although the pandemic was a stressful period, it has increased the scientific production, since distance-based working favours writing.
2. As first authors, production has decreased among the senior women, considering that they are more susceptible to doing housework and taking care of children (or elder people) at home.
3. In a collaborative work, while working remotely, the contributions of junior women seems to be disregarded and they are not included unless their contribution is predominant. This decreased of scientific production of the junior women as last authors.

2 Impact Statement

This work is doing a binary gender study. In that sense, we are simplifying the real gender spectrum (D'Ignazio and Klein, 2018). Our motivation is because we want to study the effect of COVID-19 in women, in the line of previous works (Schluter, 2018).

By highlighting the role of women in scientific contributions, we emphasize the importance of strengthening the educational programs, scientific grants and support that motivate woman in NLP and in STEM (science, technology, engineering and mathematics) in general.

[1] https://www.the-scientist.com/news-opinion/gender-gap-in-research-output-widens-during-pandemic-67665

Proceedings of the First Workshop on Language Technology for Equality, Diversity and Inclusion, pages 1–6
April 19, 2021.

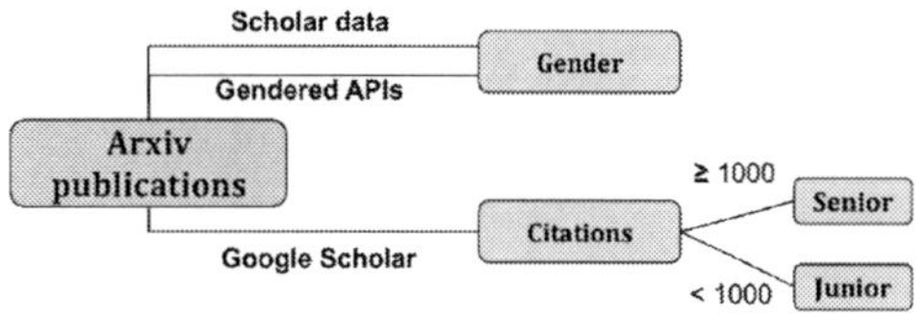

Figure 1: Data diagram

3 Related work

Several studies that show the imbalance between females/males emerge with different objectives in NLP. We can assume three main categories that show imbalances: in our data, in the automatic representations from our systems and in the professional level. Our study falls into this third category.

Data. Similar to the study of the number of video frames in computer vision, e.g., (Madaan et al., 2018b), which analyses the number of dedicated frames for women and men, there is a study in NLP that examines the gender-specific references in the literature (Madaan et al., 2018a). This study shows a higher disproportion in mentioning men more than women. More than the disproportion, it is the role that men are usually associated with "high-level" occupations compared to women who are associated with more "care-giving" occupations.

Automatic Representations. Our systems have shown that they perpetuate and amplify biases (Bolukbasi et al., 2016; Caliskan et al., 2017) as examples in word representation. We have also seen biases in applications such as machine translation (Prates et al., 2020), sentiment analysis (Kiritchenko and Mohammad, 2018) and others.

Professional level. A deep study of the *glass ceiling* (Schluter, 2018) shows profound evidence of the existence of such limitations. It is worth mentioning that while doing our study, there were parallel studies in several fields which have led to similar conclusions (Büyüm et al., 2020; Coleman et al., 2021; Ancochea et al., 2020; Ruiz-Frutos et al., 2021; Spagnolo et al., 2020; Squazzoni et al., 2020; Sohrabi et al., 2021; King and Frederickson, 2020).

4 Data

In this section, we describe the procedure for extracting the data that allows us to discuss the impact of COVID-19 on the scientific production of NLP papers in terms of gender, contribution and experience. This data is available to other researchers[2].

[2]https://github.com/ChristineBasta/Cov19PubStats

We select a source of papers, extract them, and classify the authors according to gender and experience. The contribution is measured according to the criteria of the first author and the last author: The first authors are the maximum contributors and the last authors are the collaborators or supervisors. We show a block diagram of the entire data extraction process in Figure 1 and explain the details in the following sections.

4.1 Paper selection

We have decided to get a source of publications that can be easily updated daily and overall months. Therefore, Arxiv[3], an open access archive for scientific articles, was chosen as a source with such criteria. We have extracted from the Arxiv NLP publications of the years 2019 and 2020 from August 2019 to August 2020. In order to extract those of the NLP category, we specified the category *cs.cl*, which corresponds to the field of Computer Science and Computation and Language. This category corresponds to the category ACM i.2.7 (Natural Language Processing). We found about 6760 unique articles, starting in August 2019. Given this data, we now have to infer gender and experience to the authors of the papers. The following sections describe how to infer the gender of the names and how to classify them on the experience level.

4.2 Inferring gender of names

The study (Mohammad, 2020b) examines the citations and authors of the publications of the ACL anthology. In this dataset, called NLP-scholar, we can find the gender of the first and last authors. Thus, this was the first direction to find out the gender of the authors. To investigate the gender of authors, not available in this dataset, we used two APIs[4,5], which allow extracting the gender of the name to ensure that the gender of the name is correctly recognized. We use the former to predict the names. However, if the name is predicted with less accuracy, we use the latter for verification. It is a difficult task to guess the gender from Chinese names (van de Weijer et al., 2020). While there are open tools that can make this guess[6], we are not aware of any tools for the case of Chinese names written in English. Therefore, we have decided to

[3]https://arxiv.org/

[4]https://genderize.io/

[5]https://pypi.org/project/gender-guesser/

[6]http://www.chinese-tools.com

neglect them when they do not exist in the NLP-scholar dataset.

4.3 Senior and Junior classification

Google Scholar is a free web search engine for academic literature to access metadata for authors and publications. Google Scholar does not provide an official API to extract information about authors, but we have used scholarly[7] to extract citations of the authors from their Google Scholar profile pages. A Google Scholar Profile page is the page where authors can include their papers (citations are included) and their affiliations (Mohammad, 2020a). Seniors are classified as authors with more than 1000 citations, while juniors are those with less than 1000 citations. Sometimes the same author name can have several profile pages. Accordingly, we have performed a manual inspection to ensure that the interests of the extracted author include a related field, e.g. 'computer science', 'Natural Language Processing', etc.

5 Discussion

Our discussion will target solving the hypothesis raised in section 1 together with additional ones.

What is the effect of pandemic on NLP publications? Our study examines the total production of NLP research during the year and the gender distribution. In the figure 2, we observe an increase in the number of both female and male authors during the period from March to July 2020, which confirms *hypothesis 1* from section 1. This may be explained by the fact that scientific work has gained popularity during the pandemic, together with the fact that working from a distance tends to leave more time for writing articles.

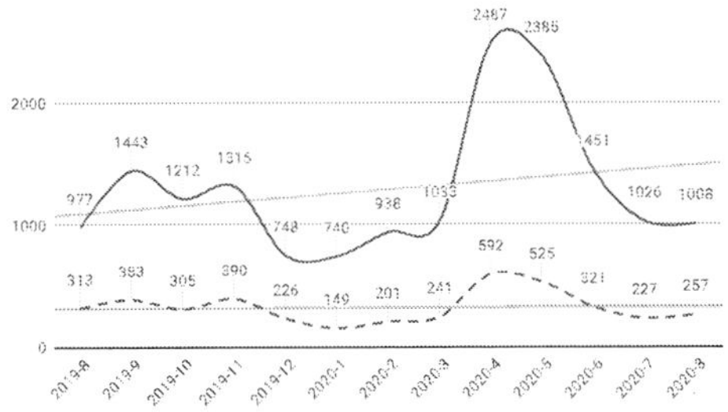

Figure 2: Total number of male (blue) and female (dashed-red) authors per month.

[7]https://pypi.org/project/scholarly/

What is the ratio of females/males contributions? There is a real gap in the contributions of females/males in NLP, which varies between 0.16 and 0.24 in monthly terms (figure 3). Within the period under study, this gap gets larger, which brings us to the next question.

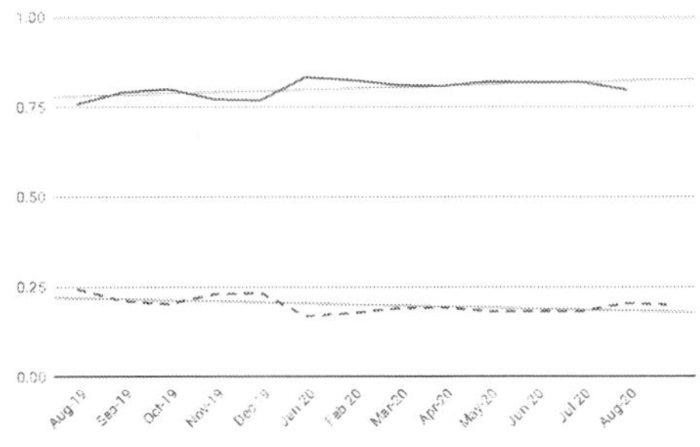

Figure 3: Ratio of men (blue) and women (dashed-red) in total authors

What is the effect of the pandemic in the ratio of females/males contributions? The tendency during this period is the reduction of the females/males ratio. We can analyze the effect in this period in two different ways, but with similar conclusions. First, if we compare production in August 2019 and 2020, the females/males ratio has decreased from 0.24 to 0.20 (figure 3). Second, a comparison of the average production in the months before the first lockdowns[8] (August 2019-February 2020) and for the months of 2020 with intermittent lockdowns (April-August). In the former case, the ratio is 0.21, whereas, in the latter, the ratio is reduced to 0.18.

What is the effect of the pandemic in the ratio of females/males first and last authors contribution? The ratio of females/males first authors is stable (figure 4 (top)), whereas the ratio of females/males last authors decreases slightly (figure 4 (bottom)).

What is the effect of the pandemic on the ratio of females/males first authors contribution related to experience? The ratio of females/males first authors during the studied period increases among juniors (figure 5 (top)) and decreases significantly among seniors (figure 5 (bottom)), confirming *hypothesis 2*. The influence of the pandemic is less relevant for junior female scientists than for senior female researchers. This reinforces the hypothesis that the productivity of senior female researchers declined. This could be explained due to the combination of "care-giving"/family and professional re-

[8]https://en.wikipedia.org/wiki/COVID-19_pandemic_lockdowns

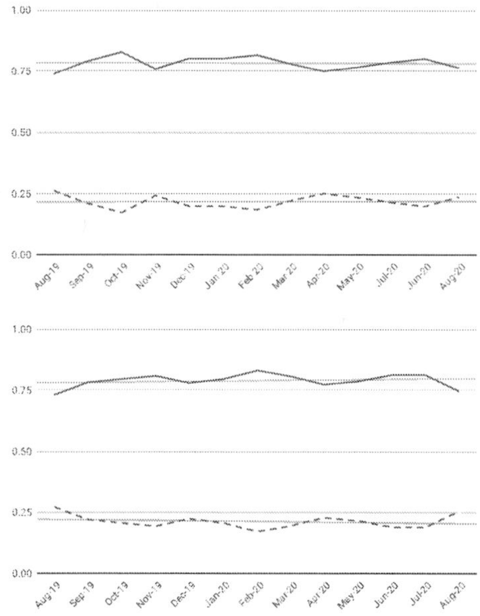

Figure 4: First (top) and last (bottom) authors.

sponsibilities (Zimmer, 2020). However, we want to make clear that there is no proven correlation between care-giving responsibilities and the level of seniority based on number of citations provided.

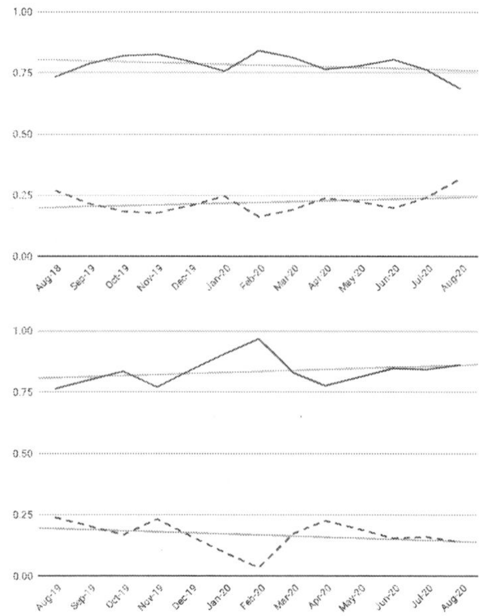

Figure 5: First authors: juniors (top); seniors (bottom)

What is the effect of the pandemic on the ratio of females/males last authors contribution related to experience? Here we see an interesting effect, which is that the ratio females/males ratio decreases in the juniors (figure 6 (top)), which confirms *hypothesis 3*, while in the seniors, the ratio is stable (figure 6 (bottom)). It is noted that there are opposite effects on junior female scientists, depending on whether they occupy the last or the first position in the publication. This is not straightforward to explain, but we can speculate about the following. In the case of leading the work as first authors (figure 5 (top)), the proportion increases compared to men. In contrast, the proportion decreases when women are the last authors. From our point of view, this could show that female junior researchers are less likely to be involved if they do not lead the work, at least during the pandemic. This could be a form of discrimination against women in the sense that some of their collaborations could be neglected. This is pure speculation, as studying the factors which support this hypothesis is out of the scope of the paper. In the case of the senior women, their production is stable as last authors (as opposed to the decline as first authors), possibly due to the fact that they supervise the work at a higher level of detail and this is less demanding in terms of dedication. Therefore, in the case of the last authors and the experience level, we do not see a decline in production during the period under study.

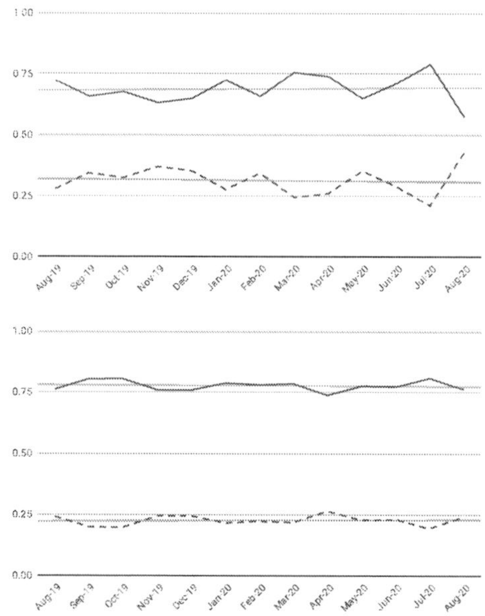

Figure 6: Last authors: juniors (top); seniors (bottom)

6 Conclusions

The main goal here is to estimate the pandemic effect on the NLP production. The impact was studied in terms of gender, contribution and experience. When combining the three criteria, different effects are noted. In the first position (maximum contribution), the females/males proportion increases for juniors and decreases for seniors. This can be explained by the fact that the senior researchers had to take on more responsibility (family, care-giving) during the crisis, which prevented them from keeping up with scientific production. In the last position (supervision or collaboration contribution) the females/males proportion decreases for juniors and is kept stable for seniors. It could be speculated that female junior researchers were more neglected than male junior researchers in terms of small contributions when working at a distance.

7 Room for improvement

Since the data is just for a year, we do not have any previous trends to show seasonal variation patterns. Without countering for seasonal variation we may at least question whether the patterns are for pandemic or part of the natural variation/fluctuation in the system. To give an example, in Figure 2, we see a spike in the number of papers during April-May-June. This could be because we have external factors just as that the camera-ready deadlines are at that time, or anonymity period ends or begins just after this period, etc. To answer these questions, we need to look at the graphs for previous few years.

We are simplifying scientific productivity by assuming that it is equal or proportional to the number of publications. We are aware that publication count is just a proxy of productivity.

However, even taking into account these limitations, our study shows the pervasive gap between women and men (also disaggregated in contribution and experience) in scientific NLP publications during the COVID-19 first year.

Acknowledgements

This work is supported in part by the Catalan Agency for Management of University and Research Grants (AGAUR) through the FI PhD Scholarship.

This work also is supported in part by the project PID2019-107579RB-I00 / AEI / 10.13039/501100011033.

References

Julio Ancochea, Jose L Izquierdo, Joan B Soriano, Savana COVID-19 Research Group, et al. 2020. Evidence of gender bias in the diagnosis and management of covid-19 patients: A big data analysis of electronic health records. *medRxiv*.

Tolga Bolukbasi, Kai-Wei Chang, James Y Zou, Venkatesh Saligrama, and Adam T Kalai. 2016. Man is to computer programmer as woman is to homemaker? debiasing word embeddings. In *Proceedings of Advances in Neural Information Processing Systems 29*, pages 4349–4357.

Ali Murad Büyüm, Cordelia Kenney, Andrea Koris, Laura Mkumba, and Yadurshini Raveendran. 2020. Decolonising global health: if not now, when? *BMJ Global Health*, 5(8):e003394.

Aylin Caliskan, Joanna J. Bryson, and Arvind Narayanan. 2017. Semantics derived automatically from language corpora necessarily contain human biases. *Science*, 356:183–186.

Julia R Coleman, Jad M Abdelsattar, Roan J Glocker, Navin G Vigneshwar, Randi Ryan, Qiong Qiu, Apoorve Nayyar, Michael R Visenio, Cheyenne C Sonntag, Pranit Chotai, et al. 2021. Covid-19 pandemic and the lived experience of surgical residents, fellows, and early-career surgeons in the american college of surgeons. *Journal of the American College of Surgeons*, 232(2):119–135.

Catherine D'Ignazio and Lauren Klein. 2018. Data feminism. MIT Press.

Molly M King and Megan Frederickson. 2020. The pandemic penalty: The gendered effects of covid-19 on scientific productivity.

Svetlana Kiritchenko and Saif M. Mohammad. 2018. Examining gender and race bias in two hundred sentiment analysis systems. In **SEM@NAACL-HLT*.

N. Madaan, Sameep Mehta, S. Mittal, and Ashima Suvarna. 2018a. Judging a book by its description : Analyzing gender stereotypes in the man bookers prize winning fiction. *ArXiv*, abs/1807.10615.

Nishtha Madaan, Sameep Mehta, Taneea Agrawaal, Vrinda Malhotra, Aditi Aggarwal, Yatin Gupta, and Mayank Saxena. 2018b. Analyze, detect and remove gender stereotyping from bollywood movies. volume 81 of *Proceedings of Machine Learning Research*, pages 92–105, New York, NY, USA. PMLR.

Saif M. Mohammad. 2020a. Examining citations of natural language processing literature. In *Proceedings of the 58th Annual Meeting of the Association for Computational Linguistics*, pages 5199–5209, Online. Association for Computational Linguistics.

Saif M. Mohammad. 2020b. NLP scholar: A dataset for examining the state of NLP research. In *Proceedings of The 12th Language Resources and Evaluation Conference*, Marseille, France. European Language Resources Association.

Marcelo O. R. Prates, Pedro H. C. Avelar, and Luis Lamb. 2020. Assessing gender bias in machine translation – a case study with google translate. *Neural Computing and Applications, 32*, page 6363–6381.

Carlos Ruiz-Frutos, Mónica Ortega-Moreno, Regina Allande-Cussó, Sara Domínguez-Salas, Adriano Dias, and Juan Gómez-Salgado. 2021. Health-related factors of psychological distress during the covid-19 pandemic among non-health workers in spain. *Safety Science*, 133:104996.

Natalie Schluter. 2018. The glass ceiling in NLP. In *Proceedings of the 2018 Conference on Empirical Methods in Natural Language Processing*, pages 2793–2798, Brussels, Belgium. Association for Computational Linguistics.

Catrin Sohrabi, Ginimol Mathew, Thomas Franchi, Ahmed Kerwan, Michelle Griffin, Jennick Soleil C Del Mundo, Syed Ahsan Ali, Maliha Agha, and Riaz Agha. 2021. Impact of the coronavirus (covid-19) pandemic on scientific research and implications for clinical academic training–a review. *International Journal of Surgery*.

Jessica Spagnolo, Lara Gautier, Mathieu Seppey, and Nicole Anne D'souza. 2020. Re-thinking global and public health projects during the covid-19 pandemic context: Considerations and recommendations for early-and not-so-early-career researchers. *Social Sciences & Humanities Open*, 2(1):100075.

Flaminio Squazzoni, Giangiacomo Bravo, Francisco Grimaldo, Daniel Garcıa-Costa, Mike Farjam, and Bahar Mehmani. 2020. No tickets for women in the covid-19 race? a study on manuscript submissions and reviews in 2347 elsevier journals during the pandemic. *SSRN Electronic Journal*.

Jeroen van de Weijer, Guangyuan Ren, Joost van de Weijer, Weiyun Wei, and Yumeng Wang. 2020. Gender identification in chinese names. *Lingua*, 234:102759.

Katarina Zimmer. 2020. Gender gap in research output widens during pandemic. *The Scientist*.

Adapting the Portuguese Braille System to Formal Semantics

Luís Filipe Cunha
Faculdade de Letras da Universidade do Porto / Centro de Linguística da Universidade do Porto (Unidade FCT PEst-OE/LIN/UI0022/2011)
Via Panorâmica, s/n, 4150-564, Porto, Portugal
luisfilipeleitecunha@gmail.com

Abstract

Since the seminal work of Richard Montague in the 1970s, mathematical and logic tools have successfully been used to model several aspects of the meaning of natural language. However, visually impaired people continue to face serious difficulties in getting full access to this important instrument. Our paper aims to present a work in progress whose main goal is to provide blind students and researchers with an adequate method to deal with the different resources that are used in formal semantics. In particular, we intend to adapt the Portuguese Braille system in order to accommodate the most common symbols and formulas used in this kind of approach and to develop pedagogical procedures to facilitate its learnability. By making this formalisation compatible with the Braille coding (either traditional and electronic), we hope to help blind people to learn and use this notation, essential to acquire a better understanding of a great number of semantic properties displayed by natural language.

1 Introduction

In their attempt to describe and understand the multiple aspects that underlie the construction of sentential meaning in natural languages, philosophers and semanticists explored different conceptions and methodologies, which gave rise to a large number of theoretical approaches.

A fruitful and promising way to tackle some of the most complex semantic problems, based on a formal notation, was initiated by Richard Montague in the decade of 1970 (see e.g., Montague, 1974). Formal approaches to semantics use logical and mathematical tools to account for various aspects of meaning in natural language. Although the initial task of formal semantics was to describe and resolve ambiguities regarding quantification in the nominal domain, it was rapidly expanded to cover other areas of interest to semanticists, from tense and aspect relations (e.g., Dowty, 1979; Bach, 1986; Moens, 1987; Parsons, 1990) to complex modal descriptions involving the interaction of time, situations, and possible worlds (cf. Portner, 2009 and the papers collected in Kratzer, 2012, for example).

The adoption of formal outlines in the context of the semantic descriptions for natural languages has the advantage of giving rise to unambiguous representations for the meaning of sentences, which facilitate the confirmation or rejection of the suggested hypotheses and postulates.

To illustrate this point, let us consider a simple example, classically discussed in the literature. A sentence like "Every student read a book" is clearly ambiguous between two interpretations: it may mean that every student read a (non-specific) book, whatever it is; or it may mean that there is a (specific) book that every student read. The formal representations in (1) and (2) unambiguously spell out these two readings:

1) $\forall$ x, student(x) $\rightarrow \exists$ y, book(y) & read(x, y)

Proceedings of the First Workshop on Language Technology for Equality, Diversity and Inclusion, pages 7–14
April 19, 2021.

(For every x, if x is a student, then there is a y which is a book so that x read y)

2) $\exists$ y, book(y) & $\forall$ x, student(x) $\rightarrow$ read(x, y) (There is a y which is a book and for every x, if x is a student, then x read y)

book)

In other words, in the representation in (1), the universal quantifier has wide scope over the existential one, which leads to the multiple book reading. Conversely, in (2), it is the existential quantifier that has wide scope over the universal one, giving rise to the unique book reading.

On the other hand, formal representations have been able to transcend the domain of simple sentences. In fact, Kamp & Reyle's (1993) Discourse Representation Theory (DRT) extends the semantic formalisation to more complex discourses and Asher & Lascarides' (2003) Segmented Discourse Representation Theory (SDRT) even deals with pragmatic-based notions such as those underlying Rhetorical Relations.

Today, formal semantics supports a significant number of theories that describe meaning in natural language. In fact, formal approaches cover almost all areas that traditionally are ascribed to semantic studies, from simple word relations to the intricacies behind discourse structures.

Irrespective of the particularities that characterise the diverse frameworks departing from formal approaches to meaning, there are, nonetheless, some important principles that bring them together. In all cases, predicates are related to their argument(s), i.e., entities that fulfil the predicative relation. Different kinds of operators are introduced in order to model the interactions that arise between the participants in a sentence or even between independent sentences in a discourse.

The variables that may be introduced in a formula correspond to entities of distinct kinds: they can be individuals, intervals of time, situations or (possible) worlds. Besides the predicative relations, entities may interact with a range of operators that include quantifiers, relations between elements and sets of elements or between two sets of elements, or even precedence or overlapping relations in the temporal domain.

Despite its undeniable relevance regarding the semantic studies on recent years, no attempt has been done, at least to our knowledge, to provide visually impaired people with adequate tools that enable them to learn and manage this kind of formalisation.

The main goal of our project is, thus, to explore some ways that could make it possible to blind students and researchers to interact with the most common and widespread representations in formal semantics. To do so, we will make use of the immense potential that is offered to us by the Braille system.

2 The Braille system: some preliminary remarks

Braille is the most widespread and efficient means for blind people to read and write texts. It was created in France by Louis Braille in 1824 in order to provide a tactile representation for the French alphabet (cf. Mellor 2006). Based on the night writing encoding system developed by Charles Barbier, the Braille system consists of rectangular cells placed sequentially. Each cell corresponds to one character and it is traditionally constituted by two columns each of which presents three "slots" . The different combinations of salient or raised dots in each cell gives rise to the several Braille characters. The six dots that form a cell are numbered, so that each character can be identified by the raised dots that represent it. For instance, the character "b" , in Braille, is identified by dots 1 and 2, the character "t" by dots

2, 3, 4 and 5, and so on. There are 64 possible combinations, including no dots at all for spaces between words.

As we have pointed out, the original purpose of the development of the Braille system was to provide a tactile transcription of the printed alphabet, enabling blind people to read and write texts. Since the languages of the world differ considerably from each other, either concerning the alphabets that are employed, or regarding the number and type of graphic accents and punctuation marks they use, Braille encoding is language-specific, i.e., it varies according to the chosen language.

Braille has proven to be an immensely powerful and flexible system in various ways.

First, it was fruitfully adapted to include a large number of languages and alphabets around the world. Moreover, it was extended to cover other notations. Music, mathematics, physics, chemistry, phonetics, or informatics are some of the multiple areas in which Braille has been successfully employed to make knowledge more accessible to visually impaired people (cf. Herlein 1975; Thompson 2005; Schweikhardt *et al.* 2006; Englebretson 2009).

Second, Braille has adapted easily to the emergence of new technologies, following its continuous development. The ancient slate and stylus – a handwriting device – has been substituted by Braille writers, and, more recently, by refreshable Braille displays, notetakers and tablets (cf. Leonardis, Claudio & Frisoli 2017).

In order to cover a greater range of symbols, as well as to be used with Braille displays and notetakers, the six-dot Braille has been enhanced with two additional dots at the bottom of the cell, giving rise to the so-called 8-dot braille system or 8-dot Braille code.

Nowadays, Braille is used with computers, tablets, and smartphones, making information and knowledge easily accessible: it allows blind persons to access technology and to write and read emails, books, newspapers, and scientific articles on practically equal terms with respect to sighted people.

Although its use is declining in some parts of the world, due mainly to the growing influence of audio media, such as speech synthesizers, Braille remains essential for the learning process and for the general literacy of visually impaired people, facilitating their inclusion in the labour market and in other important social activities, especially when it is used in combination with new technologies (see, e.g., Wiazowski 2014).

Of course, it was not our intention here to provide an in-depth approach to the internal structure and functioning of the Braille system, having limited ourselves only to leave a few brief remarks on the aspects that seem most relevant and more useful to our purposes. For more details and information, see, among many others, Hampshire (1981), Croisdale, Kamp & Werner (2012), Wiazowski (2014), and, for specific aspects of the Portuguese Braille system, Lemos & Cerqueira (1996), Baptista (2000), Reino (2000) or Pereira (2002).

3 The project

Given that our project is still at an exceedingly early stage, it will not be possible to offer here any relevant results and conclusions. Nevertheless, I will expose our main goals and the methodology that was chosen to achieve them.

3.1 Main goals

As we said earlier, although the Braille system has been successfully used in different mathematical environments (cf. Annamalai *et al.* 2003; Alonso *et al.* 2006; Archambault *et al.* 2007; Asebriy, Raghay & Bencharef 2018), there is no attempt, to our knowledge, that has been done to adapt the Braille system to account for semantic formalisation in a comprehensive and systematic way. This is perfectly reasonable, given, on the one hand, the great complexity, as well as the inherent difficulties that such task involves, and, on the other, the reduced number of blind people that study or work with formal frameworks in the semantic field.

To fight against this state of affairs, we will take as our main goal the implementation of a first approach to the application of the Braille system to formal semantics.

Bearing in mind that the existing Braille displays are typically constituted by a single line of cells (cf. Leonardis, Claudio & Frisoli 2017), we decided to give primacy to linear formal systems, having therefore excluded proposals such as the Discourse Representation Theory developed by Kamp & Reyle (1993) or the Segmented Discourse Representation Theory of Asher & Lascarides (2001) that are based on more complicated two-dimensional graphic representations. However, if Braille tablets with multiple lines become standard, the inclusion of such approaches will be easily feasible.

Besides ascribing the correspondences between the symbols used in formal semantics and Braille characters, we will try to provide a simple description of the meaning and use of such tools, in order to facilitate the comprehension of the internal coherence and functioning of formal systems by blind students.

Moreover, we will attempt to explore the better way to provide visually impaired students and researchers with tools to interpret and produce texts that include semantic formulae.

The ultimate goal of our project is, therefore, to make semantic formalisation more friendly and accessible to blind people.

3.2 A note on challenges and decisions

Before describing the different stages that constitute our project, it seems important to address a few challenges underlying our task (I thank an anonymous reviewer of this paper for pointing them to me).

The choice for the one-to-one matching between symbols used in formal semantics and braille characters was preferred to the adoption of an audio output or to their simple substitution by the corresponding words in natural language. Regarding the use of a speech synthetiser to provide a translation of the formalisation, the difficulty of retrieving and retaining information must be taken into account (Braille is much more flexible and reliable in this respect). Concerning the translation into the corresponding words in natural language, it would create some difficulties when using automatic translation of printed texts in Braille displays or Braille printers: note that each "digital" character must be assigned to a well-defined combination of dots in the Braille system in order to be appropriately read by these devices. Moreover, the system we propose is closer to the original spirit of formalisation than the translation into natural language words proposal.

So, the use of Braille (in particular the 8-dot Braille system) seems the most appropriate way to provide blind students with valuable tools to learn and manage semantic formalisation. Bear in mind that a 6-dot Braille notation is also feasible, provided that we introduce compound characters, i.e., characters made of a prefix followed by the main symbol, a practice that is current in many other Braille notations.

3.3 Brief description

In this subsection, we will provide a brief description of the steps and tasks that we will undertake to achieve the goals sketched in 3.1.

1) Mapping the characters

The first step to be performed in our project is the selection of the set of formal symbols that will constitute the base for mapping the Braille notation.

Given the quantity and the diversity of formal approaches to meaning, it will not be possible to cover the full range of existing symbols in this area. In that view, we will select only the most relevant and widespread symbols that appear in introductory textbooks dealing with formal semantics, that is, those that constitute the core subjects of the formalisation that students learn in the introductory courses of semantics. This does not mean, though, that our list will be regarded as a closed one; on the contrary, it will be considered as an open departure point that may be continuously enriched with new contributions.

Having elected the basic set of symbols, the next step will be to establish a mapping between each of them and the corresponding Braille character. Since many of these symbols come from frameworks related to mathematics and logic, we will try to attest the existence of their Braille correspondents in these systems.

If the correspondence already exists, we will incorporate it in our list; if not, we will try to propose a new Braille character, always obeying the rules that regulate the internal coherence of this system.

As we have already pointed out, the Braille rules vary considerably according to the chosen language. We will take as our working system the Portuguese notation since it is the most familiar to us. However, with the relevant adaptations, this matching procedure may be extended to cover other Braille codifications.

At the end of this stage, we hope to have a list of Braille characters (both the 6-dot characters and the 8-dot ones) that directly correspond to each of the preselected items, giving rise to a coherent "translation" of formal symbols into Braille.

2) Exemplification

Since textbooks on formal semantics do not account for Braille notation, we consider that it would be helpful to provide some explanation and exemplification of some particular aspects regarding the use of our formal system with special focus on the consequences of its adaptation to the Braille code.

Departing from some introductory texts in this area (cf., e.g., Gamut, 1991; Cann, 1992; Portner & Partee, 2002; Kearns, 2011; Winter, 2016), we will provide a simple explanation for the meaning and use of each of the symbols at hand. It is not our intention, of course, to offer a complete and detailed introduction to the semantic questions involved, as this is better done by the literature we have cited, but only to establish some bridges between the traditionally used symbology and the corresponding Braille characters, in order to facilitate the understanding of specific issues by blind people. In other words, we want to make clear some aspects of the formalisation that could pose problems to visually impaired students, due to the differences that exist between Braille and paper-printed representations.

To achieve this goal, we will construct a brief presentation of each Braille symbol, consisting of its Braille representation in 6 and 8-dot Braille, the explanation of its meaning and some examples of its use in semantic formulae. Such information may also be summarized in a table for easier and faster reference.

3) Braille tables

The last stage of our project deals with the construction of Braille tables.

To convert digital information associated with each character into Braille, screen readers and Braille displays make use of Braille tables. A Braille table is designed to make a one-to-one correspondence between ANSII (or Unicode) characters and their Braille correlates, enabling screen readers and Braille displays to represent the information through the correct combination of dots.

Screen readers, such as JAWS for Windows, Non-Visual Desktop Access (NVDA) or Windows Narrator, are a piece of software that turns the visual information that appears in the computer's screen into an audio or tactile output. The tactile output is typically conveyed by a Braille display or a Braille notetaker, electronic-mechanical devices that present a tactile surface in which the refreshable Braille text is gradually exhibited.

In the case of Braille displays, the text that is shown is controlled by an external device – a personal computer or a smartphone, for example. In the case of Braille notetakers, text can be stored in different formats in their internal memory, and, besides their usage as computer terminals, thanks to their own firmware, these devices can be operated autonomously.

In any case, the contribution of a Braille table that allows the translation of the original text into Braille is essential since it permits the correspondences between symbols and Braille characters to be correctly displayed.

Hence, our main task in this third stage of our project will be to build a Braille table that includes the symbols used in formal semantics so that blind students and researchers, employing specific electronic equipment, can produce and access texts in this field. Needless to say, the texts to be read have to be written in accordance with the standard symbology used in formal semantics. Unfortunately, texts that are based on images or graphic representations cannot be properly accounted for by these tools.

4 Conclusion

Our project aims to turn formal semantics more accessible to blind students and researchers who want to learn and investigate different aspects of this important area of linguistic knowledge. With this work, we want to contribute in some extent to a better inclusion of this part of the population into graduate and post-graduate programs, facilitating their participation in university advanced studies.

We believe that accessibility for all is the better way to spread knowledge and information, to improve social inclusion and to favour the empowerment of impaired people, contributing to a more equitable society. Our work hopes to constitute a small step to create better conditions of access and to open new horizons to blind people.

For future research, it would be interesting to provide Optical Character Recognition (OCR) software with the capacity of recognizing the symbols used in formal semantics; this would constitute an important step to turn printed texts fully accessible to screen readers. However, the complexities that this task involves are completely beyond the scope of our present work.

References

Alonso, Fernando, José Luis Fuertes, Ángel L. González & Loïc A. Martínez (2006) "SBT: A translator from Spanish mathematical Braille to MathML" . In *International Conference on Computers for Handicapped Persons*: pp. 1207-1214. Berlin / Heidelberg: Springer.

Annamalai, A., D. Gopal, G. Gupta, H. Guo & A. Karshmer (2003) "INSIGHT: a comprehensive system for converting Braille based mathematical documents to Latex" . *Universal Access in HCI – Inclusive Design in the Information Society*, 4: pp. 1245-1249.

Archambault, Dominique, Bernhard Stöger, Mario Batusic, Claudia Fahrengruber & Klaus Miesenberger (2007) "A software model to support collaborative mathematical work between Braille and sighted users" . In *Proceedings of the 9th international ACM SIGACCESS conference on Computers and accessibility*: pp. 115-122. Doi: https://doi.org/10.1145/1296843.1296864

Asebriy, Zahra, Said Raghay & Omar Bencharef (2018) "An assistive technology for Braille users to support mathematical learning: A semantic retrieval system" . Symmetry, 10 (11): 547. Doi: https://doi.org/10.3390/sym10110547

Asher, Nicholas & Lascarides, Alex (2003) *Logics of Conversation*. Cambridge: Cambridge University Press.

Bach, Emmon (1986) "The algebra of events" . *Linguistics and Philosophy*, 9 (1), pp. 5-16.

Baptista, José António (2000) *A Invenção do Braille e a sua Importância na Vida dos Cegos*. Lisboa: Gráfica, 2000 (9).

Cann, Ronnie (1992) *Formal Semantics: an Introduction*. Cambridge, Cambridge University Press.

Croisdale, D. W., H. Kamp & H. Werner (eds.) (2012) *Computerised Braille Production: Today and Tomorrow*. Springer Science & Business Media.

Dowty, David (1979) *Word Meaning and Montague Grammar: The Semantics of Verbs and Times and Generative Semantics and Montague's PTQ*. Dordrecht: Reidel.

Englebretson, Robert (2009) "An overview of IPA Braille: An updated tactile representation of the International Phonetic Alphabet" . *Journal of the International Phonetic Association* 39 (1): pp. 67-86.

Gamut, L. F. T. (1991) *Logic, Language, and Meaning. Volume 1: Introduction to Logic*. Chicago: The University of Chicago Press.

Hampshire, Barry (1981) *Working with Braille*. Paris: Unesco.

Herlein, Doris G. (1975) "Music reading for the sightless: Braille notation". *Music Educators Journal* 62 (1): pp. 42-45.

Kamp, Hans & Uwe Reyle (1993) *From Discourse to Logic. Introduction to Model-Theoretic Semantics of Natural Language, Formal Logic and Discourse Representation Theory*. Dordrecht: Kluwer Academic Publishers.

Kearns, Kate (2011) *Semantics* (2nd edition). London: Macmillan International Higher Education.

Kratzer, Angelika (2012) *Modals and Conditionals: New and Revised Perspectives*. Oxford: Oxford University Press.

Lemos, Edison Ribeiro & Jonir Bechara Cerqueira (1996) "O sistema Braille no Brasil" . *Benjamin Constant*, 2.

Leonardis, Daniele, Loconsole Claudio & Antonio Frisoli (2017) "A survey on innovative refreshable braille display technologies" . In *International Conference on Applied Human Factors and Ergonomics*: pp. 488-498. Cham: Springer.

Mellor, C. Michael. (2006) *Louis Braille: A touch of genius*. Boston: National Braille Press.

Moens, Marc (1987) *Tense, Aspect and Temporal Reference*. PhD Dissertation, Edinburgh: Edinburgh University.

Montague, Richard (1974) *Formal Philosophy. Selected Papers of Richard Montague*. R. Thomason (ed.), New Haven: Yale University Press.

Parsons, Terence (1990) *Events in the Semantics of English: a Study in Subatomic Semantics*. Cambridge Mass.: MIT Press.

Pereira, Maria de Lourdes (2002) A Deficiência Visual e a Literacia Braille. Aspectos da Grafia Braille da Língua Portuguesa. Doctoral dissertation, Lisboa: Faculdade de Motricidade Humana da Universidade Técnica de Lisboa.

Portner, Paul (2009) *Modality*. Oxford: Oxford University Press.

Portner, Paul & Barbara H. Partee (eds.) (2002) *Formal Semantics: The Essential Readings*. Oxford: Blackwell Publishing Company.

Reino, Vítor (2000) *170 Anos Depois: Algumas Considerações de Ordem Histórica, Sociológica e Psicopedagógica sobre o Sistema Braille*. Lisboa: Biblioteca Nacional de Portugal.

Schweikhardt, Waltraud, C. Bernareggi, N. Jessel, B. Encelle & M. Gut (2006) "LAMBDA: A European system to access mathematics with Braille and audio synthesis" . In *International Conference on Computers for Handicapped Persons*: pp. 1223-1230. Berlin / Heidelberg: Springer.

Thompson, David M. (2005) "LaTeX2Tri: Physics and mathematics for the blind or visually impaired" . In *Proceedings from the 20th Conference on Technology and Persons with Disabilities* (CSUN). Available online at http://citeseerx.ist.psu.edu/viewdoc/download?doi=10.1.1.90.1991& rep=rep1& type=pdf

Wiazowski, Jaroslaw (2014) "Can Braille be revived? A possible impact of high-end Braille and mainstream technology on the revival of tactile literacy medium" . *Assistive Technology*, 26 (4): pp. 227–230.

Wiazowski, Jaroslaw (2014) "Can Braille be revived? A possible impact of high-end Braille and mainstream technology on the revival of tactile literacy medium" . *Assistive Technology* 26 (4): pp. 227-230.

Winter, Yoad (2016) *Elements of Formal Semantics: An Introduction to the Mathematical Theory of Meaning in Natural Language*. Edinburgh: Edinburgh University Press.

Cross-Lingual Transfer Learning for Hate Speech Detection

Irina Bigoulaeva and **Viktor Hangya** and **Alexander Fraser**
Center for Information and Language Processing
LMU Munich
I.Bigoulaeva1@campus.lmu.de, {hangyav,fraser}@cis.lmu.de

Abstract

We address the task of automatic hate speech detection for low-resource languages. Rather than collecting and annotating new hate speech data, we show how to use cross-lingual transfer learning to leverage already existing data from higher-resource languages. Using bilingual word embeddings based classifiers we achieve good performance on the target language by training only on the source dataset. Using our transferred system we bootstrap on unlabeled target language data, improving the performance of standard cross-lingual transfer approaches. We use English as a high-resource language and German as the target language for which only a small amount of annotated corpora are available. Our results indicate that cross-lingual transfer learning together with our approach to leverage additional unlabeled data is an effective way of achieving good performance on low-resource target languages without the need for any target language annotations.

1 Introduction

Due to the increased digitization of society, the impact of online discourse on everyday life is becoming more pronounced. A single hateful message shared on social media now has the potential to incite violent offline movements, as well as exert a negative emotional impact on millions of readers. For this reason, platforms such as Twitter and Facebook have created community policies to ensure civil conduct on the part of their users. The goal is to filter hate speech, which unlike mere offensive or vulgar content, is exclusively designed to attack or denigrate entire groups of people and is generally agreed to add no constructive value to discussions. But with the sheer amount of posts being published, it is becoming difficult for humans to moderate them in a complete and timely manner. Different annotators are also not guaranteed to agree on every classification, even in the presence of well-defined annotation guidelines. Moreover, due to their repeated and prolonged exposure to negative content, many moderators experience a decline in mental health (Vidgen and Derczynski, 2020). For these reasons, automatic hate speech detection has become a field of high interest.

In general, the task of classifying hate speech has been acknowledged as difficult (de Gibert et al., 2018). One reason is data scarcity: there are currently few public hate speech datasets available, and the majority of them are for English. Thus, building systems for lower-resource languages is even more challenging (Vidgen and Derczynski, 2020). An additional difficulty of the task is the need to precisely define hate speech. While many people have an intuitive understanding of what hate speech is, this does not easily translate to a finite set of characteristics. Different hate speech datasets often deal with specific hate speech subtypes, leading to stark differences between the content of their hate speech classes and making the available resources for a given set of hate speech subtypes in a low-resource language even scarcer.

The goal of this paper is to reduce these difficulties by exploiting available resources from other languages. We address data scarcity in German, a generally high-resource language but a language for which there are not yet many hate speech datasets (only 4 labeled corpora compared to the 25 available for English (Vidgen and Derczynski, 2020)). Our method is a zero-shot setup that assumes we do not have any annotated training data in German. We develop a cross-lingual transfer learning approach based on bilingual word embeddings (BWEs) and neural classifiers to provide access to hate speech data in English. We use the English dataset of de Gibert et al. (2018) and the German dataset of the GermEval Shared Task on the Identification of Offensive Language (Ruppenhofer et al.,

Proceedings of the First Workshop on Language Technology for Equality, Diversity and Inclusion, pages 15–25
April 19, 2021.

2018) in our experiments. However, their annotation had to be modified using a few simple rules to ensure label compatibility.

In addition to training only on English, we bootstrap on two unlabeled German datasets, one of which we crawled from the web. Using a set of our English-only models we predict the labels of previously-unseen data and keep only those on which the used models agree. By using the newly-labeled data as well for training, we further improved the performance on the target language.

2 Previous Work

2.1 What is Hate Speech?

Hate speech detection is considered a subtype of offensive language detection. However, Davidson et al. (2017) note that the two concepts are often wrongly conflated due to a lack of a precise definition of hate speech. This is an undesirable strategy, given that social media is saturated with low-severity insults and comments that use rude language in a non-hostile way. Moreover, the absence of offensive words and slurs does not guarantee the absence of hate speech.

Multiple datasets have been created that feature hate speech as a distinct class from other forms of offensive language. However, these datasets nearly all differ in how they conceptualize hate speech. The dataset of Bretschneider and Peters (2017) focuses on hate speech in the sense of anti-foreigner comments. The dataset of Ross et al. (2016) contains hate speech exclusively against refugees. The three datasets of Majumder et al. (2019) do not focus on one particular target.

These discrepancies across hate speech datasets lead to an even smaller amount of available resources for building a system for hate speech detection.

Perhaps the most informative and broad definition of hate speech is given by de Gibert et al. (2018) who define it as "a deliberate attack directed towards a specific group of people motivated by aspects of the group's identity". With this definition in mind, de Gibert et al. (2018) present an English-language hate speech dataset featuring text scraped from the white-nationalist forum Stormfront. This dataset will be referred to as the Stormfront dataset. Due to the broad nature of its hate speech definition and its decent size (ca. 10,000 examples), it was chosen as the training set for this paper.

Table 1 illustrates some 'Hate' and 'noHate' sentences from the Stormfront dataset.[1] Sentences 2 and 4 are examples of racial hate speech, and Sentence 5 is an example of hate speech related to gender. Sentence 1 is not an example of hate speech, since it has a neutral sentiment and does not ascribe the qualities 'poor' and 'victimized' to an entire group of people. Finally, Sentence 3 expresses the writer's approval of a video and does not attack or mention any group.

In comparison to other languages, English has by far the largest amount of annotated hate speech data. A comprehensive online catalogue published by Vidgen and Derczynski (2020)[2] currently catalogues 25 datasets for English, with a grand total of 800,000 data samples. Other languages are left far behind: the next-best represented language, Arabic, has just over 48,000 total examples. German has four datasets totalling around 19,500 samples, found in: Bretschneider and Peters (2017), Ross et al. (2016), Wiegand et al. (2018b), and Majumder et al. (2019).

Of particular interest is the dataset of German-language tweets presented with the 2018 GermEval Shared Task on the Identification of Offensive Language (Ruppenhofer et al., 2018). The shared task focused on the detection of offensive language in general (the "coarse-grained task"), along with the detection of three of its subtypes (the "fine-grained task"): 'Insult', 'Profanity', and 'Abuse'. A tweet is assigned the 'Abuse' label if "... the target of judgment is seen as a representative of a group and it is ascribed negative qualities that are taken to be universal, omnipresent and unchangeable characteristics of the group" (Ruppenhofer et al., 2018). Importantly, this definition keeps the nature of the target group general and is therefore compatible with the hate speech definition of de Gibert et al. (2018). Thus, the GermEval dataset was used as our test set for evaluation.

2.2 Low-Resource Approaches

SVMs, CNNs and RNNs are the most commonly-used models for hate speech detection and offensive language detection in general (Waseem et al., 2017; Fišer et al., 2018; Roberts et al., 2019; Ruppenhofer et al., 2018). Two architectures from the 2018 GermEval task are particularly relevant to this paper. Xi et al. (2018) used a CNN following (Kim, 2014) to address the coarse-grained task. Wiedemann

[1]The data samples in this paper are shown for explanatory purposes and do not represent the views of the authors.

[2]https://hatespeechdata.com

	Sentence	Label
1.	This film tells the story of a poor victimised African boy (Joseph) who was allowed into Ireland .	noHate
2.	Whites in all their glory against impossibly large hordes of non-whites .	Hate
3.	The video about the "Day of honour", is really cool .	noHate
4.	But unfortunately , Maine 's become the dumping ground for Somalis and other African trash .	Hate
5.	Most White Western Women have the racial sense of a cabbage .	Hate

Table 1: Sample 'Hate' and 'noHate' comments according to de Gibert et al. (12).

et al. (2018) used a model combining CNN and BiLSTMs to achieve second-best performance in the coarse-grained task and top performance in the fine-grained task. The classifiers we use are based on these two approaches.

Data scarcity remains a relevant problem for hate speech detection, and recent work still aims to utilize resources from English to improve in languages with less hate speech data. Ranasinghe and Zampieri (2020) train transformer-based architectures on English data and use the learned weights to initialize models which are trained on target language data. Stappen et al. (2020) also utilize transformer architectures, training them on the source language and evaluating on the target language. Alternatively, they concatenate a small number of target language samples with the source language training data. Wiegand et al. (2018a) also augment their available German training set, using English-German BWEs to create a concatenated dataset with both the English and German training data. Mathur et al. (2018) utilize a cross-lingual transfer procedure for hate speech detection in Hinglish, a code-switched language that uses both Hindi and English words. By first training a CNN and an LSTM on an English dataset, then fine-tuning the models on Hinglish, better performance was achieved compared to a Hinglish-only model. In contrast to these works, our approach requires no target language annotations.

Kozareva (2006) present a bootstrapping-based approach that annotates new data for named entity recognition to improve the performance in low-resource scenarios. First a set of classifiers are trained, which are then applied to a unlabeled set with majority voting. The extended corpus is used to improve the performance by retraining the models from scratch. Rather than bootstrapping new target language data, Ghadery and Moens (2020) fine-tune an mBERT model (Devlin et al., 2019) on an augmented multilingual dataset constructed automatically by translating the English source dataset. Our approach does not require the additional resources of automatic translation, however.

We combine the bootstrapping procedure of Kozareva (2006) with the fine-tuning procedure of Mathur et al. (2018), first bootstrapping German-language data then using it to fine-tune our models. Variations of this bootstrapping procedure have been used for other tasks such as named entity recognition, using active learning instead of only source language trained models to annotate new data (Chaudhary et al., 2019). To our knowledge, we are the first to utilize such a procedure for detecting hate speech.

3 Experiment Setup

This section introduces the setup of our experiments. First the source and target datasets are discussed, along with the ways in which they were modified for maximum compatibility. This is followed by a presentation of our CNN and CNN/BiLSTM model architectures.

3.1 Datasets

The English and German datasets that we used in our experiments are listed in Table 2 and 3 respectively, along with their class distributions.

While the Stormfront and GermEval datasets have similar hate speech definitions, their annotation schemas differed. The Stormfront dataset features binary 'Hate' vs. 'noHate' labeling, along with a 'Relation' label for sentences that had to be considered in context with others to acquire a hateful meaning, and a 'Skip' label for when the sentence was either non-English or not meaningful enough to be given either of the binary labels. In contrast, the GermEval dataset features a two-tiered annotation schema: each tweet carries a coarse-grained label ('Offense' vs 'Other') as well as a

	noHate	Hate
Stormfront	9,580	1,364

Table 2: Ratio of hate to non-hate labels in the English Stormfront dataset.

	Other	Abuse	Insult	Prof.
Train	3,321	1,022	595	71
Test	2,330	773	381	48

Table 3: Distribution of the fine-grained class labels of the original German GermEval training and test datasets.

fine-grained label that specifies the subtype of offensiveness: either 'Insult', 'Profanity', or 'Abuse'. To ensure optimal cross-lingual transfer between these two datasets, we made certain modifications to their labeling schemas that were motivated by the datasets' specific class definitions.

First we simplified the annotation schema of the fine-grained GermEval data into a binary schema. As per the discussion in Section 2.1, we took GermEval's 'Abuse' label to be the counterpart of the Stormfront dataset's 'Hate', relabeling comments belonging to the 'Other', 'Insult', and 'Profanity' classes as 'noHate'.

Next, we relabeled all 'Skip' and 'Relation' samples from the Stormfront dataset to conform with the binary schema. The 92 comments that carried the label 'Skip', indicating that they were either non-English or not informative, were relabeled as 'noHate'. The 168 instances of the 'Relation' class were relabeled as 'Hate', since these sentences were always hateful when placed in context.

After relabeling was completed, we addressed the imbalanced class distributions of the English and German datasets. Examining Table 2, it is clear that the majority of samples in the Stormfront dataset are 'noHate'. This reflects the real-life observation that hate speech is less common than regular text. But this has been known to pose difficulties for machine learning models, which need plenty of data from both classes in order to be able to generalize (Madukwe et al., 2020; Vidgen and Derczynski, 2020). In our initial experiments, the 'noHate' class was so dominant over 'Hate' that the models were skewed towards assigning the 'noHate' label every time. Previous research suggests that oversampling the underrepresented class yields good model performance (De Smedt and Jaki, 2018). For this reason we oversampled

	noHate	Hate
EN-OS	9,580	9,548
DE-REL	3,345	855
DE-DEV	642	167
DE-TEST	2,759	773

Table 4: Datasets used for our experiments.

the Stormfront dataset with multiple copies of the 'Hate' examples, yielding a nearly-balanced distribution that resulted in optimal performance for our models. This oversampled version of the Stormfront dataset will be referred to as EN-OS, and is the English dataset used for training.

We split the official GermEval training set into train and dev sets following the work of Wiedemann et al. (2018). First, we transferred the final 809 samples from the full set to a new development set named DE-DEV for hyperparameter tuning. The remaining samples formed the DE-REL dataset, which will be used in the fine-tuning experiments in Section 4.2. We did not use this data anywhere else. See Table 4.

3.2 Model Architectures

All our models described below are based on BWEs. BWEs are one of the most commonly-used tools for conducting cross-lingual transfer, the other being machine translation of source language data. However, ensuring accurate machine translation requires large amounts of resources, making BWEs more interesting in general for low-resource languages. BWEs ensure that source- and target language words are represented in a common vector space, enabling neural models based on BWEs to train on the source language and test on the target language without any intermediate steps.

To produce our bilingual English-German embeddings, monolingual embeddings were first trained using FastText SkipGram (Bojanowski et al., 2017) over English and German NewsCrawl corpora (Bojar et al., 2015) which contain text dating from 2007 to 2013 and were preprocessed with Moses tools (Koehn et al., 2007). The resulting embeddings were mapped with MUSE (Conneau et al., 2018). We used the default parameters of the above mentioned tools.

Our baseline classifier was a linear SVM over these BWEs. For each training example, we calculated the average of the vector representations of the words in the given text to obtain its global

Model	Accuracy	Hate			noHate			Macro-Average		
		P	R	F1	P	R	F1	P	R	F1
SVM	47.65	22.24	55.76	31.80	78.54	45.38	57.52	50.39	50.57	50.48
CNN1	59.17	22.15	34.41	26.95	78.25	66.11	71.67	50.20	50.26	50.23
CNN2	61.04	22.47	31.82	26.34	78.38	69.23	73.52	50.42	50.53	50.47
BiLSTM1	63.22	21.90	26.52	23.99	78.12	73.50	75.74	50.01	50.01	50.01
BiLSTM2	72.88	21.71	9.18	12.91	78.10	90.72	83.94	49.90	49.95	49.93

Table 5: Cross-lingual performance on DE-TEST after training on EN-OS.

representation. Wiegand et al. (2018a) showed that SVMs based on feature engineering, e.g., using word and character n-grams or lexicon based features, perform well on hate-speech detection. However, such systems are not easily applicable in cross-lingual settings, thus we use only the BWE based SVM.

Our second model was a CNN classifier following the widely-used architecture of Kim (2014). This model accepts an embedding layer as an input and feeds it into a convolution layer with a variable number of filters. Global max-pooling is performed on the convolution output, and the result is passed through a dense layer. The input word embeddings can either be randomly-initialized, preloaded from an outside source, or fine-tuned during training. Optionally, two of these variants may be used at the same time. We used only one form of embeddings, namely our BWEs, and did not update them during training. For the remaining model hyperparameters, we used the default values [3].

Our third model was based on the neural model of Wiedemann et al. (2018), with some modifications for compatibility with our cross-lingual setup. In our version, an input layer of our BWEs was fed into a BiLSTM layer of 100 units. The output of this BiLSTM layer was then fed into a convolution layer with three feature maps of 200 units each, with respective kernel sizes of 3, 4, and 5. Global max-pooling was applied after each convolution, and the output of this step was fed to a dense layer of 100 units.

4 Results

4.1 Cross-Lingual Experiments

In the first experiment phase, the SVM, CNN, and BiLSTM architectures were trained on EN-OS. Hyperparameters such as epoch count, learning rate, and class weights were optimized on DE-DEV. The two best-performing hyperparameter settings for each of the neural models were saved, resulting in a total of four English-trained models: CNN1, CNN2, BiLSTM1, and BiLSTM2. These will form the four-model ensemble used in Section 4.2.

The models' performance is summarized in Table 5. Despite the models being trained on forum posts they achieved good results on tweets as well.

With all three of our architectures, we observed that training with a proper class weight distribution was vital to ensuring good performance. Despite the fact that EN-OS was designed to be as balanced as possible, an improper weight ratio would result in a model always predicting either 'Hate' or 'noHate' on DE-DEV. This would achieve a high macro-average F1 score on DE-DEV but poor performance within one of the two classes. Therefore we chose the weight values that produced good F1 scores for both classes, even if it meant sacrificing average F1 performance.

Table 6 shows the optimal hyperparameter values during training on EN-OS. The CNN architecture benefited from high epoch counts and a class weight distribution that was skewed towards 'noHate'. The BiLSTM architecture in contrast required a reduced epoch count due to its overfitting behavior, and resulted in a class weight distribution that was skewed towards 'Hate'.

4.2 Bootstrapping

The next phase of cross-lingual experiments centered around data augmentation and fine-tuning. In the first augmentation experiment, we treated the samples in the DE-REL training set described in Table 4 as unlabeled and used an ensemble-based approach similar to Kozareva (2006) to label them. As mentioned in Section 3.1, we did not use DE-REL at any point during the training process.

Our ensemble consisted of the four neural models mentioned in Section 4.1. Of the relabeled sentences, we collected only those for which all four

[3] `https://github.com/yoonkim/CNN_sentence/blob/master`

	noHate	Hate	Dropout	Learn Rate	Epochs
SVM	0.17	0.83	n/a	n/a	n/a
CNN1	0.6	0.4	0.7	10^{-4}	30
CNN2	0.6	0.4	0.7	10^{-4}	40
BiLSTM1	0.2	0.8	0.7	10^{-4}	15
BiLSTM2	0.2	0.8	0.7	10^{-4}	15

Table 6: Optimal hyperparameters for training on EN-OS. The first two columns represent class weights.

	noHate	Hate
noHate	1,490	113
Hate	412	30
Total	1,902	143

Table 7: Confusion matrix of the ensemble-relabeled DE-REL* compared to the original annotations in DE-REL. Gold and predicted labels are shown in the rows and columns respectively.

models agreed into a new corpus called DE-REL*. We do not include the SVM in our ensemble and only fine-tune the neural models, since the neural architectures allow us to easily control how much of the original training data to forget by means of learning rate tuning.

Table 7 shows the confusion matrix for the labels of the dataset.

The Labels of DE-REL* Table 8 shows a selection of correct and incorrect classifications in DE-REL*, according to the original gold labels of the examples. Comment 1 shows that the ensemble was able to detect a covert kind of hate speech that involved contextual hints rather than overt vulgar language. One must understand what 'Mohrenkopf' is being used to mean in order to recognize the sentence as hate speech. Comment 2 was correctly classified as 'noHate' despite the presence of the controversial word 'Scheindemokratie' (en. *fake democracy*). This suggests that the model learned hate speech features that were more complex than lexical cues.

Comment 3 was falsely labeled as 'Hate' and Comment 4 was falsely labeled as 'noHate'. A possible reason for Comment 4 could be that its hate speech target (i.e. the group of German boys) differs from the groups typically targeted in a white supremacist forum, which was the source for the EN-OS training data. As a result, our models did not associate the insults contained in the comment with a hateful meaning.

The Fine-Tuning Phase We performed fine-tuning on the four English-trained models in Table 5, loading the dataset DE-REL* and resuming training for 3 epochs. All other hyperparameters, shown in Table 10, were selected based on both class-wise and macro-average F1 performance on DE-DEV. In particular, we had to modify the class weight ratio of each model from its original optimum.

Table 9 shows the models' scores on DE-TEST after fine-tuning on DE-REL*. Three of the four models improved their macro-average F1-score after fine-tuning. The largest improvement of 1.76 points was made by the BiLSTM1, while BiLSTM2 was close behind with an improvement of 1.45 points. CNN1 improved less, achieving only an additional 0.18 points.

CNN2 was the only model to perform worse after fine-tuning, decreasing in macro-average F1 by 0.27 points. A closer look at its class-wise F1 scores for 'Hate' and 'noHate' in Table 9 shows that the model's score in the latter class improved, while its score in the former decreased. This points to the fact that the model became skewed during fine-tuning towards predicting 'noHate'.

Crawled German Stormfront Data In the second experiment, we sought a source of completely new German data from the Internet to serve as a fine-tuning dataset. As mentioned previously, German hate speech data is scarce, and most of the existing datasets deviate significantly from (de Gibert et al., 2018) in hate speech definition. To keep to the stylistic tendencies of the Stormfront dataset, we took our data from a German-language thread within the Stormfront forum.

At the time of our experiments, the thread had around 5,500 posts. These consisted predominantly of comments written in German, although many were written in English. We programmed a simple webcrawler using the Python library Scrapy[4] to browse the thread and extract the content of the

[4]`https://scrapy.org`

		Sentence	Ensemble	Gold
DE-REL*	1.	@Nacktmagazin @DuHugonotte Und zum Nachtisch einen Mohrenkopf . *en. And for dessert a Mohrenkopf (head of a Moor / a kind of candy)*	Hate	Hate
	2.	Wir leben in einer Scheindemokratie aber in keiner #Demokratie! *en. We're living in a fake democracy, but not in a democracy.*	noHate	noHate
	3.	@Dora_Bromberger @lawyerberlin Hetze haben weder Fakten noch Argumente je ersetzt. *en. Hate has never replaced facts or arguments.*	Hate	noHate
	4.	@NegohotShlomo @Frank_Pasemann Pubertierende masturbierende Pickelträger...kein Wunder das deutsche Mädels keine deutsche Jungs wollen....! *en. Pubescent masturbating pimple-faces... no wonder German girls don't want German boys!*	noHate	Hate
DE-NEW	5.	Das Motto in Deutschland heutzutage ist nicht "Deutschland, Deutschland ueber alles", aber jedoch Jude, Jude ueber alles! *en. The motto in Germany these days isn't "Germany, Germany above all" but rather "Jew, Jew above all"!*	Hate	(Hate)
	6.	Ich persönlich komme mit allen (ausser juden) besten aus und halte es mit Dr.David Duke der sagt: "I do not hate any other people." *en. Personally I get along with all people fantastically (except Jews) and hold with Dr. David Duke, who says: "I do not hate any other people."*	Hate	(Hate)
	7.	Das ist wirklich wahr, für die meisten **NS** wäre die Erfindung der Zeitmaschine ein Segen; der Punkt ist das Leute die eine Ideologie vertreten und den **Führer** religiös verehren nur wenig Zugang zur Realität haben. da skann man ja hier im Forum auch beobachten... *en. That really is true, for the majority of the **Nazis**, the invention of the time machine would have been a blessing; the point is that people who support an ideology and religiously venerate the **Führer** have only a limited grasp on reality. yo ucan[sic] observe that right here in the forum...*	noHate	(noHate)
	8.	Der in Tutzing in Oberbayern lebende kanadische **Holocaust-Leugner** Alfred Schaefer ist wegen Volksverhetzung angeklagt. Der 63-Jährige selbst hat den Verhandlungstermin am 4. Mai vor dem Amtsgericht Dresden mit den Worten er sei "vor die Inquisition geladen" publik gemacht und angekündigt, den Prozess dazu zu nutzen, in langatmiger Form den **nationalsozialistischen Völkermord** an den Juden in Frage zu stellen. *en. The Canadian **Holocaust-denier** Alfred Schaefer, who lives in Tutzing in Upper Bavaria, has been charged with sedition. On his part, the 63-year-old made his trial appointment before the court of Dresden on the 4th of May public by saying he had been "invited by the Inquisition", and announced that he would use the process to verbosely call into question the **national-socialist genocide** of the Jewish people.*	noHate	(noHate)
	9.	Eine Partei, die immernoch gegen die "boesen amerikanischen Besatzer" wettert, kann und will ich nicht verstehen. *en. A party that still continues to fume over the "evil American occupants" I cannot understand and do not want to."*	Hate	(noHate)

Table 8: Correct and incorrect ensemble labels for either DE-REL* or DE-NEW. Gold labels for DE-NEW are given by the authors in brackets.

	Model	Accuracy	Hate			noHate			Macro-Average		
			P	R	F1	P	R	F1	P	R	F1
DE-REL*	CNN1	**61.95**	**22.42**	30.01	25.66	**78.33**	**70.90**	**74.43**	**50.37**	**50.45**	**50.41**
	CNN2	**68.15**	22.24	18.24	20.04	78.19	**82.13**	**80.11**	50.22	50.19	50.20
	BiLSTM1	51.22	**23.31**	**53.69**	**32.51**	**79.57**	50.53	61.80	**51.44**	**52.11**	**51.77**
	BiLSTM2	66.53	**24.02**	**24.45**	**24.23**	**78.72**	78.33	78.52	**51.37**	**51.39**	**51.38**
DE-NEW	CNN1	**72.71**	21.99	9.70	13.46	78.13	**90.36**	**83.80**	50.06	50.03	50.05
	CNN2	**73.53**	**23.18**	9.06	13.02	78.24	**91.59**	**84.39**	**50.71**	50.32	**50.51**
	BiLSTM1	50.03	**22.63**	**53.04**	**31.72**	**78.90**	49.18	60.59	**50.76**	**51.11**	**50.94**
	BiLSTM2	22.08	**21.93**	**100.00**	**35.97**	**100.00**	0.25	0.51	**60.96**	**50.13**	**55.02**

Table 9: Model performance on DE-TEST with bootstrapping, i.e., after training on EN-OS and fine-tuning on either DE-REL* or DE-NEW. Improvements compared to the models without fine-tuning shown in bold.

		noHate	Hate	Dropout	Learn Rate	Epochs
DE-REL*	CNN1	0.1	0.9	0.4	10^{-7}	3
	CNN2	0.2	0.8	0.7	10^{-6}	3
	BiLSTM1	0.08	0.92	0.8	10^{-7}	3
	BiLSTM2	0.1	0.9	0.4	10^{-6}	3
DE-NEW	CNN1	0.1	0.9	0.2	10^{-7}	4
	CNN2	0.2	0.8	0.2	10^{-7}	4
	BiLSTM1	0.01	0.99	0.9	10^{-12}	2
	BiLSTM2	0.01	0.99	0.9	10^{-12}	3

Table 10: Optimal hyperparameters for fine-tuning on DE-REL* and DE-NEW. The first two columns represent class weights.

posts. To account for the typical prevalence of lengthy posts in a forum setting, the crawler considered each paragraph distinguished by a newline to be a separate text sample.

Before the data could be used for training, we performed some manual preprocessing to ensure compatibility with the format of a tweet. We removed the following things from the data, as much as was feasible to detect manually:

- Non-German text
- Bullet-point lists
- Quotes from books, articles, etc. over 1000 characters
- Links, i.e. to Youtube videos
- Extremely short lines: names, one-word responses, timestamps, letter salutations
- Lines or sentences that were cut off without any clear continuation

The following things were kept:

- Quotes or news article snippets under 1000 characters.
- Multi-line interview dialogue, with each line considered as a distinct text sample.
- Mixed English/German sentences, since Anglicisms were common in the GermEval tweets as well.

The following things were manually corrected and kept:

- Sentence parts that the crawler considered separate but clearly belonged together:
  - 'tut mir' and 'leid' → 'tut mir leid'
- Words broken apart by spaces:
  - 'd aß' → 'daß'

The result of this preprocessing was a corpus of 6,586 text samples, all or nearly all written in German. We refer to this corpus as DE-NEW and use it as the training set during fine-tuning.

The Labels of DE-NEW Since we had no gold labels of DE-NEW to evaluate our ensemble's classifications, we manually examined several examples and judged them strictly according to the points of the hate speech definition in de Gibert et al. (2018). Table 8 shows four classifications made by the ensemble. Comments 5 and 6 are clearly 'Hate' and were intuitively classified as such. Comments 7 and 8 were intuitively classified as 'noHate', although the comments contain several words which we bolded that might be associated with a hateful context: "NS" (*en. National-Socialist/Nazis*), "Führer", "Holocaust-Leugner", (*en. Holocaust-denier*). Despite the occurrence of these words, all four models of our ensemble were able to classify the whole text as 'noHate', indicating that the models learned deeper hate speech features than lexical cues. Finally, Comment 9 was mistakenly classified as 'Hate'. Although the statement is critical of a political party, it is not severe enough to be an attack. Table 9 illustrates the models' performance after fine-tuning on D-NEW.

As with DE-REL*, fine-tuning on DE-NEW improved the macro-average F1 scores for three of the four models. Once again a CNN performed worse, namely CNN1, whose average F1 score dropped by 0.18 points. The LSTMs once again showed the greatest improvement. Notably, BiLSTM2 managed to achieve the highest macro-average F1 score among both fine-tuned groups, due to its high precision in the 'Hate' class and high recall in the 'noHate' class.

These results were also dependent upon proper tuning of hyperparameters. The optimal values are shown in Table 10. Importantly, we decreased the dropout rates of the CNNs compared to the first fine-tuning setup and trained for four epochs instead of three. This procedure did not work for the

BiLSTMs, however, as it caused them to ovefit to DE-NEW and predict only 'Hate'. This resulted in a rapid decrease in macro-average F1 performance on DE-DEV. Therefore, to optimize performance for the BiLSTMs, we significantly lowered the learning rate, increased the dropout, and skewed the class weights strongly towards 'Hate', leaving the weight for 'noHate' nearly zero.

Discussion Our results align with the findings in Mathur et al. (2018), where fine-tuning on cross-lingual data improved classifier performance. In the same vein, both of our fine-tuning experiments improved the macro-average F1 performance of English-trained neural hate speech classifiers. However, ensuring good performance in our fine-tuning setups required proper hyperparameter tuning. Sub-optimal hyperparameter settings caused the models to overfit to the fine-tuning data and decrease in macro-average F1 performance. We noted that in each of the fine-tuning setups, one of our two CNN models worsened in macro-average F1 performance despite hyperparameter tuning. Moreover, borrowing the hyperparameter settings from the CNN that did improve its score did not help. A reason for this could be that the CNNs were originally trained for a different number of epochs. In general, however, we found that the CNN architecture was robust at handling the fine-tuning data without overfitting. In both fine-tuning rounds, the optimal class weight distributions for CNN1 and CNN2 remained the same as during their initial training, and when fine-tuning on DE-NEW they could afford to be trained for four epochs instead of three. The BiLSTMs in contrast required low learning rates, low epoch counts, and high dropout rates, particularly when being fine-tuned on DE-NEW. Nevertheless, when we tuned the hyperparameters for these models correctly, we achieved macro-average F1 improvements by far surpassing those of the CNNs.

We observe that the average F1 scores of the SVM, CNNs and BiLSTMs were relatively similar before fine-tuning, and also to a lesser degree after fine-tuning the neural models. This is in line with previous results in (Bachfischer et al., 2018), where the macro-average F1 scores of an SVM, CNN, and LSTM differed in around three points from each other. This is most likely the result of too little data for the neural networks, and may indicate the merits of procuring even more training data than we presently did to benefit from these models' full potential.

A caveat to training on a specialized dataset such as the Stormfront dataset is that the hate speech examples will typically have a characteristic target group, in this case non-white individuals. The effects of this were observed in our ensemble's mislabeling of Comment 4 in Table 8, where the hate speech target was the group of German boys. This underscores the importance of training on multiple subtypes of hate speech.

5 Conclusion

Building automatic hate speech detection systems for low-resource languages is problematic due to the small amount of available datasets. Our goal was to investigate whether cross-lingual transfer learning could be used to mitigate the problem of data scarcity. We chose an English dataset with a broad hate speech definition for training and a similar German corpus for testing. Although the datasets were similar, we had to simplify the complex annotation schema of the target language dataset into the binary schema of the source dataset to make them compatible for the cross-lingual experiments. Our results showed that cross-lingual transfer learning is indeed an effective tool for hate speech detection in low-resource languages. Additionally, we assembled two corpora of previously-unseen, unlabeled target language data and applied an ensemble of trained classifiers to them. We showed that fine-tuning on these automatically labeled examples improves classification performance. Our goal for the future is to apply cross-lingual transfer learning to other language pairs with greater syntactic differences than German and English, as well as employing current state-of-the-art transformer models such as BERT. In addition, since the differences of labeling schemas across various datasets could prevent the application of transfer learning methods, we aim at bridging the gap between incompatibly-labeled train and test datasets.

Acknowledgments

This work was supported by the European Research Council (ERC) under the European Union's Horizon 2020 research and innovation programme (grant agreement No. 640550) and by German Research Foundation (DFG; grant FR 2829/4-1).

References

Matthias Bachfischer, Uchenna Akujuobi, and Xiangliang Zhang. 2018. KAUSTmine - Offensive Comment Classification on German Language Microposts. In *Proceedings of the GermEval 2018 Workshop*, pages 33–37.

Piotr Bojanowski, Edouard Grave, Armand Joulin, and Tomas Mikolov. 2017. Enriching Word Vectors with Subword Information. *Transactions of the Association for Computational Linguistics*, pages 135–146.

Ondřej Bojar, Rajan Chatterjee, Christian Federmann, Barry Haddow, Chris Hokamp, Matthias Huck, Varvara Logacheva, and Pavel Pecina, editors. 2015. *Proceedings of the Tenth Workshop on Statistical Machine Translation.*

Uwe Bretschneider and Ralf Peters. 2017. Detecting offensive statements towards foreigners in social media. In *50th Hawaii International Conference on System Sciences, HICSS 2017, Hilton Waikoloa Village, Hawaii, USA, January 4-7, 2017*, pages 1–10. ScholarSpace / AIS Electronic Library (AISeL).

Aditi Chaudhary, Jiateng Xie, Zaid Sheikh, Graham Neubig, and Jaime G. Carbonell. 2019. A little annotation does a lot of good: A study in bootstrapping low-resource named entity recognizers. In *Proceedings of the 2019 Conference on Empirical Methods in Natural Language Processing and the 9th International Joint Conference on Natural Language Processing (EMNLP-IJCNLP)*, pages 5164–5174.

Alexis Conneau, Guillaume Lample, Marc'Aurelio Ranzato, Ludovic Denoyer, and Hervé Jégou. 2018. Word Translation Without Parallel Data. In *Proceedings of the International Conference on Learning Representations.*

Thomas Davidson, Dana Warmsley, Michael Macy, and Ingmar Weber. 2017. Automated hate speech detection and the problem of offensive language. In *Proceedings of the 11th International AAAI Conference on Web and Social Media*, ICWSM '17, pages 512–515.

Tom De Smedt and Sylvia Jaki. 2018. Challenges of Automatically Detecting Offensive Language Online: Participation Paper for the Germeval Shared Task 2018 (HaUA). In *Proceedings of the GermEval 2018 Workshop*, pages 27–32.

Jacob Devlin, Ming-Wei Chang, Kenton Lee, and Kristina Toutanova. 2019. BERT: Pre-training of Deep Bidirectional Transformers for Language Understanding. In *Proceedings of the 2019 Conference of the North American Chapter of the Association for Computational Linguistics: Human Language Technologies*, pages 4171–4186.

Darja Fišer, Ruihong Huang, Vinodkumar Prabhakaran, Rob Voigt, Zeerak Waseem, and Jacqueline Wernimont, editors. 2018. *Proceedings of the 2nd Workshop on Abusive Language Online (ALW2).* Association for Computational Linguistics, Brussels, Belgium.

Erfan Ghadery and Marie-Francine Moens. 2020. Liir at semeval-2020 task 12: A cross-lingual augmentation approach for multilingual offensive language identification. In *Proceedings of the Fourteenth Workshop on Semantic Evaluation*, pages 2073–2079.

Ona de Gibert, Naiara Perez, Aitor García-Pablos, and Montse Cuadros. 2018. Hate speech dataset from a white supremacy forum. In *Proceedings of the 2nd Workshop on Abusive Language Online (ALW2)*, pages 11–20.

Yoon Kim. 2014. Convolutional neural networks for sentence classification. In *Proceedings of the 2014 Conference on Empirical Methods in Natural Language Processing (EMNLP)*, pages 1746–1751.

Philipp Koehn, Hieu Hoang, Alexandra Birch, Chris Callison-Burch, Marcello Federico, Nicola Bertoldi, Brooke Cowan, Wade Shen, Christine Moran, Richard Zens, et al. 2007. Moses: Open source toolkit for statistical machine translation. In *Proceedings of the 45th annual meeting of the ACL on interactive poster and demonstration sessions*, pages 177–180.

Zornitsa Kozareva. 2006. Bootstrapping named entity recognition with automatically generated gazetteer lists. In *Student Research Workshop.*

Kosisochukwu Madukwe, Xiaoying Gao, and Bing Xue. 2020. In data we trust: A critical analysis of hate speech detection datasets. In *Proceedings of the Fourth Workshop on Online Abuse and Harms*, pages 150–161, Online. Association for Computational Linguistics.

Prasenjit Majumder, Daksh Patel, Sandip Modha, and Thomas Mandl. 2019. Overview of the HASOC track at FIRE 2019: Hate Speech and Offensive Content Identification in Indo-European Languages. In *Proceedings of the 11th forum for information retrieval evaluation*, pages 14–17.

Puneet Mathur, Ramit Sawhney, Meghna Ayyar, and Rajiv Shah. 2018. Did you offend me? classification of offensive tweets in Hinglish language. In *Proceedings of the 2nd Workshop on Abusive Language Online (ALW2)*, pages 138–148, Brussels, Belgium. Association for Computational Linguistics.

Tharindu Ranasinghe and Marcos Zampieri. 2020. Multilingual offensive language identification with cross-lingual embeddings. In *Proceedings of the 2020 Conference on Empirical Methods in Natural Language Processing (EMNLP)*, pages 5838–5844.

Sarah T. Roberts, Joel Tetreault, Vinodkumar Prabhakaran, and Zeerak Waseem, editors. 2019. *Proceedings of the Third Workshop on Abusive Language Online.* Association for Computational Linguistics, Florence, Italy.

Björn Ross, Michael Rist, Guillermo Carbonell, Benjamin Cabrera, Nils Kurowsky, and Michael Wojatzki. 2016. Measuring the Reliability of Hate Speech Annotations: The Case of the European Refugee Crisis. In *Proceedings of NLP4CMC III: 3rd Workshop on Natural Language Processing for Computer-Mediated Communication*, volume 17 of *Bochumer Linguistische Arbeitsberichte*, pages 6–9.

Josef Ruppenhofer, Melanie Siegel, and Michael Wiegand, editors. 2018. *Proceedings of the GermEval 2018 Workshop*. Austrian Academy of Sciences.

Lukas Stappen, Fabian Brunn, and Björn Schuller. 2020. Cross-lingual Zero- and Few-shot Hate Speech Detection Utilising Frozen Transformer Language Models and AXEL.

Bertie Vidgen and Leon Derczynski. 2020. Directions in abusive language training data, a systematic review: Garbage in, garbage out. *PLOS ONE*, 15(12):e0243300.

Zeerak Waseem, Wendy Hui Kyong Chung, Dirk Hovy, and Joel Tetreault, editors. 2017. *Proceedings of the First Workshop on Abusive Language Online*. Association for Computational Linguistics, Vancouver, BC, Canada.

Gregor Wiedemann, Eugen Ruppert, Raghav Jindal, and Chris Biemann. 2018. Transfer Learning from LDA to BiLSTM-CNN for Offensive Language Detection in Twitter. In *Proceedings of the GermEval 2018 Workshop*.

Michael Wiegand, Anastasija Amann, Tatiana Anikina, Aikaterini Azoidou, Anastasia Borisenkov, Kirstin Kolmorgen, Insa Kröger, and Christine Schäfer. 2018a. Saarland University's Participation in the GermEval Task 2018 (UdSW) - Examining Different Types of Classifiers and Features. In *Proceedings of the GermEval 2018 Workshop*, pages 21–26.

Michael Wiegand, Melanie Siegel, and Josef Ruppenhofer. 2018b. Overview of the germeval 2018 shared task on the identification of offensive language. In *Proceedings of GermEval 2018, 14th Conference on Natural Language Processing (KONVENS 2018)*, pages 1–10.

Jian Xi, Michael Spranger, and Dirk Labudde. 2018. CNN-Based Offensive Language Detection. In *Proceedings of the GermEval 2018 Workshop*.

hBert + BiasCorp - Fighting Racism on the Web

Olawale Onabola[1], Zhuang Ma[2]
Yang Xie[3], Benjamin Akera[1], Abdulrahman Ibraheem[1],
Jia Xue[4], Dianbo Liu[1], and Yoshua Bengio[1,5]
[1]Montreal Institute for Learning Algorithms (Mila), [2]Carnegie Mellon University, CMU,
[3]Independent Researcher, [4]University of Toronto,
[5]CIFAR Program Co-director
walexi4great@gmail.com, liudianbo@gmail.com
yoshua.bengio@mila.quebec

Abstract

Subtle and overt racism is still present both in physical and online communities today and has impacted many lives in different segments of the society. In this short piece of work, we present how we're tackling this societal issue with Natural Language Processing. We are releasing BiasCorp [12], a dataset containing 139,090 comments and news segment from three specific sources - Fox News, BreitbartNews and YouTube. The first batch (45,000 manually annotated) is ready for publication. We are currently in the final phase of manually labelling the remaining dataset using Amazon Mechanical Turk. BERT has been used widely in several downstream tasks. In this work, we present hBERT, where we modify certain layers of the pretrained BERT model with the new Hopfield Layer. hBert generalizes well across different distributions with the added advantage of a reduced model complexity. We are also releasing a JavaScript library [3] and a Chrome Extension Application [4], to help developers make use of our trained model in web applications (say chat application) and for users to identify and report racially biased contents on the web respectively.

1 Introduction

The internet has evolved to become one of the main sources of textual information for many people. Through social media, reviews, and comment sections across the internet, people are continuously consuming information through text. With this, racially biased content has become more entrenched within the language of the internet. Racially biased content in this context refers to the attitudes or stereotypes expressed against marginalized races. This is often as a result of implicit bias resulting into hate speech. In this work, we attempt to automatically detect this racially biased content from data collected from the web, including comments from online news outlets such as Fox News and and comments from YouTube videos. We label this dataset with pointers to racial bias and use machine learning techniques to automate this task. Specifically, we implement BERT as a base model to do this. We also implement a browser extension as a tool to help people identify racially biased content in the information they are consuming. We will also be releasing our curated dataset - BiasCorp to allow more research to be done in this direction.

2 Related works

One of the earliest papers to investigate machine learning approaches for the automatic detection of racially-biased online content is (Greevy and Smeaton, 2004). The paper identified the potential use of bag-of-words, n-grams, and distributions of parts-of-speech tags as features for the task. Their bag-of-words features are informed by ideas from the field of information retrieval, and involve either word frequencies or counts of word occurrences. Using an SVM classifier, for bag-of-words features, they found that the use of frequency of words, rather than number of occurrence of words, yielded greater classification accuracies. The n-grams and parts-of-speech tags techniques were unavailable as of the time of their writing.

In (Warner and Hirschberg, 2012), authors

[1]corresponds to:dianbo.liu/ yoshua.bengio@mila.quebec
[2]https://doi.org/10.7910/DVN/KPBRLC
[3]https://github.com/walexi/biasjs
[4]https://github.com/walexi/biasjs-chrome-extension

Proceedings of the First Workshop on Language Technology for Equality, Diversity and Inclusion, pages 26–33
April 19, 2021. ©2020 Association for Computational Linguistics

followed the definition of (Nockleby and John, 2000) by defining hate speech as "any communication that disparages a person or a group on the basis of some characteristic such as race, color, ethnicity, gender, sexual orientation, nationality, religion, or other characteristic." Their work focused more on detecting anti-Semitic hate speech. For their work, they created a dataset containing hate speech obtained from Yahoo! and the American Jewish Congress. Following the work of (Yarowsky, 1994), they employed hand-crafted template-based features. Apart from the fact that these features are hand-engineered, a potential drawback is their sheer size: a total of 3,537 features, which is prone to the curse of dimensionality. A counter-intuitive result reported by the paper is that the uni-gram features contributed best to classification accuracies. They used linear-kernel SVMs for classification.

The work of (C. et al., 2016) dealt with the broad category of abusive language. Authors of the work gave definitions for distinguishing between three categories of abusive language: hate speech which subsumes racial bias, derogatory remarks and profanity. Further, they described reasons why automatic detection of abusive language, which subsumes racial bias, is difficult. Reasons include: clever evasion of detection engines by users via the use of mischievous permutations of words (e.g. Niggah written as Ni99ah); evolution of ethnic slurs with time; role of cultural context in the perception and interpretation of slurs, as a phrase that is considered derogative in one culture might be perfectly neutral in another culture. Towards building their classification model, they employed four categories of features namely, n-grams, lexical features, syntactic/parser features, and word-level as well as comment-level embeddings. They found that character-level n-grams gave the highest contribution to the model's accuracy.

The authors of (Burnap and Williams, 2016) also developed techniques for detecting multiple hate speech categories including the racially-based category. Towards creating their datasets, they harnessed hate speech event-triggers. For example, to create their racial bias dataset, they collected tweets in a two-week interval following the re-election of Barrack Obama as U.S president. They explored a number of potential features towards building their classification algorithm: bag of words, lexicon of hateful terms, and typed dependencies. In addition, they experimented into classification via SVMs versus classification via random forests, and reported that the former yielded superior performance over the latter. Also, they compared the use of classifiers trained for each hate speech category against the use of a single classifier trained on data spanning all categories. As expected, the specialized classifiers outperformed their multi-category counterpart. (Hasanuzzaman et al., 2017) followed the definition of (Gelber and Stone, 2007), which states that hate speech is: "speech or expression which is capable of instilling or inciting hatred of, or prejudice towards, a person or group of people on a specified ground, including race, nationality, ethnicity, country of origin, ethno-religious identity, religion, sexuality, gender identity or gender." The main research thrust of their work was to apply demographic embeddings (Bamman et al., 2014) , (Hovy, 2015), for the task of racial bias detection in tweets. Compared to other works such as (Burnap and Williams, 2016), for instance, a particularly distinguishing result of (Hasanuzzaman et al., 2017) is how their data extraction procedure is able to arrive at a better balanced ratio of racially-biased to non-racially-biased comments. For example, in the work, 40.58 percent of Canadian tweets were judged racially-biased by human annotators, whereas in (Burnap and Williams, 2016) only about 3.73 percent of the comments in the dataset are racially biased. Classification results using an SVM classifier revealed benefits of their proposed demographic embeddings over traditional features and embeddings. In (Saleh et al., 2020), the authors explored the detection of hate speech in White supremacist forums. They explored BiLSTM, logistic regression and BERT for their task. Also, they compared the use of domain-agnostic pre-trained word embedding (such as GloVe.6B.300d) versus the use of a domain-aware 300-dimensional word2vec embedding trained on the specific dataset used in the work. Results showed that BERT yields better results than both logistic regression and BiLSTM. Further, results proved the domain-aware embeddings to be superior to the pre-trained embeddings.

3 Method

3.1 Data curation and processing

The datasets used for training were obtained from discussion channels of online news media by programmed web crawler based on Scrapy framework with all crawled data stored in PostgreSQL database. Since existing comments of online article were generally loaded by asynchronous API accessed by a specific key hidden in the articles before presenting them on website, the web crawler parsed keys for each article after completing a list with URLs of all articles waiting to be further crawled and then matched the keys with their corresponding API to retrieved stored comments for each article.

First, sentences containing neural racial words from a curated list were selected. Second, the sentiment score of each comment was calculated according to two lookup tables: a combined and augmented (Jockers, 2015) and Rinker's augmented Hu and Liu (Tyler Rinker, 2016) (Hu and Liu, 2004) positive/negative word list as sentiment lookup values, and a racial-related English lookup table from Hatebase[5]. To guarantee these two tables influence the sentiment score consistently, the lookup values of the Hatebase table were adjusted by percentage. Then we extracted the data with bottom 20 percent of the sentiment score, and matched them up with other randomly selected comments appearing under the same articles or videos as random control. Finally, equal numbers of random controls are added into the data set, to ensure that approximately half of the data is racially discriminatory.

3.2 Model Architecture

Attention-based Transformer network (Vaswani et al., 2017) has been used widely across different natural language processing tasks. Based on the previous successes of the transformer network, we decided to use the BERT Architecture (Devlin et al., 2019) as our base model. Unlike previous variant of the attention-based language models such as (Radford et al., 2018), BERT learns to jointly conditions on the right and left context of the input representation at all the layers by randomly masking out segments of the input token. This is particularly useful for extracting contextual information from the input representation, and it's very applicable to our use case. We aim to build a variant of the model that can generalize *sufficiently* well across different data distributions[6]. The notion of *sufficiency* is evaluated by training, validating and testing our model on data across the different sources. We fine-tune the pretrained BERT model on our curated dataset rather than training from scratch (this choice was based on empirical results). We are releasing a JavaScript library for developers to use our pretrained model in front facing applications such as chat app, to flag down racially biased comments. Consequently, we need to optimize for the model complexity without sacrificing performance gain. BERT has a huge number of parameters / large model size. Other methods have been employed to reduce the complexity without hurting the performance, such as knowledge distillation (Sanh et al., 2019) and quantization (Zafrir et al., 2019). It has also been proven that pruning the weights of the pretrained model do not necessarily affect the model performance, within acceptable 'thresholds' (Gordon et al., 2020). In a similar fashion, we aim to reduce the complexity of BERT without sacrificing performance by replacing certain layers with the Hopfield layer (Ramsauer et al., 2020). Hopfield layer can be used to replace the attention-based layer of the BERT model; as it has been shown to approximate the functionality of the attention mechanism with a new Energy update rule (modified version of the Hopfield network extended to continuous state representation). The learning dynamics of BERT as shown in (Ramsauer et al., 2020) shows that the attention heads in the higher layers are mostly responsible for extracting task-specific features from the input representation. We replaced the self-attention mechanism in the last X layers of the pretrained BERT model with a Hopfield layer, where X is an hyperparameter. In a similar approach described in (Vaswani et al., 2017), we use residual connection around the Hopfield sub-layer, followed by layer normalization (Ba et al., 2016). It has been shown that residual connections help propagate positional information across layers. The replaced Hopfield layer drastically reduced the parameter size of our model. To further improve the performance of the model, we use the Hopfield Pooling layer which acts as both a permutation equivariant layer and pools generated embedding from the modified BERT model. The Hopfield pooling layer also acts as a form of memory to store the hidden state of the last layer in the modified BERT model. Finally, we add a classification layer on top of the pooling layer for the task in question.

[5] https://hatebase.org/

[6] distributions here implies different use cases or data environments/sources

3.3 Model Training

Given the disparity between the annotators for each sample in our dataset, averaging the labels with the confidence scores as weights might be noisy. We computed the coefficient of variation CV among annotators for each sample in our dataset. Using the recommended (JUDICE et al., 1999) (Veit et al., 2017) CV of 0.2 for the bias scores would imply dropping 90% of the dataset as seen in 2. In order to fully utilize the dataset and effectively manage the disparity between the annotators, we formulate a loss function $\mathcal{L}_{model}$ given by

$$L_{model} = 1/N \sum_{i=1}^{N} CE\Big(p(x_i), q(x_i)\Big) \quad (1)$$

where $CE(p(x_i), q(x_i))$ is the cross entropy between $p(x_i)$ and $q(x_i)$ for the ith sample, and N is the size of the dataset.

$$CE(p,q) = -\sum_{i=1}^{c} p_c(x) \log(\epsilon + q_c(x)) \quad (2)$$

$q_c(x)$ is the predicted probability of sample x in class c, equivalently, the output probabilities from the model and ϵ is for numerical stability. $p_c(x)$ is the probability of sample x in class c, equivalently, $p_c(x)$ is a $c - length$ vector with entries such that $\sum_{i=1}^{c} p_c(x) = 1$. The entries of $p_c(x)$ are the normalized confidence scores of the annotators with indices given by the respective voted classes. As an example, following the algorithm described in 1, for a given sample shown in figure 1; the bias scores of the 3 different annotators with their confidence level is represented with an array of tuples, X where each tuple, (b_i, s_i) is the bias score b_i with the associated confidence score, s_i by annotator i. To calculate $p_c(x)$, we first normalize the confidence scores across the 3 different annotators such that $\sum_{i=1}^{3} s_i = 1$. The resulting $p_c(x)$ for the entry, S, shown in 1 is

$$X = \Big[(4,4),(3,3),(2,5)\Big]$$

$$X_{norm} = \Big[(4, 0.3333), (3, 0.25), (2, 0.4167)\Big]$$

$$p_c(X) = [0., 0., 0.4167, 0.25, 0.3333, 0.]$$

3.4 Evaluation Task and Metrics

We evaluate the model performance across the validation and test set, given that they are from different distributions or sources. The test set contains only comments from YouTube while the validation set was randomly sampled from Fox News and BreitbartNews. The particular choices were due to the fact that the first batch of the dataset used for training contained very relatively few samples from YouTube. We evaluate our approach using two methods; multiclass classification and multiclass-multilabel classification.

Using the multiclass approach, for a given sample, k and using the method described previously in calculating the target class, the class with the maximum confidence score was used as the target. We calculate the average precision for each class, AP_c and the mean average precision MAP averaged over the entire dataset with size N along the class dimension d as described in (Veit et al., 2017)

$$AP_c = \frac{\sum_{k=1}^{N} Precision(k,c) \cdot rel(k,c)}{numberofpositives} \quad (3)$$

$$MAP = 1/d \sum_{c=1}^{d} AP_c \quad (4)$$

Algorithm 1: Compute $p_c(x)$ for a sample x

Result: $p_c(x)$

Input: An array of target scores ***t***, and array of confidence scores ***s*** where ***s[i]*** is the confidence score by ***annotator i*** for choosing target score ***t[i]***

Both arrays are of equal length N where N is the number of annotators. ***C*** is the number of classes (equivalently the range/max of possible target scores if scores are integer.)

Step 1: Initialize

$p_c \leftarrow [\ .0$ **for** _ **in** $C]$

Step 2: Calculate normalizing constant K

K $\leftarrow \sum_{i=1}^{N} s_i$;

Step 3: Set the values of p_c

for i in N **do**

  $class\_index \leftarrow t[i]$;

  $p_c[class\_index] \xleftarrow{+} \frac{s[i]}{K}$;

end

	text	bias_1	bias_2	bias_3	confidence_1	confidence_2	confidence_3
0	" Democrats needed someone like Obama, half w...	4	3	2	4	3	5

Figure 1: Sample annotation

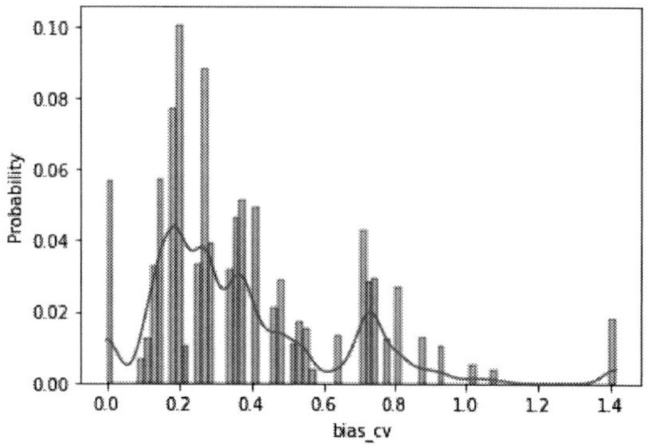

(a) Bias Score

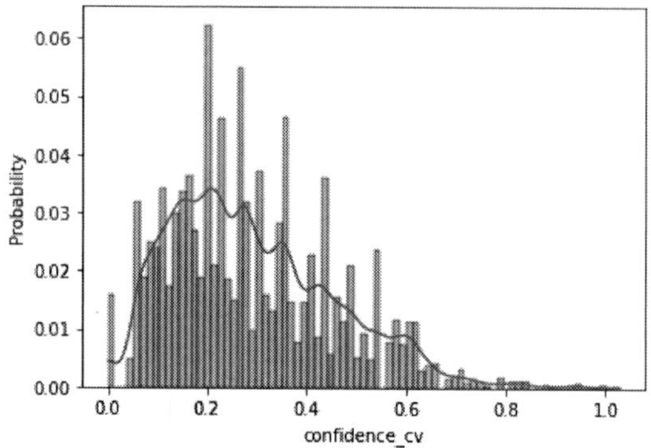

(b) Confidence Score

Figure 2: Confidence of Variation

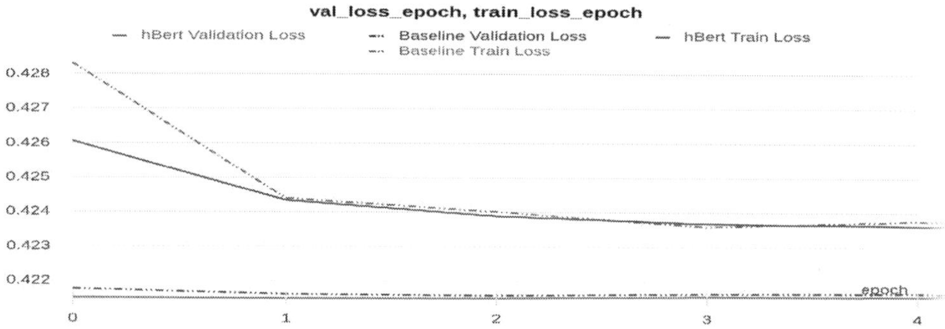

(a) Train Vs Validation Loss

Model	TopK Accuracy			mAP	F1 @ k			IoU @ k		
	1	2	3		1	2	3	1	2	3
Baseline	0.6015625	0.703125	0.7890625	0.29355	0.5859	0.6953	0.7734	0.2102	0.2114	0.2102
hBert	**0.0.640625**	0.703125	0.765625	**0.3501**	**0.6562**	**0.7109**	**0.8125**	**0.2266**	**0.2165**	**0.2281**

Table 1: Test Metrics for selected trial for each model configuration

Model	AP					
	0	1	2	3	4	5
Baseline	0.2205	0.0967	0.1344	0.9564	0.1103	0.2340
hBert	0.1195	**0.1111**	**0.2132**	**0.9607**	**0.5049**	0.1914

Table 2: The Average Precision (AP) for the different classes

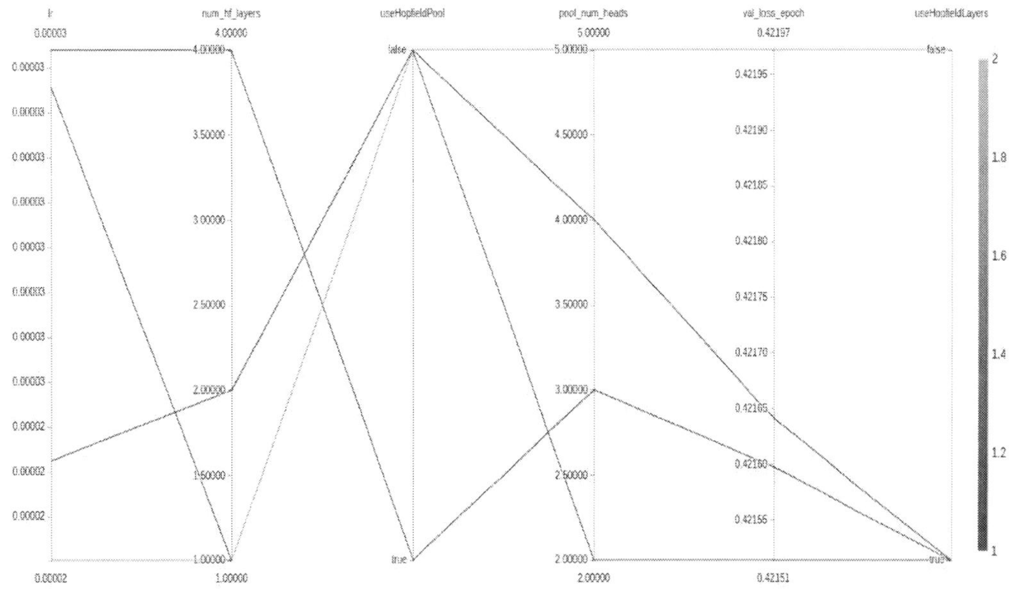

Figure 3: Parallel Coordinate Graph for multiple runs/trials across model configurations
The model configuration is the Baseline when the target variable (***useHopfieldLayers*** in the graph is False.
The ***useHopfieldPool*** variable denotes whether the Hopfield Pooling layer was used
The ***lr, pool_num_heads, num_hf_layers, val_loss_epoch*** variables in the graph are the learning rate, the number of heads in the Hopfield Pooling Layer (if used), the number of Hopfield Layer and the validation loss respectively
. With a reduced model complexity, the hBert performs relatively as good as the baseline

where $Precision(k, c)$ is the precision for class c for the kth sample and $rel(k, c)$ is an indicator function that is 1 if the predicted and the target class for sample k is positive. We also report the $topK$ accuracy, for $k = [1, 3]$ since we had a max of 3 annotators for each k.

Using the multilabel approach, for a given sample, k and using the method described previously in calculating the target class, we take the top k classes as the target classes. We do the same for the predictions (obtained after passing the output logits through a softmax function). We compute the AP_c (for each class), mAP, $F1$ score, and IoU

4 Experiments

4.1 Training Details & Result

We run a multi-objective hyperparameter search (using Optuna(Akiba et al., 2019)) optimizing for the following parameters: validation loss, FLOPs (indicative of the model complexity and ultimately the inference time), mAP on the validation and test set, and the Intersection over Union IoU scores (also known as the Jaccard Index) for the *topk* for $k = [1, 3]$ transformations described above. We use 4 NVidia V100SXM2 (16G memory) GPUs on a single node, with batch size of 32. We reduced the batch size (instead of say 64) because we had to run multiple trials and to avoid the notorious OOM error. For each model configuration, we run 10 trials with 5 epochs each. As seen in 3, the hBert perform relatively better with a reduced model complexity. In 1, the models predictions were more accurate for an increasing k. The hBert perform better than the Baseline for the Top1 accuracy. The F1 scores and Jaccard Index (IoU) for the hBert were relatively higher for $k = [1, 3]$. The mAP, which is the average of the AP_c over the classes, is relatively low because of the low performing classes as seen in 2

4.2 Data statistics

The data set contains 139,090 rows, and 67.70 percent of their sentiment scores are negative. Their average sentiment score is -0.1422, and the median value is -0.1203, ranging from -3.6206 to 2.1414. 66,998 of them are comments from Fox News, with an average sentiment score of -0.0997 and a median of -0.0884, ranging from -2.8591 to 2.1414. And 63,948 of the data are comments from Breitbart News, with an average sentiment score of -0.1760 and a median of -0.1721, ranging from -3.6206 to 1.3576. And 8,144 of the data are comments from YouTube, with an average sentiment score of -0.2259 and a median of -0.2694, ranging from -3.3000 to 1.4673. In this work, we used the first batch of the dataset; which have been manually annotated using Amazon Mechanical Turk. After pre-processing the input text (removing irrelevant tokens such as mentions), the maximum length was 478 (it was 623 before preprocessing).

5 Discussion

In this work we have shown a way to detect racial bias in text. We experimented with a BERT-based model as we aim to reduce model complexity without sacrificing much of the performance. We also discussed the BiasCorp, a manually labelled dataset containing racially biased comments from Fox News, BreitbartNews and YouTube. To enable developers make use of our pretrained hBERT model, we are releasing a Javascript Library, optimized for inference on the edge. A Chrome Extension will also be available for users to help report and identify racially bias text on the web. We also plan to extend this work to other forms of biases such as Gender. In a future work, we plan to further reduce the model complexity by using Gaussian Kernel as described in (Ramsauer et al., 2020) and other quantization tricks.

Acknowledgments

This research was enabled in part by support provided by Calcul Québec (www.calculquebec.ca) and Compute Canada (www.computecanada.ca)

References

Takuya Akiba, Shotaro Sano, Toshihiko Yanase, Takeru Ohta, and Masanori Koyama. 2019. Optuna: A next-generation hyperparameter optimization framework. In *Proceedings of the 25rd ACM SIGKDD International Conference on Knowledge Discovery and Data Mining*.

Jimmy Lei Ba, Jamie Ryan Kiros, and Geoffrey E. Hinton. 2016. Layer normalization.

David Bamman, Chris Dyer, and Noah A. Smith. 2014. Distributed representations of geographically situated language. In *Proceedings of the Association for Computational Linguistics*, pages 828–834.

Pete Burnap and Mathew Williams. 2016. Us and them: identifying cyber hate on twitter across multiple protected characteristics. *EPJ Data Science*, 5:1817–1853.

Nobata C., Tetreault J., Thomas A., Y. Mehdad, and Chang Y. 2016. Abusive language detection in online user content. In *Proceedings of the 25th international conference on world wide web*, pages 145–153.

Jacob Devlin, Ming-Wei Chang, Kenton Lee, and Kristina Toutanova. 2019. Bert: Pre-training of deep bidirectional transformers for language understanding.

Katharine Gelber and Adrienne Sarah Ackary Stone. 2007. *Hate Speech and Freedom of Speech in Australia*. Federation Press.

Mitchell A. Gordon, Kevin Duh, and Nicholas Andrews. 2020. Compressing bert: Studying the effects of weight pruning on transfer learning.

Edel Greevy and Alan Smeaton. 2004. Text categorisation of racist texts using a support vector machine. *JADT 2004 : 7es Journées internationales d'Analyse statistique des Données Textuelles*, pages 533–544.

Mohammed Hasanuzzaman, Gael Dias, and Andy Way. 2017. Demographic word embeddings for racism detection on twitter. In *Proceedings of the 8th International Joint Conference on Natural Language Processing*, pages 926–936.

Dirk Hovy. 2015. Demographic factors improve classification performance. In *Proceedings of the Association for Computational Linguistics*, pages 752–762.

Minqing Hu and Bing Liu. 2004. Mining and summarizing customer reviews. pages 168–177.

Matthew L. Jockers. 2015. *Syuzhet: Extract Sentiment and Plot Arcs from Text*.

MARCELO JUDICE, Muniz Augusto, and Roberto Carvalheiro. 1999. Avaliação do coeficiente de variação na experimentação com suínos. *Ciência e Agrotecnologia*, 23.

Nockleby and John. 2000. Hate speech. In *Encyclopedia of the American Constitution*, pages 1277–1279.

Alec Radford, Karthik Narasimhan, Tim Salimans, and Ilya Sutskever. 2018. Improving language understanding with unsupervised learning.

Hubert Ramsauer, Bernhard Schäfl, Johannes Lehner, Philipp Seidl, Michael Widrich, Thomas Adler, Lukas Gruber, Markus Holzleitner, Milena Pavlović, Geir Kjetil Sandve, Victor Greiff, David Kreil, Michael Kopp, Günter Klambauer, Johannes Brandstetter, and Sepp Hochreiter. 2020. Hopfield networks is all you need.

Hind Saleh, Areej Alhothali, and Kawthar Moria. 2020. Detecting white supremacist hate speech using domain specific word embedding with deep learning and bert. *In Submission to Information Processing and Management*, pages 533–544.

Victor Sanh, Lysandre Debut, Julien Chaumond, and Thomas Wolf. 2019. Distilbert, a distilled version of BERT: smaller, faster, cheaper and lighter. *CoRR*, abs/1910.01108.

Vitalie Spinu Tyler Rinker. 2016. sentimentr: Dictionary based sentiment analysis that considers valence shifters.

Ashish Vaswani, Noam Shazeer, Niki Parmar, Jakob Uszkoreit, Llion Jones, Aidan N. Gomez, Lukasz Kaiser, and Illia Polosukhin. 2017. Attention is all you need.

Andreas Veit, Neil Alldrin, Gal Chechik, Ivan Krasin, Abhinav Gupta, and Serge J. Belongie. 2017. Learning from noisy large-scale datasets with minimal supervision. *CoRR*, abs/1701.01619.

J. Warner and J. Hirschberg. 2012. Detecting hate speech on the world wide web. In *Proceedings of the Second Workshop on Language in Social Media*, pages 19–26.

David Yarowsky. 1994. Decision lists for lexical ambiguity resolution: Application to accent restoration in spanish and french. In *Proceedings of the ACL*, pages 88–95.

Ofir Zafrir, Guy Boudoukh, Peter Izsak, and Moshe Wasserblat. 2019. Q8BERT: quantized 8bit BERT. *CoRR*, abs/1910.06188.

An Overview of Fairness in Data – Illuminating the Bias in Data Pipeline

Senthil Kumar B [1], **Chandrabose Aravindan** [1], **Bharathi Raja Chakravarthi** [2]
[1] Sri Sivasubramaniya Nadar College of Engineering, Tamil Nadu
[2] National University of Ireland Galway
senthil@ssn.edu.in

Abstract

Data in general encodes human biases by default; being aware of this is a good start, and the research around how to handle it is ongoing. The term 'bias' is extensively used in various contexts in NLP systems. In our research the focus is specific to biases such as gender, racism, religion, demographic and other intersectional views on biases that prevail in text processing systems responsible for systematically discriminating specific population, which is not ethical in NLP. These biases exacerbate the lack of equality, diversity and inclusion of specific population while utilizing the NLP applications. The tools and technology at the intermediate level utilize biased data, and transfer or amplify this bias to the downstream applications. However, it is not enough to be colourblind, gender-neutral alone when designing a unbiased technology – instead, we should take a conscious effort by designing a unified framework to measure and benchmark the bias. In this paper, we recommend six measures and one augment measure based on the observations of the bias in data, annotations, text representations and debiasing techniques.

1 Introduction

Irrespective of the data sources, the majority of the bias prevails in data itself (Lam et al., 2011; Fine et al., 2014; Jones et al., 2020). The inherent bias in data affects the core NLP tasks such as Part-Of-Speech (POS) tagging, POS Chunking (Manzini et al., 2019), and dependency parsing (Garimella et al., 2019). Other than data bias, the techniques used to represent the data also pose a threat to NLP systems (Bolukbasi et al., 2016; Caliskan et al., 2017; Ethayarajh et al., 2019; Zhou et al., 2019). Eventually the bias magnifies itself due to these biased data representation in downstream applications such as Named Entity Recognition (NER) (Manzini et al., 2019), coreference resolution (Zhao et al., 2017; Rudinger et al., 2018; Zhao et al., 2019), sentiment analysis (Kiritchenko and Mohammad, 2018), machine translation (Stanovsky et al., 2019; Escudé Font et al., 2019), social data analysis (Waseem and Hovy, 2016; Davidson et al., 2017; Sap et al., 2019; Hasanuzzaman et al., 2017), and bio-medical language processing (Rios et al., 2020). However,a very little attention is given to data collection and processing. Wikipedia seems like a diverse data source but fewer than 18% of the site's biographical entries represents women(Wagner et al., 2015).

Olteanu et al. (2019) observed that the dataset extracted from social media data has its own bias in various aspects such as age, gender, racism, location, job, and religion. Existing research classified biases at various levels, including the bias in data - source itself, the bias in the data analysis pipeline, and the biased data in building the systems. For example, using a biased abusive language detection system may result in discrimination against a group of minority peoples such as African-American (Waseem and Hovy, 2016).

The survey by Blodgett and O'Connor (2017) on bias in NLP systems found that works related to bias failed to explain why the system behaviours are 'biased', harmful, what kind of behaviours lead to bias, in what ways, to whom and why. The paper also discusses the need to conceptualise bias better by linking the languages and social hierarchies in the society. Another survey by Sun et al. (2019) analyses the bias framework and issues with the current debiasing methods. Their study reveals that the gender bias in NLP is still at a nascent level and lacks unified metrics and benchmark evaluation methods. This paper audits or surveys the present situation in analysing the bias at various levels of data.

This paper has been divided into four section. In

Proceedings of the First Workshop on Language Technology for Equality, Diversity and Inclusion, pages 34–45
April 19, 2021. ©2020 Association for Computational Linguistics

section 2, we analyse the bias in language resources or corpora, in word representations, in pre-trained language models. In section 3, based on the observation of bias in corpora level, social data, text representations, metric to measure and mitigate bias, we infer six recommendations and one measure augmenting the existing one. In section 4, we conclude with the need of practicing standard procedures across the data pipeline in NLP systems to support ethical and fairness usage of data.

2 Data Bias

Language resources are present in two forms: 1) Online digital data 2) Annotated corpus. In fact language technologies are data-driven methods based on statistical learning techniques. There needs to be a framework to monitor the flow of data from the source to the NLP system and to measure the bias emanating at each level. The dataset can be representative of a specific genre or domain and a balanced one to avoid selectional bias as noted by Søgaard et al. (2014). The bias also emanates from labelling the corpus by annotators. Dickinson and Meurers (2003) observed bias in widely-used Penn Treebank annotated corpora which contain many errors. Apart from the linguistic experts, using non-experts in the annotation process through crowd-sourcing platforms also leads to considerable bias in data (Waseem, 2016). Figure.1 shows the effects of bias in data which leads to bias in gender, bias in syntactic and shallow parsing across domains, bias due to the disparity in language resources represented by tree hierarchy.

2.1 Fallacies in Language resources or corpora

As language resources or corpora are crucial for any NLP systems, the following show the gender and domain bias in data itself, occurred due to tagging and parsing, annotation issues in corpus creation.

Bias in Diversity and Inclusion of languages:

- The quantitative analysis by Joshi et al. (2020) reveals the disparity amongst language resources. The taxonomy of languages in the aspect of resource distributions (Joshi et al., 2020) shows that among six classes of languages, the Class-0, which contains the largest section of languages – 2,191 languages – are still ignored in the aspect of language technologies, and there is no resource present. This non-availability of language resources aggravates the disparity in language resources.
- Hence the Diversity and Inclusion (DI) score should be recommended to measure the diversity of NLP system methods to apply for different languages and the system's contributions to the inclusivity of poorly resourced or less represented languages Joshi et al. (2020).
- As languages are dynamic, Hovy and Søgaard (2015) warned the consequence of using age-old limited training data to train a model which could be evaluated on new data.

Bias across domain:

- Fine et al. (2014) investigated bias across five annotated corpora: Google Ngram, BNC (written, spoken), CELEX (written, spoken), Switchboard (Penn Treebank) using psycholinguistic measures identified domain bias in the corpora. Google appears to be familiar with terminology dealing with adult material and technology related terms. Similarly, BNC is biased towards Briticisms. The Switchboard corpus overestimates how quickly humans will react to colloquialisms and backchannels during telephone conversations.

Bias in annotating social data:

- Davidson et al. (2017) found a substantial racial bias that exists among all datasets and recommended the way to measure the origin of bias during collection and labelling.
- The bias in social data cripples during the labelling process as noted by Waseem (2016). The author criticized the decision by annotators by labelling the words from African-American English (AAE) as offensive since it is being used widely among its users. The models built on expert annotations perform comparatively better than the amateur annotators as they are more likely to label an item as hate speech. Indeed annotating task for social data is complex if the task is to categorize the abusive behaviour, as there is no standard procedure, and what qualifies as abusive is still not clear (Founta et al., 2018).
- The dialect-based bias in the corpora was observed by Sap et al. (2019). Amazon Mechanical Turk annotators were asked to find whether

Twitter user's dialect and race are offensive to themselves or others. The result showed that dialect and race are less significant to label AAE tweet as offensive to someone. Thus the racial bias emanates from skew annotation process can be removed by not having skewed demographics of annotators.

Gender bias in data / corpus:

- After 2010, Wikipedia is aimed at closing the gender gap by rolling out several projects, which includes WikiProject women, WikiProject gender studies, Women in Red. To determine the type and quality of material that is acceptable in Wikipedia articles, the content on Wikipedia must be written from a neutral point of view (NPOV) [1].

- But still, there is a large gender gap among the Wikipedia editors. Findings by Lam et al. (2011) indicate a male-skewed gender imbalance in English Wikipedia editors. Females are more likely to exit from Wikipedia than males before accumulating many edits. Hence the proportion of males who become administrators is more than females. Based on eight interest areas, females and males are focused on different content, females concentrate more on People and Art areas, while males focus more on Geography and Science.

Figure 1: Data bias tree hierarchy

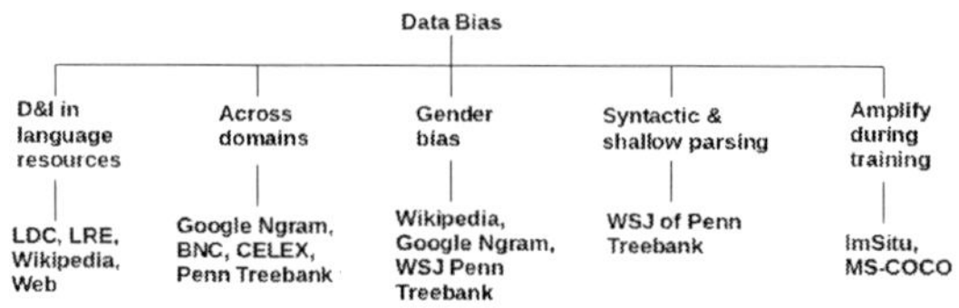

- How gender bias has developed in the Wikipedia was analysed by Schmahl et al. (2020) using four categories: Career, Science, Family and Arts. The stereotypical gender bias in the categories family and science is decreasing, and art-related words are becoming more biased towards females. Their findings also reveal that the selection of corpus for word embedding depends on the task. For example, to have a gender-neutral word embedding related to Science, one may best use the corpus of 2018.

- Analysis on the word embedding representation of the Google Ngram corpus shows that stereotypical gender associations in languages have decreased over time but still exists (Jones et al., 2020).

Bias in syntactic and shallow parsing:

- Apart from the labelling bias in Penn Treebank, Garimella et al. (2019) observed a gender bias in syntactic labelling and parsing for the Wall Street Journal (WSJ) articles from Penn Treebank with gender information. The POS taggers, syntactic parsers trained on any data performed well when tested with female-authored articles. Whereas the male writings performed better only on sufficient male-authored articles as training data. This highlights the grammatical differences between gender and the need for better tools for syntactic annotation.

- Off-the-shelf POS taggers show differences in performance for languages of the people in different age groups, and the linguistic differences are not solely on lexical but also grammatical (Hovy and Søgaard, 2015).

2.2 Fallacies in Word Representations

Bias is pervasive in word embeddings and neural models in general. Apart from analysing the language resources and corpora, the bias in the language can also be studied by using the word embeddings – distributed representation of words in vector form. Biases in word embeddings may, in turn, have unwanted consequences in downstream applications.

Bias in word representations:

- A pioneer work in the detection of bias on word embeddings by Bolukbasi et al. (2016) proposed two debiasing techniques: hard and soft-debias. They showed that gender bias could be captured by identifying the direction in embedding subspace and could be neutralised. The hard-debiasing effectively reduce gender stereotypes when compared with the soft-debiasing technique.

- Caliskan et al. (2017) measured the bias in the Word2Vec embeddings on Google News corpus and pre-trained GloVe using WEAT, WEFAT score. The authors noted that the gender association strength of occupation words is highly correlated.

[1] https://en.wikipedia.org/wiki&/Wikipedia:Neutral_point_of_view

- Using the notion of bias subspace, the WEAT shows systemic error in overestimating the bias (Ethayarajh et al., 2019). Even though Bolukbasi et al. (2016) shown that removing bias by subspace projection method, there is no theoretical guarantee that the debiased vectors are entirely unbiased or the method works for embedding models other than the skip-gram with negative sampling (SGNS). Proposed the measure relational inner product association (RIPA) that analyses how much gender association in embedding space is due to embedding model and training corpus. For further notion on the impact of bias, subspace and debiasing refer Ethayarajh et al. (2019).

Representation bias in social data:

- The Twitter data was analysed using demographic embeddings (location, age, location), which shows that the gender variable has a small impact when compared with the location variable in classifying the racism tweets (Hasanuzzaman et al., 2017).
- The Word2Vec trained on L2-Reddit shows bias in the dataset using multi-class for a race, gender and religion (Manzini et al., 2019). Embeddings are debiased using hard, and soft-debias and its downstream effect shows decreased performance by POS tagging and an increase in NER and Chunking.

Representation bias in applications:

- To detect an unintended bias in word embeddings Sweeney and Najafian (2019) proposed a Relative Negative Sentiment Bias (RNSB) framework. WEAT score shows that the Word2vec and GloVe word embeddings are biased with respect to national origin, whereas RNSB measure the discrimination with respect to more than two demographics within a protected group. The study also reveals that the unintended bias is more in GloVE embeddings.

Representation bias in language resources:

- Brunet et al. (2019) used PPMI, Word2Vec and GloVe embeddings to train the two corpora Wikipedia and NYT, used WEAT metric to quantify the amount of bias contributed by the data in training.
- Using Word2vec trained on Google News, GloVe on NYT and COHA embeddings for temporal analysis Garg et al. (2018) found the occupational and demographic shifts over time. The embeddings are leveraged to quantify the attitude towards women and ethnic minorities.
- Zhao et al. (2019) reported that bias gets amplified while training the biased dataset. For example, some of the training set verbs have small bias and are heavily biased towards females after training. Kitchen and technology-oriented categories in MS-COCO are aligned towards females and males, respectively that have been amplified during training.

2.3 Fallacies in Pre-trained Language Models

Instead of using the word embeddings directly from the models for classification, the embeddings from pre-trained language models (LM) such as GloVe, ELMo, BERT, GPT can be used to train the task-specific datasets using transfer learning.

Pre-trained LM in MT:

- Escudé Font et al. (2019) found gender bias in the translation of English-Spanish in the news domain. The baseline system is trained with GloVe and use hard-debias along with GN-GloVE embeddings for debiasing. The BLEU score increased for the pre-trained embedding and improved slightly for the debiased model using transfer learning which means the translation is preserved while enhancing the gender debias.
- Embeddings of gendered languages such as Spanish and French contain gender bias. For English, Zhou et al. (2019) used the fastText monolingual embeddings pre-trained on Wikipedia corpora. For word translation, the bilingual embeddings ES-EN and FR-EN from MUSE aligns the fastText monolingual embeddings. The bias in bilingual embeddings is observed using MWEAT and mitigated using Shift_EN method.

Pre-trained LM in Coreference:

- Zhao et al. (2019) used ELMo pre-trained embeddings to represent OntoNotes to train the LSTM model. The bias is evaluated using the WinoBias dataset. Data augmentation and

Data	Resource/Task/Techniques	Work by
Bias in Diversity, Inclusivity of Language Resources	Class-0: 2191 languages virtually no unlabelled data to use	(Joshi et al., 2020)
Bias in Language Resources	Wikipedia Google Books Ngram Corpus	(Lam et al., 2011) (Schmahl et al., 2020) (Jones et al., 2020)
Bias in Domain	Google Ngram, BNC(written,spoken), CELEX(written, spoken), Switchboard(Penn Treebank)	(Fine et al., 2014)
Bias amplify in training	Bias in embeddings gets amplified while training the datasets – imSitu	(Zhao et al., 2017)
Lexicons to detect dialects in social data	AAE	(Davidson et al., 2017), (Sap et al., 2019), (Blodgett and O'Connor, 2017)
	HateBase	(Davidson et al., 2017)
	Slur DB, ethnic slur by Wikipedia	(Hasanuzzaman et al., 2017)
Data design/schema-level constructs	WinoBias-gender bias in Coref. Winogender-gender bias in Coref. WinoMT - gender bias in MT EEC-gender/race bias in SA	(Zhao et al., 2018, 2019) (Rudinger et al., 2018) (Stanovsky et al., 2019) (Hasanuzzaman et al., 2017)

Table 1: Survey on the research done in the bias in data

Neutralization are used to fine-tune the embeddings, which reduces bias.

Pre-trained LM in Social data analysis:

- Park and Fung (2017) trained the Twitter dataset on CNN, GRU and Bi-directional GRU with attention models using FastText, Word2vec pre-trained embeddings. The gender bias on models trained with sexist and abusive tweets was mitigated by debiased word embeddings, data augmentation and fine-tuning with a large corpus. Result concluded that debiased word embeddings alone do not effectively correct the bias, while fine-tuning bias with a less biased source dataset greatly improves the performance with drop-in bias.

3 Observations and Inferences

The biases that are much extensively experimented can be categorized as: fine-grained such as gender, racism, religion, and location; coarse-grained such as demographic and gender+occupation. Most experiments or analysis are performed on observing gender bias and its stereotypes from data and through word representations. The other types of bias, such as racism, sexism, and religion, are extensively studied in social data. The other biases from intersectional bias attributes such as demographic (age, gender, location), gender+racism, and gender+location+job are not extensively studied. Much attention is needed to study the other types and bias based on the intersectional view.

3.1 Bias in data / corpora

A standard process has to be defined on how data are collected, processed and organized. Gebru et al. (2020) recommended that every dataset should have datasheets that are metadata that documents its motivation, composition, collection process, recommended uses, and so on. Every training dataset should be accompanied by information on how the data were collected and annotated. If data contain information about people, then summary statistics on geography, gender, ethnicity and other demographic information should be provided. Specifically, steps should be taken to ensure that such datasets are diverse and do not represent any particular groups. The model performance may hinder if the dataset reflects unwanted biases or its deployment domain does not match its training or evaluation domain. Table 1 shows the analysis of

Labelling / Annotations	Resource/Task/Techniques	Work by
Bias in labelling	POS Tag, Dependency parse in WSJ Penn Treebank	(Garimella et al., 2019)
Bias in social data annotations	Inter-Annotator agreement for Twitter data collection	(Waseem, 2016),(Sap et al., 2019)
	Misleading label in financial tweets by annotators	(Chen et al., 2020)

Table 2: Analysis of bias in labelling / annotation

bias in data.

1. **Datasheets & Data Statements**: Datasheet for data should be documented well, to avoid the misuse of data sets for unmatched domains and tasks (Gebru et al., 2020). Bender and Friedman (2018) proposed data statements to be included in all NLP systems' publication and documentation. These data statements will address exclusion and bias in language technologies that do not misrepresent the users from others.

2. **D&I metric for corpora**: The metric to measure the language diversity and inclusivity is necessary for each corpus that helps to measure the language support by the corpora and its power to include poor-resource languages (Joshi et al., 2020).

3. **Data design – Schema templates**: The schema-level constructs such as WinoBias, Winogender for coreference systems, WinoMT for MT and EEC for sentiment analysis are used to measure and mitigate the bias for task / application-specific purposes. These schemas provide semantic cues in sentences apart from syntactic cues to detect the bias.

4. **Metric for subset selection** - The subset selection is a fundamental task that does not consider the metric to select the set of instances from a more extensive set. Mitchell et al. (2019) formalized how these subsets can be measured for diversity and inclusion for image datasets. There should be a similar kind of metrics that should be formulated for text datasets too.

5. **Bias through an Intersectional view** – Bias also emanates due to the cross-section of the gender and racism. Solomon et al. (2018) demands the study of bias through the intersection of race and gender, which would alleviate the problem experienced by Black Women. This is done by analysing multiple identities through an intersectional lens. Research shows that Black or women are not inclusive of Black women's unique perspectives.

Our recommendations based on the above:

- **Recommendation-1:** Research on various semantic-level constructs specific to applications is needed. Like data design practiced in database systems to capture the semantics of data using schema representations, schema-level constructs are needed for task-specific applications to mitigate bias.

- **Recommendation-2:** The need for Taxonomy of bias for LT w.r.t EDI – which focus other than binary gender such as transgender, LGBTQ, and bias through an intersectional view.

- **Recommendation-3:** Biases defined for linguistic resources can not be used or may unmatch for the data from other domains such as bio-medical, science and law. Need of domain-wise bias study as it may differ in its own perspectives.

3.2 Bias in corpus labelling or annotations

If the data labelling is done through crowdsourcing, then necessary information about the crowd participants should be included, alongside the exact request or instructions that they were given. To help identify sources of bias, annotators should systematically label the content of training data sets with standardised metadata. Table 2 shows the analysis of bias in labelling corpora, social data annotations.

1. **Is Social data fair enough?** – Some bias is inherent in social data, which are unique. Many researchers have warned

Representation / Embedding	Technique / Model	Work by
Commonly used word representations to measure bias	Word2Vec, GloVe, ELMo, PPMI, TF-IDF, Character n-grams	-
Bias in word representations	Word2Vec GloVe	(Bolukbasi et al., 2016) (Caliskan et al., 2017)
Bias among word representations	Word2Vec Vs. GloVe GloVe, Word2Vec Vs. ConceptNet	(Brunet et al., 2019) (Sweeney and Najafian, 2019)
Bias in bilingual embeddings	ES-EN, FR-EN	(Zhou et al., 2019)
Word representations to neutralize bias	HistWords – Embed on historic data GN-GloVe – Gender-neutral embed GeoSGLM – demographic embed	(Garg et al., 2018) (Zhao et al., 2018) (Escudé Font et al., 2019) (Hasanuzzaman et al., 2017)
Pre-trained LM	ELMo, BERT, GPT	(Park and Fung, 2017) (Escudé Font et al., 2019) (Zhao et al., 2019) (Liang et al., 2020)

Table 3: Analysis of bias in text representations

against the naive use of social data in NLP tasks (Jørgensen et al., 2015). Olteanu et al. (2019) categorised four biases that occur at the source level and how biases manifest themselves. Applications using social data must be validated and audited, effectively identifying biases introduced at various levels in a data pipeline. Other harmful blind spots along a data analysis pipeline further require better auditing and evaluation frameworks.

Our recommendation based on the above:

- **Recommendation-4:** The need for the study on bias in social data by NLP research community: Social data contains diverse dialects, which is not a norm in language resources. There are methodological limitations, and pitfalls (Jørgensen et al., 2015) as well as ethical boundaries and unexpected consequences (Olteanu et al., 2019) in social data. Hence the propagation and amplification of bias in the data pipeline of social data differ, which needs to be addressed.

3.3 Bias in text representations

Word embeddings contain bias and amplify bias present in the data, such as stereotypes. Word embeddings trained on different models produce different results. Bias in word embeddings is noted by (Bolukbasi et al., 2016) in Word2Vec, which represents a stereotypical bias among the pair of words using word analogy. Recently word embeddings specifically to neutralize the gender in embeddings – GN-GloVe, embeddings on demographic attributes – GeoSGLM are used to detect and mitigate bias in word representations. Table 3 shows the analysis of bias in text representations for monolingual, bilingual and embeddings to neutralize the bias.

1. **Limitations in Transformer Models** - Limitations of this models are noted in computational abilities (Hahn, 2020), multilingual embeddings produced by BERT (Singh et al., 2019), mBERT (Wu and Dredze, 2020), bilingual embeddings by MUSE (Zhou et al., 2019).

2. **Fairness in pre-trained LM** – The model cards proposed by Mitchell et al. (2019) are recommended to the pre-trained LM that can substantiate the context in which the models can be used and can provide a benchmarked evaluation on various bias types. Currently, the GPT-2 model card [2] have not mentioned the type of bias in the dataset used to train and the model fitness for specific applications.

3. **Is pre-trained LM bias-free?** – Dale (2021)

[2] https://github.com/openai/gpt-2/blob/master/model_card.md

Measure/Mitigate	Metric/Techniques	Work by
Metric proposed to evaluate bias	WEAT – for SGNS model	(Caliskan et al., 2017)
	Relative norm distance	(Garg et al., 2018)
	WEAT1, WEAT2 – bias b/w embeddings	(Brunet et al., 2019)
	SEAT – bias in sentence embeddings	(May et al., 2019)
	RIPA – for any embedding model	(Ethayarajh et al., 2019)
	MWEAT – bias in MT	(Zhou et al., 2019)
	RNSB – bias in Sentiment Analysis	(Sweeney and Najafian, 2019)
Debiasing techniques proposed	Hard-debias, Soft-debias	(Bolukbasi et al., 2016)
	RBA	(Zhao et al., 2017)
	Auxiliary dataset	(Zhao et al., 2018)
	Named Entity anonymization	
	Data Augmentation	(Zhao et al., 2019)
	Neutralization	
	SENT-DEBIAS	(Liang et al., 2020)

Table 4: Metric/Methods used to evaluate bias and debias

found that the pre-trained LM such as GPT-3 has the output embody all the biases that might be found in its training data.

4. **Transfer learning is ecological?**– Training the language models is costly to train financially and environmentally, which uses more carbon dioxide than the manufacturing and lifetime use of a car (Strubell et al., 2019).

Our recommendation and augmentation based on the above:

- **Recommendation-5:** A semantic-aware neural architecture to generate debiased embeddings for monolingual, cross-lingual and multi-lingual applications.
- **Augmentation-1:** We augment Gebru et al. (2020) to adopt and extend Datasheets for the language resources, annotated corpora and Model cards by Mitchell et al. (2019) for the algorithms used in pre-train LM and techniques for debiasing.

3.4 Measuring and mitigating bias

Since the plurality in languages inherently carries bias, it is essential to analyze the normative procedure's bias. Because of the complexity and types of bias, the detection and quantification of bias are not always possible by using formal mathematical techniques. Table 4 shows the metrics or methods used to measure and mitigate the bias.

1. **Fairness in bias metric** – Gonen and Goldberg (2019) observed that the bias emanating from word stereotypes and learned from the corpus is ingrained much more deeply in the word embeddings. Ethayarajh et al. (2019) found that the commonly used WEAT does not measure the bias appropriately for the embeddings other than the SGNS model. May et al. (2019) proposed SEAT to measure bias in sentence embeddings. This implies the need of a specific algorithm or method that can be used across all the embeddings to measure the bias (Gonen and Goldberg, 2019; Davidson et al., 2017).

2. **Application specific bias** – The bias can also be measured specific to the applications. For example, RNSB, TGBI (Cho et al., 2019) are proposed to measure the bias in Sentiment Analysis, MT, respectively.

3. **Fairness in debiasing** – The experiment on GN-GloVE and hard-debias reveals the presence of systemic bias in the embeddings independent of gender directions measure the gender association (Gonen and Goldberg, 2019). Even though many systems use hard-debias or soft-debias as de-facto standards to mitigate bias, they do not effectively remove it from the word representations. This requires a standardized framework that effectively measures and mitigate the bias across the domains and applications.

Our recommendation based on the above:

- **Recommendation-6:** An Unified and End-to-End Framework – there is a need for a unified framework to measure and mitigate the bias based on benchmark metrics and methods at various levels data pipeline.

4 Conclusion

The above analysis at various levels reveals that most NLP systems consider bias at a nascent level. Computer scientists should strive to develop algorithms that are more robust to biases in the data. Various approaches are being pursued. Such debiasing approaches are promising, but they need to be refined and evaluated in the real world. All need to think about appropriate notions of fairness in data. Should the data be representative of the world as it is, or of a world that many would aspire to? To address these questions and evaluate the broader impact of training data and algorithms, machine-learning researchers must engage with social scientists, and experts in other domains. Based on the observations of methods used at various levels, we recommend six measures and augment one measure to support ethical practice and fairness in the usage of data. Practising and adopting various normative procedures across the data pipeline in NLP systems would enhance the Equality, Diversity and Inclusion of different subgroups of peoples and their languages.

References

Emily M. Bender and Batya Friedman. 2018. Data statements for natural language processing: Toward mitigating system bias and enabling better science. *Transactions of the Association for Computational Linguistics*, 6:587–604.

Su Lin Blodgett and Brendan O'Connor. 2017. Racial disparity in natural language processing: A case study of social media african-american english.

Tolga Bolukbasi, Kai-Wei Chang, James Zou, Venkatesh Saligrama, and Adam Kalai. 2016. Man is to computer programmer as woman is to homemaker? debiasing word embeddings. In *Proceedings of the 30th International Conference on Neural Information Processing Systems*, NIPS'16, page 4356–4364, Red Hook, NY, USA. Curran Associates Inc.

Marc-Etienne Brunet, Colleen Alkalay-Houlihan, Ashton Anderson, and Richard Zemel. 2019. Understanding the origins of bias in word embeddings. In *Proceedings of the 36th International Conference on Machine Learning*, volume 97 of *Proceedings of Machine Learning Research*, pages 803–811. PMLR.

Aylin Caliskan, Joanna J. Bryson, and Arvind Narayanan. 2017. Semantics derived automatically from language corpora contain human-like biases. *Science*, 356(6334):183–186.

Chung-Chi Chen, Hen-Hsen Huang, and Hsin-Hsi Chen. 2020. Issues and perspectives from 10,000 annotated financial social media data. In *Proceedings of the 12th Language Resources and Evaluation Conference*, pages 6106–6110, Marseille, France. European Language Resources Association.

Won Ik Cho, Ji Won Kim, Seok Min Kim, and Nam Soo Kim. 2019. On measuring gender bias in translation of gender-neutral pronouns. In *Proceedings of the First Workshop on Gender Bias in Natural Language Processing*, pages 173–181, Florence, Italy. Association for Computational Linguistics.

Robert Dale. 2021. Gpt-3: What's it good for? *Natural Language Engineering*, 27(1):113–118.

T. Davidson, Dana Warmsley, M. Macy, and Ingmar Weber. 2017. Automated hate speech detection and the problem of offensive language. In *ICWSM*.

Markus Dickinson and W. Detmar Meurers. 2003. Detecting errors in part-of-speech annotation. In *Proceedings of the Tenth Conference on European Chapter of the Association for Computational Linguistics - Volume 1*, EACL '03, page 107–114, USA. Association for Computational Linguistics.

Joel Escudé Font, Marta Costa-jussa, and R. 2019. Equalizing gender bias in neural machine translation with word embeddings techniques. In *Proceedings of the First Workshop on Gender Bias in Natural Language Processing*, pages 147–154, Florence, Italy. Association for Computational Linguistics.

Kawin Ethayarajh, David Duvenaud, and Graeme Hirst. 2019. Understanding undesirable word embedding associations. In *Proceedings of the 57th Annual Meeting of the Association for Computational Linguistics*, pages 1696–1705, Florence, Italy. Association for Computational Linguistics.

Alex B. Fine, Austin F. Frank, T. Florian Jaeger, and Benjamin Van Durme. 2014. Biases in predicting the human language model. In *Proceedings of the 52nd Annual Meeting of the Association for Computational Linguistics (Volume 2: Short Papers)*, pages 7–12, Baltimore, Maryland. Association for Computational Linguistics.

Antigoni-Maria Founta, Constantinos Djouvas, Despoina Chatzakou, Ilias Leontiadis, Jeremy Blackburn, Gianluca Stringhini, Athena Vakali, Michael Sirivianos, and Nicolas Kourtellis. 2018. Large scale crowdsourcing and characterization of twitter abusive behavior. *CoRR*, abs/1802.00393.

Nikhil Garg, Londa Schiebinger, Dan Jurafsky, and James Zou. 2018. Word embeddings quantify 100 years of gender and ethnic stereotypes. *Proceedings of the National Academy of Sciences*, 115(16):E3635–E3644.

Aparna Garimella, Carmen Banea, Dirk Hovy, and Rada Mihalcea. 2019. Women's syntactic resilience and men's grammatical luck: Gender-bias in part-of-speech tagging and dependency parsing. In *Proceedings of the 57th Annual Meeting of the Association for Computational Linguistics*, pages 3493–3498, Florence, Italy. Association for Computational Linguistics.

Timnit Gebru, Jamie Morgenstern, Briana Vecchione, Jennifer Wortman Vaughan, Hanna Wallach, Hal Daumé III au2, and Kate Crawford. 2020. Datasheets for datasets.

Hila Gonen and Yoav Goldberg. 2019. Lipstick on a pig: Debiasing methods cover up systematic gender biases in word embeddings but do not remove them. In *Proceedings of the 2019 Conference of the North American Chapter of the Association for Computational Linguistics: Human Language Technologies, Volume 1 (Long and Short Papers)*, pages 609–614, Minneapolis, Minnesota. Association for Computational Linguistics.

Michael Hahn. 2020. Theoretical limitations of self-attention in neural sequence models. *Transactions of the Association for Computational Linguistics*, 8:156–171.

Mohammed Hasanuzzaman, Gaël Dias, and Andy Way. 2017. Demographic word embeddings for racism detection on Twitter. In *Proceedings of the Eighth International Joint Conference on Natural Language Processing (Volume 1: Long Papers)*, pages 926–936, Taipei, Taiwan.

Dirk Hovy and Anders Søgaard. 2015. Tagging performance correlates with author age. In *Proceedings of the 53rd Annual Meeting of the Association for Computational Linguistics and the 7th International Joint Conference on Natural Language Processing (Volume 2: Short Papers)*, pages 483–488, Beijing, China. Association for Computational Linguistics.

Jason Jeffrey Jones, M. Amin, Jessica Kim, and S. Skiena. 2020. Stereotypical gender associations in language have decreased over time. *Sociological Science*, 7:1–35.

Anna Jørgensen, Dirk Hovy, and Anders Søgaard. 2015. Challenges of studying and processing dialects in social media. In *Proceedings of the Workshop on Noisy User-generated Text*, pages 9–18, Beijing, China. Association for Computational Linguistics.

Pratik Joshi, Sebastin Santy, Amar Budhiraja, Kalika Bali, and Monojit Choudhury. 2020. The state and fate of linguistic diversity and inclusion in the NLP world. In *Proceedings of the 58th Annual Meeting of the Association for Computational Linguistics*.

Svetlana Kiritchenko and Saif Mohammad. 2018. Examining gender and race bias in two hundred sentiment analysis systems. In *Proceedings of the Seventh Joint Conference on Lexical and Computational Semantics*, pages 43–53, New Orleans, Louisiana. Association for Computational Linguistics.

Shyong (Tony) K. Lam, Anuradha Uduwage, Zhenhua Dong, Shilad Sen, David R. Musicant, Loren Terveen, and John Riedl. 2011. Wp:clubhouse? an exploration of wikipedia's gender imbalance. In *Proceedings of the 7th International Symposium on Wikis and Open Collaboration*, WikiSym '11, page 1–10, New York, NY, USA. Association for Computing Machinery.

Paul Pu Liang, Irene Mengze Li, Emily Zheng, Yao Chong Lim, Ruslan Salakhutdinov, and Louis-Philippe Morency. 2020. Towards debiasing sentence representations. In *Proceedings of the 58th Annual Meeting of the Association for Computational Linguistics*, pages 5502–5515, Online. Association for Computational Linguistics.

Thomas Manzini, Lim Yao Chong, Alan W Black, and Yulia Tsvetkov. 2019. Black is to criminal as caucasian is to police: Detecting and removing multiclass bias in word embeddings. In *Proceedings of the 2019 Conference of the North American Chapter of the Association for Computational Linguistics: Human Language Technologies, Volume 1 (Long and Short Papers)*, pages 615–621, Minneapolis, Minnesota. Association for Computational Linguistics.

Chandler May, Alex Wang, Shikha Bordia, Samuel R. Bowman, and Rachel Rudinger. 2019. On measuring social biases in sentence encoders. In *Proceedings of the 2019 Conference of the North American Chapter of the Association for Computational Linguistics: Human Language Technologies, Volume 1 (Long and Short Papers)*, pages 622–628, Minneapolis, Minnesota. Association for Computational Linguistics.

Margaret Mitchell, Simone Wu, Andrew Zaldivar, Parker Barnes, Lucy Vasserman, Ben Hutchinson, Elena Spitzer, Inioluwa Deborah Raji, and Timnit Gebru. 2019. Model cards for model reporting. In *Proceedings of the Conference on Fairness, Accountability, and Transparency*, FAT* '19, page 220–229, New York, NY, USA. Association for Computing Machinery.

Alexandra Olteanu, Carlos Castillo, Fernando Diaz, and Emre Kiciman. 2019. Social data: Biases, methodological pitfalls, and ethical boundaries. *Frontiers in Big Data*, 2.

Ji Ho Park and Pascale Fung. 2017. One-step and two-step classification for abusive language detection on Twitter. In *Proceedings of the First Workshop on Abusive Language Online*, pages 41–45, Vancouver, BC, Canada. Association for Computational Linguistics.

Anthony Rios, Reenam Joshi, and Hejin Shin. 2020. Quantifying 60 years of gender bias in biomedical research with word embeddings. In *Proceedings of the 19th SIGBioMed Workshop on Biomedical Language Processing*, pages 1–13, Online. Association for Computational Linguistics.

Rachel Rudinger, Jason Naradowsky, Brian Leonard, and Benjamin Van Durme. 2018. Gender bias in coreference resolution. In *Proceedings of the 2018 Conference of the North American Chapter of the Association for Computational Linguistics: Human Language Technologies, Volume 2 (Short Papers)*, pages 8–14, New Orleans, Louisiana. Association for Computational Linguistics.

Maarten Sap, Dallas Card, Saadia Gabriel, Yejin Choi, and Noah A. Smith. 2019. The risk of racial bias in hate speech detection. In *Proceedings of the 57th Annual Meeting of the Association for Computational Linguistics*, pages 1668–1678, Florence, Italy. Association for Computational Linguistics.

Katja Geertruida Schmahl, Tom Julian Viering, Stavros Makrodimitris, Arman Naseri Jahfari, David Tax, and Marco Loog. 2020. Is Wikipedia succeeding in reducing gender bias? assessing changes in gender bias in Wikipedia using word embeddings. In *Proceedings of the Fourth Workshop on Natural Language Processing and Computational Social Science*, pages 94–103, Online. Association for Computational Linguistics.

Jasdeep Singh, Bryan McCann, Richard Socher, and Caiming Xiong. 2019. BERT is not an interlingua and the bias of tokenization. In *Proceedings of the 2nd Workshop on Deep Learning Approaches for Low-Resource NLP (DeepLo 2019)*, pages 47–55, Hong Kong, China. Association for Computational Linguistics.

Anders Søgaard, Barbara Plank, and Dirk Hovy. 2014. Selection bias, label bias, and bias in ground truth. In *Proceedings of COLING 2014, the 25th International Conference on Computational Linguistics: Tutorial Abstracts*, pages 11–13, Dublin, Ireland. Dublin City University and Association for Computational Linguistics.

A. Solomon, D. Moon, A. L. Roberts, and J. E. Gilbert. 2018. Not just black and not just a woman: Black women belonging in computing. In *2018 Research on Equity and Sustained Participation in Engineering, Computing, and Technology (RESPECT)*, pages 1–5.

Gabriel Stanovsky, Noah A. Smith, and Luke Zettlemoyer. 2019. Evaluating gender bias in machine translation. In *Proceedings of the 57th Annual Meeting of the Association for Computational Linguistics*, pages 1679–1684, Florence, Italy. Association for Computational Linguistics.

Emma Strubell, Ananya Ganesh, and Andrew McCallum. 2019. Energy and policy considerations for deep learning in NLP. In *Proceedings of the 57th Annual Meeting of the Association for Computational Linguistics*, pages 3645–3650, Florence, Italy. Association for Computational Linguistics.

Tony Sun, Andrew Gaut, Shirlyn Tang, Yuxin Huang, Mai ElSherief, Jieyu Zhao, Diba Mirza, Elizabeth Belding, Kai-Wei Chang, and William Yang Wang. 2019. Mitigating gender bias in natural language processing: Literature review. In *Proceedings of the 57th Annual Meeting of the Association for Computational Linguistics*, pages 1630–1640, Florence, Italy. Association for Computational Linguistics.

Chris Sweeney and Maryam Najafian. 2019. A transparent framework for evaluating unintended demographic bias in word embeddings. In *Proceedings of the 57th Annual Meeting of the Association for Computational Linguistics*, pages 1662–1667, Florence, Italy. Association for Computational Linguistics.

Claudia Wagner, D. García, M. Jadidi, and M. Strohmaier. 2015. It's a man's wikipedia? assessing gender inequality in an online encyclopedia. In *ICWSM*.

Zeerak Waseem. 2016. Are you a racist or am I seeing things? annotator influence on hate speech detection on Twitter. In *Proceedings of the First Workshop on NLP and Computational Social Science*, pages 138–142, Austin, Texas. Association for Computational Linguistics.

Zeerak Waseem and Dirk Hovy. 2016. Hateful symbols or hateful people? predictive features for hate speech detection on Twitter. In *Proceedings of the NAACL Student Research Workshop*, pages 88–93, San Diego, California. Association for Computational Linguistics.

Shijie Wu and Mark Dredze. 2020. Are all languages created equal in multilingual BERT? In *Proceedings of the 5th Workshop on Representation Learning for NLP*, pages 120–130, Online. Association for Computational Linguistics.

Jieyu Zhao, Tianlu Wang, Mark Yatskar, Ryan Cotterell, Vicente Ordonez, and Kai-Wei Chang. 2019. Gender bias in contextualized word embeddings. In *Proceedings of the 2019 Conference of the North American Chapter of the Association for Computational Linguistics: Human Language Technologies, Volume 1 (Long and Short Papers)*, pages 629–634, Minneapolis, Minnesota. Association for Computational Linguistics.

Jieyu Zhao, Tianlu Wang, Mark Yatskar, Vicente Ordonez, and Kai-Wei Chang. 2017. Men also like shopping: Reducing gender bias amplification using corpus-level constraints. In *Proceedings of the 2017 Conference on Empirical Methods in Natural Language Processing*, pages 2979–2989, Copenhagen, Denmark. Association for Computational Linguistics.

Jieyu Zhao, Tianlu Wang, Mark Yatskar, Vicente Ordonez, and Kai-Wei Chang. 2018. Gender bias in coreference resolution: Evaluation and debiasing methods. In *Proceedings of the 2018 Conference of the North American Chapter of the Association for*

Computational Linguistics: Human Language Technologies, Volume 2 (Short Papers), pages 15–20. Association for Computational Linguistics.

Pei Zhou, Weijia Shi, Jieyu Zhao, Kuan-Hao Huang, Muhao Chen, Ryan Cotterell, and Kai-Wei Chang. 2019. Examining gender bias in languages with grammatical gender. In *Proceedings of the 2019 Conference on Empirical Methods in Natural Language Processing and the 9th International Joint Conference on Natural Language Processing (EMNLP-IJCNLP)*, pages 5276–5284, Hong Kong, China. Association for Computational Linguistics.

GEPSA, a tool for monitoring social challenges in digital press

Iñaki San Vicente, Xabier Saralegi, Nerea Zubia
Elhuyar Foundation
Zelai Haundi 3,
20170 Usurbil, Spain
{i.sanvicente,x.saralegi,n.zubia}@elhuyar.eus

Abstract

This papers presents a platform for monitoring press narratives with respect to several social challenges, including gender equality, migrations and minority languages. As narratives are encoded in natural language, we have to use natural processing techniques to automate their analysis. Thus, crawled news are processed by means of several NLP modules, including named entity recognition, keyword extraction,document classification for social challenge detection, and sentiment analysis. A Flask powered interface provides data visualization for a user-based analysis of the data. This paper presents the architecture of the system and describes in detail its different components. Evaluation is provided for the modules related to extraction and classification of information regarding social challenges.

1 Introduction

Today society presents several challenges concerning equality, diversity and inclusion. Among them, this paper focuses on gender equality, migration and minority languages.

When developing policies to address these challenges, evidence-based diagnostics are necessary, and the digital press is a source of evidence or more specifically the narratives of reality that they offer. This type of analysis has already been carried out for several social challenges such as immigration (Chouliaraki and Zaborowski, 2017; Lee, 2019), gender equality (Lansdall-Welfare et al., 2017) and armed conflicts (Khaldarova and Pantti, 2016).

In these narratives we can analyze different aspects or indicators referring to social challenges (importance of the challenge, agents involved, relevant issues in each challenge, etc.). However, narratives are encoded in natural language which implies that to automate their analysis we have to use natural language processing techniques.

In this paper we describe GEPSA, a tool that facilitates the analysis of social challenges on the narratives built in the digital press. For that aim, it automates the analysis of several macro key indicators (KI) associated with each challenge. It also offers navigation to inspect the different indicators at the micro level. Automation is possible thanks to the use of different NLP techniques: entity extraction, keyword extraction, polarity, and text classification. The current demo includes models and resources developed for Basque and Spanish languages.

From here on the paper is organized as follows: the next section gives details about the main features of the system and the indicators extracted for each social challenge analyzed. Section 3 describes the architecture of the tool and its main modules. Section 4 discusses the validation of the tool. The last section summarizes the paper contribution and conclusions drawn from this work.

2 Features

GEPSA is a tool that allows permanent listening of digital press sources. Sources are customizable to each use case, and are defined at the beginning of the monitoring, depending on variables such as the geographical scope or the type of publications to include in the analysis.

Listening is permanent and consists of analyzing different macro indicators for three social challenges: immigration, gender equality, and minority languages. Table1 lists the macro KIs defined for each of the social challenges.

Different filters may be applied interactively to the indicators, thus allowing micro-analysis through access to specific news:

- Time period: Specific time periods may be selected.

Proceedings of the First Workshop on Language Technology for Equality, Diversity and Inclusion, pages 46–50
April 19, 2021.

Social challenge / indicator	Gender equality	Immigration	Minority Languages
Importance of the challenge on news per source	x	x	x
Importance of the challenge on front-page news per source	x	x	x
Importance of the challenge on news per thematic section		x	x
Gender balance on news	x		
Gender balance among news main characters	x		
Gender balance in front page news	x		
Most relevant persons and organizations in news	x	x	x
Most relevant keywords in news	x	x	x
Most relevant polar words in news	x	x	x

Table 1: Macro key indicators defined for monitoring gender equality, immigration and minority languages.

- Language: System includes news in Basque and Spanish.
- Source: Data corresponding to one or more specific sources may be analyzed.
- Thematic section: News from specific categories (politics, sports, etc.) may be analyzed.

3 System architecture

GEPSA is designed as a pipeline working on a document basis. Its first module is responsible for crawling news data, and retrieved documents are passed through the various modules for information extraction. Each module adds new enriched metadata to a common database.

Figure 1 offers a detailed view of the system components. Lemmatization and Named Entity recognition and classification (NERC) module is responsible for extracting the people and organizations involved in an specific news article, and it also assigns male or female gender to extracted people named entities. Keyword extraction module extracts most salient terms in a document and detects polar words among them. The next module uses supervised classifiers to label the thematic section of a document. The last module detects if a news article belongs to any of the analyzed challenges.

3.1 Crawling

As mentioned earlier, our data source are digital press publications. We mine a set of predefined press sources[1] by means of an in-house RSS feed reader. This reader takes care of gathering news articles periodically[2], removing boilerplate and extracting specific new features (i.e. front page news, photographs).

In order to effectively remove boilerplate from a large number of sources, a hybrid approach has been implemented combining page-level and site-level strategies. In a first step we extract content candidates from the DOM tree using a page-level approach (Kohlschütter et al., 2010), and a second step prunes wrong candidates based on site-level patterns. Those patterns are automatically discovered and updated regularly for each source. Evaluation over 100 random documents (from 20 different sources) shows that the second step improves the number of completely clean documents from 30% to 93%, and benefit is observed for all the types of boilerplate analyzed: banners, breadcrumbs, sharing options, related contents, author/source/date data and photographs.

3.2 NERC

NERC is performed by means of BERT-based (Devlin et al., 2018) neural models. Specifically, BERTeus (Agerri et al., 2020) and BETO (Cañete et al., 2020) models are applied. The Basque model achieves 87.06% Fscore on EIEC corpus (Alegria et al., 2004), while the Spanish model achieves 88.24% Fscore on the CONLL2003 dataset (Tjong Kim Sang and De Meulder, 2003).

In addition to extracting NEs, we detect and classify the gender of person type entities. Detection is done based on gazetteers composed of 6,500 male and 6,500 female names. Those lists were compiled from various sources including international

[1] 180+ sources for the described use case.

[2] Twice a day for the current use case.

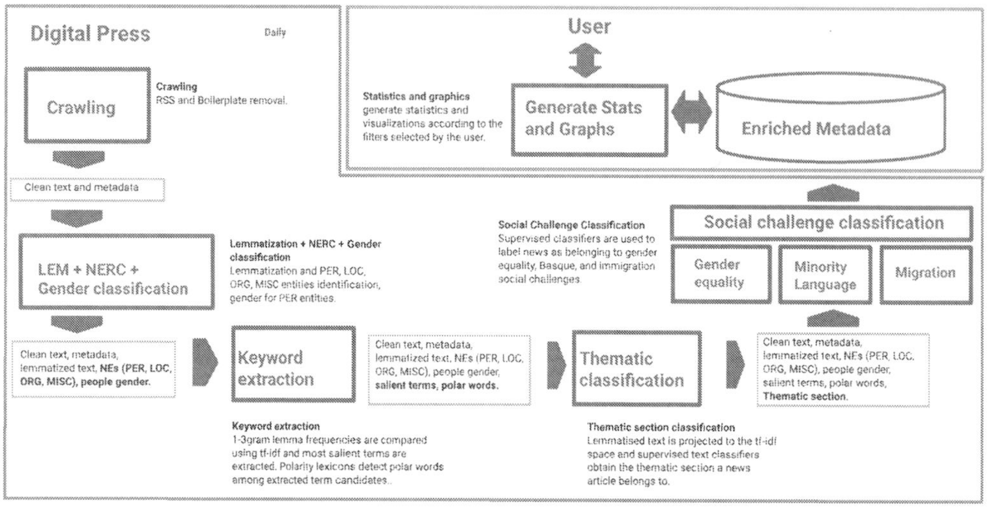

Figure 1: Architecture of GEPSA tool.

and local name lists and news corpora.

3.3 Keyword Extraction

Keyword extraction is done by identifying noun-phrases from the document and computing their representativeness according to TFIDF or Log Likelihood Ratio measures (Dunning, 1993).

For evaluation, keywords were extracted from all the news in annotated challenge datasets (see section 3.5 for details on these datasets), and we manually evaluated the rankings of the most frequent 50 keywords, generated by taking the top n best candidates from each document ($n = [5, 10]$). Precision at different cut offs ($P@[1, 5, 1020, 50]$ was computed. The best performing setup was TFIDF and $n = 5$. P@50 for Spanish was 1 for all social challenges, and ranged from 0.9 to 0.96 for Basque.

Among the keywords extracted, we also detect polar keywords, based on existing polarity lexicons. We used Basque (San Vicente and Saralegi, 2016) and Spanish (Saralegi and San Vicente, 2013) Elh-Polar lexicons.

3.4 Thematic Section Classification

News articles are classified in thematic sections such as politics, culture, sports, etc. There is no standard section taxonomy, press sources have their own criteria and taxonomies. However, it is important to have unified field labels, as this facilitates analyses of the whole narratives depending on the thematic section (e.g. Is it a gender equality diagnostic the same for politics and culture?).

Hence we trained a supervised multi-class classifier in order to classify the crawled news according to a single unique set of eight section classes ([*Economy, Society, Sports, Culture, World, Politics, Technology, Science*]). For that aim we built two news datasets (one per language) by mapping classified news from certain sources to our set of classes. Spanish and Basque datasets contain 156K and 300K classified news, respectively. Systems are trained with 80% of the dataset and evaluated with the rest 20%. Results are reported in table 2. Between Logistic Regression (LR) and Support Vector Machine classifiers (SVM) the former showed better performance, achieving a micro-average F-score of 0.81 and 0.92 for Basque and Spanish, respectively. Representation of news is done by bag-of-words model and TFIDF. Table 2 shows the results by category. Science and Technology classes perform notably worse than the rest due to the lack of examples from those categories in the datasets (less than 1%).

3.5 Social Challenge Classification

Supervised classifiers are used to label news as belonging to gender equality, minority language, and Immigration social challenges. In order to assign a news article to one or more social challenges, supervised binary classifiers were trained. Logistic Regression classifiers are used, using bag-of-words

Category	P	R	F1
Basque			
Economy	0.66	0.84	0.74
Society	0.78	0.68	0.73
Sports	0.92	0.89	0.90
Culture	0.84	0.88	0.86
World	0.80	0.94	0.86
Politics	0.74	0.75	0.74
Technology	0.44	0.87	0.59
Science	0.14	0.24	0.18
micro avg	0.81	0.81	0.81
macro avg	0.66	0.76	0.70
Spanish			
Economy	0.88	0.92	0.90
Society	0.70	0.83	0.76
Sports	0.99	0.98	0.98
Culture	0.93	0.92	0.93
World	0.93	0.92	0.9
Politics	0.93	0.88	0.91
Technology	0.61	0.81	0.69
Science	0.53	0.82	0.64
micro avg	0.92	0.92	0.92
macro avg	0.84	0.84	0.84

Table 2: Precision (P), Recall(R) and F1 score (F1) results for the thematic section classifiers by category.

representations of the documents projected into the TFIDF space. Apart from LR, SVM was tested. LR was chosen over SVM because the latter obtained very low recall values for positive examples of news corresponding to social challenges.

For each social challenge and language, training datasets were created manually. Annotation was carried out by two experts in social research from an specialized consulting service. In order to unify annotation criteria, a first annotation of 100 documents per social challenge was carried out by both annotators, and disagreements were discussed. This resulted in narrowing the scope of some social challenges. From there on each document was annotated once. A minimum of 2,000 documents (per language and challenge) were annotated. In some cases annotation further continued until at least 200 positive examples were found. Datasets were split into 80% for training and 20% for testing. Training sets were oversampled to reach class balance.

Table 3 presents the performance achieved by the classifiers, for each social challenge. Macro averaged measures are reported in this case, because test datasets are highly skewed towards negative

Language	P	R	F1
Basque	0.84	0.80	0.81
Spanish	0.85	0.85	0.85

(a) P, R and Macro-average F-score values achieved by the gender equality classifier on the test sets.

Language	P	R	F1
Basque	0.78	0.83	0.80
Spanish	0.76	0.74	0.75

(b) P, R and Macro-average F-score values achieved by the immigration classifier on the test sets.

Language	P	R	F1
Basque	0.78	0.79	0.78
Spanish	0.83	0.86	0.85

(c) P, R and Macro-average F-score values achieved by the minority language classifier on the test sets.

Table 3: P, R and Macro-average F1 score values achieved by the classifier on the test sets.

examples.

3.6 Data Visualization

User can navigate the data using a user interface developed with Flask Web Application framework[3]. GEPSA implements a number of visualizations aimed to represent the indicators defined in section 2. The main visualizations include: news distributions per source and thematic sections; gender balance in overall news, front page news and among protagonists of the articles; most comparison, evolution of mentions across time, most mentioned entities, terms and polar words. All the visualizations include interactions that provide further analysis such as looking at the specific news regarding an specific entity, term or polar word, or filtering the data according to various criteria such as language, time period, data source or thematic section.

4 User validation

A tool such as GEPSA should be validated by users in real case scenarios, if we want such automatic analysis tools to be adopted by social researchers and policy makers. In order to validate GEPSA, a pilot study is being conducted using the tool as diagnostic tool for the aforementioned challenges. There are 5 participants in the study: the two social researchers that participated in the annotation of the datasets, two data scientists and a policy maker. The pilot will last for the first half of 2021 and is

[3]https://palletsprojects.com/p/flask/

expected to generate an intermediate and a final report on aspects such as the validity of the data gathered, the indicators measured, and the usability of the interface. Although we can not yet draw conclusions, preliminary feedback from participants shows that they find the interface intuitive and easy to use, and indicators provide accurate results both for macro and micro analysis.

5 Conclusions

This paper presents a tool that assists researchers analyzing the narratives built by the press respect to specific social challenges, including gender equality, migrations and minority languages.

The developed tool is an example of how by combining various NLP techniques we can automate the process of narrative analysis focused on social challenges.

Moreover, the tool is a showcase of how policy makers may observe those narratives based on evidences collected from a big data environment, according to several predefined key indicators and their temporal evolution. This is useful both to enact more inclusive policies and also to observe the impact of those policies.

Lastly, the user interface and access to data gathered since the beginning of 2020 are publicly available at `https://talaia.elhuyar.eus:8978`

Acknowledgements

This work has been partially funded by the Basque Government (Gepsa, Hazitek grant no. ZL-2020/00584) and by the Spanish Government (DeepReading, RTI2018-096846-B-C21, MCIU/AEI/FEDER, UE).

References

Rodrigo Agerri, Iñaki San Vicente, Jon Ander Campos, Ander Barrena, Xabier Saralegi, Aitor Soroa, and Eneko Agirre. 2020. Give your text representation models some love: the case for basque. In *Proceedings of The 12th Language Resources and Evaluation Conference*, pages 4781–4788.

Inaki Alegria, Olatz Arregi, Irene Balza, Nerea Ezeiza, Izaskun Fernandez, and Ruben Urizar. 2004. Design and development of a named entity recognizer for an agglutinative language. In *First International Joint Conference on NLP (IJCNLP-04). Workshop on Named Entity Recognition.*

José Cañete, Gabriel Chaperon, Rodrigo Fuentes, Jou-Hui Ho, Hojin Kang, and Jorge Pérez. 2020. Spanish pre-trained bert model and evaluation data. In *PML4DC at ICLR 2020.*

Lilie Chouliaraki and Rafal Zaborowski. 2017. Voice and community in the 2015 refugee crisis: A content analysis of news coverage in eight european countries. *International Communication Gazette*, 79(6-7):613–635.

Jacob Devlin, Ming-Wei Chang, Kenton Lee, and Kristina Toutanova. 2018. Bert: Pre-training of deep bidirectional transformers for language understanding. *arXiv preprint arXiv:1810.04805.*

Ted E Dunning. 1993. Accurate methods for the statistics of surprise and coincidence. *Computational linguistics*, 19(1):61–74.

Irina Khaldarova and Mervi Pantti. 2016. Fake news: The narrative battle over the ukrainian conflict. *Journalism practice*, 10(7):891–901.

Christian Kohlschütter, Peter Fankhauser, and Wolfgang Nejdl. 2010. Boilerplate detection using shallow text features. In *Proceedings of the third ACM international conference on Web search and data mining*, pages 441–450.

Thomas Lansdall-Welfare, Saatviga Sudhahar, James Thompson, Justin Lewis, FindMyPast Newspaper Team, and Nello Cristianini. 2017. Content analysis of 150 years of british periodicals. *Proceedings of the National Academy of Sciences*, 114(4):E457–E465.

Changsoo Lee. 2019. How are 'immigrant workers' represented in korean news reporting?—a text mining approach to critical discourse analysis. *Digital Scholarship in the Humanities*, 34(1):82–99.

Iñaki San Vicente and Xabier Saralegi. 2016. Polarity lexicon building: to what extent is the manual effort worth? In *Proceedings of the Tenth International Conference on Language Resources and Evaluation (LREC 2016).*

Xabier Saralegi and Iñaki San Vicente. 2013. Elhuyar at tass 2013. In *Proceedings of the TASS 2013 Workshop at SEPLN.*

Erik F. Tjong Kim Sang and Fien De Meulder. 2003. Introduction to the CoNLL-2003 shared task: Language-independent named entity recognition. In *Proceedings of the Seventh Conference on Natural Language Learning at HLT-NAACL 2003*, pages 142–147.

Finding Spoiler Bias in Tweets by Zero-shot Learning and Knowledge Distilling from Neural Text Simplification

Avi Bleiweiss
BShalem Research
Sunnyvale, CA, USA
avibleiweiss@bshalem.onmicrosoft.com

Abstract

Automatic detection of critical plot information in reviews of media items poses unique challenges to both social computing and computational linguistics. In this paper we propose to cast the problem of discovering spoiler bias in online discourse as a text simplification task. We conjecture that for an item-user pair, the simpler the user review we learn from an item summary the higher its likelihood to present a spoiler. Our neural model incorporates the advanced transformer network to rank the severity of a spoiler in user tweets. We constructed a sustainable high-quality movie dataset scraped from unsolicited review tweets and paired with a title summary and meta-data extracted from a movie specific domain. To a large extent, our quantitative and qualitative results weigh in on the performance impact of named entity presence in plot summaries. Pretrained on a split-and-rephrase corpus with knowledge distilled from English Wikipedia and fine-tuned on our movie dataset, our neural model shows to outperform both a language modeler and monolingual translation baselines.

1 Introduction

People who expose themselves to the process of satisfying curiosity expect to enhance the pleasure derived from obtaining new knowledge (Loewenstein, 1994; Litman, 2005). Conversely, induced revelatory information about a plot of a motion picture, TV program, video game, or book can spoil the viewer sense of surprise and suspense, and thus greatly diminish the enjoyment in consuming the media. As social media has thrived into a medium for self-expression, live tweets, opinion dumps, or even hashtags tend to proliferate within minutes of the media reaching the public, and hence the risk of uncovering a spoiler widens rapidly. Spoilers on review websites may inevitably contain undesired information and disclose critical plot twists that evoke far less interest to users who consult online reviews first, and later engage with the media itself.

Social media platforms have placed elaborate policies to better guard viewers from spoilers. On the producer side, some sites adopted a strict convention of issuing a spoiler alert to be announced in the subject of the post (Boyd-Graber et al., 2013). Recently, Twitter started to offer provisions for the tweet consumer to manually mute references to specific keywords and hashtags and stop displaying tweets containing them (Golbeck, 2012). But despite these intricate mechanisms that aim to preemptively ward off unwanted spoilers, the solutions proposed lack timely attraction of consumers and may not scale, as spoilers remain a first-class problem in online discourse. Rather than solicit spoiler annotations from users, this work motivates automatic detection of spoiler bias in review tweets, of which spoiler annotations are unavailable or scarce.

Surprisingly, for the past decade spoiler detection only drew little notice and remained a relatively understudied subject. Earlier work used machine learning techniques that incorporated human-curated features in a supervised settings, including a Latent Dirichlet Allocation (LDA) based model that combines simple bag-of-words (BOA) with linguistic cues to satisfy spoiler detection in review commentary (Guo and Ramakrishnan, 2010), baseline n-gram features augmented with binary meta-data that was extracted from their review dataset showed dramatically improved performance of spoiler detection in text (Boyd-Graber et al., 2013), and while frequent verbs and named entities play a critical role in identifying spoilers, adding objectivity and main sentence tense improved classification accuracy by about twelve percentage points (Jeon et al., 2013; Iwai et al., 2014).

More recently researchers started to apply deep learning methods to detect spoiler sentences in review corpora. The study by Chang et al. (2018) pro-

Proceedings of the First Workshop on Language Technology for Equality, Diversity and Inclusion, pages 51–60
April 19, 2021.

poses a model architecture that consists of a convolutional neural network (CNN) based genre encoder and a sentence encoder that uses a bidirectional gated recurrent unit (bi-GRU) (Cho et al., 2014). A genre-aware attention layer aids in learning spoiler relations that tend to vary by the class of the item reviewed. Their neural model was shown to outperform spoiler detection of machine-learning baselines that use engineered features. Using a book review dataset with sentence-level spoiler tags, Wan et al. (2019) followed a similar architecture explored by Chang et al. (2018) and introduced SpoilerNet that comprises a word and sentence encoders, each realizing a bi-GRU network. We found their error analysis interesting in motivating the rendition of spoiler detection as a ranking task rather than a conventional binary classification. Although only marginally related, noteworthy is an end-to-end similarity neural-network with a variance attention mechanism (Yang et al., 2019), proposed to address real-time spoiled content in time-sync comments that are issued in live video viewing. In this scenario, suppressing the impact of often occurring noisy-comments remains an outstanding challenge.

In our approach we propose to cast the task of spoiler detection in online discourse as ranking the quality of sentence simplification from an item description to a multitude of user reviews. We used the transformer neural architecture that dispenses entirely of recurrence to learn the mapping from a compound item summarization to the simpler tweets. The contributions of this work are summarized as follows:

- A high-quality and sustainable movie review dataset we constructed to study automatic spoiler detection in social media microblogs. The data was scraped from unsolicited Twitter posts and paired with a title caption and meta-data we extracted from the rich Internet Movie Database (IMDb). [1] We envision the dataset to facilitate future related research.
- We propose a highly effective transformer model for ranking spoiler bias in tweets. Our novelty lies in applying a preceding text simplification stage that consults an external paraphrase knowledge-base, to aid our downstream NLP task. Motivated by our zero-shot learning results (Table 1), we conjectured that the more simplified tweet, predicted from the movie caption, is likely to make up a spoiler.
- Through exhaustive experiments that we conducted, we provide both qualitative analysis and quantitative evaluation of our system. The results show that our method accomplished performance that outperforms strong baselines.

[1] www.imdb.com

✓	i literally tried everything the force is strong with daisy ridley theriseofskywalker *(p=0.08)*
×	nfcs full podcast breakdown of star wars episode ix the rise of skywalkerstarwars *(p=0.18)*
×	new theriseofskywalker behindthescenes images show the kijimi set see more locations here *(p=0.27)*
✓	weekend box office report for janfebbadboysforlifemoviedolittlegret *(p=0.12)*
×	in my latest for the officialsite i examine some of the themes from theriseofskywalker and how they reinforce some *(p=0.23)*

Table 1: Zero-shot classification of unlabeled tweets about the movie The Rise of the Skywalker (annotating spoiler free ✓ and spoiler biased × posts). Along with text simplification ranking of spoiler bias $p \in [0, 1]$.

2 Related Work

Text simplification is an emerging NLP discipline with the goal to automatically reduce diction complexity of a sentence while preserving its original semantics. Inspired by the success of neural machine translation (NMT) models (Sutskever et al., 2014; Cho et al., 2014), sentence simplification has been the subject of several neural architectural efforts in recent years. Zhang and Lapata (2017) addressed the simplification task with a long short-term memory (LSTM) (Hochreiter and Schmidhuber, 1997) based encoder-decoder network, and employed a reinforcement learning framework to inject prior knowledge and reward simpler outputs. In their work, Vu et al. (2018) propose to combine Neural Semantic Encoders (NSE) (Munkhdalai and Yu, 2017), a novel class of memory augmented neural networks which offer a variable sized encoding memory, with a trailing LSTM-based decoder architecture. Their automatic evaluation suggests that by allowing access to the entire input sequence, NSE present an effective solution to simplify highly complex sentences. More recently, Zhao et al. (2018) incorporated a hand-crafted knowledge base of simplification rules into the self-attention transformer network (Vaswani et al., 2017). This model accurately selects simplified words and shows empiri-

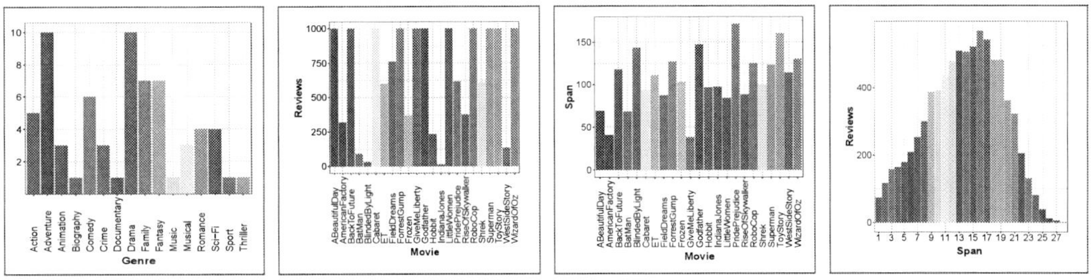

(a) (b) (c) (d)

Figure 1: Distributions across the entire movie dataset of (a) genre, (b) user reviews (capped per title at 1,000), and span length in words of (c) plot summaries, and (d) user reviews.

cally to outperform previous simplification models.

Title Name	Year	Title Name	Year
A Beautiful Day	2019	The Hobbit	2012
American Factory	2019	Indiana Jones	1981
Back to the Future	1985	Little Women	2019
Batman	1989	Pride and Prejudice	1995
Blinded by the Light	2019	The Rise of Skywalker	2019
Cabaret	1972	RoboCop	1987
ET	1982	Shrek	2001
Field of Dreams	1989	Superman	1978
Forrest Gump	1994	Toy Story	1995
Frozen	2013	West Side Story	1961
Give Me Liberty	2019	The Wizard of Oz	1939
The Godfather	1972		

Table 2: Movie title names and release dates.

3 Dataset

Our task requires a dataset that pairs user reviews obtained from discourse on social media with a summarization record collected from an item specific domain. By and large, a user-item model implies distinct review authors for each item. In this study we chose the movie media as the item, or the subject to review, of which a plot description lets users read about the title before watching the film. To the extent of our knowledge, publicly accessible spoiler corpora to date include the dataset used in the work by Guo and Ramakrishnan (2010) that consists of four movies and a total of 2,148 review comments, and more recently, the IMDb Spoiler Dataset, a large-scale corpus provided by Kaggle. [2] However, these datasets were entirely collected from IMDb. Instead, we scraped unlabeled movie reviews from Twitter and matched them with short-text descriptions we assembled from IMDb.

Movies posted on IMDb are each linked with a storyline at different plot detail, including keywords, outlines, summaries, and a single synopsis. Plot summaries are reasonably brief, about a paragraph or two long, and tend to contain small spoilers. Conversely, a plot synopsis contains a detailed description about the entire story of the film, excluding commentary, and may include spoilers that give away important plot points. In casting our spoiler detection task as sentence simplification, we chose to use for our model input to simplify the most comprehensive plot summary of each movie.

We constructed a new dataset for our experiments that comprises meta-data and a total of 15,149 user reviews across twenty three movies. [3] We selected movies released as early in 1939 till 2019 (Table 2), thus spanning an extended period of eighty years. In our title selection we attempted to obtain content coverage and represent a broad range of sixteen genre types. Figure 1a shows genre distribution across movies and highlights adventure and drama motion pictures the most popular, whereas biography, documentary, music, sport, and thriller narratives were anticipated more lower key with each holding a moderate single title presence. We used the Twitter API to search movie hashtags of which we fetched authorized tweets. In scraping user reviews, we placed an upper bound of one thousand asking tweets per movie item. The distribution in Figure 1b shows eleven out of twenty three, close to half the titles, have 1,000 reviews each, however for the remaining films we retrieved less tweets than were requested. On average there were about 658 reviews per title (Table 3).

We viewed our movie corpus as a parallel drawn between a single elaborate plot summary and many simpler review tweets. A text simplification system learns to split the compound passage into several

[2] www.kaggle.com/rmisra/imdb-spoiler-dataset

[3] We made meta-data and tweets publicly available at: https://github.com/bshalem/mst

Property	Min	Max	Mean	StdDev
Reviews	12	1,000	658.7	379.7
Summary Span	38	171	105.8	33.9
Review Span	1	28	13.7	5.4

Table 3: Statistics for distributions across our movie dataset of (a) number of reviews and (b) span length in words for plot summaries and user reviews.

small text sequences further rewritten to preserve meaning (Narayan et al., 2017). To perform lexical and syntactic simplification requires to sustain a reasonable span length ratio of the plot summary to a user review. This predominately motivated our choice of using review tweets that are extremely short-text sequences of 240 characters at most. Distributions of span length in words for both plot summaries and user reviews are shown in Figure 1c and Figure 1d, respectively. Review spans affecting at least 200 tweets are shown to range from 6 to 22 words and apportion around 46 percent of total reviews. Still, the minimum summary span-length has 38 words that is larger than the maximum review span-length at 28 words. As is evidenced in Table 3, at 7.7 on average, the span split ratio of complex to simple text sequences is most plausible.

4 Model

Neural text simplification (NTS) models prove successful to jointly perform compelling lexical simplification and content reduction (Nisioi et al., 2017). Combined with SARI (Xu et al., 2016), a recently introduced metric to measure the goodness of sentence simplification, NTS models are encouraged to apply a wide range of simplification operations, and moreover, their automatic evaluation was shown empirically to correlate well with human judgment of simplicity. Unlike BLEU (Papineni et al., 2002) that scores the output by counting n-gram matches with the reference, i.e. the simplified version of the complex passage, SARI principally compares system output against both the reference and input sentences and returns an arithmetic average of n-gram precisions and recalls of addition, copy, and delete rewrite operations. [4] SARI that correctly rewards models like ours which make changes that simplify input text sequences has inspired us to cast the spoiler detection task as a form of sentence simplification. We hypothesized that the better simplification of a user review from a plot summary, the higher the likelihood of the tweet to contain a spoiler. Moreover, our system is designed to not just confirm the presence or absence of a spoiler, but rather rank the plot revealing impact of a review tweet in a fine-grained scale.

Using a colon notation, we denote our collection of n movie objects $m_{1:n} = \{m_1, \ldots, m_n\}$, each incorporating a plot summary S and k user reviews $r_{1:k} = \{r_1, \ldots, r_k\}$. Thus the input movie m_i we feed our model consists of $k^{(i)}$ pairs $\{S, r_j\}^{(i)}$, where $1 \geq j \leq k^{(i)}$. Given S, a linearly l-split text sequence $s_{1:l} = \{s_1, \ldots, s_l\}$, our model predicts a simplified version $\hat{r}$ of an individual split s.

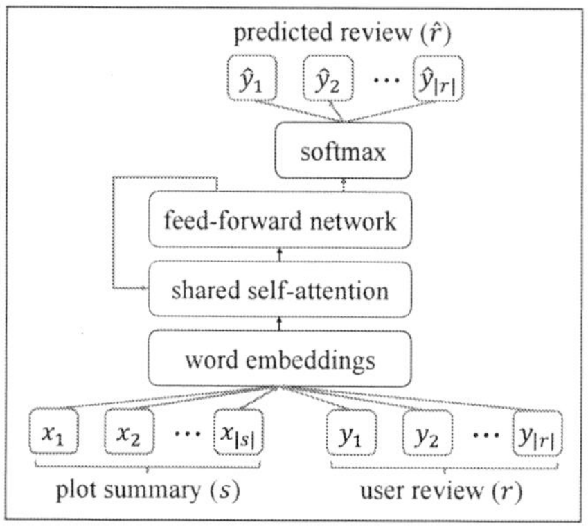

Figure 2: Architecture overview of the transformer (encoder path shown in blue, decoder in brown).

Neural sentence simplification is a form of text-to-text generation closely resembling the task of machine translation in the confines of a single language. In our study we used the self-attention transformer architecture that requires less computation to train and outperforms both recurrent and convolutional system configurations on many language translation tasks (Vaswani et al., 2017). In Figure 2, we present an overview of the transformer architecture. Stacked with several network layers, the transformer encoder and decoder modules largely operate in parallel. In the text simplification framework, the input sequences to the transformer consist of the compound passage words x_i, obtained from a summary split s, and the simple reference words y_i from the current user review r_j. To represent the lexical information of words x_i and y_i, we use pretrained embedding vectors that are shared across our entire movie corpus. The transformer network facilitates complex-to-simple attention communication and a softmax layer operates on the decoder hidden-state outputs to produce the predicted simplified output $\hat{y}_i$. Our training objective is to minimize the cross-entropy loss of the reference-output review pairs.

[4]https://github.com/cocoxu/simplification

5 Experimental Setup

In this section, we provide preprocessing steps we applied to our movie corpus and details of our training methodology.

5.1 Corpus

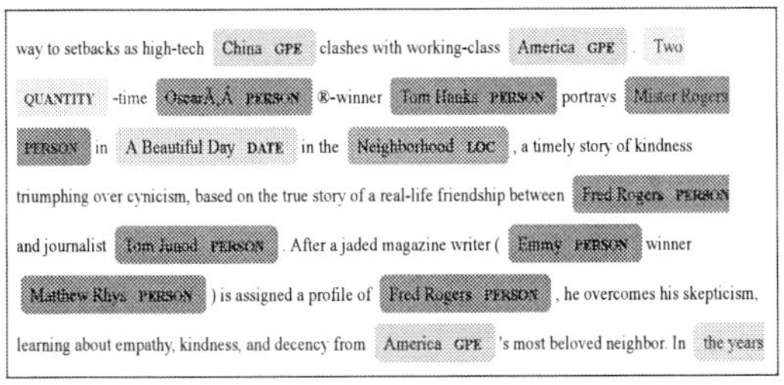

Figure 3: Highlighted named entities in the plot summary of the movie A Beautiful Day in the Neighborhood.

In building our movie dataset, we limited the language of tweets to English. Made of unstructured text, tweets tend to be noisy and often presented with incomplete sentences, irregular expressions, and out of vocabulary words. This involved scraped reviews to undergo several cleanup steps, including the removal of duplicate tweets and any hashtags, replies and mentions, retweets, and links. In addition, we pulled out punctuation symbols and numbers, and lastly converted the text to lowercase. [5] We used the Microsoft Translator Text API for language detection and retained tweets distinguished as English with certainty greater than 0.1. At this stage, we excluded empty and single-word tweets from our review collection, and all in all this reduced the total number of posts from our initial scraping of 15,149 down to 7,928 tweets. In contrast, plot summaries are well-defined and only required the conversion to lowercase. Respectively, vocabularies of plot summaries and user reviews consisted of 863 and 24,915 tokens.

In our evaluation, we compared the quality of text simplification between compound-simple pairs provided with named entities, and pairs of which named entities has been removed altogether. We used the spaCy library that excels at large-scale information extraction tasks, [6] and implements a fast statistical named entity recognition (NER) system. spaCy NER strongly depends nonetheless on the examples its model was trained on. Hence, to address unidentified or misinterpreted named entities in our corpus, we have extended the default training set of spaCy with our specific examples. For instance, we made *Sith* an organization class, *Jo March* a person rather than a date, and *IQ* a quantity. In Figure 3, we highlight the representation of the spaCy named entity visualizer for the plot summary of the movie A Beautiful Day in the Neighborhood. Labels shown include person, geopolitical (GPE) and non-GPE locations, date, and quantity.

5.2 Training

After replicating plot summaries to match the number of user reviews for each movie, we apportion the data by movie into train, validation, and test sets with an 80-10-10 split that amounts to 6,334, 781, and 813 summary-tweet pairs, respectively. To initialize shared vector representations for words that make up both plot summaries and user reviews, we chose GloVe 200-dimensional embeddings pretrained on the current largest accessible Twitter corpus that contains 27B tokens from uncased 2B tweets, with a vocabulary of 1.2M words. [7] Given the fairly small vocabulary size of plot summaries, we expected the embedding matrix generated from the large tweet corpus to perform vector lookup with a limited number of instances that flag unknown tokens.

Hyperparameter settings of the transformer included the number of encoder and decoder layers $N = 6$, the parallel attention head-count $h = 8$, and the model size $d_{model} = 512$. Then, the dimensionality of the query, key, and value vectors were set uniformly to $d_{model}/h = 64$, and the inner feed-forward network size $d_{ff} = 2,048$. Using a cross-entropy loss, we chose the Adam optimizer (Kingma and Ba, 2014) and varied the learning rate, and for network regularization we applied both a fixed model dropout of 0.1 and label smoothing.

6 Experiments

Our evaluation comprises both a spoiler classification and ranking components. First, we applied zero-shot learning (Lampert et al., 2014) to our unlabeled tweets and identified the presence or absence of a spoiler bias. Then, our proposed NTS model produced probability for each summary-post pair to rank the bias of spoilers in tweets. Performance of our NTS approach is further compared to a language modeling and monolingual translation baselines. Moreover, our study analyzes the

[5] All our tweets were rendered on February 2nd 2020.

[6] https://spacy.io

[7] https://nlp.stanford.edu/projects/glove/

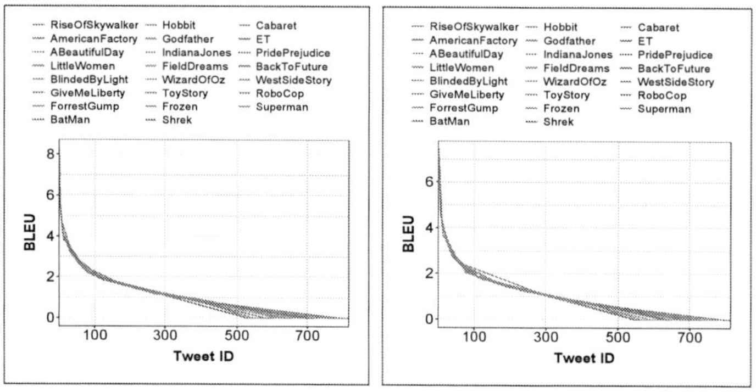

(a) Named Entity Removal

(b) Named Entity Inclusion

Figure 4: Monolingual Translation Baseline: Spoiler rank in BLEU scores for unsplit plot summaries with (a) named entities removed and (b) named entities included.

quality impact of named entity presence in the plot summary and offers an explanation to model behavior once named entities were removed from the text. We have conducted both automatic and human evaluation to demonstrate the effectiveness of the SARI metric, and suggest possible computation paths forward to improve performance.

	Precision	Recall	F1-Score	Support
Negative	0.48	0.41	0.44	388
Positive	0.51	0.59	0.55	425

Table 4: Zero-shot classification of our tweets. The support column identifies the number of user posts for a given category— spoiler free (negative) or biased (positive).

Zero-shot Spoiler Classification Baseline. We used a pretrained model on natural language inference (NLI) tasks to perform zero-shot classification of our unlabeled tweets. [8] To classify the presence or absence of a spoiler in tweets, we provided the NLI pretrained model premise-hypothesis pairs to predict entailment or contradiction. Table 4 summarizes our zero-shot classification results for spoilers in tweets with 388 and 425 user posts categorized negative and positive, respectively. In contrast with human judgment that had a fairly even distribution of spoiler free and spoiler biased user posts at 410 at 403, respectively. We achieved 0.51 accuracy compared to 0.74 on SpoilerNet (Wan et al., 2019) that uses a fully labeled, tenfold larger dataset.

Language Modeling Baseline. We built a language modeling baseline and trained it on a flattened dataset we produced by concatenating all our user reviews into one long text sequence and thus leaving out movie labels, title names, and IDs altogether. Respectively, dataset splits were of 99,575, 12,078, and 12,794 word long for the train, validation, and test sets. The neural network we trained for the language modeling task consisted of a transformer encoder module with its output sent to a linear transform layer that follows a log-softmax activation function. The function assigns a probability for the likelihood of a given word or a sequence of words to follow a sequence of text.

In this experiment, we extracted non-overlapping sub-phrases from each of the plot summaries, and performed on each sub-phrase sentence completion using our language modeling baseline. Uniformly we divided a plot text-sequence into sub-phrases of ten words each, thus leading to a range of four to seventeen sub-phrases per plot summary (Table 3), and a total of 243 phrases to complete for all the 23 titles. We configured our neural model to generate twenty completion words for each sub-phrase and expected one of three scenarios: (i) completion text is contained in one of the review tweets for the title described by the current plot summary, (ii) words partially matching a non-related movie review, and (iii) no completion words were generated. Respectively, these outcomes represent true positives, false positives, and false negatives of which we drew a 0.11 F1-score for sentence completion of plot summaries.

Monolingual Translation Baseline. The baseline for text simplification by monolingual machine translation uses a transformer based neural model that employs both an encoder and decoder modules (Figure 2). To train this model, we used the publicly

[8]https://huggingface.co/transformers/

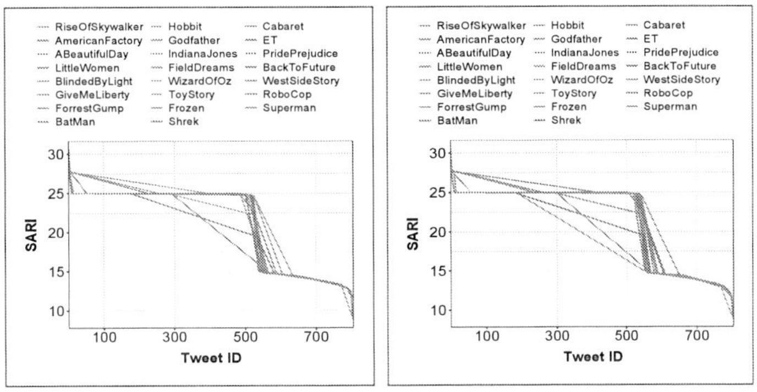

(a) Named Entity Removal (b) Named Entity Inclusion

Figure 5: Text Simplification Mainline: Spoiler rank in SARI scores for linearly-split plot summaries with (a) named entities removed and (b) named entities included. Scores render the mean over all splits of a plot summary.

available dataset introduced by Surya et al. (2019). The data comprises 10,000 sentence pairs extracted from the English Normal-Simple Wikipedia corpus (Hwang et al., 2015) and the Split-Rephrase dataset (Narayan et al., 2017). [9] The Wikipedia dataset, with a large proportion of biased simplifications, was further filtered down to 4,000 randomly picked samples from good and partial matches with similarity scores larger than a 0.45 threshold (Nisioi et al., 2017). Whereas each of the remaining 6,000 Split-Rephrase records comprised one compound source sentence and two simple target sentences.

Using domain adaptation, our model was trained on distilled text simplification data and directly validated and inferred on our movie-review development and test sets, respectively. Noting that for this baseline we avoided a hyperparameter fine-tuning step on our title-review train set. Following NMT practices, we used the BLEU metric for automatic evaluation of our model, and in Figure 4, we show baseline spoiler ranking for unsplit plot summaries without (4a) and with (4b) named entities. BLEU scores ranged from zero to 8.3 with a mean of 0.9. As evidenced, the absence or presence of named entities has a relatively subtle performance impact.

Text Simplification Mainline. As the first stage for evaluating our mainline model, we conducted qualitative analysis to assess the simpleness of user reviews across our entire movie dataset. We classified tweets based on readability scores and used the Flesch Readability Ease (FRE) metric (Flesch, 1948). In Table 5, we provide statistics for user reviews categorized into seven readability grade-levels, and showing for each the number of tweets, FRE range, and average FRE rate. A standard FRE classification renders reviews into simple and complex groups of 990 and 6,930 tweets, respectively. While FRE has its shortcomings to fully qualify sentence simpleness, we found the bias in user reviews toward complex sentences extremely useful.

Grade Level	Tweets	Min	Max	Mean
Very Easy	40	90.7	100	97.4
Easy	126	80.1	89.9	84.1
Fairly Easy	274	70.3	79.1	74.5
Standard	550	60.0	69.9	64.4
Fairly Difficult	642	50.2	59.4	54.6
Difficult	1,503	30.3	49.8	40.1
Very Confusing	4,793	0	29.8	6.3

Table 5: Statistics of Flesch Readability Ease (FRE) scores for user reviews. Showing for each grade the number of tweets, FRE range, and average FRE rate.

Our mainline model starts off with the checkpoint of hyperparameter state from training the monolingual translation baseline on the text simplification dataset from Surya et al. (2019). We then followed with a fine-tuning step on the train and validation sets from our review dataset. In Figure 5 we show mainline spoiler ranking for plot summaries without (5a) and with (5b) named entities. We ran inference on the movie-review test set and report SARI scores for automatic evaluation. SARI scores range from 8.9 to 30.5 with an average rate of 21.3. Although the metrics we used for each baseline and mainline models differ, our results show that the mainline system outperforms the baselines by a considerable margin, owing to linearly-split plot summaries, the extra review-specific training step, and the use of the SARI metric that is effective for tuning and evaluating simplification systems.

[9] https://github.com/shashiongithub

The Rise of the Skywalker	Back to the Future	A Beautiful Day in the Neighborhood
did you know the scene in therise-ofskywalker when rey hears the voices of jedi past during her battle with palpatine was	what do marty mcfly dorothy gale and sadaharu oh have in common a propensity to exceed the established boundarie	tomhanks turns in a fine performance to bring the us childrens tv legend fred rogers to the big screen as matthewrhy

Table 6: A sample of test review tweets for distinct titles with highlighted named entities.

In Figure 6, we analyze the impact of FRE scores on our model performance. Test tweets are shown predominately to fall in two distinct clusters centered around SARI scores of about 14 and 25. Inexplicable at first observation, this rendition is presumably posed by the broadcast nature of online discourse that lets tweets to easily share peer content. On the other hand, FRE grades are shown scattered fairly evenly with no indication to affect performance adversely. We also inspected the reward of automatically extracting named entities from plot summaries and tweets for conducting spoiler identification effectively. In Table 6, we list a sample of user reviews with their named entities highlighted. The correlation between SARI scores obtained from removing and including named entities in plot summaries is presented in Figure 7. About half of the SARI scores turned identical, but the inclusion of named entities produced a marked eighteen percentage points with higher SARI scores.

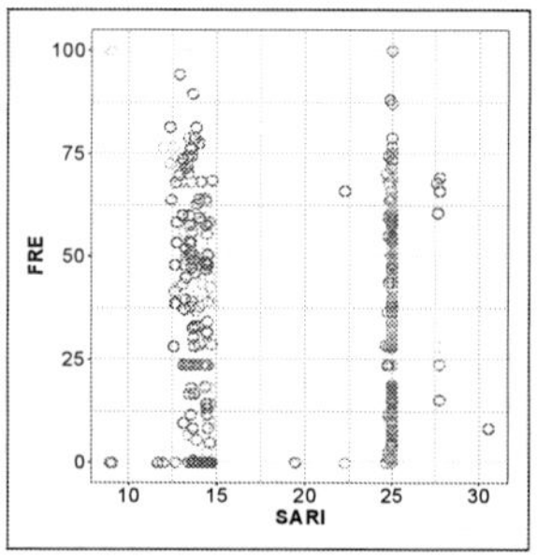

Figure 6: Correlation between FRE and SARI scores.

Data	Min	Max	Mean	SD
Plot Summaries	4	39	16.4	7.4
Reviews	1	12	5.2	2.2

Table 7: Statistics of named entity presence in unsplit plot summaries and reviews.

We also conducted human evaluation by manually rating the spoiledness of individual user reviews in our test set. To this extent, we built a vocabulary V_{ne} of the distinct named entities that are

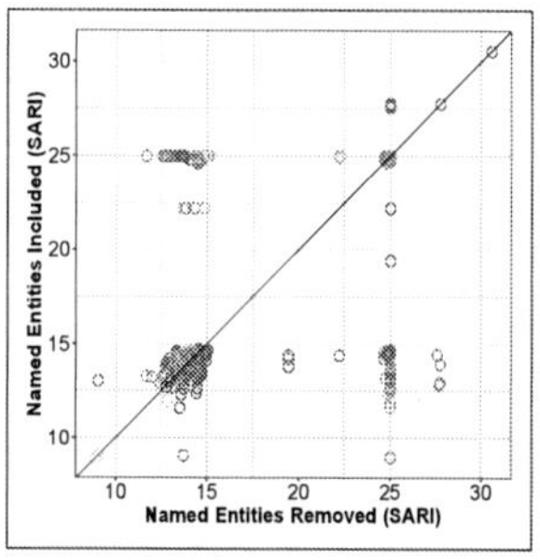

Figure 7: Correlation between SARI scores for plot summaries with named entities removed and included.

present in the entire collection of plot summaries. Our metric for human judgment then follows to rank spoiledness by computing the cosine similarity between two named entity vectors of dimensionality $|V_{ne}| = 274$ that represent a plot summary and a tweet, respectively. Human mediation was essential to inspect the integrity of named entities in tweets that were often misspelled, as evidenced in Table 6. Named entity distribution in unsplit plot summaries and test tweets were at an average ratio of 3 to 1 (Table 7) that correlates well with our SARI automatic scores.

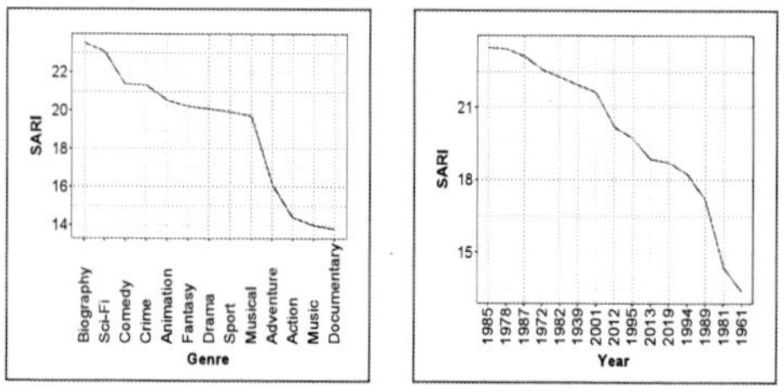

(a) (b)

Figure 8: SARI spoiledness average scores as a function of the movie (a) major genre and (b) year.

In the absence of work with similar goals, we are unable to provide a fair performance comparison.

7 Discussion

Given its proven record of state-of-the-art performance for various NLP tasks, we considered the use of the BERT architecture (Devlin et al., 2019)—

a transformer based language model that was pre-trained on a large-scale corpus of English tweets (BERTweet) (Nguyen et al., 2020). However, the smaller number of 850M tweets BERTweet employs compared to 2B posts in our corpus, along with the dearth of support for NTS at the time of publication precluded further use of BERTweet in our study.

Of great practical importance is the answer to how the genre of a movie or the year in which it was released weigh in on the amount of spoiler bias. Average SARI scores of spoiledness as a function of the primary movie genre (family, romance, and thriller considered secondary) are shown in Figure 8a. Somewhat surprisingly, biography and science fiction types came most vulnerable, as adventure and action titles scored lower by about 8 SARI points, and documentary category appears the most immune to spoilers. In Figure 8b, we reviewed bias impact of the year the movie was launched. Most biased are movies of the seventies and eighties, as the more recent twenty first century movies are clustered in the middle, and West Side Story (1961) ranked the least biased.

8 Conclusions

We proposed a new dataset along with applying advanced language technology to discover emerging spoiler bias in tweets that represent a diverse population with different cultural values. Performing text simplification, our model principally drew on named entity learning in an item-user paradigm for media review and showed through correlational studies plausible performance gains.

The results we presented in this study carve several avenues of future research such as minimizing spoiler bias before user comments reach their audience, and incorporating novel pretrained language models and training schemes to improve bias ranking quality. When supplied with the proper dataset, we foresee our generic method aid researchers to address a broader bias term in text.

Acknowledgments

We would like to thank the anonymous reviewers for their insightful suggestions and feedback.

References

Jordan Boyd-Graber, Kimberly Glasgow, and Jackie Sauter Zajac. 2013. Spoiler alert: Machine learning approaches to detect social media posts with revelatory information. *American Society for Information Science and Technology (ASIS&T)*, 50(1):1–9.

Buru Chang, Hyunjae Kim, Raehyun Kim, Deahan Kim, and Jaewoo Kang. 2018. A deep neural spoiler detection model using a genre-aware attention mechanism. In *Advances in Knowledge Discovery and Data Mining (PAKDD)*, pages 183–195. Springer Verlag.

Kyunghyun Cho, Bart van Merriënboer, Caglar Gulcehre, Dzmitry Bahdanau, Fethi Bougares, Holger Schwenk, and Yoshua Bengio. 2014. Learning phrase representations using RNN encoder–decoder for statistical machine translation. In *Empirical Methods in Natural Language Processing (EMNLP)*, pages 1724–1734, Doha, Qatar.

Jacob Devlin, Ming-Wei Chang, Kenton Lee, and Kristina Toutanova. 2019. BERT: Pre-training of deep bidirectional transformers for language understanding. In *North American Chapter of the Association for Computational Linguistics: Human Language Technologies (NAACL)*, pages 4171–4186, Minneapolis, Minnesota.

Rudolf Franz Flesch. 1948. A new readability yardstick. *The Journal of applied psychology*, 32 3:221–233.

Jennifer Golbeck. 2012. The twitter mute button: A web filtering challenge. In *Conference on Human Factors in Computing Systems (SIGCHI)*, page 2755–2758, Austin, Texas.

Sheng Guo and Naren Ramakrishnan. 2010. Finding the storyteller: Automatic spoiler tagging using linguistic cues. In *Conference on Computational Linguistics (COLING)*, pages 412–420, Beijing, China.

Sepp Hochreiter and Jürgen Schmidhuber. 1997. Long short-term memory. *Neural Computation*, 9:1735–1780.

William Hwang, Hannaneh Hajishirzi, Mari Ostendorf, and Wei Wu. 2015. Aligning sentences from standard Wikipedia to simple Wikipedia. In *North American Chapter of the Association for Computational Linguistics (NAACL)*, pages 211–217, Denver, Colorado.

Hidenari Iwai, Yoshinori Hijikata, Kaori Ikeda, and Shogo Nishida. 2014. Sentence-based plot classification for online review comments. In *Web Intelligence (WI) and Intelligent Agent Technologies (IAT)*, page 245–253, Warsaw, Poland.

Sungho Jeon, Sungchul Kim, and Hwanjo Yu. 2013. Don't be spoiled by your friends: Spoiler detection in tv program tweets. In *Conference on Weblogs and Social Media (ICWSM)*, pages 681–684.

Diederik P. Kingma and Jimmy Ba. 2014. Adam: A method for stochastic optimization. *CoRR*, abs/1412.6980. http://arxiv.org/abs/1412.6980.

C. H. Lampert, H. Nickisch, and S. Harmeling. 2014. Attribute-based classification for zero-shot visual object categorization. *IEEE Transactions on Pattern Analysis and Machine Intelligence*, 36(3):453–465.

Jordan Litman. 2005. Curiosity and the pleasures of learning: Wanting and liking new information. *Cognition and Emotion*, 19(6):793–814.

George Loewenstein. 1994. The psychology of curiosity: A review and reinterpretation. *Psychological Bulletin*, 116(1):75–98.

Tsendsuren Munkhdalai and Hong Yu. 2017. Neural semantic encoders. In *European Chapter of the Association for Computational Linguistics (EACL)*, pages 397–407, Valencia, Spain.

Shashi Narayan, Claire Gardent, Shay B. Cohen, and Anastasia Shimorina. 2017. Split and rephrase. In *Conference on Empirical Methods in Natural Language Processing (EMNLP)*, pages 606–616, Copenhagen, Denmark.

Dat Quoc Nguyen, Thanh Vu, and Anh Tuan Nguyen. 2020. BERTweet: A pre-trained language model for English tweets. In *Proceedings of the 2020 Conference on Empirical Methods in Natural Language Processing: System Demonstrations*, pages 9–14, Online.

Sergiu Nisioi, Sanja Štajner, Simone Paolo Ponzetto, and Liviu P. Dinu. 2017. Exploring neural text simplification models. In *Annual Meeting of the Association for Computational Linguistics (ACL)*, pages 85–91, Vancouver, Canada.

Kishore Papineni, Salim Roukos, Todd Ward, and Wei-Jing Zhu. 2002. BLEU: a method for automatic evaluation of machine translation. In *Annual Meeting of the Association for Computational Linguistics (ACL)*, pages 311–318, Philadelphia, Pennsylvania.

Sai Surya, Abhijit Mishra, Anirban Laha, Parag Jain, and Karthik Sankaranarayanan. 2019. Unsupervised neural text simplification. In *Annual Meeting of the Association for Computational Linguistics (ACL)*, pages 2058–2068, Florence, Italy.

Ilya Sutskever, Oriol Vinyals, and Quoc V. Le. 2014. Sequence to sequence learning with neural networks. In *Neural Information Processing Systems*, page 3104–3112, Montreal, Canada.

Ashish Vaswani, Noam Shazeer, Niki Parmar, Jakob Uszkoreit, Llion Jones, Aidan N Gomez, Ł ukasz Kaiser, and Illia Polosukhin. 2017. Attention is all you need. In *Advances in Neural Information Processing Systems (NIPS)*, pages 5998–6008. Curran Associates, Inc., Red Hook, NY.

Tu Vu, Baotian Hu, Tsendsuren Munkhdalai, and Hong Yu. 2018. Sentence simplification with memory-augmented neural networks. In *North American Chapter of the Association for Computational Linguistics (NAACL)*, New Orleans, Louisiana.

Mengting Wan, Rishabh Misra, Ndapa Nakashole, and Julian McAuley. 2019. Fine-grained spoiler detection from large-scale review corpora. In *Annual Meeting of the Association for Computational Linguistics (ACL)*, pages 2605–2610, Florence, Italy.

Wei Xu, Courtney Napoles, Ellie Pavlick, Quanze Chen, and Chris Callison-Burch. 2016. Optimizing statistical machine translation for text simplification. *Transactions of the Association for Computational Linguistics*, 4:401–415.

Wenmian Yang, Weijia Jia, Wenyuan Gao, Xiaojie Zhou, and Yutao Luo. 2019. Interactive variance attention based online spoiler detection for time-sync comments. In *Conference on Information and Knowledge Management (CIKM)*, pages 1241–1250, Beijing, China. ACM.

Xingxing Zhang and Mirella Lapata. 2017. Sentence simplification with deep reinforcement learning. In *Empirical Methods in Natural Language Processing (EMNLP)*, pages 584–594, Copenhagen, Denmark.

Sanqiang Zhao, Rui Meng, Daqing He, Andi Saptono, and Bambang Parmanto. 2018. Integrating transformer and paraphrase rules for sentence simplification. In *Empirical Methods in Natural Language Processing (EMNLP)*, pages 3164–3173, Brussels, Belgium.

Findings of the Shared Task on Hope Speech Detection for Equality, Diversity, and Inclusion

Bharathi Raja Chakravarthi[♥] **and Vigneshwaran Muralidaran**[♣]
[♥]Data Science Institute, National University of Ireland Galway
[♣]Cardiff University, Cardiff, United Kingdom
bharathi.raja@insight-centre.org

Abstract

Hope plays a crucial role in the well-being, recuperation and restoration of human life. Hope speech reflects the belief that one can discover pathways to their desired objectives and become motivated to utilise those pathways. We created a hope speech detection dataset to encourage research in Natural Language Processing (NLP) towards reinforcement of positivity rather than minimising negativity (through control of hate speech etc.). In this paper, we report the findings of the shared task of hope speech detection for Tamil, English, and Malayalam languages conducted as a part of the EACL 2021 workshop on Language Technology for Equality, Diversity, and Inclusion (LT-EDI-2021). We also present an overview of the methods and results of the competing systems. The datasets for this challenge are openly available[1]. To the best of our knowledge, this is the first shared task to conduct hope speech detection.

1 Introduction

In the recent years, there has been an exponential rise in the number of studies focusing on the detection and management of hate speech and offensive language in social media (Kumar et al., 2018; Mandl et al., 2020; Zampieri et al., 2020). However, this has led to controlling user expression instead of improving user experience. (Ghanghor et al., 2021a; Hegde et al., 2021; Yasaswini et al., 2021). This has also resulted in putting barriers on modes of expression of different groups of people resulting in the violation of the principles of Equality, Diversity, and Inclusion (EDI). For instance, some NLP systems have classified the comments made in African American English as offensive language without accommodating the linguistic features peculiar to the dialect. Hence there is a need for a shift in the approaches taken to handle hate speech without compromising on the principles of EDI.

We propose to shift the prevailing research direction in Natural Language Processing from controlling negativity (curbing hate speech etc.) to encouraging positivity (promoting hope speech). Hope speech is any expression that is positive, encouraging, supportive, and / or inspires promise of the future (Chakravarthi, 2020a). For the shared task organised in this connection, participants were provided with development, training and test dataset in English as well as in two under-resourced languages - Tamil and Malayalam. Tamil (ISO 639-3: tam) belongs to the Dravidian language family and is widely spoken in the southern state of Tamil Nadu in India, Sri Lanka, Malaysia and Singapore (Krishnamurti, 2003; Kolipakam et al., 2018; Chakravarthi, 2020b; Thavareesan and Mahesan, 2019, 2020a,b). Malayalam (ISO 639-3: mal) also belongs to the Dravidian language family and is spoken in the Indian state of Kerala and the Union Territories of Lakshdweep and Puducherry (Chakravarthi et al., 2020). Both Tamil and Malayalam have their own scripts which are alphasyllabaries like other Indic scripts i.e. they are partially alphabetic and partially syllabic. The Tamil language was written using Tamili, Vattezhuthu, Chola, Pallava and Chola-Pallava scripts at different points in history. The modern Tamil script descended from the Chola-Pallava script that was conceived around the 6th century CE (Srinivasan, 2019). Malayalam was first written with Vattezhuthu script that evolved from Tamili script around 4-5th century CE (Mahadevan, 2003). Modern Malayalam is written using the Vattezhuttu alphabets extended with symbols from the Grantha script to accomodate non-native Sanskrit sounds (Krishnamurti, 2003). Although they have their own scripts, the social media comments in these languages are often written in Latin script as it is

[1]https://competitions.codalab.org/competitions/27653

Proceedings of the First Workshop on Language Technology for Equality, Diversity and Inclusion, pages 61–72
April 19, 2021.

easy to input.

Our dataset for the hope speech for EDI shared task was created from user-generated content in Tamil, Malayalam, and English (Chakravarthi and Muralidaran, 2021). The user-generated comments in our dataset for Tamil and Malayalam were code-mixed (Chakravarthi, 2020a). We proposed a comment/post level classification task. The goal for the participants was to classify a given Youtube comment into either 'Hope_speech', 'Non_hope_speech' or 'Not_Tamil / Not_Malayalam / Not_English'. Our CodaLab website will remain open to allow researchers to access the data and build upon this work.

2 Task Description

We define the hope speech for our problem as "YouTube comments/posts that offer support, reassurance, suggestions, inspiration and insight". A comment/post within the corpus may contain more than one sentence, but the average sentence length of the corpus is one. The annotations in the corpus are made at a comment/post level. The participants were provided with development, training and test dataset in English, Tamil, and Malayalam. A few examples from the dataset are given below along with their translations and hope speech class annotations.

- **kashtam thaan. irundhaalum muyarchi seivom** - *It is indeed difficult. Let us try it out though.* Hope speech.
- **uff. China mon vannallo**- *Phew! Here comes the Chinese guy* Non-hope speech
- **paambu kari saappittu namma uyirai vaanguranunga**- *These guys (Chinese) eat snake meat and make our lives miserable* Non-hope speech
- **Enthinennariyilla karanjupoy.sooryamma.you.are grate**- *I do not know what is the reason but I cried. Dear Soorya, you are great.* Hope speech
- **Plz talk slowly**- *Please talk slowly* Not Tamil
- **Gd msg.. thanks dr.**- *It is a good message. Thanks Doctor.* Not Malayalam

2.1 Datasets

We have used the HopeEDI datasets from Chakravarthi (2020a) for this shared task. Our dataset contained user-generated comments from the social media platform YouTube with 28,451, 20,198 and 10,705 comments in English, Tamil and Malayalam, respectively, manually labelled as hope speech or not. The inter-annotator agreement of the dataset labels was verified using Krippendorff's alpha. We will now briefly describe the annotation process and the statistics of the collected dataset. For detailed explanation of the datasets, please refer to the works of Chakravarthi (2020a). The data was collected on a wide range of socially relevant topics related to EDI, including LGBTIQ issues, COVID-19, women in STEM, Black Lives Matter, Dravidian languages, and the Indo-China war. The data for English was collected from English-speaking regions across the world. For Tamil and Malayalam, we collected the data from the states of Tamil Nadu and Kerala in India. Full consideration was given to minimize the risk associated with breach of privacy by removing the information related to individual identity from a comment before it was sent for annotation. The annotators were educated about EDI and a minimum of three annotators labelled each comment. Our diverse annotator base was from Australia, the Republic of Ireland, the United Kingdom, the United States of America, Tamil Nadu, Kerala (in India) and Sri Lanka. The inter-annotator agreement in terms of Krippendorff's alpha (α) was 0.63, 0.76, anad 0.85 for English, Tamil and Malayalam.

In total, HopeEDI dataset contains 59,354 comments with 28,451 comments in English, 20,198 comments in Tamil, and 10,705 comments in Malayalam. Table 1 and Table 2 show the distribution of HopeEDI dataset by language and annotation label respectively. To calculate corpus statistics *nltk* tool (Bird et al., 2009) was used to tokenise the sentences in the comments. The vocabulary size of the Tamil and Malayalam dataset was high due to different types of code-mixing in the user-generated content.

Most of the comments fell under the 'Not_hope' category because of how we defined hope speech and hence the distribution of classes in the dataset was skewed. It is typical for user-generated content from online social media platforms to be skewed and the systems should be able to handle imbalanced data common in real-life setting. 'not_Tamil' and 'not_Malayalam' labels are found in considerably large amount due to high code-mixing. The fully annotated dataset was split into training, de-

Language	English	Tamil	Malayalam
Number of Words	522,717	191,242	122,917
Vocabulary Size	29,383	46,237	40,893
Number of Comments/Posts	28,451	20,198	10,705
Number of Sentences	46,974	22935	13,643
Average number of words per sentences	18	9	11
Average number of sentences per post	1	1	1

Table 1: Corpus statistics

Class	English	Tamil	Malayalam
Hope	2,484	7,899	2,052
Not Hope	25,940	9,816	7,765
Other lang	27	2,483	888
Total	28,451	20,198	10,705

Table 2: Classwise Data Distribution

	English	Tamil	Malayalam
Training	22,762	16,160	8564
Development	2,843	2,018	1070
Test	2,846	2,020	1071
Total	28,451	20,198	10,705

Table 3: Train-Development-Test Data Distribution

velopment and test sets. The training, development and test sets respectively contain 80%, 10% and 10% of the data as shown in Table 3.

2.2 Training Phase

In this first phase, training, validation and development data were released for the participants to train and develop hope speech detection for one or more of the three languages. The participants could choose to perform cross-validation on the training data or use the validation dataset for preliminary evaluations and use the development set for hyper-parameter sharing. The goal of this phase was to ensure that the systems developed by the participants be ready for evaluation before the release of the test data. In total, 137 participants registered for all the three languages and downloaded the data.

2.3 Testing Phase

In this phase, the test dataset was released in CodaLab without the gold labels. Participants were instructed to submit their predictions using Google Forms. They were allowed to submit their results as many times as they wanted to and their best submission was chosen for evaluation and preparation of rank list. The predictions were evaluated against the gold standard labels. The performance of the classification system was measured in terms of weighted averaged Precision, Recall and F-Score across all the classes. Weighted averaged scores calculate the support-weighted mean per label. The metric used for the preparing the rank list was the weighted F1 score. Participants were encouraged to check their system with Sklearn classification report [2]. For Tamil, Malayalam and English languages, the number of participants were 30, 31 and 31 respectively for the final test.

3 Systems

We first describe the baseline systems from the HopeEDI paper. Next, we briefly describe the general approach taken by each participating team. We encourage the readers to refer to the individual papers of each team for more details.

3.1 Baseline Classifiers

We used the prior published work as the baseline for hope speech detection from social media. More details about the baseline system description and results can be seen in Chakravarthi (2020a). In this prior work, we described in detail our dataset and presented our baseline results by employing a wide range of standard classifiers on the unbalanced settings of the dataset. The experiment was applied on the token frequency-inverse document frequency (Tf-Idf) of tokens. We used sklearn [3] library to create baseline classifiers. We used a grid search for the k-nearest neighbours (KNN), support vector machine (SVM), decision tree and logistic regression. For the multinomial Naive Bayes, we set alpha = 0.7. More details about the parameters

[2] https://scikit-learn.org/stable/modules/generated/sklearn.metrics.classification_report.html

[3] https://scikit-learn.org/stable/

of the classifier will be published in the code.

3.2 System Descriptions

In this section we summarise the systems implemented by the participants for the shared task. For more details, please refer to the shared task papers submitted by the authors.

- Chinnappa (2021) participated in identifying hope speech classes in English, Tamil, and Malayalam datasets. They presented a two-phase mechanism to detect hope speech. In the first phase, they built a classifier to identify the language of the text. In the second phase, they created a classifier to identify the class labels. The author used language Models SBERT, FNN and BERT inference. They achieved 3rd, 4th, and 2nd ranks in Tamil, Malayalam and English respectively.

- M K and A P (2021) used context-aware string embeddings for word representations and Recurrent Neural Network (RNN) and pooled document embeddings for text representation. Their proposed methodology achieved higher performance than baseline results. The highest weighted average F-scores of 0.93, 0.56, and 0.84 for English, Tamil, and Malayalam were reported on the final evaluation test set. The proposed models outperformed baselines by 3%, 2% and 11% in absolute terms for English, Tamil, and Malayalam.

- Dowlagar and Mamidi (2021) performed experiments by taking advantage of preprocessing and transfer-learning models. They have shown that the pre-trained multilingual-BERT model with convolution neural networks gave the best results. Their model ranked 1st , 3rd , and 4th on English, Malayalam-English, and Tamil-English code-mixed datasets respectively.

- S et al. (2021a) trained the data using transformer models, specifically mBERT for Tamil and Malayalam and BERT for English, and achieved weighted average F1-scores of 0.38, 0.81, 0.92 for Tamil, Malayalam, and English respectively. They achieved the rank of 14, 4, 2 for Tamil, Malayalam, English respectively.

- Puranik et al. (2021) experimented with several transformer-based models including BERT, ALBERT, DistilBERT, XLM-RoBERTa, MuRIL to classify dataset in English, Malayalam and Tamil languages. ULMFiT achieved a weighted average F1-score of 0.91 on English data, mBERT achieved 0.57 on Malayalam data, and distilmBERT achieved 0.37 on Tamil data. They secured 15th, 12th, and 3rd ranks for predictions on Tamil, Malayalam, and English datasets respectively.

- Saumya and Mishra (2021) used various machine learning and deep learning-based models (support vector machine, logistics regression, convolutional neural network, recurrent neural network) to identify the hope speech in the given youTube comments. The best performing model on English data was 2-parallel CNN-LSTM with GloVe and Word2Vec embeddings, and it reported a weighted average F1 score 0.91 and 0.90 for development and test sets respectively. Similarly, the best performing model of Tamil and Malayalam was obtained from 3-parallel Bi-LSTM. For Tamil, the reported F1 scores were 0.56 and 0.54 on development and test dataset respectively. Similarly, for Malayalam, the reported weighted F1 was 0.78 and 0.79 on development and test datasets.

- Dave et al. (2021) used TF-IDF character n-grams and pretrained MuRIL embeddings for text representation and Logistic Regression and Linear SVM for classification. Their best approach achieved 2nd, 8th and 5th rank with a weighted F1 scores of 0.92, 0.75 and 0.57 in English, Malayalam-English and Tamil-English on test dataset.

- Zhou (2021) fine-tuned the Roberta pre-training model based on three data sets English, Tamil, and Malayalam. The F1 scores of their models in Tamil and Malayalam sub-tasks reached 0.56 and 0.78, respectively, and the F1 score in English sub-task reached 0.93, achieving the first rank.

- Zhao (2021) used attention mechanism to adjust the weights of all the output layers of XLM-RoBERTa to make full use of the information extracted from each layer, and used the weighted sum of all the output layers to complete the classification task. They used

Team-Name	Precision	Recall	F1 Score	Rank
spartans (Sharma and Arora, 2021)	0.62	0.62	0.61	1
TeamUNCC (Mahajan et al., 2021)	0.61	0.61	0.61	1
NLP@CUET (Hossain et al., 2021)	0.61	0.61	0.6	2
res - si sun	0.61	0.6	0.6	2
team-hub (Huang and Bai, 2021)	0.61	0.61	0.59	3
MUCS (Balouchzahi et al., 2021)	0.59	0.59	0.59	3
ZYJ (Zhao, 2021)	0.59	0.59	0.59	3
dhivya-hope-detection (Chinnappa, 2021)	0.59	0.59	0.59	3
GCDH (Ziehe et al., 2021)	0.62	0.6	0.58	4
e8ijs	0.59	0.59	0.58	4
EDIOne - suman (Dowlagar and Mamidi, 2021)	0.58	0.58	0.58	4
IIITK (Ghanghor et al., 2021b)	0.58	0.58	0.58	4
HopeIsAllYouNeed	0.59	0.59	0.57	5
IRNLP-DAIICT-LR (Dave et al., 2021)	0.59	0.59	0.57	5
KBCNMUJAL	0.59	0.59	0.57	5
KU-NLP (M K and A P, 2021)	0.62	0.6	0.56	6
Zeus (Zhou, 2021)	0.59	0.59	0.56	6
CFILT-IITB-Submission	0.55	0.55	0.55	7
IIIT-DWD (Saumya and Mishra, 2021)	0.54	0.54	0.54	8
hopeful-nlp (Awatramani, 2021)	0.57	0.56	0.53	9
MUM	0.53	0.53	0.53	9
snehan-coursera	0.53	0.55	0.52	10
TeamX - Olawale Onabola	0.55	0.55	0.52	10
Hopeful-Men (Upadhyay et al., 2021)	0.52	0.55	0.49	11
SIMON (Que, 2021)	0.63	0.56	0.49	11
result	0.63	0.56	0.49	11
Amrita-CEN-NLP (S et al., 2021b)	0.48	0.49	0.47	12
mIGeng	0.42	0.42	0.42	13
ssn-diBERTsity (S et al., 2021a)	0.43	0.44	0.38	14
IIITT - Karthik Puranik (Puranik et al., 2021)	0.38	0.39	0.37	15

Table 4: Rank list based on F1-score along with other evaluation metrics (Precision and Recall) for Tamil language

Team-Name	Precision	Recall	F1 Score	Rank
NLP@CUET(Hossain et al., 2021)	0.86	0.85	0.85	1
MUCS (Balouchzahi et al., 2021)	0.85	0.85	0.85	1
GCDH (Ziehe et al., 2021)	0.84	0.85	0.85	1
ZYJ (Zhao, 2021)	0.84	0.84	0.84	2
team-hub (Huang and Bai, 2021)	0.84	0.85	0.84	2
res - si sun	0.84	0.85	0.84	2
KU-NLP (M K and A P, 2021)	0.84	0.85	0.84	2
CFILT-IITB-Submission	0.84	0.85	0.84	2
TeamUNCC (Mahajan et al., 2021)	0.83	0.83	0.83	3
IIITK (Ghanghor et al., 2021b)	0.83	0.84	0.83	3
HopeIsAllYouNeed	0.83	0.83	0.83	3
EDIOne - suman t (Dowlagar and Mamidi, 2021)	0.83	0.83	0.83	3
e8ijs	0.83	0.84	0.83	3
ssn-diBERTsity (S et al., 2021a)	0.82	0.81	0.81	4
snehan-coursera	0.82	0.81	0.81	4
KBCNMUJAL	0.81	0.82	0.81	4
hopeful-nlp (Awatramani, 2021)	0.82	0.81	0.81	4
dhivya-hope-detection (Chinnappa, 2021)	0.81	0.82	0.81	4
IIIT-DWD (Saumya and Mishra, 2021)	0.79	0.79	0.79	5
Zeus (Zhou, 2021)	0.79	0.81	0.78	6
MUM	0.76	0.78	0.77	7
TeamX - Olawale Onabola	0.77	0.74	0.75	8
IRNLP-DAIICT-LR (Dave et al., 2021)	0.78	0.79	0.75	8
Hopeful-Men (Upadhyay et al., 2021)	0.76	0.79	0.75	8
Amrita-CEN-NLP (S et al., 2021b)	0.78	0.73	0.75	8
Amrita (S et al., 2021b)	0.76	0.72	0.73	9
spartans (Sharma and Arora, 2021)	0.62	0.62	0.61	10
mIGeng	0.58	0.61	0.59	11
IIITT - Karthik Puranik (Puranik et al., 2021)	0.57	0.57	0.57	12
SIMON (Que, 2021)	0.63	0.56	0.49	13
result	0.63	0.56	0.49	13

Table 5: Rank list based on F1-score along with other evaluation metrics (Precision and Recall) for Malayalam language

Team-Name	Precision	Recall	F1 Score	Rank
Zeus (Zhou, 2021)	0.93	0.94	0.93	1
TeamUNCC (Mahajan et al., 2021)	0.93	0.94	0.93	1
team-hub (Huang and Bai, 2021)	0.93	0.93	0.93	1
res - si sun	0.93	0.93	0.93	1
NLP@CUET(Hossain et al., 2021)	0.93	0.93	0.93	1
KU-NLP (M K and A P, 2021)	0.92	0.93	0.93	1
Hopeful-men (Upadhyay et al., 2021)	0.93	0.93	0.93	1
GCDH	0.93	0.93	0.93	1
EDIOne - suman t (Dowlagar and Mamidi, 2021)	0.93	0.94	0.93	1
cs-english (Chen and Kong, 2021)	0.93	0.94	0.93	1
Autobots (Gundapu and Mamidi, 2021)	0.93	0.93	0.93	1
Hopeful-nlp (Awatramani, 2021)	0.93	0.94	0.93	1
ZYJ (Zhao, 2021)	0.92	0.93	0.92	2
ssn-diBERTsity (S et al., 2021a)	0.91	0.93	0.92	2
MUCS (Balouchzahi et al., 2021)	0.92	0.93	0.92	2
IRNLP-DAIICT-LR (Dave et al., 2021)	0.92	0.93	0.92	2
IIITK (Ghanghor et al., 2021b)	0.92	0.92	0.92	2
HopeIsAllYouNeed	0.92	0.93	0.92	2
dhivya-hope-detection (Chinnappa, 2021)	0.92	0.92	0.92	2
CFILT-IITB-Submission	0.92	0.93	0.92	2
snehan-coursera	0.92	0.91	0.91	3
IIITT - Karthik Puranik (Puranik et al., 2021)	0.92	0.91	0.91	3
MUM	0.89	0.91	0.9	4
IIIT-DWD (Saumya and Mishra, 2021)	0.9	0.91	0.9	4
e8ijs	0.91	0.92	0.9	4
wrecking-crew	0.9	0.91	0.87	5
HopeFighters	0.83	0.91	0.87	5
Amrita-CEN-NLP (S et al., 2021b)	0.83	0.91	0.87	5
mlGeng	0.86	0.85	0.85	6
TeamX - Olawale Onabola	0.9	0.77	0.81	7
KBCNMUJAL	0.88	0.5	0.61	8

Table 6: Rank list based on F1-score along with other evaluation metrics (Precision and Recall) for English language

the Stratified-K-Fold method to address class imbalance. They achieved a weighted average F1-score of 0.59, 0.84, and 0.92 for Tamil, Malayalam, and English languages, which ranked 3rd, 2nd, and 2nd respectively.

- Huang and Bai (2021) used the method and model that combines the XLM-RoBERTa preraining language model and the TF-IDF algorithm. They got 1st, 2nd, and 3rd ranks on the English, Malayalam, and Tamil dataset respectively.
- Chen and Kong (2021) used fine-tuned BERT and K fold cross-validation to accomplish classification on English dataset. They achieved a final F1 score of 0.93, and got 1st rank for English language.
- Ziehe et al. (2021) demonstrated that even very simple baseline algorithms perform reasonably well on this task if provided with enough training data. However, their best performing algorithm is a cross-lingual transfer learning approach in which they fine-tuned XLM-RoBERTa. The model achieved the 1st rank for Malayalam and English and the 4th rank for Tamil.
- Mahajan et al. (2021), in their paper, described their approach of fine-tuning RoBERTa for Hope Speech detection in English and fine-tuning XLM-RoBERTa for Hope Speech detection in Tamil and Malayalam languages. They ranked 1st in English (F1 = 0.93), 1st in Tamil (F1 = 0.61) and 3rd in Malayalam (F1 = 0.83).
- Gundapu and Mamidi (2021) describe a Transformer-based BERT model for Hope speech detection. Their model achieved a weighted averaged F1-score of 0.93 on the test set for English. They showed that BERT model helped for better contextual representation of words in a comment, and the language identification model- assisted in detecting 'Other language' comments. They also explored with other transformer models like RoBERTa, XLNet, Albert, FLAIR, and ELMo for a superior hope speech detection.
- S et al. (2021b) proposed a BiLSTM with attention based approach in solving hope speech detection and using this approach they achieved an F1 score of 0.73 (9th rank) in Malayalam-English dataset.
- Upadhyay et al. (2021) experimented with two approaches. In the first approach, they used contextual embeddings to train classifiers using logistic regression, random forest, SVM, and LSTM based models. The second approach involved using a majority voting ensemble of 11 models which were obtained by fine-tuning pre-trained transformer models (BERT, AL-BERT, RoBERTa, IndicBERT) after adding an output layer. They found that the second approach was superior for English, Tamil and Malayalam. They got a weighted F1 score of 0.93, 0.75 and 0.49 for English,Malayalam and Tamil respectively. They ranked 1st in English, 8th in Malayalam and 11th in Tamil.
- Awatramani (2021) achieved an F-score of 0.93, ranking 1st on the leaderboard for English comments. The paper used pre-trained transformers and Paraphrasing Generation for Data Augmentation.
- Hossain et al. (2021) employed various machine learning (SVM, LR, ensemble), deep learning (CNN+BiLSTM) and transformer (m-BERT, Indic-BERT, XLNet, XLM-R) based methods. They showed that XLM-R outperformed all other techniques by gaining a weighted F1-score of 0.93, 0.60 and 0.85 respectively for English, Tamil and Malayalam language. Their team achieved 1st , 2nd and 1st rank in these three tasks respectively.
- Que (2021) used XLM- Roberta model and proposed an excellent multilingual model to achieve the classification task.
- Balouchzahi et al. (2021) created three models namely, CoHope-ML, CoHope-NN, and CoHope-TL based on Ensemble of classifiers, Keras Neural Network (NN) and BiLSTM with Conv1D model. CoHope-ML, CoHope-NN models were trained on a feature set comprising of char sequences extracted from sentences combined with words for Ma-En and Ta-En code-mixed texts and a combination of word and char ngrams along with syntactic word ngrams for English text. CoHope-TL model consisted of three major parts: training tokenizer, BERT Language Model (LM)

training and then using pre-trained BERT LM as weights in BiLSTM- Conv1d model. Out of the three proposed models, CoHope-ML model (best one among the models proposed) obtained 1st, 2nd, and 3rd ranks with weighted F1-scores of 0.85, 0.92, and 0.59 for Ma-En, English and Ta-En texts respectively.

- Sharma and Arora (2021) extends that of (Arora, 2020a) as they used their strategy to synthetically generate code-mixed data for training a transformer-based model RoBERTa and used it in an ensemble along with their pre-trained ULMFiT. They presented RoBERTa language model for code-mixed Tamil which they pre-trained from scratch. Using transfer learning they fine-tune RoBERTa and ULM-FiT language models on down- stream tasks of OLI and HSD. They got Rank 4 in the former task using an ensemble of classifiers trained on RoBERTa and ULMFiT and Rank 1 in the latter task using classifier based on ULMFiT.

4 Results and Discussion

Overall, we received a total of 31,31 and 30 submissions for English, Malayalam and Tamil tasks. It is interesting to note that the top performing teams in all the three languages predominantly used XLM-Roberta to complete the shared task. One of the top ranking teams for English used context-aware string embeddings for word representations and Recurrent Neural Networks and pooled document embeddings for text representation. Among the other submissions, although Bi-LSTM was popular, there were other machine learning and deep learning models that were used. However, they did not achieve good results compared to the Roberta based models.

The top scores were 0.61, 0.85 and 0.93 for Tamil, Malayalam and English respectively. The range of scores was between 0.37 to 0.61, 0.49 to 0.85 and 0.61 to 0.93 for Tamil, Malayalam and English datasets respectively. It can be seen that the F1 scores of all the submissions on the Tamil dataset were considerably lower than those of Malayalam and English. It is not suprising that the English scores were better because many approaches used variations of pretrained transformer based models trained on English data. Due to code-mixing at various levels the scores are naturally lower for Malayalam and Tamil datasets. Among these two, the systems submitted performed badly on Tamil data. The identification of the exact reasons for the bad performance in Tamil requires further research. However, one possible explanation for this could be that the distribution of 'Hope_speech', 'Non_hope_speech' and 'not-Tamil' classes is starkly different from those of English and Malayalam. In the English dataset there were just 27 out of 28,451 comments which were labelled as not-English by the annotators. In the remaining two classes, the number of non-hope speech comments were significantly higher than hope speech comments. Similarly in Malayalam there were only 888 out of 10,705 comments that were not Malayalam and overwhelmingly higher proportion of non-hope speech in the dataset. However in Tamil dataset, there were 2,483 comments out of 20,198 comments that were not Tamil. Moreover the proportion of Non-hope speech comments in Tamil (9,816 comments) is close enough to the number of hope speech labels (7,899 comments). This made the classifications in English and Malayalam a binary prediction task rather than a three class classification and naturally the former systems performed better than the latter.

The participants rarely faced challenges during the training, testing and submission phase. However, there were minor inconsistencies in the labelling of classes that was duly rectified on Codalab immediately. The intial round of peer review offered significant suggestions to the participants in terms of rewriting paper in a more presentable way. These suggestions of the reviewers were duly incorporated before the final submissions.

5 Conclusion

In this paper, we have presented the first shared task results on hope speech detection for equality, diversity, and inclusion. We received a wide range of entries that satisfied the goals of the shared task. We hope that HopeEDI shared task makes a lasting contribution to the NLP field.

References

Vasudev Awatramani. 2021. Hopeful NLP@LT-EDI-EACL2021: Finding Hope in YouTube Comment Section. In *Proceedings of the First Workshop on Language Technology for Equality, Diversity and Inclusion*, Online. Association for Computational Linguistics.

Fazlourrahman Balouchzahi, Aparna B K, and H L Shashirekha. 2021. MUCS@LT-EDI-

EACL2021:CoHope-Hope Speech Detection for Equality, Diversity, and Inclusion in Code-Mixed Texts. In *Proceedings of the First Workshop on Language Technology for Equality, Diversity and Inclusion*, Online. Association for Computational Linguistics.

Steven Bird, Ewan Klein, and Edward Loper. 2009. *Natural language processing with Python: analyzing text with the natural language toolkit.* " O'Reilly Media, Inc.".

Bharathi Raja Chakravarthi. 2020a. HopeEDI: A multilingual hope speech detection dataset for equality, diversity, and inclusion. In *Proceedings of the Third Workshop on Computational Modeling of People's Opinions, Personality, and Emotion's in Social Media*, pages 41–53, Barcelona, Spain (Online). Association for Computational Linguistics.

Bharathi Raja Chakravarthi. 2020b. *Leveraging orthographic information to improve machine translation of under-resourced languages.* Ph.D. thesis, NUI Galway.

Bharathi Raja Chakravarthi, Navya Jose, Shardul Suryawanshi, Elizabeth Sherly, and John P McCrae. 2020. A sentiment analysis dataset for code-mixed Malayalam-English. In *Proceedings of the 1st Joint Workshop of SLTU (Spoken Language Technologies for Under-resourced languages) and CCURL (Collaboration and Computing for Under-Resourced Languages) (SLTU-CCURL 2020)*, Marseille, France. European Language Resources Association (ELRA).

Bharathi Raja Chakravarthi and Vigneshwaran Muralidaran. 2021. Findings of the shared task on Hope Speech Detection for Equality, Diversity, and Inclusion. In *Proceedings of the First Workshop on Language Technology for Equality, Diversity and Inclusion*. Association for Computational Linguistics.

Shi Chen and Bing Kong. 2021. cs-english@LT-EDI-EACL2021: Hope Speech Detection Based On Fine-tuning AlBERT Model. In *Proceedings of the First Workshop on Language Technology for Equality, Diversity and Inclusion*, Online. Association for Computational Linguistics.

Dhivya Chinnappa. 2021. Multilingual Hope Speech Detection for Code-mixed and Transliterated Texts. In *Proceedings of the First Workshop on Language Technology for Equality, Diversity and Inclusion*, Online. Association for Computational Linguistics.

Bhargav Dave, Shripad Bhat, and Prasenjit Majumder. 2021. IRNLP-DAIICT@LT-EDI-EACL2021: Hope Speech detection in Code Mixed text using TF-IDF Char N-grams and MuRIL. In *Proceedings of the First Workshop on Language Technology for Equality, Diversity and Inclusion*, Online. Association for Computational Linguistics.

Suman Dowlagar and Radhika Mamidi. 2021. EDIOne@LT-EDI-EACL2021: Pre-trained Transformers with Convolutional Neural Networks for Hope Speech Detection. In *Proceedings of the First Workshop on Language Technology for Equality, Diversity and Inclusion*, Online. Association for Computational Linguistics.

Nikhil Kumar Ghanghor, Parameswari Krishnamurthy, Sajeetha Thavareesan, Ruba Priyadharshini, and Bharathi Raja Chakravarthi. 2021a. IIITK@DravidianLangTech-EACL2021: Offensive Language Identification and Meme Classification in Tamil, Malayalam and Kannada. In *Proceedings of the First Workshop on Speech and Language Technologies for Dravidian Languages*, Online. Association for Computational Linguistics.

Nikhil Kumar Ghanghor, Rahul Ponnusamy, Prasanna Kumar Kumaresan, Ruba Priyadharshini, Sajeetha Thavareesan, and Bharathi Raja Chakravarthi. 2021b. IIITK@LT-EDI-EACL2021: Hope Speech Detection for Equality, Diversity, and Inclusion in Tamil, Malayalam and English. In *Proceedings of the First Workshop on Language Technology for Equality, Diversity and Inclusion*, Online.

Sunil Gundapu and Radhika Mamidi. 2021. Autobots@LT-EDI-EACL2021: All Lives Matter! Hope Speech Detection with BERT Transformer Model. In *Proceedings of the First Workshop on Language Technology for Equality, Diversity and Inclusion*, Online. Association for Computational Linguistics.

Siddhanth U Hegde, Adeep Hande, Ruba Priyadharshini, Sajeetha Thavareesan, and Bharathi Raja Chakravarthi. 2021. UVCE-IIITT@DravidianLangTech-EACL2021: Tamil Troll Meme Classification: You need to Pay more Attention. In *Proceedings of the First Workshop on Speech and Language Technologies for Dravidian Languages*. Association for Computational Linguistics.

Eftekhar Hossain, Omar Sharif, and Mohammed Moshiul Hoque. 2021. NLP-CUET@LT-EDI-EACL2021: Multilingual Code-Mixed Hope Speech Detection using Cross-lingual Representation Learner . In *Proceedings of the First Workshop on Language Technology for Equality, Diversity and Inclusion*, Online. Association for Computational Linguistics.

Bo Huang and Yang Bai. 2021. TEAM HUB@LT-EDI-EACL2021: Hope Speech Detection Based On Pre-trained Language Model. In *Proceedings of the First Workshop on Language Technology for Equality, Diversity and Inclusion*, Online. Association for Computational Linguistics.

Vishnupriya Kolipakam, Fiona M Jordan, Michael Dunn, Simon J Greenhill, Remco Bouckaert, Russell D Gray, and Annemarie Verkerk. 2018. A

Bayesian phylogenetic study of the Dravidian language family. *Royal Society open science*, 5(3):171504.

Bhadriraju Krishnamurti. 2003. *The Dravidian languages*. Cambridge University Press.

Ritesh Kumar, Atul Kr. Ojha, Shervin Malmasi, and Marcos Zampieri. 2018. Benchmarking aggression identification in social media. In *Proceedings of the First Workshop on Trolling, Aggression and Cyberbullying (TRAC-2018)*, pages 1–11, Santa Fe, New Mexico, USA. Association for Computational Linguistics.

Junaida M K and Ajees A P. 2021. KU-NLP@LT-EDI-EACL2021: A Multilingual Hope Speech Detection for Equality, Diversity, and Inclusion using Context Aware Embeddings. In *Proceedings of the First Workshop on Language Technology for Equality, Diversity and Inclusion*, Online. Association for Computational Linguistics.

Iravatham Mahadevan. 2003. Early tamil epigraphy. *From the earliest times to the sixth century ad*.

Khyati Mahajan, Erfan Al-Hossami, and Samira Shaikh. 2021. TeamUNCC@LT-EDI-EACL2021: Hope Speech Detection using Transfer Learning with Transformers. In *Proceedings of the First Workshop on Language Technology for Equality, Diversity and Inclusion*, Online. Association for Computational Linguistics.

Thomas Mandl, Sandip Modha, Anand Kumar M, and Bharathi Raja Chakravarthi. 2020. Overview of the HASOC Track at FIRE 2020: Hate Speech and Offensive Language Identification in Tamil, Malayalam, Hindi, English and German. In *Forum for Information Retrieval Evaluation*, FIRE 2020, page 29–32, New York, NY, USA. Association for Computing Machinery.

Karthik Puranik, Adeep Hande, Ruba Priyadharshini, Sajeetha Thavareesan, and Bharathi Raja Chakravarthi. 2021. IIITT@LT-EDI-EACL2021-Hope Speech Detection: There is always hope in Transformers. In *Proceedings of the First Workshop on Language Technology for Equality, Diversity and Inclusion*, Online. Association for Computational Linguistics.

Qinyu Que. 2021. Simon @ LT-EDI-EACL2021: Detecting Hope Speech with BERT. In *Proceedings of the First Workshop on Language Technology for Equality, Diversity and Inclusion*, Online. Association for Computational Linguistics.

Arunima S, Akshay Ramakrishnan, Avantika Balaji, Thenmozhi D, and Senthil Kumar B. 2021a. ssn-diBERTsity@LT-EDI-EACL2021:Hope Speech Detection on multilingual YouTube comments via transformer based approach. In *Proceedings of the First Workshop on Language Technology for Equality, Diversity and Inclusion*, Online. Association for Computational Linguistics.

Thara S, Ravi Teja Tasubilli, and Kothamasu Sai Rahul. 2021b. Amrita@LT-EDI-EACL2021: Hope Speech Detection on Multilingual Text. In *Proceedings of the First Workshop on Language Technology for Equality, Diversity and Inclusion*, Online. Association for Computational Linguistics.

Sunil Saumya and Ankit Kumar Mishra. 2021. IIIT-DWD@LT-EDI-EACL2021: Hope Speech Detection in YouTube multilingual comments. In *Proceedings of the First Workshop on Language Technology for Equality, Diversity and Inclusion*, Online. Association for Computational Linguistics.

Megha Sharma and Gaurav Arora. 2021. Spartans@LT-EDI-EACL2021: Inclusive Speech Detection using Pretrained Language Models. In *Proceedings of the First Workshop on Language Technology for Equality, Diversity and Inclusion*, Online. Association for Computational Linguistics.

Ramya Srinivasan. 2019. Reinventing tamil script.

Sajeetha Thavareesan and Sinnathamby Mahesan. 2019. Sentiment Analysis in Tamil Texts: A Study on Machine Learning Techniques and Feature Representation. In *2019 14th Conference on Industrial and Information Systems (ICIIS)*, pages 320–325.

Sajeetha Thavareesan and Sinnathamby Mahesan. 2020a. Sentiment Lexicon Expansion using Word2vec and fastText for Sentiment Prediction in Tamil texts. In *2020 Moratuwa Engineering Research Conference (MERCon)*, pages 272–276.

Sajeetha Thavareesan and Sinnathamby Mahesan. 2020b. Word embedding-based Part of Speech tagging in Tamil texts. In *2020 IEEE 15th International Conference on Industrial and Information Systems (ICIIS)*, pages 478–482.

Ishan Sanjeev Upadhyay, Nikhil E, Anshul Wadhawan, and Radhika Mamidi. 2021. Hopeful Men@LT-EDI-EACL2021: Hope Speech Detection Using Indic Transliteration and Transformers. In *Proceedings of the First Workshop on Language Technology for Equality, Diversity and Inclusion*, Online. Association for Computational Linguistics.

Konthala Yasaswini, Karthik Puranik, Adeep Hande, Ruba Priyadharshini, Sajeetha Thavareesan, and Bharathi Raja Chakravarthi. 2021. IIITT@DravidianLangTech-EACL2021: Transfer Learning for Offensive Language Detection in Dravidian Languages. In *Proceedings of the First Workshop on Speech and Language Technologies for Dravidian Languages*. Association for Computational Linguistics.

Marcos Zampieri, Preslav Nakov, Sara Rosenthal, Pepa Atanasova, Georgi Karadzhov, Hamdy Mubarak, Leon Derczynski, Zeses Pitenis, and Çağrı Çöltekin. 2020. SemEval-2020 task 12: Multilingual offensive language identification in social media (OffensEval 2020). In *Proceedings of the Fourteenth*

Workshop on Semantic Evaluation, pages 1425–1447, Barcelona (online). International Committee for Computational Linguistics.

Yingjia Zhao. 2021. ZYJ@LT-EDI-EACL2021:XLM-RoBERTa-Based Model with Attention for Hope Speech Detection. In *Proceedings of the First Workshop on Language Technology for Equality, Diversity and Inclusion*, Online. Association for Computational Linguistics.

Siyao Zhou. 2021. Zeus@LT-EDI-EACL2021: Hope speech detection based on Pre-training Mode. In *Proceedings of the First Workshop on Language Technology for Equality, Diversity and Inclusion*, Online. Association for Computational Linguistics.

Stefan Ziehe, Franziska Pannach, and Aravind Krishnan. 2021. cs-english@GCDH@LT-EDI-EACL2021: XLM-RoBERTa for Hope Speech Detection in English, Malayalam, and Tamil. In *Proceedings of the First Workshop on Language Technology for Equality, Diversity and Inclusion*, Online. Association for Computational Linguistics.

dhivya-hope-detection@LT-EDI-EACL2021: Multilingual Hope Speech Detection for Code-mixed and Transliterated Texts

Dhivya Chinnappa
Thomson Reuters
dhivya.infant@gmail.com

Abstract

In this paper describe the shared task on hope speech detection. We present a unified framework to predict hope speech in the English, Tamil, and Malayalam datasets. Our mechanism follows a two phase approach to detect hope speech. In the first phase we build a classifier to identify the language of the text. In the second phase, we build a classifier to detect *hope speech*, *non hope speech* or *not lang* labels. Experimental results show that hope speech detection is challenging and there is scope for improvement.

1 Introduction

Artificial Intelligence models are criticized for their bias against the protected classes (Rudinger et al., 2017; Davidson et al., 2019). These biases are shown to arise from data or the model itself. There are several efforts taken to mitigate bias from the data and model perspectives (Park et al., 2018; Bender and Friedman, 2018; Mitchell et al., 2019) . Mozafari et al. (2020) present a bias alleviation mechanism evaluating the performance following a cross-domain approach.

Hope speech detection is the task of automatically detecting web content that may play a positive role in diffusing hostility on social media triggered by heightened political tensions during a conflict (Palakodety et al., 2020). We hypothesize that hope speech detection datasets could be used in evaluating the aforementioned bias alleviation mechanisms. These datasets and mechanisms could help in building AI systems that are diverse and inclusive. Additionally, with divisiveness spread across social media platforms, identifying hope speech and enhancing them would help mitigate divisiveness and animosity.

English	
God accepts everyone.	Hope
the tech industry is tough for everyone.	Non hope
CASA. LA. FEMMEnWesT.	Not Eng.
Tamil	
G..... semester exam ah pathi video uploade pannunga	Hope
Background மொக்கையா irruku	Non hope
love u mg bye.. bye... take care!!	Not Tam.
Malayalam	
Surya good. കഴിഞ്ഞ കാലം ഓക്കുന്നതാണ് ഏറ്റവും വലിയ കാര്യം. God bless u	Hope
കമ്മി ആണല്ലേ??	Non hope
I am made in India.	Not Mal.

Table 1: Examples of hope speech, non hope speech, and not *lang* in English, Tamil and Malayalam.

In this paper, we describe our approach on the hope detection shared task. We work with a multilingual corpora aiming to detect hope speech. We follow a two phase approach to accomplish the task. In the first phase, we identify the language of the input text. In the second phase we classify if the text is *hope speech* or not. We begin with describing the corpora, then analyze the datasets, explain the experimental setup, and finally discuss the results.

2 Data

We work with the hope speech detection corpora from Chakravarthi (2020). Unlike most

Proceedings of the First Workshop on Language Technology for Equality, Diversity and Inclusion, pages 73–78
April 19, 2021.

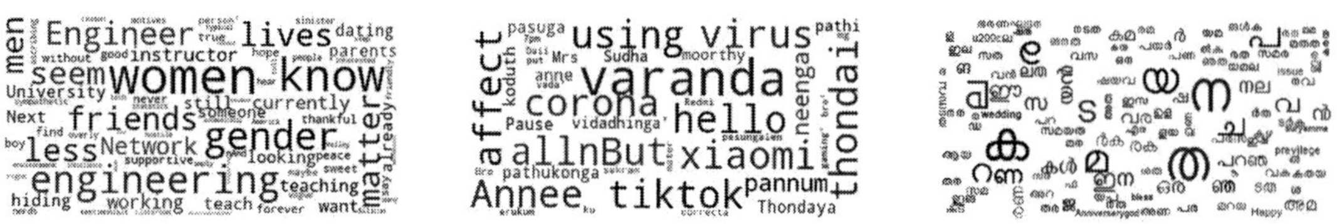

Figure 1: Wordcloud generated from the hope speech instances of the English (left), Tamil (center), and Malayalam (right) datasets.

Figure 2: Wordcloud generated from the non hope speech instances of the English (left), Tamil (center), and Malayalam (right) datasets. Note that the Tamil wordclouds consistently have English words.

other corpora that target English texts, this corpora focuses on diversity and inclusion including two dravidian languages apart from English. The corpora contains hope speech detection datasets in three languages (i) English, (ii) Tamil, and (iii) Malayalam.

The datasets are generated from YouTube comments, and manually labeled for the three labels *hope speech*, *non hope speech*, and *not lang*. The *hope speech* label and the *non hope speech* label are self-explanatory. The *not lang* label indicates that the YouTube comment does not belong to the specific language. That is, the datasets include *not English*, *not Tamil*, and *not Malayalam* instances depending on the language of the dataset they belong. This label becomes important as the Tamil and Malayalam dataset instances are generated by social media users who are usually bilingual (English and their mother tongue). Throughout this paper, we use the label *not lang* to refer that the text does not belong to the specific language. Table 1 presents examples of *hope speech*, *non hope speech*, and *not lang* from the three datasets.

3 Analysis

The English dataset includes 28,451 instances (*hope*: 2,484; *non hope*: 25,940; *not lang*: 27), the Tamil dataset includes 20,198 instances (*hope*: 7,899; *non hope*: 9,816; *not lang*: 2,483), and the Malayalam dataset includes 10,705 instances (*hope*: 2,052; *non hope*: 7,765; *not lang*: 888). Find more about the statistics of the corpora in the original paper (Chakravarthi, 2020).

Analyzing the datasets reveal that there are several Tamil and Malayalam instances that include code-mixed or English transliterated texts. For instance, the *non hope* example for Tamil dataset in Table 1 shows a combination of code-mixed (English and Tamil) and English transliteration of Tamil. It is common for bilingual speakers around the Indian subcontinent to use several English words when uttering a sentence in their mother tongue. Additionally, as several devices did not provide easy non-English typing in the beginning of the smart phone era, most users adapted to type English transliteration of non-English sentences. This phenomena is profoundly reflected in the Tamil and the Malayalam hope speech detection datasets. In case of the English dataset, this phenomena is uncommon and there was only 0.1% of *not lang* labels. We attribute these labels to the error caused by the language detector.

Figure 1 presents wordclouds for the *hope speech* instances in the three datasets English, Tamil, and Malayalam. As we can see, the English hope wordcloud (left) has hopeful words like good, teach, etc. Interstingly, the Tamil wordcloud (center) is filled with English words and Tamil words translitered to English like *pathukonga*, *neenga*, etc. Tamil social media users tend to use code-mixed (Tamil and English) and English transliterations of Tamil texts, causing this behavior. In case of Malay-

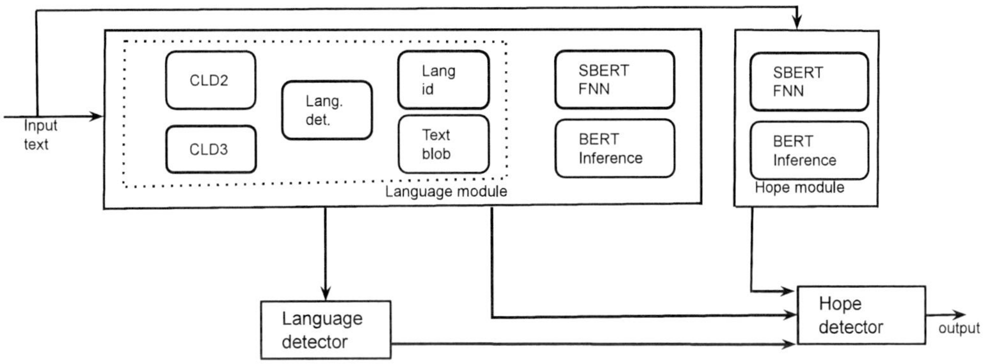

Figure 3: Architecture diagram describing the two phase hope detection process. The language detector identifies the language of the model, and the hope detector classifies the text into *hope speech*, *non hope speech*, or *not lang*.

alam, the wordcloud(right) includes both English and Malayalam words.

Figure 2 presents wordclouds for the *non hope speech* instances in the three datasets English, Tamil, and Malayalam. Unsurprisingly, the wordclouds for non hope speech instances include words with negative connotations. It is to be noted that Tamil social media users have more English influence than Malayalam social media users, despite both languages being Dravidian.

4 Experiments

As the number of *not lang* labels are considerably less than (English: 0.1%, Tamil: 12%, Malayalam: 11%) the other two labels, we specifically target to identify *not lang* labels by building a dedicated classifier. Thus we follow a two-phase approach to detect hope speech. We argue a two-phase language identification approach might be helpful as the datasets include a *not lang* label despite corresponding to a specific language. In phase 1, we identify the language of the text using a language detector. In phase 2, we use the results from phase 1 in addition to other features, to identify hope speech or not using a hope detector. The architecture is described in Figure 1.

4.1 Language detection

In this phase, we convert all *hope speech* and *not-hope speech* labels to *lang* labels, and keep the *not lang* labels as they are. Thus, we build a binary classifier using a feedforward neural network (FNN) to predict *lang* or *not lang*. We call this FNN as the language detector. The language detector takes as input (i) outputs from five language models (ii) probabilities from a vanilla feedforward network classifying *lang* and *not lang*with SBERT (Reimers and Gurevych, 2019) inputs, (iii) BERT (Devlin et al., 2019) inferences for *lang* and *not lang*.

Language models. We use five language models that take text as input and return the language of the text. The language detectors used are Compact Language Detector 2(CLD2, 2015), Compact Language Detector 3(CLD3, 2020), langid (Lui and Baldwin, 2012), textblob language detector (Loria, 2018), and langdetect (Nakatani, 2010). We use multiple language models rather than one language model improve the performance of the language detector. We follow the same approach for all language datasets including English, Tamil, and Malayalam.

SBERT FNN. We generate SBERT embeddings for each input text and feed it to a vanilla feedforward network that predicts *lang* or *not lang*. The output probabilities are passed to the language detector FNN. For the English dataset we use the *bert-base-nli-stsb-mean-tokens* model (Reimers and Gurevych, 2019) to generate SBERT embeddings. For Tamil and Malayalam datasets, we use the *distiluse-base-multilingual-cased* model (Sanh et al., 2019).

BERT inference. Here, we fine tune BERT models to predict *lang* or *not lang* obtaining BERT inferences. We hypothesize that hate speech models are useful in identifying hope speech detection, and use hate speech

	English			Tamil			Malayalam		
	P	R	F	P	R	F	P	R	F
Hope speech	0.56	0.56	0.56	0.56	0.52	0.54	0.63	0.46	0.54
Non hope speech	0.96	0.96	0.96	0.61	0.66	0.63	0.85	0.92	0.88
Not lang	0.00	0.00	0.00	0.61	0.54	0.58	0.83	0.66	0.74
W. avg.	0.92	0.92	0.92	0.59	0.59	0.59	0.81	0.82	0.81

Table 2: Results obtained with hope speech identified from text (YouTube comments) across the three languages English, Tamil, and Malyalam.

BERT models if present for a specific language. For English, we use the BERT models *dehatebert-mono-english* (Aluru et al., 2020) and *twitter-roberta-base-hate* (Barbieri et al., 2020). For Tamil, we use the BERT models *tamillion* (Doiron, 2020) and *bert-base-multilingual-uncased* (Devlin et al., 2018). For Malayalam we use the BERT model *bert-base-multilingual-uncased* (Devlin et al., 2018). Thus we have two BERT inferences results for English (*dehatebert-mono-english, twitter-roberta-base-hate*) and Tamil (*tamillion, bert-base-multilingual-uncased*), and one result for Malayalam (*bert-base-multilingual-uncased*).

The outputs from language models, probabilities from the SBERT vanilla FNN, and the BERT inferences make up the language module. The outputs from the language module is fed as an input to the language detector and the hope detector.

4.2 Hope detection

In this phase we predict the labels *hope speech, non hope speech*, or *not lang* using the hope detector. Similar to the language detector, the hope detector is a FNN that takes as input (i) outputs from the language module, (ii) outputs from the hope module, and (iii) probabilities from language detector.

Outputs from the language module. The same ouputs from the language module as described in 4.1 is given as the input to the hope detector.

SBERT FNN. This is similar to the SBERT FNN described in 4.1 except that it predicts *hope speech, non hope speech*, or *not lang*.

BERT inference. This is also very similar to the SBERT inferences described in 4.1, except that the BERT models are finetuned to predict *hope speech, non hope speech*, or *not lang*.

This **SBERT FNN** and **BERT inference** make up the hope module. We note that the probabilities from the **SBERT FNN** and **BERT inference** for language module and the hope module are different, as they were trained with different labels (language labels vs. hope labels).

5 Results

We present test results for English, Tamil, and Malayalam datasets in Table 2. Regarding the English dataset, the *non hope speech* labels achieve higher performance than *hope speech* labels (F1: .95 vs. .56). None of the *not lang* labels are predicted correctly. This poor performance for the *not lang* labels can be attributed to the imbalanced label distribution. There were only 3 *not lang* labels in the test set.

Regarding the Tamil dataset, the performance on all the three labels are comparable (F1: .52 vs. .66 vs. .54). Note that the Tamil dataset includes several code-mixed and transliterated texts. This phenomena can be attributed to why the classifier struggles in identifying the correct label.

Regarding the Malayalam dataset the performance of the label *hope speech* is worse than the others. Additionally, it is relatively easier to predict *not lang* labels in Malayalam.

The experimental results show detecting *hope speech* is difficult regardless of the language. Even in the English dataset where there are no transliterations or code-mixing, the classifier struggles. While we infer that hope detection is a difficult task, code-mixing and transliterations in Tamil and Malayalam increases the complexity of the problem. Chakravarthi and Muralidaran (2021) describe the results and techniques from the other participants of the hope speech detection shared task.

6 Conclusion

This paper describes the shared task on hope speech detection It targets to detect hope speech from a multilingual corpora. The corpora includes datasets in three languages English, Tamil, and Malayalam. First we conduct an analysis over the corpora finding code-mix and transliterated texts in the Tamil and Malayalam datasets. Next, we build a two phase mechanism to identify hope speech. In the first phase we detect the language of the text. In the next phase, we classify the text into *hope speech*, *non hope speech*, or *not lang*. Finally, we discuss the results concluding that hope detection is a challenging task.

References

Sai Saket Aluru, Binny Mathew, Punyajoy Saha, and Animesh Mukherjee. 2020. Deep learning models for multilingual hate speech detection. *arXiv preprint arXiv:2004.06465*.

Francesco Barbieri, Jose Camacho-Collados, Luis Espinosa Anke, and Leonardo Neves. 2020. TweetEval: Unified benchmark and comparative evaluation for tweet classification. In *Findings of the Association for Computational Linguistics: EMNLP 2020*, pages 1644–1650, Online. Association for Computational Linguistics.

Emily M. Bender and Batya Friedman. 2018. Data statements for natural language processing: Toward mitigating system bias and enabling better science. *Transactions of the Association for Computational Linguistics*, 6:587–604.

Bharathi Raja Chakravarthi. 2020. HopeEDI: A multilingual hope speech detection dataset for equality, diversity, and inclusion. In *Proceedings of the Third Workshop on Computational Modeling of People's Opinions, Personality, and Emotion's in Social Media*, pages 41–53, Barcelona, Spain (Online). Association for Computational Linguistics.

Bharathi Raja Chakravarthi and Vigneshwaran Muralidaran. 2021. Findings of the shared task on Hope Speech Detection for Equality, Diversity, and Inclusion. In *Proceedings of the First Workshop on Language Technology for Equality, Diversity and Inclusion*. Association for Computational Linguistics.

CLD2. 2015. Compact language detector 2. `https://github.com/CLD2Owners/cld2`.

CLD3. 2020. Compact language detector 3. `https://github.com/google/cld3`.

Thomas Davidson, Debasmita Bhattacharya, and Ingmar Weber. 2019. Racial bias in hate speech and abusive language detection datasets. In *Proceedings of the Third Workshop on Abusive Language Online*, pages 25–35, Florence, Italy. Association for Computational Linguistics.

Jacob Devlin, Ming-Wei Chang, Kenton Lee, and Kristina Toutanova. 2018. BERT: pre-training of deep bidirectional transformers for language understanding. *CoRR*, abs/1810.04805.

Jacob Devlin, Ming-Wei Chang, Kenton Lee, and Kristina Toutanova. 2019. BERT: Pre-training of deep bidirectional transformers for language understanding. In *Proceedings of the 2019 Conference of the North American Chapter of the Association for Computational Linguistics: Human Language Technologies, Volume 1 (Long and Short Papers)*, pages 4171–4186, Minneapolis, Minnesota. Association for Computational Linguistics.

Nick Doiron. 2020. Tamillion bert. `https://huggingface.co/monsoon-nlp/tamillion`.

Steven Loria. 2018. textblob documentation. *Release 0.15*, 2.

Marco Lui and Timothy Baldwin. 2012. langid.py: An off-the-shelf language identification tool. In *Proceedings of the ACL 2012 System Demonstrations*, pages 25–30, Jeju Island, Korea. Association for Computational Linguistics.

Margaret Mitchell, Simone Wu, Andrew Zaldivar, Parker Barnes, Lucy Vasserman, Ben Hutchinson, Elena Spitzer, Inioluwa Deborah Raji, and Timnit Gebru. 2019. Model cards for model reporting. *Proceedings of the Conference on Fairness, Accountability, and Transparency*.

Marzieh Mozafari, Reza Farahbakhsh, and Noel Crespi. 2020. Hate speech detection and racial bias mitigation in social media based on bert model.

Shuyo Nakatani. 2010. Language detection library for java.

Shriphani Palakodety, Ashiqur R. KhudaBukhsh, and Jaime G. Carbonell. 2020. Hope speech detection: A computational analysis of the voice of peace.

Ji Ho Park, Jamin Shin, and Pascale Fung. 2018. Reducing gender bias in abusive language detection. In *Proceedings of the 2018 Conference on Empirical Methods in Natural Language Processing*, pages 2799–2804, Brussels, Belgium. Association for Computational Linguistics.

Nils Reimers and Iryna Gurevych. 2019. Sentence-bert: Sentence embeddings using siamese bert-networks. In *Proceedings of the 2019 Conference on Empirical Methods in Natural Language*

Processing. Association for Computational Linguistics.

Rachel Rudinger, Chandler May, and Benjamin Van Durme. 2017. Social bias in elicited natural language inferences. In *Proceedings of the First ACL Workshop on Ethics in Natural Language Processing*, pages 74–79, Valencia, Spain. Association for Computational Linguistics.

Victor Sanh, Lysandre Debut, Julien Chaumond, and Thomas Wolf. 2019. Distilbert, a distilled version of bert: smaller, faster, cheaper and lighter. *ArXiv*, abs/1910.01108.

KU_NLP@LT-EDI-EACL2021: A Multilingual Hope Speech Detection for Equality, Diversity, and Inclusion using Context Aware Embeddings

Junaida M K
Department of Information Technology
Kannur University
Kerala, India
junaidashukoor@gmail.com

Ajees A P
Department of Information Technology
Kannur University
Kerala, India
ajeesap87@gmail.com

Abstract

Hope speech detection is a new task for finding and highlighting positive comments or supporting content from user-generated social media comments. For this task, we have used a Shared Task multilingual dataset on Hope Speech Detection for Equality, Diversity, and Inclusion (HopeEDI) for three languages English, code-switched Tamil and Malayalam. In this paper, we present deep learning techniques using context-aware string embeddings for word representations and Recurrent Neural Network (RNN) and pooled document embeddings for text representation. We have evaluated and compared the three models for each language with different approaches. Our proposed methodology works fine and achieved higher performance than baselines. The highest weighted average F-scores of 0.93, 0.58, and 0.84 are obtained on the task organisers' final evaluation test set. The proposed models are outperforming the baselines by 3%, 2% and 11% in absolute terms for English, Tamil and Malayalam respectively.

1 Introduction

In recent years, social media became an integral part of human life and people started spending more time on these platforms. But people are mindful of social media behaviour and putting less personal information in the public domain (Thavareesan and Mahesan, 2019, 2020a,b). Now social media behaviors changed quite dramatically and we are living not just in a pandemic, but also in an "infodemic", where fake news is becoming more common (Lima et al., 2020). Conversations on the internet are often a reflection of the conversations that one makes offline.

Several AI techniques are adopted to analyse the online comments in social media, which are intensified on the detection of negative comments such as hate speech detection, offensive language identification and abusive language detection (Chakravarthi, 2020a). Hate speech is widely used in media, internet and public discourse which seen or read in the media expressing disapproval, hatred, or aggression towards minorities, could lead to violence and form negative impact on minorities. Hope speech detection is a new task related to Hate speech detection for finding and highlighting positive comments or supporting content, rather than just filtering hostile content (Chakravarthi et al., 2020a). For this task, YouTube comments/posts that offer support, reassurance, suggestions, inspiration and insight are recognized as hope speech. In bilingual and multilingual communities linguistic code-switching occurs in social groups (Chakravarthi et al., 2018, 2019; Chakravarthi, 2020b). It is incredibly important in many social groups, When an individual uses a group's dialect or accent, the audience is more receptive to the content (Jose et al., 2020; Priyadharshini et al., 2020). Recently, many researchers are focused on high resource languages using monolingual corpora but less attention is given to code-switching languages especially under resourced languages like Indian languages (Chakravarthi et al., 2020b; Mandl et al., 2020). In our work, we used Hope Speech dataset for Equality, Diversity and Inclusion (HopeEDI) not only in English but also code-switched Tamil and Malayalam (Chakravarthi, 2020a).

2 Related Work

The authors (Puranik et al., 2021; Ghanghor et al., 2021) introduced a novel task for detecting hostility diffusing content from comments in social media, dubbed hope-speech detection. The authors analysed and studied the importance of automatic identification of user-generated hope speech web content that diffuse tension and violence among

Proceedings of the First Workshop on Language Technology for Equality, Diversity and Inclusion, pages 79–85
April 19, 2021.

Language	Train	Dev	Test	Total
English	22,762	2,843	2,846	28,451
Tamil	16,160	2,018	2,020	20,198
Malayalam	8564	1070	1071	10,705

Table 1: Train-Devolopment-Test Split

people in an international crisis. Finally, the obtained results are very promising and automatic recognition of hope speech may also find applications in many other contexts. But they restricted the definition of hope into diffuse tension and violence not considering the other perspectives of hope.

Chakravarthi (2020a) constructed a multilingual Hope Speech dataset for Equality, Diversity and Inclusion (HopeEDI) containing user-generated comments from YouTube for English and two low-resource languages, Malayalam and Tamil. The authors considered much more perspectives support, reassurance, suggestions, inspiration and insight of the hope and EDI. To facilitate future research on encouraging positivity, the authors make this dataset publicly available and created several baselines to benchmark the proposed dataset.

3 Materials and Methods

This section describes the dataset used for our experiments and technical description of the proposed methodology.

3.1 Dataset

For our work, we used the Shared Task dataset on Hope Speech Detection for Equality, Diversity, and Inclusion at LT-EDI 2021- EACL 2021 (Chakravarthi and Muralidaran, 2021). The dataset contains YouTube comments from English, code-switched Tamil and Malayalam. This is considered a multilingual resource to allow cross-lingual studies and approaches. The corpus consists of a total of 59,354 comments from YouTube videos, where 28,451 comments are in English, 20,198 comments are in Tamil, and the remaining 10,705 comments are in Malayalam. The dataset was manually annotated with three different labels: Hope Speech, Not-Hope Speech and Other languages, where Other languages refer to comments that were not in the intended language. The Figure 1 shows, distribution of three classes in shared task dataset. For our work, we have used the training, validation and test set of the shared task as depicted in Table 1.

3.2 Methods

Hope speech detection is a form of text classification, which classify sentences or documents into specified categories. Most current state of art approaches to text classification rely on a technique called text embedding. The embeddings of words in a sentence is used to make a vector representation of the sentence. The sentence embeddings can be achieved in many ways. It could be done by convolutional neural networks (CNN) (Kim, 2014), by averaging word vectors (Iyyer et al., 2015) or by using Recurrent Neural Networks(RNNs) (Dai and Le, 2015).

In our proposed method we have used Deep contextual and fixed (non-contextual) embeddings to derive word representations. Then, puts them into an RNN or does a pooling operation on overall word embeddings to obtain a text representation. Finally, a softmax layer accepts the text representations to get the actual class label (Akbik et al., 2019b). We have implemented three models for each language using contextualized string embeddings (*flair*) in a **FLAIR** framework (Akbik et al., 2019a).

Contextualized String Embedding (*Flair*) : (Akbik et al., 2018) proposed a novel word embedding from internal states of a trained character language model and termed as *contextual string embeddings*. The two primary factors powering contextual string embeddings (*Flair*) are, words are trained as characters and embeddings are contextualised by their surrounding text. Hence, it is treated as character language model(charLM) and it perhaps the biggest benefit of using over a word-based language model when a word has not been seen in the training data. The Flair embeddings are obtained by training two LSTM -based language models, forward and backward. The final word embedding is the concatenation of two specific hidden states from two language models. Let, t_1, t_2 ...., t_n be the character indices. Furthermore, let $h^f{}_t$, $h^b{}_t$ be the hidden states at character position t for forward and backward LM respectively. The *Flair* embedding $\mathbf{w}_k$ for the word w_k is defined as given in Equation 1.

$$\mathbf{w}_k = \left[h^f_{t_{k+1}-1}; \quad h^b_{t_k-1} \right] \tag{1}$$

Stacked Embedding : In this method we combine different embeddings, such as *word2vec*, *Glove*, *FastText* along with embeddings generated from *Flair* language models(Akbik et al., 2019a).

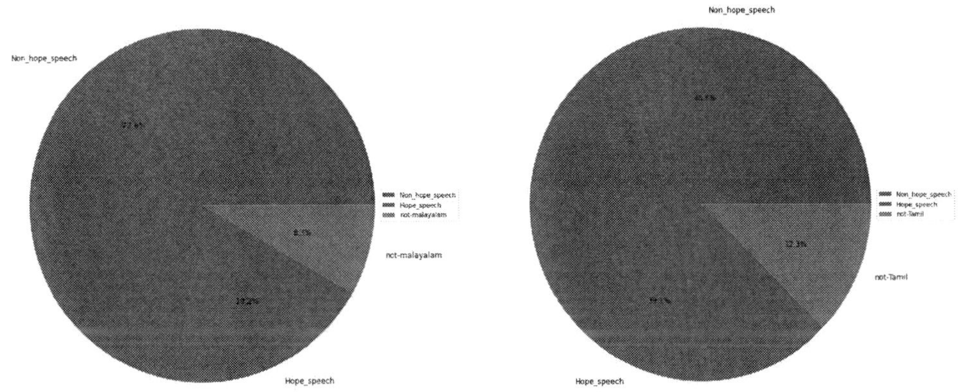

(a) Malayalam (b) Tamil

Figure 1: Distribution of three classes over the Hope Speech Detection for Equality, Diversity, and Inclusion at LT-EDI 2021-EACL 2021 Shared Task dataset for English, Malayalam and Tamil languages

Document Pool Embeddings : It is a simple document embedding, calculate a pooling operation (mean or max or min) over a list of token embeddings in a document. The default operation is mean which gives the mean of all words in the sentence (Akbik et al., 2019a).

4 Experiments

4.1 Experimental Setup

We have utilized the FLAIR framework (Akbik et al., 2019a) for all our experiments with GPU (12 GB) provided by Google Colab. We have trained three models for each language. The first model employed a pretrained *flair* LM for word representation and RNN for text representation (*FLAIR+RNN*). The second model combines pretrained *flair* LM and pretrained word embeddings (PWE) for word representaion and RNN is used for text representaion (*FLAIR+PWE+RNN*). The third model apply the same word representation and pooled document embedding for text representation (*FLAIR+PWE+Pooled*). The Gated Recurrent Unit (GRU) is used for document RNN embedding and max pool operation is used for pooled document embedding. The Table 2 shows the hyperparameters settings for all our experiments.

For all three languages, We have adopted pretrianed *flair* embeddings from FLAIR framework (*en-forward, en-backward, ml-forward, ml-backward, ta-forward* and *ta-backward*) (Akbik et al., 2019a). For PWE in English we have also taken the twitter embeddings from same framework. The Malayalam and Tamil langauge used the PWE from IndicFT, FastText-based word embeddings (11 languages), which is a 300-dimensional word embeddings for each language on IndicCorp, recently published large monolingual sentence level corpora for 11 Indian languages (Kakwani et al., 2020).

Parameter	Value
Learning rate	0.1
Patience	5
Batch size	32
Anneal factor	0.5
Word dropout	0.05
Loss function	Cross Entropy
Epochs	20

Table 2: Hyper Parameters

4.2 Evaluation

The performance of a text classification model is usually noted as F1-score (harmonic mean of precision and recall) since accuracy can often be misleading in an imbalanced class distribution (Akosa, 2017). For this task, the dataset having imbalanced class distribution as in Figure 1. Due to the imbalance problem, we measured our system performance in terms of weighted averaged Precision, weighted averaged Recall and weighted averaged F-Score across all the three classes. Weighted averaged calculations use average of the support-weighted mean per label.

Language	Classifier	Weighted avg		
		P	**R**	**F**
English	*DT*	0.90	0.90	0.90
	MNB	0.60	0.58	0.56
Tamil	*LR*	0.58	0.57	0.56
Malayalam	*DT*	0.73	0.76	0.73

Table 3: Baseline results from (Chakravarthi, 2020a).

Language	Model	Weighted avg		
		P	**R**	**F**
	FLAIR+RNN	0.91	0.92	0.91
English	*FLAIR+PWE+RNN*	0.92	0.93	0.91
	FLAIR+PWE+Pooled	0.92	0.93	**0.93**
	FLAIR+RNN	0.58	0.58	0.56
Tamil	*FLAIR+PWE+RNN*	0.60	0.59	**0.58**
	FLAIR+PWE+Pooled	0.62	0.60	0.56
	FLAIR+RNN	0.78	0.82	0.79
Malayalam	*FLAIR+PWE+RNN*	0.82	0.86	0.83
	FLAIR+PWE+Pooled	0.84	0.85	**0.84**

Table 4: Our models results from proposed methodology.

5 Results and Analysis

This section presents the results and analysis of our experiments, which we have explained in the previous sections. As well as, we present the baseline results obtained by the authors (Chakravarthi, 2020a), to compare the performance with our proposed models. The final evaluation results obtained for participants' submissions by task organisers are also presented in overview paper (Chakravarthi and Muralidaran, 2021). The best-performing classifiers on HopeEDI datasets are considered as baseline models for this task (See Table 3). The Table 4 depict the precision, recall and F-score results of trained models for three languages described in section 4.1.

As shown, all our proposed models for Hope EDI detection task in three languages work well and show significant improvement than the best-performed baseline models. The results indicate that a Hope EDI detection classifier with good precision and recall can be constructed using deep learning approaches. It may be due to the representational power of pre-trained word embeddings or language models to capture semantic and lexical structure. It has virtually replaced the feature engineering part of supervised machine learning classifiers.

For English and Malayalam, our model with stacked word embeddings and pooled document embedding achieved the highest performance on the HopeEDI dataset with a weighted average F-Score of 0.93 and 0.84 respectively. But in Tamil, stacked PWE with RNN document embedding performed better than other models with weighted average F-Score of 0.58. Furthermore, it can be seen that all Malayalam language models (0.79,0.83,0.84) achieved greater improvement than baseline models(0.73). Other two languages exhibit slight improvement in proposed models than baseline models.

In most cases, it can be observed from the Table 4 that the *flair* embedding with PWE gives higher performance than the standalone embeddings. This indicates that combining contextual embedding with non-contextual embeddings achieves noticeably better outcomes. This finding is in line with the findings of (Akbik et al., 2018). The Figures 2 and 3 represents the class level precision, recall and f-scores of best-performed baseline models and best performed proposed models for all three languages. It can be noticed from these figures that the class "not-english" have no significant performance in both models due to the imbalance in shared task dataset (Chakravarthi, 2020a).

Also, we can observe that the "Non-hope-speech" class for English shows similar perfor-

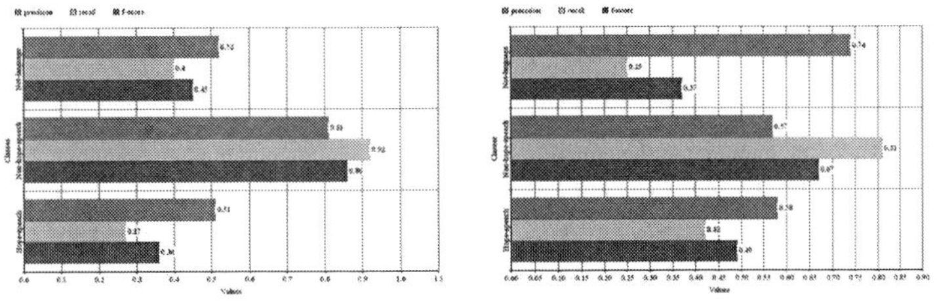

(a) Malayalam (b) Tamil

Figure 2: Class level precision, recall and f-scores of baselines models (Chakravarthi, 2020a) for three languages.

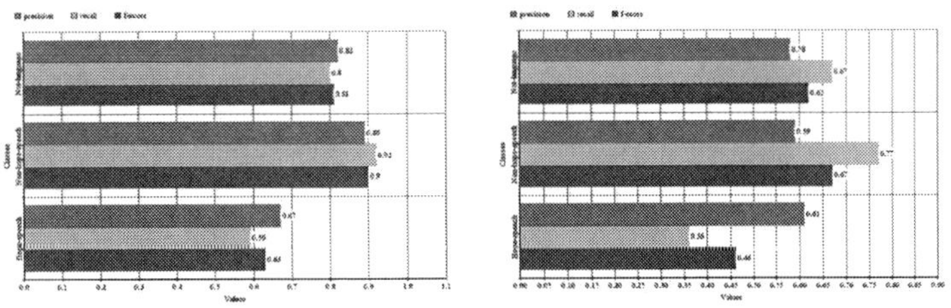

(a) Malayalam (b) Tamil

Figure 3: Class level precision, recall and f-scores of best-performed models from our experiments for three languages.

mance in both models and "Hope-speech" class hold a remarkable improvement over baseline models. In Tamil and Malayalam the majority class "Non-hope-speech" possesses approximately similar F-scores for baseline and proposed the best model. Another notable and interesting observation from Figure 2 and 3 is that the two minority classes in Malayalam dataset, "Hope-speech" and "not-malayalam" shows comparable performance approximately 30% above F-score than the baseline model. Also, "not-Tamil" class shows approximately 25% above F-score than the baseline model.

These higher scores indicate that deep learning techniques can classify the correct class regardless of label distribution better than traditional machine learning technique. This may because our deep learning techniques rely on pre-trained embeddings and language model, which is a contextualized word representation allowing a word to be associated with multiple word vectors, whereas the classical techniques rely on merely manually selected features.

6 Conclusion

We have presented a deep learning technique with contextual aware embeddings for Hope speech detection task in three languages: English, Malayalam and Tamil (code-switched). We have used contextual string embedding (flair) and pre-trained word embeddings (PWE) for word representations and Recurrent Neural Network (RNN) and pooled document embedding with max pool operation for text representations. All the three models were evaluated for each language and compared the baseline models using the dataset given by Hope Speech Detection for Equality, Diversity, and Inclusion (HopeEDI) Shared Task organizers. All model performances are measured using weighted average F-score due to the imbalanced class distribution in the dataset.

We have obtained the highest F-scores 0.93, 0.58 and 0.84 for three languages English, Tamil and Malayalam respectively, which significantly improved performance over baselines (0.90, 0.56, and 0.73). For the minority class 'not-language', the proposed best model improved 35% and 25% performance than baselines for Malayalam and Tamil, respectively. Based on these observations, we conclude that the deep learning models with contextual string embeddings are well suited for HopeEDI detection task with an imbalanced dataset. We could also achieve good performance results with moderate resources (one GPU and a small corpus), even without optimizing hyperparameters.

The performance can be improved further by fine-tuning hyperparameters and pre-trained contextual embeddings, incorporating different attention mechanisms and increasing the size of the training dataset.

References

Alan Akbik, Tanja Bergmann, Duncan Blythe, Kashif Rasul, Stefan Schweter, and Roland Vollgraf. 2019a. FLAIR: An easy-to-use framework for state-of-the-art NLP. In *Proceedings of the 2019 Conference of the North American Chapter of the Association for Computational Linguistics (Demonstrations)*, pages 54–59, Minneapolis, Minnesota. Association for Computational Linguistics.

Alan Akbik, Tanja Bergmann, and Roland Vollgraf. 2019b. Pooled contextualized embeddings for named entity recognition. In *Proceedings of the 2019 Conference of the North American Chapter of the Association for Computational Linguistics: Human Language Technologies, Volume 1 (Long and Short Papers)*, pages 724–728, Minneapolis, Minnesota. Association for Computational Linguistics.

Alan Akbik, Duncan Blythe, and Roland Vollgraf. 2018. Contextual string embeddings for sequence labeling. In *Proceedings of the 27th International Conference on Computational Linguistics*, pages 1638–1649, Santa Fe, New Mexico, USA. Association for Computational Linguistics.

J. Akosa. 2017. Predictive accuracy : A misleading performance measure for highly imbalanced data.

Bharathi Raja Chakravarthi. 2020a. HopeEDI: A multilingual hope speech detection dataset for equality, diversity, and inclusion. In *Proceedings of the Third Workshop on Computational Modeling of People's Opinions, Personality, and Emotion's in Social Media*, pages 41–53, Barcelona, Spain (Online). Association for Computational Linguistics.

Bharathi Raja Chakravarthi. 2020b. *Leveraging orthographic information to improve machine translation of under-resourced languages*. Ph.D. thesis, NUI Galway.

Bharathi Raja Chakravarthi, Mihael Arcan, and John P. McCrae. 2018. Improving wordnets for under-resourced languages using machine translation. In *Proceedings of the 9th Global Wordnet Conference*, pages 77–86, Nanyang Technological University (NTU), Singapore. Global Wordnet Association.

Bharathi Raja Chakravarthi, Mihael Arcan, and John P. McCrae. 2019. WordNet gloss translation for under-resourced languages using multilingual neural machine translation. In *Proceedings of the Second Workshop on Multilingualism at the Intersection of Knowledge Bases and Machine Translation*, pages 1–7, Dublin, Ireland. European Association for Machine Translation.

Bharathi Raja Chakravarthi, M Anand Kumar, John Philip McCrae, Premjith B, Soman KP, and Thomas Mandl. 2020a. Overview of the track on HASOC-Offensive Language Identification-DravidianCodeMix. In *Working Notes of the Forum for Information Retrieval Evaluation (FIRE 2020). CEUR Workshop Proceedings. In: CEUR-WS. org, Hyderabad, India*.

Bharathi Raja Chakravarthi and Vigneshwaran Muralidaran. 2021. Findings of the shared task on Hope Speech Detection for Equality, Diversity, and Inclusion. In *Proceedings of the First Workshop on Language Technology for Equality, Diversity and Inclusion*. Association for Computational Linguistics.

Bharathi Raja Chakravarthi, Ruba Priyadharshini, Vigneshwaran Muralidaran, Shardul Suryawanshi, Navya Jose, Elizabeth Sherly, and John P. McCrae. 2020b. Overview of the Track on Sentiment Analysis for Dravidian Languages in Code-Mixed Text. In *Forum for Information Retrieval Evaluation*, FIRE 2020, page 21–24, New York, NY, USA. Association for Computing Machinery.

Andrew M. Dai and Quoc V. Le. 2015. Semi-supervised sequence learning.

Nikhil Kumar Ghanghor, Rahul Ponnusamy, Prasanna Kumar Kumaresan, Ruba Priyadharshini, Sajeetha Thavareesan, and Bharathi Raja Chakravarthi. 2021. IIITK@LT-EDI-EACL2021: Hope Speech Detection for Equality, Diversity, and Inclusion in Tamil, Malayalam and English. In *Proceedings of the First Workshop on Language Technology for Equality, Diversity and Inclusion*, Online.

Mohit Iyyer, Varun Manjunatha, Jordan Boyd-Graber, and Hal Daumé III. 2015. Deep unordered composition rivals syntactic methods for text classification. In *Proceedings of the 53rd Annual Meeting of the Association for Computational Linguistics and the 7th International Joint Conference on Natural Language Processing (Volume 1: Long Papers)*, pages 1681–1691, Beijing, China. Association for Computational Linguistics.

Navya Jose, Bharathi Raja Chakravarthi, Shardul Suryawanshi, Elizabeth Sherly, and John P. McCrae. 2020. A Survey of Current Datasets for Code-Switching Research. In *2020 6th International Conference on Advanced Computing and Communication Systems (ICACCS)*, pages 136–141.

Divyanshu Kakwani, Anoop Kunchukuttan, Satish Golla, Gokul N.C., Avik Bhattacharyya, Mitesh M. Khapra, and Pratyush Kumar. 2020. IndicNLPSuite: Monolingual corpora, evaluation benchmarks and pre-trained multilingual language models for Indian languages. In *Findings of the Association for Computational Linguistics: EMNLP 2020*, pages 4948–4961, Online. Association for Computational Linguistics.

Yoon Kim. 2014. Convolutional neural networks for sentence classification. In *Proceedings of the 2014 Conference on Empirical Methods in Natural Language Processing (EMNLP)*, pages 1746–1751, Doha, Qatar. Association for Computational Linguistics.

Diego Laurentino Lima, Maria Antonieta Albanez A. de Medeiros Lopes, and Ana Maria Brito. 2020. Social media: friend or foe in the COVID-19 pandemic? *Clinics*, 75.

Thomas Mandl, Sandip Modha, Anand Kumar M, and Bharathi Raja Chakravarthi. 2020. Overview of the HASOC Track at FIRE 2020: Hate Speech and Offensive Language Identification in Tamil, Malayalam, Hindi, English and German. In *Forum for Information Retrieval Evaluation*, FIRE 2020, page 29–32, New York, NY, USA. Association for Computing Machinery.

Ruba Priyadharshini, Bharathi Raja Chakravarthi, Mani Vegupatti, and John P. McCrae. 2020. Named Entity Recognition for Code-Mixed Indian Corpus using Meta Embedding. In *2020 6th International Conference on Advanced Computing and Communication Systems (ICACCS)*, pages 68–72.

Karthik Puranik, Adeep Hande, Ruba Priyadharshini, Sajeetha Thavareesan, and Bharathi Raja Chakravarthi. 2021. IIITT@LT-EDI-EACL2021-Hope Speech Detection: There is always hope in Transformers. In *Proceedings of the First Workshop on Language Technology for Equality, Diversity and Inclusion*. Association for Computational Linguistics.

Sajeetha Thavareesan and Sinnathamby Mahesan. 2019. Sentiment Analysis in Tamil Texts: A Study on Machine Learning Techniques and Feature Representation. In *2019 14th Conference on Industrial and Information Systems (ICIIS)*, pages 320–325.

Sajeetha Thavareesan and Sinnathamby Mahesan. 2020a. Sentiment Lexicon Expansion using Word2vec and fastText for Sentiment Prediction in Tamil texts. In *2020 Moratuwa Engineering Research Conference (MERCon)*, pages 272–276.

Sajeetha Thavareesan and Sinnathamby Mahesan. 2020b. Word embedding-based Part of Speech tagging in Tamil texts. In *2020 IEEE 15th International Conference on Industrial and Information Systems (ICIIS)*, pages 478–482.

EDIOne@LT-EDI-EACL2021: Pre-trained Transformers with Convolutional Neural Networks for Hope Speech Detection.

Suman Dowlagar
LTRC
IIIT-Hyderabad
suman.dowlagar
@research.iiit.ac.in

Radhika Mamidi
LTRC
IIIT-Hyderabad
radhika.mamidi
@iiit.ac.in

Abstract

Hope is an essential aspect of mental health stability and recovery in every individual in this fast-changing world. Any tools and methods developed for detection, analysis, and generation of hope speech will be beneficial. In this paper, we propose a model on hope-speech detection to automatically detect web content that may play a positive role in diffusing hostility on social media. We perform the experiments by taking advantage of pre-processing and transfer-learning models. We observed that the pre-trained multilingual-BERT model with convolution neural networks gave the best results. Our model ranked 1st, 3rd, and 4th ranks on English, Malayalam-English, and Tamil-English code-mixed datasets.

1 Introduction

Nowadays, people often use social media websites to share their views and thoughts. The thoughts might be positive or negative. Much work has been done towards identifying the negative thoughts, i.e., hate speech and offensive content identification on social media (Schmidt and Wiegand, 2017; Davidson et al., 2017). Research is now shifting to the field of analyzing positivity via hope speech detection on social media.

Hope is a positive state of mind, an expectation of positive outcomes concerning events and circumstances in one's life (Youssef and Luthans, 2007). Hope drives an individual to move forward. Hope can be a useful tool for each individual to maintain a stable and optimistic attitude towards life.

In a multilingual society, people usually express their thoughts by mixing two or more languages in a single utterance. This form of language contact is known as code-mixing (Di Sciullo et al., 1986). Code mixed data is real-world unprocessed data that has non-standard variations of spelling and does not follow a grammatical structure (Bali et al., 2014). Any automated hope-speech detection tool will face challenges in this aspect. So the analysis of code-mixed hope speech detection is necessary to handle the real-time social media data.

The European Association of Computational Linguistics 2021 has organized a Language Technology workshop for Equality, Diversity, and Inclusion (Chakravarthi and Muralidaran, 2021) with a shared task to cultivate positivity and promote research on code-mixed hope speech data. The goal of this task is to identify whether a given comment contains hope-speech or not.

In this work, we address the issue of hope-speech detection on code-mixed Dravidian youtube comments. This paper presents a pre-trained multilingual BERT encoder with CNN as a classifier for the hope speech classification data.

The paper is organized as follows. Section 2 provides related work on hope speech detection. Section 3 provides information on the task and datasets Section 4 describes the proposed work. Section 5 presents the experimental setup and the performance of the model. Section 6 concludes our work.

2 Related Work

Hope speech detection is a novel topic with a significantly limited amount of research done in this field.

(Palakodety et al., 2019) propose a novel task to automatically detect hope speech on web content that may play a positive role in diffusing hostility on social media triggered by heightened political tensions during a conflict between two nuclear power nations.

(Chakravarthi, 2020) created a multilingual, hostility-diffusing hope speech dataset for equality, diversity, and inclusion. It is a new large-scale English, Tamil (code-switched) dataset, and Malay-

Proceedings of the First Workshop on Language Technology for Equality, Diversity and Inclusion, pages 86–91
April 19, 2021.

Dataset	#Train	#Dev	#Test	#Total
English	22762	2843	2846	28451
Malayalam-English	8564	1070	1071	10705
Tamil-English	16160	2018	2020	20198

Table 1: Data Statistics

alam (code-switched) YouTube comments. They have experimented on the dataset by using traditional machine learning classifiers.

3 Task Description

We need to identify the hope in the code-mixed English, Tamil-English, and Malayalam-English youtube comments for hope speech detection. For the English language, data was collected related to the following issues, including women in STEM, LGBTIQ issues, COVID-19 pandemic, Racism, and Black Lives Matters, United Kingdom (UK) versus China, United States of America (USA) versus China, and Australia versus China from YouTube video comments. For Tamil and Malayalam, we collected data from India on the recent topics regarding LGBTIQ issues, COVID-19, women in STEM, the Indo-China border dispute. Each comment or post is annotated with hope-speech or non-hope-speech and not-Tamil/not-Malayalam labels. The dataset is divided into train, development, and test sets for the given hope speech task. The details of the dataset are given in the table 1.

4 Our method

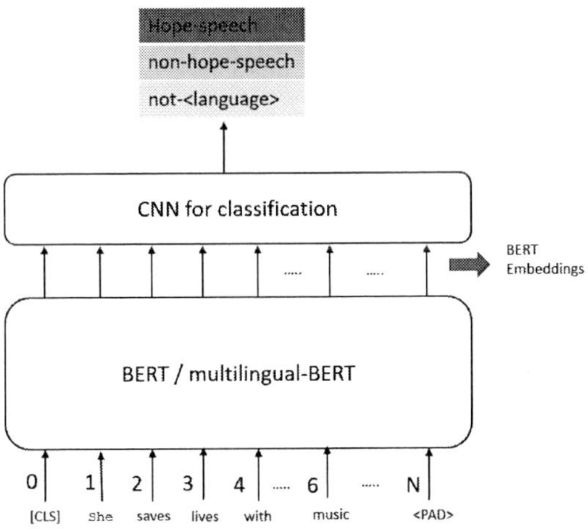

Figure 1: Pretrained BERT with CNN for Hope Speech Detection

In this section, we present the pre-processing and the use of pre-trained multilingual BERT embeddings with CNN classification model for hope speech identification.

4.1 Pre-processing

The data set is a code-mixed real-time dataset, and it has issues related to transliterated script with variations in the spelling, excessive use of emoticons, mentions, and hashtags in the corpus. Pre-processing will help to solve these issues to some extent. While pre-processing,

1. We removed all punctuations, emotions, hashtags
2. We back-transliterated the script to its native language using linguistic rules, transliteration, and language detection libraries.

4.2 Pre-trained BERT model for embeddings

Bi-directional Encoder Representations with Transformers (BERT) (Devlin et al., 2018) is a language model. BERT uses a transformer (Vaswani et al., 2017), multi-headed attention with a point-wise feed-forward network, to learn contextual relations between words (or sub-words) in a text. In its vanilla form, the transformer includes two separate mechanisms, an encoder that reads the text input and a decoder that produces a prediction for the task.

Using BERT, each sentence is tokenized using a sub-word level tokenizer and uses a layer of transformers to encode the word in a sentence into a vector of size 1x768, where 768 is the length of BERT embedding. The BERT uses [CLS] token to indicate the beginning of the sentence and [SEP] token to indicate the end of the sentence. In our approach, we used a small version of the pre-trained multilingual BERT model called *bert-base-multilingual-cased* obtained from the transformers library (Wolf et al., 2019).

4.3 Convolutional Neural Network (CNN)

CNN is a category of Neural Networks that uses convolution and pooling operations and performs

Classifier	Hope	Non-Hope	not-English	macro-F1	weighted-F1	Acc
SVM	0.53	0.95	0.00	0.49	0.91	0.91
SVM *processed*	0.53	0.95	0.00	0.49	0.91	0.91
mBERT	**0.54**	0.96	0.00	0.53	0.92	0.92
mBERT *processed*	**0.54**	0.96	0.00	0.53	0.92	0.92
Our approach	**0.54**	**0.97**	0.00	**0.54**	**0.94**	**0.94**

Table 2: Classification performance of Our approach w.r.t Baselines on English Data

Classifier	Hope	Non-Hope	not-Malayalam	macro-F1	weighted-F1	Acc
SVM	0.61	0.88	0.70	0.73	0.81	0.81
SVM *processed*	0.60	0.87	0.71	0.73	0.80	0.80
mBERT	**0.66**	0.91	0.83	0.80	0.86	0.86
mBERT *processed*	0.65	**0.92**	**1.00**	**0.84**	0.86	**0.87**
Our approach	**0.66**	**0.92**	**1.00**	**0.84**	**0.87**	**0.87**

Table 3: Classification performance of Our approach w.r.t Baselines on Malayalam Data

Classifier	Hope	Non-Hope	not-Tamil	macro-F1	weighted-F1	Acc
SVM	0.57	0.61	0.60	0.57	0.57	0.57
SVM *processed*	0.46	0.60	0.59	0.55	0.55	0.55
mBERT	0.57	0.56	0.58	0.57	0.56	0.56
mBERT *processed*	**0.51**	0.64	**0.60**	**0.59**	**0.60**	**0.59**
Our approach	**0.51**	**0.65**	**0.60**	**0.59**	**0.60**	**0.59**

Table 4: Classification performance of Our approach w.r.t Baselines on Tamil Data

parameter sharing. Compared to its predecessors, CNN's main advantage is that it automatically detects the important features using convolution operations.

In our paper, we used the convolutional model developed for sentence classification by (Kim, 2014). In this CNN, We take a word embedding obtained of size (n,d), where n is the number of tokens in a sentence, and d is the embedding dimensionality. We apply convolution operations on those embeddings with three kernels of sizes (2,d), (3,d), and (4,d). We consider these kernel sizes as it takes combinations of 2, 3, 4 tokens and extracts the feature representation. We use a ReLU activation function after each convolutional layer. Then we apply max-pooling over convolutions to down-sample the input representation and to avoid overfitting. Concatenate the kernels of different sizes. Then we pass those convolutions through a forward feed network for output representation and add a dropout layer to avoid overfitting.

5 Implementation

We give the input text to the pre-trained multilingual BERT model, and the pre-trained BERT model gives encoded information as output. Now we need to learn a classification model for the given encoded information. We pass the encoded information as embeddings to the above CNN classifier. The classifier applies convolutions, max-pooling, and finally, a feed-forward network for classification with dropout.

6 Experiments

The section presents the baselines, hyper-parameter settings, and analysis of observed results.

The baselines used for the proposed work is,

1. **SVM with TF-IDF and sub-word level tokenization:** This baseline uses term frequency and inverse document frequency-based vectorization (Ramos et al., 2003) for feature representation and the support vector machine (Cortes and Vapnik, 1995) to classify the data. The code-mixed data contains transliterated text with a non-standard representation of words. We used sub-word-level tokenization to extract the tokens to capture a better sentence representation.

2. **Pre-trained multilingual BERT (mBERT):**

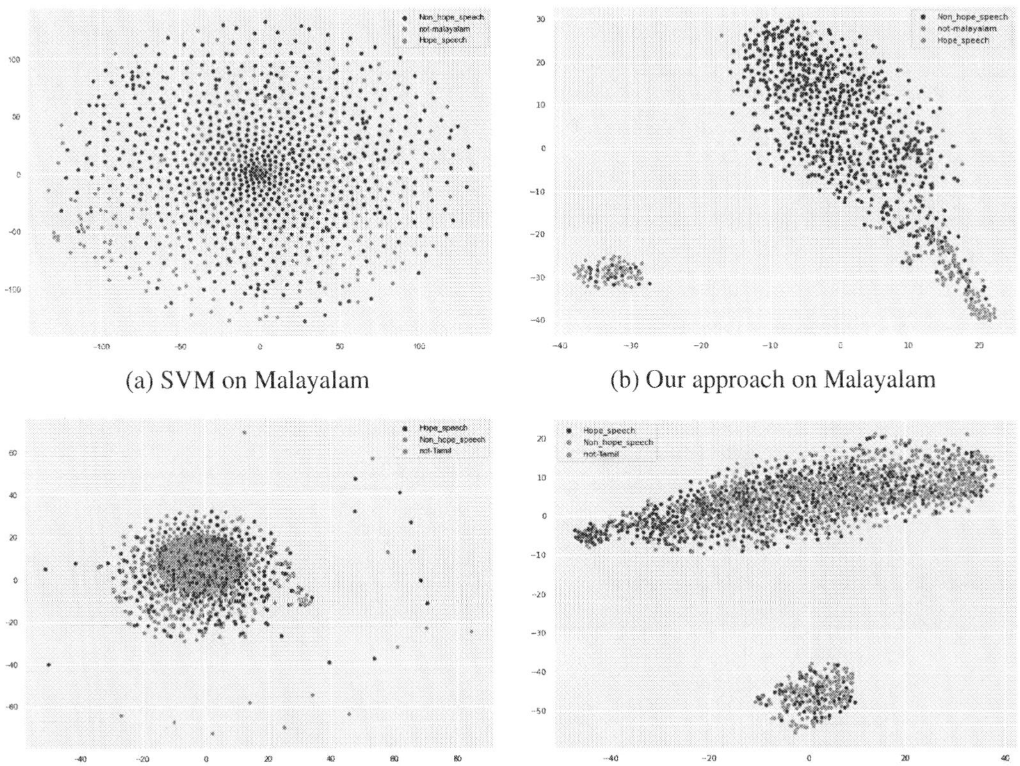

(a) SVM on Malayalam

(b) Our approach on Malayalam

(c) SVM on Tamil

(d) Our approach on Tamil

Figure 2: Comparison of SVM classifier and our approach on Tamil Data

This baseline uses a pre-trained multilingual BERT model with a feed-forward network for classification.

Note: We consider two formats, *processed* and original data for comparing the baselines, where "processed" refers to applying the pre-processing method on the original data.

6.1 Hyperparameters and libraries

Bert is a non-regressive model and uses positional embeddings along with token embeddings, so BERT specifies the model to consider the default sentence length of 512. In our model, we kept the default sentence length as 128. The number of class labels for classification is given as three (hope_speech, non_hope_speech, and not_English // not_Tamil // not_Malayalam). The dropout is kept at 0.5. We train the model for 30 epochs with batch size set to 128 and the learning rate to 1e-5. We use Adam optimizer with the cross-entropy.

We used the ai4bharat-transliteration [1], a deep learning-based transliteration tool to back transliterate the identified Malayalam and Tamil words. We used the hugging face transformers library to download the pre-trained BERT for English data and the pre-trained multilingual BERT model for Malayalam and Tamil data to obtain the encoded representations of the tokens. The PyTorch library is used to model the convolutional neural networks. The TF-IDF feature representation, SVM classifiers, and the classification metrics are obtained from the scikit-learn library. The Sentencepiece (Kudo and Richardson, 2018) achieves the subword level tokenization.

6.2 Results

Tables 2, 3, and 4 present the f1-score and accuracy of the models on the English and Dravidian code-mixed datasets.

From the above results, it is clear that our approach of the multilingual pre-trained BERT model to extract the embeddings and CNN to sentence classification and transliteration based pre-processing to handle the code-mixed data works

[1] https://pypi.org/project/ai4bharat-transliteration/

best for the given datasets.

Preprocessing helped the BERT model to focus on the relevant information and back-transliteration helped the BERT to obtain the embeddings based on the native script.

In SVM "processed" classifier did not perform better after back transliteration because the TF-IDF feature representation used in the SVM classifier and TF-IDF works on statistical counts of words rather than extraction of embeddings based on the native script. When TF-IDF vectorization was performed on the original data, the feature vector was very big, i.e., there were many unique words in the data. The words present in both native and transliterated forms are mapped to a single word after back transliteration. This reduced the feature space of each word and affected the feature representation of the word.

We have plotted the TSNE distribution 2 on the Malayalam and Tamil data to better visualize our approach compared to the baseline SVM classifier on the original data. As the plots obtained from pre-trained BERT and our approach are visually similar, we compared the SVM and our approach for better visualization. The plots on the Malayalam data show the effectiveness of our approach when compared to the SVM model. We can see a better distinction of classes (*hope-speech, non-hope-speech, and not-Malayalam*) compared to the SVM classifier.

Tamil data shows a very slight distinction between hope-speech and non-hope speech data but a clear distinction of classes for not-Tamil data. The words in the *not-Tamil* label are not back-transliterated into the Tamil language. It ensured the script of such words being different from the Tamil script, followed by different embedding representations of the words, and improved accuracy for the not-Tamil class label.

7 Conclusion

In this paper, we addressed hope speech identification in English and Dravidian code-mixed languages. We used pre-trained multilingual bidirectional encoder representations to obtain the word embeddings, and we used convolutional neural networks for classification. We compared the method with other baselines. The results showed that using back-transliteration helped the model capture the pre-trained word embeddings based on the native script. CNN helped the model extract feature representations better than feed-forward networks, which increased the model's performance. In the future, we will work on cross-lingual meta word embeddings to handle the multilingual scenario in the code-mixed datasets.

References

Kalika Bali, Jatin Sharma, Monojit Choudhury, and Yogarshi Vyas. 2014. "i am borrowing ya mixing?" An Analysis of English-Hindi Code Mixing in Facebook. In *Proceedings of the First Workshop on Computational Approaches to Code Switching*, pages 116–126.

Bharathi Raja Chakravarthi. 2020. HopeEDI: A multilingual hope speech detection dataset for equality, diversity, and inclusion. In *Proceedings of the Third Workshop on Computational Modeling of People's Opinions, Personality, and Emotion's in Social Media*, pages 41–53, Barcelona, Spain (Online). Association for Computational Linguistics.

Bharathi Raja Chakravarthi and Vigneshwaran Muralidaran. 2021. Findings of the shared task on Hope Speech Detection for Equality, Diversity, and Inclusion. In *Proceedings of the First Workshop on Language Technology for Equality, Diversity and Inclusion*. Association for Computational Linguistics.

Corinna Cortes and Vladimir Vapnik. 1995. Support-vector networks. *Machine learning*, 20(3):273–297.

Thomas Davidson, Dana Warmsley, Michael Macy, and Ingmar Weber. 2017. Automated hate speech detection and the problem of offensive language. In *Proceedings of the International AAAI Conference on Web and Social Media*, volume 11.

Jacob Devlin, Ming-Wei Chang, Kenton Lee, and Kristina Toutanova. 2018. Bert: Pre-training of deep bidirectional transformers for language understanding. *arXiv preprint arXiv:1810.04805*.

Anne-Marie Di Sciullo, Pieter Muysken, and Rajendra Singh. 1986. Government and code-mixing. *Journal of linguistics*, 22(1):1–24.

Yoon Kim. 2014. Convolutional neural networks for sentence classification. *arXiv preprint arXiv:1408.5882*.

Taku Kudo and John Richardson. 2018. Sentencepiece: A simple and language independent subword tokenizer and detokenizer for neural text processing. *arXiv preprint arXiv:1808.06226*.

Shriphani Palakodety, Ashiqur R KhudaBukhsh, and Jaime G Carbonell. 2019. Hope speech detection: A computational analysis of the voice of peace. *arXiv preprint arXiv:1909.12940*.

Juan Ramos et al. 2003. Using tf-idf to determine word relevance in document queries. In *Proceedings of the first instructional conference on machine learning*, volume 242, pages 29–48. Citeseer.

Anna Schmidt and Michael Wiegand. 2017. A survey on hate speech detection using natural language processing. In *Proceedings of the Fifth International workshop on natural language processing for social media*, pages 1–10.

Ashish Vaswani, Noam Shazeer, Niki Parmar, Jakob Uszkoreit, Llion Jones, Aidan N Gomez, Łukasz Kaiser, and Illia Polosukhin. 2017. Attention is all you need. In *Advances in neural information processing systems*, pages 5998–6008.

Thomas Wolf, Lysandre Debut, Victor Sanh, Julien Chaumond, Clement Delangue, Anthony Moi, Pierric Cistac, Tim Rault, Rémi Louf, Morgan Funtowicz, et al. 2019. Huggingface's transformers: State-of-the-art natural language processing. *ArXiv*, pages arXiv–1910.

Carolyn M Youssef and Fred Luthans. 2007. Positive organizational behavior in the workplace: The impact of hope, optimism, and resilience. *Journal of management*, 33(5):774–800.

ssn_diBERTsity@LT-EDI-EACL2021:Hope Speech Detection on multilingual YouTube comments via transformer based approach

Arunima S, Akshay R, Avantika Balaji, Thenmozhi D, Senthil Kumar B
Sri Sivasubramaniya Nadar College of Engineering
{theni_d, senthil}@ssn.edu.in

Abstract

In recent times, there exists an abundance of research to classify abusive and offensive texts focusing on negative comments but only minimal research using the positive reinforcement approach. The task was aimed at classifying texts into 'Hope_speech', 'Non_hope_speech', and 'Not in language'. The datasets were provided by the LT-EDI organisers in English, Tamil, and Malayalam languages with texts sourced from YouTube comments. We trained our data using transformer models, specifically mBERT for Tamil and Malayalam and BERT for English, and achieved weighted average F1-scores of 0.46, 0.81, 0.92 for Tamil, Malayalam, and English respectively. In the task results, our approach ranked second, fourth and fourteenth place in English, Malayalam and Tamil respectively.

1 Introduction

The world today is rife with uncertainty. With the new COVID'19 strain proliferating across the globe, our chances to return to normalcy soon seem rather bleak. It is during testing times like these when people in general, crave for positive reinforcement. Even apart from this pandemic, one can argue that we cannot get enough inspiration and more often than not, employees are burdened with stress in the workplace. Moreover, there are marginalized communities, such as but not limited to, LGBTIQ (Lesbian, Gay, Bisexual, Transgender, Intersex, and Questioning), racial and ethnic minorities, which mostly rely on having faith and being hopeful for their complete acceptance in society (Puranik et al., 2021; Ghanghor et al., 2021). With the wide usage of the internet, now intensified by the ongoing pandemic, there are more people seeking the same kind of reinforcement through online forums.

YouTube, being a platform connecting billions of users across the internet, has gained an outstanding popularity across the globe (Thavareesan and Mahesan, 2019, 2020a,b). With almost 30,000 hours of content uploaded every hour, the videos from YouTube are updated showcasing the latest trends (Chakravarthi et al., 2020c,a). With the commenting facility available, one can glean a plethora of opinions from different people through this. Given the flexibility of speech in most nations in the world, this can be touted as a bane as well leading to rigorous research in Offensive Speech Detection and Hate Speech Detection (Chakravarthi et al., 2020d; Mandl et al., 2020; Chakravarthi et al., 2020b, 2021; Suryawanshi and Chakravarthi, 2021). However, there hasn't been a proportionate amount of research focusing on Hope Speech Detection. Research focusing on positive speech can have a variety of applications. With the growing concerns over mental health, recommendation engines can tailor content in a way which spreads positive comments and hope.

In our paper, we have approached Hope Speech Detection using models trained from the dataset provided by the LT-EDI organisers with the data obtained from YouTube comments in English, Tamil and Malayalam. We have tried traditional models like SVM, Logistic Regressions and Naive Bayes as well as transformers like MT5 and BERT. We achieved promising results using multilingual BERT for Tamil and Malayalam, and BERT for English YouTube comments and the task was implemented using the same.

Proceedings of the First Workshop on Language Technology for Equality, Diversity and Inclusion, pages 92–97
April 19, 2021.

2 Related Works

The Hope Speech Dataset for Equality, Diversity and Inclusion was constructed by Chakravarthi (2020), from YouTube comments, in an attempt to encourage research on detecting positive content online. With the increasing usage of social media amongst different communities across the globe, this dataset encompasses two Indian regional languages, namely Tamil and Malayalam, along with English. The work done by Palakodety et al. (2019) focused on how Hope Speech Detection can be used to diffuse tension between politically hostile nations. One of the authors' main contributions include a novel language detection technique using Polygot word embeddings and a study analysing the temporal shifts between pro-war and pro-peace intentions of social-media users.

Recently, mining data from social media has been of interest in the field of NLP. Roy et al. (2021) has proposed a transformer based approach for Hate Speech Detection on twitter tweets for multiple languages, namely English, German and Hindi. They further classify the detected negative tweets into Hate Speech, Offensive and Profane speech. Vashistha and Zubiaga (2021) have performed a comparative study between transformer models such as BERT and XLM-RoBERTa and traditional models such as Logistic Regression to classify multilingual text in two languages, Hindi and English from online platforms, into three classes, Abusive, Hateful or Neither. The authors have also presented information regarding different model sizes and their impact on the training and inference times.

The worldwide impact of the COVID'19 virus has led to the surge of varied news articles disseminated without much scientific backing. The detection of COVID'19 fake news in English and hostile posts in Hindi has been done by Sharif et al. (2021). Various techniques such as SVM, CNN and Bi-LSTM have been employed for these tasks. In order to tackle Out-of-Vocabulary words, Dong and Huang (2018) proposed a methodology combining the pre-trained word embeddings from a large general text corpus with the ones generated from the training corpus based on word2vec. The proposed new representation contains information from both the sources and using vector concatenation, the authors were able to integrate them effectively.

3 Data Analysis

The dataset released by LT-EDI 2021 (Chakravarthi and Muralidaran, 2021) for the three languages, English, Malayalam and Tamil consisted of 28451, 10705 and 20198 YouTube comments respectively. This was distributed amongst the Training, Validation and Test datasets in the following way:

Language	Training	Validation	Test
English	22,762	2,843	2,846
Malayalam	8,564	1,070	1,071
Tamil	16,162	2,018	2,020

Table 1: Data distribution

Language	Hope	Non_Hope	Other Lan
English	2,484	25,940	27
Malayalam	2,052	7,765	888
Tamil	7,899	9,816	2,483

Table 2: Class-wise distribution of data

The training and the validation dataset consisted of two columns each, "Sentence" and "label". The preprocessing performed for all three languages had a few common steps including:

- Removing extra spaces, punctuations and special characters such as '@'.
- Replace the emojis with text using the demoji[1] library. The emojis were converted into text in English. For Malayalam and Tamil, these text strings were further translated into Malayalam and Tamil scripts respectively. For example,

  ഇത് മലയാളത്തിലാണ് 👍 ➡

  ഇത് മലയാളത്തിലാണ് thumbs up ➡

  ഇത് മലയാളം തംസ് അപ്പിലാണ്

- Label encoding for the train and validation dataset.

Additionally, for the English language, we handled Out Of Vocabulary words (OOV). OOV words are words that are not present in the training dataset. These may be words that are abbreviated or misspelled, and by extension, not present in the English

[1] https://pypi.org/project/demoji/

language dictionary. These words do not have embeddings and increase the randomness in the input and can cause misclassifications. To handle this problem, we created a dictionary of length 70, containing the most frequently occurring OOV words in the train dataset and replaced them with their corrected usage. Apart from this, we also normalized contractions using a predefined list. For example, "couldn't" is replaced with "could not". Substituting these contractions makes the text standardized.

For English and Malayalam, Synthetic Minority Oversampling Technique (SMOTE (Chawla et al., 2002)) is used for oversampling the imbalanced classes present in the dataset. This is achieved by oversampling the minority class present in the dataset. SMOTE chooses data points that are nearby in the feature space, draws a line between the data points and draws a new sample at a point along that line. The model submitted for all three languages is BERT (multilingual BERT for Tamil and Malayalam). To overcome the problem of class imbalance, balanced weights were calculated using the scikit-learn[2] library and given as an argument to the model.

4 Methodology

We have employed traditional and transformer based approaches to detect the hope speech present in YouTube comments.

4.1 Traditional Learning Approach

In this approach, we use the classifiers, Support Vector Machine (Cortes and Vapnik, 1995), Naive Bayes (Rish et al., 2001) and Logistic Regression[3] to build the models for all the languages. SVM works on the principle of finding a hyperplane in an N-dimensional space, where N denotes the number of features that distinctly classifies the data points. The objective is to maximize the margin distance between the hyperplane and all data points so that classifying in the future can be done with more confidence. NB is a supervised learning algorithm based on the Bayes theorem i.e. it assumes that features are independent of each other and there is no correlation between them. It is responsible for finding the class of observation (data point) given the values of features. Logistic regression (LR) is a statistical method which finds an equation that predicts an outcome for a binary variable, Y, from one or more response variables, X. LR uses the log odds ratio and an iterative maximum likelihood method which makes it more appropriate for non normally distributed data.

These models are trained using the preprocessed train data and tested against the dev dataset. TF-IDF scores are used for performing word vectorization and a maximum of 5000 unique features are obtained. SMOTE is used for oversampling the imbalanced classes present in the English and Malayalam datasets. The below mentioned tables contain the validation results of the traditional learning models of the three languages.

Model	Accuracy	F1-Score
SVM	0.75	0.80
NB	0.74	0.79
LR	0.79	0.82

Table 3: English Validation Results

Model	Accuracy	F1-Score
SVM	0.82	0.80
NB	0.79	0.75
LR	0.81	0.79

Table 4: Malayalam Validation Results

Model	Accuracy	F1-Score
SVM	0.60	0.59
NB	0.60	0.59
LR	0.59	0.58

Table 5: Tamil Validation Results

Using SMOTE, we were able to obtain more balanced result, improving the recall scores for minority classes in the English and Malayalam validation set. The recall for the English language improved by two-fold upon using SMOTE and the Malayalam language saw a 53% increase in the same.

4.2 Transformer Based Approach

For this approach, we used BERT (Bidirectional Encoder Representations from Transformers) (Devlin et al., 2018) for English and mBERT(multilingual BERT) for the Tamil and

[2] https://scikit-learn.org/stable/modules/generated/sklearn.utils.class_weight.compute_class_weight.html

[3] https://scikit-learn.org/stable/modules/generated/sklearn.linear_model.LogisticRegression.html

Malayalam languages. The BERT model operates on the principle of an attention mechanism to learn contextual relations between words. The transformer encoder used is bidirectional, as opposed to directional models, which reads the text input sequentially. This bidirectional behavior is responsible for allowing the model to learn the context of a word based on all of its surroundings (left and right of the word). This makes it very useful for classification tasks. To perform multilingual tasks, the mBERT model provides sentence representations for 104 languages.

We also implemented the Multilingual Text-to-Text Transfer Transformer (mT5) (Xue et al., 2020) for Tamil and Malayalam datasets. The mT5 is a multilingual variant of the "Text-to-Text Transfer Transformer" (T5) model. The mT5 model is trained on 101 languages and has achieved state-of-the-art results on a wide variety of cross-lingual NLP tasks. For both these transformer models, the preprocessed train data was given as input for training and the dev set was given for validation. In order to overcome the class imbalance problem, balanced weights were assigned to all three classes during the training of the respective models.

Model	Language	Accuracy	F1-Score
BERT	English	0.93	0.92
mBERT	Tamil	0.58	0.56
mBERT	Malayalam	0.78	0.79
mT5	Tamil	0.44	0.35
mT5	Malayalam	0.77	0.76

Table 6: Validation Results

The BERT model performed extremely well on the validation dataset for all the languages. mBERT outperformed the mT5 model for Tamil and Malayalam languages by a fair margin. The BERT and mBERT model outperformed the traditional learning models on the validation dataset based on the classwise scores. For the Tamil and Malayalam languages, there was a 38% and 27% increase in the F1-score of the minority class on the Validation datasets.

5 Results

In the LT-EDI-EACL-2021 task on Hope Speech Detection, our team, ssn_diBERTsity, achieved a top submission rank of 2nd in English, 4th in Malayalam and 14th in Tamil.

Lang	Precision	Recall	F1	Rank
Eng	0.91	0.93	0.92	2
Mal	0.82	0.81	0.81	4
Tam	0.50	0.53	0.46	14

Table 7: Weighted average precision, recall and F1-score on hope speech in English, Malayalam and Tamil text.

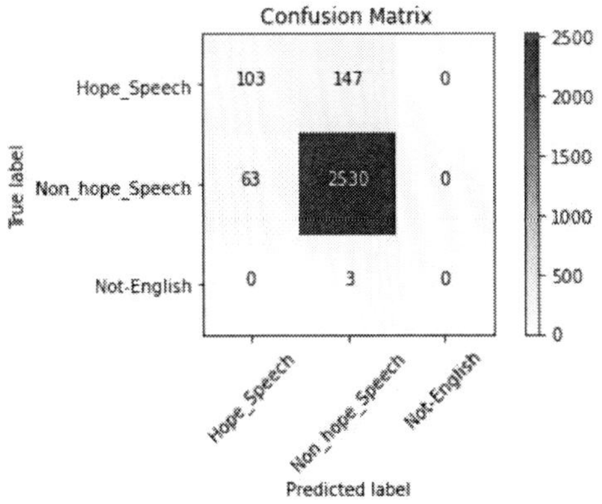

Figure 1: Confusion Matrix for English test set

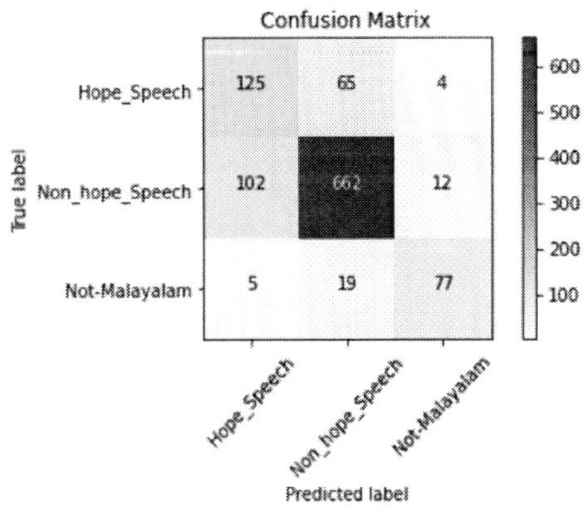

Figure 2: Confusion Matrix for Malayalam test set

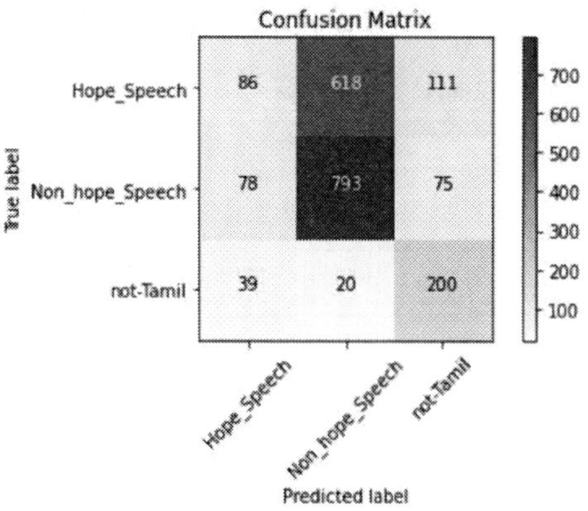

Figure 3: Confusion Matrix for Tamil test set

From Figure 1, we can conclude that out of the 2846 instances in the test set, our model for the English language has predicted 2633 true positives. From Figure 2, we can see that out of the 1071 instances in the Malayalam test set, our model has correctly predicted 864 instances. From Figure 3, we observe that out of the 2020 instances in the Tamil test set, our model has predicted 1079 true positives accurately.

Our implementation was based on the transformer model BERT for the English language and Multilingual BERT for Tamil and Malayalam. Our submission was evaluated against the test data provided by LT-EDI and achieved F1-scores of 0.92, 0.81, 0.46 for English, Malayalam and Tamil respectively.

6 Conclusion

Our implementation consists of two approaches, namely the transformer-based approach and the traditional-based approach. The model submitted for the task is BERT which outperformed the other transformer and traditional models. The validation accuracy achieved by the BERT model is 93%, 78% and 58% for English, Malayalam and Tamil respectively. BERT's capabilities extend to making more accurate predictions when dealing with newer documents even when the type of document differs significantly in key properties such as length and vocabulary. This attribute of BERT makes it the perfect choice when dealing with multiple languages and code-switching within text. In the future, we would like to extend our research in order to create a language model suitable for code-switched content and experiment with different model architectures in the hope for better performance.

References

Bharathi Raja Chakravarthi. 2020. HopeEDI: A multilingual hope speech detection dataset for equality, diversity, and inclusion. In *Proceedings of the Third Workshop on Computational Modeling of People's Opinions, Personality, and Emotion's in Social Media*, pages 41–53, Barcelona, Spain (Online). Association for Computational Linguistics.

Bharathi Raja Chakravarthi, Navya Jose, Shardul Suryawanshi, Elizabeth Sherly, and John Philip McCrae. 2020a. A sentiment analysis dataset for code-mixed Malayalam-English. In *Proceedings of the 1st Joint Workshop on Spoken Language Technologies for Under-resourced languages (SLTU) and Collaboration and Computing for Under-Resourced Languages (CCURL)*, pages 177–184, Marseille, France. European Language Resources association.

Bharathi Raja Chakravarthi, M Anand Kumar, John Philip McCrae, Premjith B, Soman KP, and Thomas Mandl. 2020b. Overview of the track on HASOC-Offensive Language Identification-DravidianCodeMix. In *Working Notes of the Forum for Information Retrieval Evaluation (FIRE 2020). CEUR Workshop Proceedings. In: CEUR-WS. org, Hyderabad, India.*

Bharathi Raja Chakravarthi and Vigneshwaran Muralidaran. 2021. Findings of the shared task on Hope Speech Detection for Equality, Diversity, and Inclusion. In *Proceedings of the First Workshop on Language Technology for Equality, Diversity and Inclusion*. Association for Computational Linguistics.

Bharathi Raja Chakravarthi, Vigneshwaran Muralidaran, Ruba Priyadharshini, and John Philip McCrae. 2020c. Corpus creation for sentiment analysis in code-mixed Tamil-English text. In *Proceedings of the 1st Joint Workshop on Spoken Language Technologies for Under-resourced languages (SLTU) and Collaboration and Computing for Under-Resourced Languages (CCURL)*, pages 202–210, Marseille, France. European Language Resources association.

Bharathi Raja Chakravarthi, Ruba Priyadharshini, Navya Jose, Anand Kumar M, Thomas Mandl, Prasanna Kumar Kumaresan, Rahul Ponnusamy, Hariharan V, Elizabeth Sherly, and John Philip McCrae. 2021. Findings of the shared task on Offensive Language Identification in Tamil, Malayalam, and Kannada. In *Proceedings of the First Workshop on Speech and Language Technologies for Dravidian Languages*. Association for Computational Linguistics.

Bharathi Raja Chakravarthi, Ruba Priyadharshini, Vigneshwaran Muralidaran, Shardul Suryawanshi, Navya Jose, Elizabeth Sherly, and John P. McCrae. 2020d. Overview of the Track on Sentiment Analysis for Dravidian Languages in Code-Mixed Text. In *Forum for Information Retrieval Evaluation*, FIRE 2020, page 21–24, New York, NY, USA. Association for Computing Machinery.

Nitesh V. Chawla, Kevin W. Bowyer, Lawrence O. Hall, and W. Philip Kegelmeyer. 2002. Smote: synthetic minority over-sampling technique. *Journal of artificial intelligence research*, 16:321–357.

Corinna Cortes and Vladimir Vapnik. 1995. Support-vector networks. *Machine learning*, 20(3):273–297.

Jacob Devlin, Ming-Wei Chang, Kenton Lee, and Kristina Toutanova. 2018. BERT: pre-training of deep bidirectional transformers for language understanding. *CoRR*, abs/1810.04805.

Jianxiong Dong and Jim Huang. 2018. Enhance word representation for out-of-vocabulary on ubuntu dialogue corpus.

Nikhil Kumar Ghanghor, Rahul Ponnusamy, Prasanna Kumar Kumaresan, Ruba Priyadharshini, Sajeetha Thavareesan, and Bharathi Raja Chakravarthi. 2021. IIITK@LT-EDI-EACL2021: Hope Speech Detection for Equality, Diversity, and Inclusion in Tamil, Malayalam and English. In *Proceedings of the First Workshop on Language Technology for Equality, Diversity and Inclusion*, Online.

Thomas Mandl, Sandip Modha, Anand Kumar M, and Bharathi Raja Chakravarthi. 2020. Overview of the HASOC Track at FIRE 2020: Hate Speech and Offensive Language Identification in Tamil, Malayalam, Hindi, English and German. In *Forum for Information Retrieval Evaluation*, FIRE 2020, page 29–32, New York, NY, USA. Association for Computing Machinery.

Shriphani Palakodety, Ashiqur R. KhudaBukhsh, and Jaime G. Carbonell. 2019. Kashmir: A computational analysis of the voice of peace. *CoRR*, abs/1909.12940.

Karthik Puranik, Adeep Hande, Ruba Priyadharshini, Sajeetha Thavareesan, and Bharathi Raja Chakravarthi. 2021. IIITT@LT-EDI-EACL2021-Hope Speech Detection: There is always hope in Transformers. In *Proceedings of the First Workshop on Language Technology for Equality, Diversity and Inclusion*. Association for Computational Linguistics.

Irina Rish et al. 2001. An empirical study of the naive bayes classifier. In *IJCAI 2001 workshop on empirical methods in artificial intelligence*, volume 3, pages 41–46.

Sayar Ghosh Roy, Ujwal Narayan, Tathagata Raha, Zubair Abid, and Vasudeva Varma. 2021. Leveraging multilingual transformers for hate speech detection.

Omar Sharif, Eftekhar Hossain, and Mohammed Moshiul Hoque. 2021. Combating hostility: Covid-19 fake news and hostile post detection in social media.

Shardul Suryawanshi and Bharathi Raja Chakravarthi. 2021. Findings of the shared task on Troll Meme Classification in Tamil. In *Proceedings of the First Workshop on Speech and Language Technologies for Dravidian Languages*. Association for Computational Linguistics.

Sajeetha Thavareesan and Sinnathamby Mahesan. 2019. Sentiment Analysis in Tamil Texts: A Study on Machine Learning Techniques and Feature Representation. In *2019 14th Conference on Industrial and Information Systems (ICIIS)*, pages 320–325.

Sajeetha Thavareesan and Sinnathamby Mahesan. 2020a. Sentiment Lexicon Expansion using Word2vec and fastText for Sentiment Prediction in Tamil texts. In *2020 Moratuwa Engineering Research Conference (MERCon)*, pages 272–276.

Sajeetha Thavareesan and Sinnathamby Mahesan. 2020b. Word embedding-based Part of Speech tagging in Tamil texts. In *2020 IEEE 15th International Conference on Industrial and Information Systems (ICIIS)*, pages 478–482.

Neeraj Vashistha and Arkaitz Zubiaga. 2021. Online multilingual hate speech detection: experimenting with hindi and english social media. *Information*, 12(1):5.

Linting Xue, Noah Constant, Adam Roberts, Mihir Kale, Rami Al-Rfou, Aditya Siddhant, Aditya Barua, and Colin Raffel. 2020. mt5: A massively multilingual pre-trained text-to-text transformer.

IIITT@LT-EDI-EACL2021-Hope Speech Detection: There is always Hope in Transformers

Karthik Puranik[1], **Adeep Hande**[1], **Ruba Priyadarshini**[2],
Sajeetha Thavareesan[3], **Bharathi Raja Chakravarthi**[4]
[1]Indian Institute of Information Technology Tiruchirappalli
[2]ULTRA Arts and Science College, India,[3]Eastern University, Sri Lanka
[4]National University of Ireland Galway
karthikp18c@iiitt.ac.in

Abstract

In a world filled with serious challenges like climate change, religious and political conflicts, global pandemics, terrorism, and racial discrimination, an internet full of hate speech, abusive and offensive content is the last thing we desire for. In this paper, we work to identify and promote positive and supportive content on these platforms. We work with several transformer-based models to classify social media comments as hope speech or not-hope speech in English, Malayalam and Tamil languages. This paper portrays our work for the Shared Task on Hope Speech Detection for Equality, Diversity, and Inclusion at LT-EDI 2021- EACL 2021. The codes for our best submission can be viewed[1].

1 Introduction

Social Media has inherently changed the way people interact and carry on with their everyday lives as people using the internet (Jose et al., 2020; Priyadharshini et al., 2020). Due to the vast amount of data being available on social media applications such as YouTube, Facebook, an Twitter it has resulted in people stating their opinions in the form of comments that could imply hate or negative sentiment towards an individual or a community (Chakravarthi et al., 2020c; Mandl et al., 2020). This results in people feeling hostile about certain posts and thus feeling very hurt (Bhardwaj et al., 2020).

Being a free platform, social media runs on user-generated content. With people from multifarious backgrounds present, it creates a rich social structure (Kapoor et al., 2018) and has become an exceptional source of information. It has laid it's roots so deeply into the lives of people that they count on it for their every need. Regardless, this tends to mislead people in search of credible information. Certain individuals or ethnic groups also fall prey to people utilizing these platforms to foster destructive or harmful behaviour which is a common scenario in cyberbullying (Abaido, 2020).

The earliest inscription in India dated from 580 BCE was the Tamil inscription in pottery and then, the Asoka inscription in Prakrit, Greek and Aramaic dating from 260 BCE. Thunchaththu Ramanujan Ezhuthachan split Malayalam from Tamil after the 15th century CE by using Pallava Grantha script to write religious texts. Pallava Grantha was used in South India to write Sanskrit and foreign words in Tamil literature. Modern Tamil and Malayalam have their own script. However, people use the Latin script to write on social media (Chakravarthi et al., 2018, 2019; Chakravarthi, 2020b).

The automatic detection of hateful, offensive, and unwanted language related to events and subjects on gender, religion, race or ethnicity in social media posts is very much necessary (Rizwan et al., 2020; Ghanghor et al., 2021a,b). Such harmful content could spread, stimulate, and vindicate hatred, outrage, and prejudice against the targeted users. Removing such comments was never an option as it suppresses the freedom of speech of the user and it is highly unlikely to stop the person from posting more. In fact, he/she/they would be prompted to post more of such comments[2] (Yasaswini et al., 2021; Hegde et al., 2021). This brings us to our goal to spread positivism and hope and identify such posts to strengthen an open-minded, tolerant, and unprejudiced society.

[1] https://github.com/karthikpuranik11/Hope-Speech-Detection-

[2] https://www.qs.com/negative-comments-on-social-media/

Proceedings of the First Workshop on Language Technology for Equality, Diversity and Inclusion, pages 98–106
April 19, 2021.

Text	Language	Label
God gave us a choice my choice is to love, I would die for that kid	English	Hope
The Democrats are.Backed powerful rich people like Soros	English	Not hope
ESTE PSICÃ"PATA MASÃ"N LUCIFERIANO ES HOMBRE TRANS	English	Not English
Neega podara vedio nalla iruku ana subtitle vainthuchu ahh yella language papaga	Tamil	Hope
Avan matum enkita maatunan... Avana kolla paniduven	Tamil	Not hope
I can't uninstall mY Pubg	Tamil	Not Tamil
oooorutharum avarude ishtam pole jeevikatte . k.	Malayalam	Hope
Etraem aduthu nilkallae Arunae	Malayalam	Not hope
Phoenix contact me give you're mail I'd I hope I can support you sure!	Malayalam	Not Malayalam

Table 1: Examples of hope speech or not hope speech

2 Related Works

The need for the segregation of toxic comments from social media platforms has been identified back in the day. Founta et al. (2018) has tried to study the textual properties and behaviour of abusive postings on Twitter using a Unified Deep Learning Architecture. Hate speech can be classified into various categories like hatred against an individual or group belonging to a race, religion, skin colour, ethnicity, gender, disability, or nation[3] and there have been studies to observe it's evolution in social media over the past thirty years (Tontodimamma et al., 2021). Deep Learning methods were used to classify hate speech into racist, sexist or neither in Badjatiya et al. (2017).

Hope is support, reassurance or any kind of positive reinforcement at the time of crisis (Chakravarthi, 2020a). Palakodety et al. (2020) identifies the need for the automatic detection of content that can eliminate hostility and bring about a sense of hope during times of wrangling and brink of a war between nations. There have also been works to identify hate speech in multilingual (Aluru et al., 2020) and code-mixed data in Tamil, Malayalam, and Kannada language (Chakravarthi et al., 2020b,a; Hande et al., 2020). However, there have been very fewer works in Hope speech detection for Indian languages.

3 Dataset

The dataset is provided by (Chakravarthi, 2020a) (Chakravarthi and Muralidaran, 2021) and contains 59,354 comments from the famous online video sharing platform YouTube out of which 28,451 are in English, 20,198 in Tamil, and 10,705 comments are in Malayalam (Table 2) which can be classified as Hope speech, not hope speech and other languages. This dataset is split into train (80%), development (10%) and test (10%) dataset (Table 3).

Subjects like hope speech might raise confusions and disagreements between annotators belonging to different groups. The dataset was annotated by a minimum of three annotators and the inter-annotator agreement was determined using Krippendorff's alpha (krippendorff, 2011). Refer table 1 for examples of hope speech, not hope speech and other languages for English, Tamil and Malayalam datasets respectively.

Class	English	Tamil	Malayalam
Hope	2,484	7,899	2,052
Not Hope	25,940	9,816	7,765
Other lang	27	2,483	888
Total	28,451	20,198	10,705

Table 2: Classwise Data Distribution

Split	English	Tamil	Malayalam
Training	22,762	16,160	8564
Development	2,843	2,018	1070
Test	2,846	2,020	1071
Total	28,451	20,198	10,705

Table 3: Train-Development-Test Data Distribution

4 Experiment Setup

In this section, we give a detailed explanation of the experimental conditions upon which the models are developed.

[3] http://www.ala.org/advocacy/intfreedom/hate (Accessed January 16, 2021)

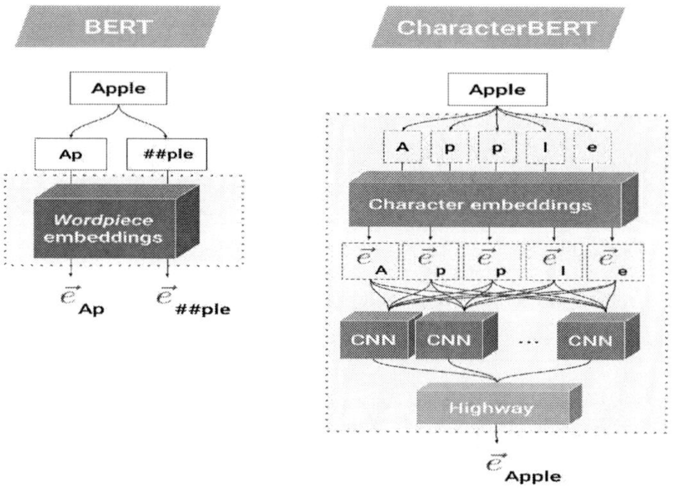

Figure 1: Context-independent representations in BERT and CharacterBERT (Source: El Boukkouri et al. (2020))

4.1 Architecture

4.1.1 Dense

The dense layers used in CNN (convolutional neural networks) connects all layers in the next layer with each other in a feed-forward fashion (Huang et al., 2018). Though they have the same formulae as the linear layers i.e. wx+b, the output is passed through an activation function which is a non-linear function. We implemented our models with 2 dense layers, rectified linear units (ReLU) (Agarap, 2019) as the activation function and dropout of 0.4.

4.1.2 Bidirectional LSTM

Bidirectional LSTM or biLSTM is a sequence processing model (Schuster and Paliwal, 1997). It uses both the future and past input features at a time as it contains two LSTM's, one taking input in the forward direction and another in the backward direction (Schuster and Paliwal, 1997). The backward and forward pass through the unfolded network just like any regular network. However, BiLSTM requires us to unfold the hidden states for every time step. It produces a drastic increase in the size of information being fed thus, improving the context available (Huang et al., 2015). Refer Table 4 for the parameters used in the BiLSTM model.

Parameter	Value
Number of LSTM units	256
Dropout	0.4
Activation Function	ReLU
Max Len	128
Batch Size	32
Optimizer	AdamW
Learning Rate	2e-5
Loss Function	cross-entropy
Number of epochs	5

Table 4: Parameters for the BiLSTM model

4.2 Embeddings

4.2.1 BERT

Bidirectional Encoder Representations from Transformers (BERT) (Devlin et al., 2019). The multilingual base model is pretrained on the top 104 languages of the world on Wikipedia (2.5B words) with 110 thousand shared wordpiece vocabulary. The input is encoded into vectors with BERT's innovation of bidirectionally training the language model which catches a deeper context and flow of the language. Furthermore, novel tasks like Next Sentence Prediction (NSP) and Masked Language Modelling (MLM) are used to train the model.

The pretrained BERT Multilingual model ***bert-base-multilingual-uncased*** (Pires et al., 2019) from Huggingface[4] (Wolf et al., 2020) is executed in PyTorch (Paszke et al., 2019). It consists of 12-layers, 768 hidden, 12 attention heads and 110M parameters which are fine-tuned by concatenating with bidirectional LSTM layers. The BiLSTM layers take the embeddings from the transformer encoder as the input which increases the information being fed, which in turn betters the context and accuracy. Adam algorithm with weight decay fix is used as an optimizer. We train our models with the default learning rate of $2e-5$. We use the cross-entropy loss as it is a multilabel classification task.

4.2.2 ALBERT

It has a similar architecture as that of BERT but due to memory limitations and longer training periods, ALBERT or A Lite BERT introduces two parameter reduction techniques (Chiang et al., 2020). ALBERT distinguishes itself from BERT with features like factorization of the embedding matrix, cross-layer parameter sharing and inter-sentence coherence prediction. We implemented ***albert-base-v2*** pretrained model with 12 repeating layers, 768 hidden, 12 attention heads, and 12M parameters for the English dataset.

4.2.3 DistilBERT

DistilBERT is a distilled version of BERT to make it smaller, cheaper, faster, and lighter (Sanh et al., 2019). With up to 40% less number of parameters than ***bert-base-uncased***, it promises to run 60% faster while preserving 97% of it's performance. We employ ***distilbert-base-uncased*** for the English dataset and ***distilbert-base-multilingual-cased*** for the Tamil and Malayalam datasets. Both models have 6-layers, 768-hidden, 12-heads and while the former has 66M parameters, the latter has 134M parameters.

4.2.4 RoBERTa

A Robustly optimized BERT Pretraining Approach (RoBERTa) is a modification of BERT (Liu et al., 2020). RoBERTa is trained for longer, with larger batches on 1000% more data than BERT. The Next Sentence Prediction (NSP) task employed in BERT's pre-training is removed and dynamic masking during training is introduced. It's additionally trained on a 76 GB large new dataset (CC-NEWS). ***roberta-base*** follows the BERT architecture but has 125M parameters and is used for the English dataset.

4.2.5 CharacterBERT

CharacterBERT (CharBERT) (El Boukkouri et al., 2020) is a variant of BERT (Devlin et al., 2019) which uses CharacterCNN (Zhang et al., 2015) like ELMo (Peters et al., 2018), instead of relying on WordPieces (Wu et al., 2016). CharacterBERT is highly desired as it produces a single embedding for any input token which is more suitable than having an inconstant number of WordPiece vectors for each token. It furthermore replaces BERT from domain-specific wordpiece vocabulary and enables it to be more robust to noisy inputs.

We use the pretrained model ***general-character-bert***[5] which was pretrained on the same corpus of that of BERT, but with a different tokenization approach. A CharacterCNN module is used that produces word-level contextual representations and it can be re-adapted to any domain without needing to worry about the suitability of any wordpieces (Figure 1). This approach helps for superior robustness by approaching the character of the inputs.

4.2.6 ULMFiT

Universal Language Model Fine-tuning, or ULMFiT, was a transfer learning method introduced to perform various NLP tasks (Howard and Ruder, 2018). Training of ULMFiT involves pretraining the general language model on a Wikipedia-based corpus, fine-tuning the language model on a target text, and finally, fine-tuning the classifier on the target task. Discriminative fine-tuning is applied to fine-tune the model as different layers capture the different extent of information. It is then trained using the learning rate scheduling strategy, Slanted triangular learning rates (STLR), where the learning rate increases initially and then drops. Gradual unfreezing is used to fine-tune the target classifier rather than training all layers at once, which might lead to catastrophic forgetting.

Pretrained model, **AWD-LSTM** (Merity et al., 2017) with 3 layers and 1150 hidden activation per layer and an embedding size of 400 is used as the language model for the English dataset. Adam optimizer with $\beta_1 = 0.9$ and $\beta_2 = 0.99$ is implemented. Later, the start and end learning rates are

[4]https://huggingface.co/transformers/pretrained_models.html

[5]https://github.com/helboukkouri/character-bert

Architecture	Embeddings	F1-Score validation	F1-Score test
BiLSTM	bert-base-uncased	0.9112	0.9241
Dense	bert-base-uncased	0.9164	0.9240
	albert-base	0.9143	0.9210
	distilbert-base-uncased	0.9238	0.9283
	roberta-base	0.9141	0.9235
	character-bert	**0.9264**	0.9220
	ULMFiT	0.9252	0.9356

Table 5: Weighted F1-scores of hope speech detection classifier models on English dataset

Architecture	Embeddings	F1-Score validation	F1-Score test
BiLSTM	mbert-uncased	**0.8436**	0.8545
	mbert-cased	0.8280	0.8482
	xlm-roberta-base	0.8271	0.8233
	MuRIL	0.8089	0.8212
Dense	mbert-uncased	0.8373	0.8433
	indic-bert	0.7719	0.8264
	xlm-roberta-base	0.7757	0.7001
	distilmbert-cased	0.8312	0.8395
	MuRIL	0.8023	0.8187

Table 6: Weighted F1-scores of hope speech detection classifier model on Malayalam dataset

Architecture	Embeddings	F1-Score Validation	F1-Score test
BiLSTM	mbert-uncased	0.6124	0.5601
	mbert-cased	**0.6183**	0.5297
	xlm-roberta-base	0.5472	0.5738
	MuRIL	0.5802	0.5463
Dense	mbert-uncased	0.5916	0.4473
	mbert-cased	0.5946	0.4527
	indic-bert	0.5609	0.5785
	xlm-roberta-base	0.5481	0.3936
	distilmbert-cased	0.6034	0.5926
	MuRIL	0.5504	0.5291

Table 7: Weighted F1-scores of hope speech detection classifier models on Tamil dataset

set to *1e-8 and 1e-2* respectively and fine-tuned by gradually unfreezing the layers to produce better results. Dropouts with a multiplier of 0.5 were applied.

4.2.7 XLM-RoBERTa

XLM-RoBERTa (Ruder et al., 2019) is a pre-trained multilingual language model to execute diverse NLP transfer tasks. It's trained on over 2TB of filtered CommonCrawl data in 100 different languages. It was an update to the XLM-100 model (Lample and Conneau, 2019) but with increased training data. As it shares the same training routine with the RoBERTa model, "RoBERTa" was included in the name. ***xlm-roberta-base*** with 12 layers, 768 hidden, 12 heads, and 270M parameters were used. It is fine-tuned for classifying code-mixed Tamil and Malayalam datasets.

4.2.8 MuRIL

MuRiL[6] was introduced by Google Research India to enhance Indian NLU (Natural Language Understanding). The model has a BERT based architecture trained on 17 Indian languages with

[6] https://tfhub.dev/google/MuRIL/1

Language	Hope-Speech	Not-hope speech	Other Language	Macro Avg	Weighted Avg
Precision					
English	0.9464	0.6346	0.0000	0.5270	0.9193
Malayalam	0.6540	0.9032	0.8941	0.8171	0.572
Tamil	0.4824	0.5819	0.5709	0.5451	0.5403
Recall					
English	0.9781	0.4108	0.0000	0.4630	0.9293
Malayalam	0.7113	0.9021	0.7525	0.7886	0.8534
Tamil	0.2687	0.7812	0.6525	0.5675	0.5579
F1-Score					
English	0.9620	0.4987	0.0000	0.4869	0.9220
Malayalam	0.6815	0.9026	0.8172	0.8004	0.8545
Tamil	0.3452	0.6670	0.6090	0.5404	0.5207

Table 8: Classification report for our system models based on the results of test set

Wikipedia, Common Crawl[7], PMINDIA[8] and Dakshina[9] datasets. MuRIL is trained on translation and transliteration segment pairs which give an advantage as the transliterated text is very common in social media. It is used for the Malayalam and Tamil datasets.

4.2.9 IndicBERT

IndicBERT (Kakwani et al., 2020) is an ALBERT model pretrained on 12 major Indian languages with a corpus of over 9 billion tokens. It performs as well as other multilingual models with considerably fewer parameters for various NLP tasks. It's trained by choosing a single model for all languages to learn the relationship between languages and understand code-mixed data. ***ai4bharat/indic-bert*** model was employed for the Tamil and Malayalam task.

5 Results

In this section, we have compared the F1-scores of our transformer-based models to successfully classify social media comments/posts into hope speech or not hope speech and detect the usage of other languages if any. We have tabulated the weighted average F1-scores of our various models for validation and test dataset for English, Malayalam and Tamil languages in tables 5, 6 and 7 respectively.

Table 5 demonstrates that the character-aware model CharacterBERT performed exceptionally well for the validation dataset. It beat ULMFiT (Howard and Ruder, 2018) by a mere difference of 0.0012, but other BERT-based models like BERT (Devlin et al., 2019) with dense and BiLSTM architecture, ALBERT (Chiang et al., 2020), DistilBERT (Sanh et al., 2019) and RoBERTa (Liu et al., 2020) by about a percent. This promising result shown by character-bert for the validation dataset made it our best model. Unfortunately, few models managed to perform better than it for the test dataset. The considerable class imbalance of about 2,484 hope to 25,940 not hope comments and the interference of comments in other languages have significantly affected the results.

Similar transformer-based model trained on multilingual data was used to classify Malayalam and Tamil datasets. Models like multilingual BERT, XLM-RoBERTa (Ruder et al., 2019), MuRIL, IndicBERT [10] and DistilBERT multilingual with both BiLSTM and Dense architectures. mBERT (Multilingual BERT) uncased with BiLSTM concatenated to it outperformed the other models for the Malayalam validation dataset and continued its dominance for the test data as well.

The data distribution for the Tamil dataset seemed a bit balanced with an approximate ratio of 4:5 between hope and not-hope. mBERT cased with BiLSTM architecture appeared to be the best model with an F1-score of 0.6183 for validation but dropped drastically by 8% for the test data. We witnessed a considerable fall in the scores of other models like mBERT and XLM-RoBERTa with linear layers of up to 15%.

Multilingual comments experience an enor-

[7]http://commoncrawl.org/the-data/

[8]http://lotus.kuee.kyoto-u.ac.jp/WAT/indic-multilingual/index.html

[9]https://github.com/google-research-datasets/dakshina

[10]https://indicnlp.ai4bharat.org/indic-bert/

mous variety of text as people tend to write in code-mixed data and other non-native scripts which are inclined to be mispredicted. A variation in the concentration of such comments between train, validation and test can result in a fluctuation in the test results. The precision, recall and F1-scores of CharacterBERT, mBERT-uncased, and mBERT-cased are tabulated under English, Malayalam, and Tamil respectively, as shown in Table 8. They were the best performing models on the validation set.

6 Conclusion

During these unprecedented times, there is a need to detect positive, enjoyable content on social media in order to help people who are combating depression, anxiety, melancholy, etc. This paper presents several methodologies that can detect hope in social media comments. We have traversed through transfer learning of several state-of-the-art transformer models for languages such as English, Tamil, and Malayalam. Due to its superior fine-tuning method, ULMFiT achieves an F1-score of 0.9356 on English data. We observe that mBERT achieves 0.8545 on Malayalam test set and distilmBERT achieves 0.5926 weighted F1-score on Tamil test set.

References

Ghada M. Abaido. 2020. Cyberbullying on social media platforms among university students in the united arab emirates. *International Journal of Adolescence and Youth*, 25(1):407–420.

Abien Fred Agarap. 2019. Deep learning using rectified linear units (relu).

Sai Saketh Aluru, Binny Mathew, Punyajoy Saha, and Animesh Mukherjee. 2020. Deep learning models for multilingual hate speech detection.

Pinkesh Badjatiya, Shashank Gupta, Manish Gupta, and Vasudeva Varma. 2017. Deep learning for hate speech detection in tweets. *Proceedings of the 26th International Conference on World Wide Web Companion - WWW '17 Companion*.

Mohit Bhardwaj, Md Shad Akhtar, Asif Ekbal, Amitava Das, and Tanmoy Chakraborty. 2020. Hostility detection dataset in hindi.

Bharathi Raja Chakravarthi. 2020a. HopeEDI: A multilingual hope speech detection dataset for equality, diversity, and inclusion. In *Proceedings of the Third Workshop on Computational Modeling of People's Opinions, Personality, and Emotion's in Social Media*, pages 41–53, Barcelona, Spain (Online). Association for Computational Linguistics.

Bharathi Raja Chakravarthi. 2020b. *Leveraging orthographic information to improve machine translation of under-resourced languages*. Ph.D. thesis, NUI Galway.

Bharathi Raja Chakravarthi, Mihael Arcan, and John P. McCrae. 2018. Improving wordnets for under-resourced languages using machine translation. In *Proceedings of the 9th Global Wordnet Conference*, pages 77–86, Nanyang Technological University (NTU), Singapore. Global Wordnet Association.

Bharathi Raja Chakravarthi, Mihael Arcan, and John P. McCrae. 2019. WordNet gloss translation for under-resourced languages using multilingual neural machine translation. In *Proceedings of the Second Workshop on Multilingualism at the Intersection of Knowledge Bases and Machine Translation*, pages 1–7, Dublin, Ireland. European Association for Machine Translation.

Bharathi Raja Chakravarthi, Navya Jose, Shardul Suryawanshi, Elizabeth Sherly, and John Philip McCrae. 2020a. A sentiment analysis dataset for code-mixed Malayalam-English. In *Proceedings of the 1st Joint Workshop on Spoken Language Technologies for Under-resourced languages (SLTU) and Collaboration and Computing for Under-Resourced Languages (CCURL)*, pages 177–184, Marseille, France. European Language Resources association.

Bharathi Raja Chakravarthi and Vigneshwaran Muralidaran. 2021. Findings of the shared task on Hope Speech Detection for Equality, Diversity, and Inclusion. In *Proceedings of the First Workshop on Language Technology for Equality, Diversity and Inclusion*. Association for Computational Linguistics.

Bharathi Raja Chakravarthi, Vigneshwaran Muralidaran, Ruba Priyadharshini, and John Philip McCrae. 2020b. Corpus creation for sentiment analysis in code-mixed Tamil-English text. In *Proceedings of the 1st Joint Workshop on Spoken Language Technologies for Under-resourced languages (SLTU) and Collaboration and Computing for Under-Resourced Languages (CCURL)*, pages 202–210, Marseille, France. European Language Resources association.

Bharathi Raja Chakravarthi, Ruba Priyadharshini, Vigneshwaran Muralidaran, Shardul Suryawanshi, Navya Jose, Elizabeth Sherly, and John P. McCrae. 2020c. Overview of the Track on Sentiment Analysis for Dravidian Languages in Code-Mixed Text. In *Forum for Information Retrieval Evaluation*, FIRE 2020, page 21–24, New York, NY, USA. Association for Computing Machinery.

Cheng-Han Chiang, Sung-Feng Huang, and Hung-yi Lee. 2020. Pretrained language model embryology: The birth of ALBERT. In *Proceedings of the 2020*

Conference on Empirical Methods in Natural Language Processing (EMNLP), pages 6813–6828, Online. Association for Computational Linguistics.

Jacob Devlin, Ming-Wei Chang, Kenton Lee, and Kristina Toutanova. 2019. BERT: Pre-training of deep bidirectional transformers for language understanding. In *Proceedings of the 2019 Conference of the North American Chapter of the Association for Computational Linguistics: Human Language Technologies, Volume 1 (Long and Short Papers)*, pages 4171–4186, Minneapolis, Minnesota. Association for Computational Linguistics.

Hicham El Boukkouri, Olivier Ferret, Thomas Lavergne, Hiroshi Noji, Pierre Zweigenbaum, and Jun'ichi Tsujii. 2020. CharacterBERT: Reconciling ELMo and BERT for word-level open-vocabulary representations from characters. In *Proceedings of the 28th International Conference on Computational Linguistics*, pages 6903–6915, Barcelona, Spain (Online). International Committee on Computational Linguistics.

Antigoni-Maria Founta, Despoina Chatzakou, Nicolas Kourtellis, Jeremy Blackburn, Athena Vakali, and Ilias Leontiadis. 2018. A unified deep learning architecture for abuse detection.

Nikhil Kumar Ghanghor, Parameswari Krishnamurthy, Sajeetha Thavareesan, Ruba Priyadharshini, and Bharathi Raja Chakravarthi. 2021a. IIITK@DravidianLangTech-EACL2021: Offensive Language Identification and Meme Classification in Tamil, Malayalam and Kannada. In *Proceedings of the First Workshop on Speech and Language Technologies for Dravidian Languages*, Online. Association for Computational Linguistics.

Nikhil Kumar Ghanghor, Rahul Ponnusamy, Prasanna Kumar Kumaresan, Ruba Priyadharshini, Sajeetha Thavareesan, and Bharathi Raja Chakravarthi. 2021b. IIITK@LT-EDI-EACL2021: Hope Speech Detection for Equality, Diversity, and Inclusion in Tamil, Malayalam and English. In *Proceedings of the First Workshop on Language Technology for Equality, Diversity and Inclusion*, Online. Association for Computational Linguistics.

Adeep Hande, Ruba Priyadharshini, and Bharathi Raja Chakravarthi. 2020. KanCMD: Kannada CodeMixed dataset for sentiment analysis and offensive language detection. In *Proceedings of the Third Workshop on Computational Modeling of People's Opinions, Personality, and Emotion's in Social Media*, pages 54–63, Barcelona, Spain (Online). Association for Computational Linguistics.

Siddhanth U Hegde, Adeep Hande, Ruba Priyadharshini, Sajeetha Thavareesan, and Bharathi Raja Chakravarthi. 2021. UVCE-IIITT@DravidianLangTech-EACL2021: Tamil Troll Meme Classification: You need to Pay more Attention. In *Proceedings of the First Workshop on Speech and Language Technologies for Dravidian Languages*. Association for Computational Linguistics.

Jeremy Howard and Sebastian Ruder. 2018. Universal language model fine-tuning for text classification. In *Proceedings of the 56th Annual Meeting of the Association for Computational Linguistics (Volume 1: Long Papers)*, pages 328–339, Melbourne, Australia. Association for Computational Linguistics.

Gao Huang, Zhuang Liu, Laurens van der Maaten, and Kilian Q. Weinberger. 2018. Densely connected convolutional networks.

Zhiheng Huang, Wei Xu, and Kai Yu. 2015. Bidirectional lstm-crf models for sequence tagging.

Navya Jose, Bharathi Raja Chakravarthi, Shardul Suryawanshi, Elizabeth Sherly, and John P. McCrae. 2020. A Survey of Current Datasets for Code-Switching Research. In *2020 6th International Conference on Advanced Computing and Communication Systems (ICACCS)*, pages 136–141.

Divyanshu Kakwani, Anoop Kunchukuttan, Satish Golla, Gokul N.C., Avik Bhattacharyya, Mitesh M. Khapra, and Pratyush Kumar. 2020. IndicNLPSuite: Monolingual Corpora, Evaluation Benchmarks and Pre-trained Multilingual Language Models for Indian Languages. In *Findings of EMNLP*.

Kawaljeet Kapoor, Kuttimani Tamilmani, Nripendra Rana, Pushp Patil, Yogesh Dwivedi, and Sridhar Nerur. 2018. Advances in social media research: Past, present and future. *Information Systems Frontiers*, 20.

klaus krippendorff. 2011. Computing krippendorff's alpha-reliability.

Guillaume Lample and Alexis Conneau. 2019. Cross-lingual language model pretraining.

Yinhan Liu, Myle Ott, Naman Goyal, Jingfei Du, Mandar Joshi, Danqi Chen, Omer Levy, Mike Lewis, Luke Zettlemoyer, and Veselin Stoyanov. 2020. Ro{bert}a: A robustly optimized {bert} pretraining approach.

Thomas Mandl, Sandip Modha, Anand Kumar M, and Bharathi Raja Chakravarthi. 2020. Overview of the HASOC Track at FIRE 2020: Hate Speech and Offensive Language Identification in Tamil, Malayalam, Hindi, English and German. In *Forum for Information Retrieval Evaluation*, FIRE 2020, page 29–32, New York, NY, USA. Association for Computing Machinery.

Stephen Merity, Nitish Shirish Keskar, and Richard Socher. 2017. Regularizing and optimizing lstm language models.

Shriphani Palakodety, Ashiqur R. KhudaBukhsh, and Jaime G. Carbonell. 2020. Hope speech detection: A computational analysis of the voice of peace.

Adam Paszke, Sam Gross, Francisco Massa, Adam Lerer, James Bradbury, Gregory Chanan, Trevor Killeen, Zeming Lin, Natalia Gimelshein, Luca Antiga, Alban Desmaison, Andreas Kopf, Edward Yang, Zachary DeVito, Martin Raison, Alykhan Tejani, Sasank Chilamkurthy, Benoit Steiner, Lu Fang, Junjie Bai, and Soumith Chintala. 2019. Pytorch: An imperative style, high-performance deep learning library. In *Advances in Neural Information Processing Systems*, volume 32, pages 8026–8037. Curran Associates, Inc.

Matthew Peters, Mark Neumann, Mohit Iyyer, Matt Gardner, Christopher Clark, Kenton Lee, and Luke Zettlemoyer. 2018. Deep contextualized word representations. In *Proceedings of the 2018 Conference of the North American Chapter of the Association for Computational Linguistics: Human Language Technologies, Volume 1 (Long Papers)*, pages 2227–2237, New Orleans, Louisiana. Association for Computational Linguistics.

Telmo Pires, Eva Schlinger, and Dan Garrette. 2019. How multilingual is multilingual BERT? In *Proceedings of the 57th Annual Meeting of the Association for Computational Linguistics*, pages 4996–5001, Florence, Italy. Association for Computational Linguistics.

Ruba Priyadharshini, Bharathi Raja Chakravarthi, Mani Vegupatti, and John P. McCrae. 2020. Named Entity Recognition for Code-Mixed Indian Corpus using Meta Embedding. In *2020 6th International Conference on Advanced Computing and Communication Systems (ICACCS)*, pages 68–72.

Hammad Rizwan, Muhammad Haroon Shakeel, and Asim Karim. 2020. Hate-speech and offensive language detection in Roman Urdu. In *Proceedings of the 2020 Conference on Empirical Methods in Natural Language Processing (EMNLP)*, pages 2512–2522, Online. Association for Computational Linguistics.

Sebastian Ruder, Anders Søgaard, and Ivan Vulić. 2019. Unsupervised cross-lingual representation learning. In *Proceedings of the 57th Annual Meeting of the Association for Computational Linguistics: Tutorial Abstracts*, pages 31–38, Florence, Italy. Association for Computational Linguistics.

Victor Sanh, Lysandre Debut, Julien Chaumond, and Thomas Wolf. 2019. Distilbert, a distilled version of bert: smaller, faster, cheaper and lighter.

M. Schuster and K. K. Paliwal. 1997. Bidirectional recurrent neural networks. *IEEE Transactions on Signal Processing*, 45(11):2673–2681.

Mike Schuster and K. Paliwal. 1997. Bidirectional recurrent neural networks. *IEEE Trans. Signal Process.*, 45:2673–2681.

Alice Tontodimamma, Eugenia Nissi, Annalina Sarra, and Lara Fontanella. 2021. Thirty years of research into hate speech: topics of interest and their evolution. *Scientometrics*, 126(1):157–179.

Thomas Wolf, Lysandre Debut, Victor Sanh, Julien Chaumond, Clement Delangue, Anthony Moi, Pierric Cistac, Tim Rault, Rémi Louf, Morgan Funtowicz, Joe Davison, Sam Shleifer, Patrick von Platen, Clara Ma, Yacine Jernite, Julien Plu, Canwen Xu, Teven Le Scao, Sylvain Gugger, Mariama Drame, Quentin Lhoest, and Alexander M. Rush. 2020. Huggingface's transformers: State-of-the-art natural language processing.

Y. Wu, Mike Schuster, Z. Chen, Quoc V. Le, Mohammad Norouzi, Wolfgang Macherey, M. Krikun, Yuan Cao, Q. Gao, Klaus Macherey, Jeff Klingner, Apurva Shah, M. Johnson, X. Liu, L. Kaiser, S. Gouws, Y. Kato, Taku Kudo, H. Kazawa, K. Stevens, G. Kurian, Nishant Patil, W. Wang, C. Young, J. Smith, Jason Riesa, Alex Rudnick, Oriol Vinyals, G. S. Corrado, Macduff Hughes, and J. Dean. 2016. Google's neural machine translation system: Bridging the gap between human and machine translation. *ArXiv*, abs/1609.08144.

Konthala Yasaswini, Karthik Puranik, Adeep Hande, Ruba Priyadharshini, Sajeetha Thavareesan, and Bharathi Raja Chakravarthi. 2021. IIITT@DravidianLangTech-EACL2021: Transfer Learning for Offensive Language Detection in Dravidian Languages. In *Proceedings of the First Workshop on Speech and Language Technologies for Dravidian Languages*. Association for Computational Linguistics.

Xiang Zhang, Junbo Zhao, and Yann LeCun. 2015. Character-level convolutional networks for text classification. In *Advances in Neural Information Processing Systems*, volume 28, pages 649–657. Curran Associates, Inc.

IIIT_DWD@LT-EDI-EACL2021: Hope Speech Detection in YouTube multilingual comments

Sunil Saumya[1] and **Ankit Kumar Mishra**[2]
[1]Indian Institute of Information Technology Dharwad Karnataka, India
[2]Magadh University, Bodh Gaya, Bihar, India
sunil.saumya@iiitdwd.ac.in, ankitmishra.in.com@gmail.com,

Abstract

Language as a significant part of communication should be inclusive of equality and diversity. The internet user's language has a huge influence on peer users all over the world. People express their views through language on virtual platforms like Facebook, Twitter, YouTube, etc. People admire the success of others, pray for their well-being, and encourage in their failure. Such inspirational comments are hope speech comments. At the same time, a group of users promotes discrimination based on gender, race, sexual orientation, persons with a disability, and other minorities. The current paper aims to identify hope speech comments which are very important to move on in life. Various machine learning and deep learning-based models (such as support vector machine, logistics regression, convolutional neural network, recurrent neural network) are employed to identify the hope speech in the given YouTube comments. The YouTube comments are available in English, Tamil, and Malayalam languages and are part of the task "*EACL-2021:Hope Speech Detection for Equality, Diversity, and Inclusion*".

1 Introduction

In the current era, there are two lives we live; a real one and a virtual one. In a real case, we interact, communicate and exchange our emotions physi cally. On the other hand in virtual cases, we interact with others through a computer-based simulated environment, social media is one such example. In both cases, to exchange information a language is required such as English, Hindi, Spanish, German, and so on. Through these languages, we share our moments such as happiness, joy, anger, sadness, appreciation for success, motivation on failure, and others which everyone needs in their hard time. These comments convey the well-being of someone and are termed as "hope speech". The other categories of comments that discourage, abuse, demotivate based on gender, race, sexual orientation, persons with a disability, and other minorities are termed as "not hope speech". In the physical scenario, the reachability and effect of these comments mitigate with region and time. On the other hand, on virtual platforms (especially social media) their effects are long-lasting across the geographical region.

Hope speech reflects the idea that you will find paths to the desired goals and be encouraged to use them. A few examples of hope speech on social media platforms are; i) product-leverage reviews, ii) election campaign comments, iii) disaster or crisis-informed decision-making comments, and so on. Since there is a large number of comments and suggestions on a specific topic, the overall difference in the sentiment of the topic is created (Lee et al., 2017). Many times hope speech of a product leads to its great success, for example, introducing a number of helpful votes received by product reviews on Amazon leads to additional \$2.7 billion revenue[1]. Similarly, a number of likes, shares, and hope speech comments received by YouTube video can make it the most viewed video and so on. Also, if the video content or quality is not up to the mark, the hopeful suggestions received by other users help to boost the content or consistency of the video. On the other hand, the not hope speech comments can lower the subject's value and demotivates the person. Considering the higher impact of hope and not hope comments in social media contexts, it is therefore important to identify them for an informed decision.

The current paper identifies the hope speech comments on the YouTube platform. The dataset used in this study is a part of "*EACL-2021: Hope Speech Detection for Equality, Diversity, and Inclusion*". The comments are in three different languages English, Tamil, and Malayalam. The problem proposed is a classification problem in three groups, where all comments are marked with hope

[1]https://articles.uie.com/magicbehindamazon/

Proceedings of the First Workshop on Language Technology for Equality, Diversity and Inclusion, pages 107–113
April 19, 2021.

or not hope or not in the intended language. For classification of comments, several classification models based on conventional machine learning (e.g. support vector machine, logistic regression), deep learning (e.g. convolutional neural network (CNN), long short term memory network (LSTM)), and hybrid learning (parallel CNN-LSTM network, three parallel Bi-LSTM network) are developed. The results from the experiments showed that a model based on the CNN-LSTM network having 2 parallel layers worked best for the English dataset, with Bi-LSTM having three parallel layers performed best for Tamil and Malayalam [2].

The rest of the article is organized as follows; Section 2 discusses the related works for monolingual dataset classification. Section 3 describes the given task and data dimension. This is followed by the methodology of the current paper in Section 4. The results are explained in Section 5. Finally, Section 6 concludes the paper by highlighting some future scope.

2 Related work

According to the best of our knowledge, this is the first task on hope speech detection. Therefore, there are no previous works in this category. However, the current work is a monolingual classification problem, one of the highly researched problems in the processing of natural languages. In this section, we identify a few state-of-art papers for monolingual classification.

There are many applications of monolingual contexts such as sentiment classification, hate speech identification, fake content identification, and others. (Pak and Paroubek, 2010) performed sentiment analysis of English text from Twitter. They use a multi-nominal naive Bayes classifier to classify each tweet into positive, negative, and neutral. The features used were n-grams and POS-tags. They found that POS-tags are a strong predictor of sentiments. (Saumya and Singh, 2018) used the sentiment analysis approach to identify spam reviews on the e-commerce platform. Three classifiers random forest, gradient boosting, and support vector machine was trained on Amazon reviews. The best performance was reported by random forest with an F1-score of 0.91. (Davidson et al., 2017) proposed a hate speech classifier for English corpus (25000 tweets). (Pitsilis et al., 2018) trained a recurrent neural network on 16K tweet for hate speech identification. A comparative analysis of machine learning, deep learning, and transfer models is presented by (Plaza-del Arco et al., 2021) for the hate speech Spanish dataset. Similarly, for fake news detection on German data (Vogel and Jiang, 2019) used convolutional network and support vector machine classifiers on 4500 news articles. A fake news hostility detection dataset was proposed by (Bhardwaj et al., 2020) in the Hindi language. They trained several machine learning models like logistic regression, support vector machine, random forest, and multilayer perceptron network with m-BERT embedding for classifying hostility contents.

In line with the above literature, the current paper employs several machine learning and deep learning models for the classification of monolingual hope speech comments into three classes. The detailed methodology of the proposed model is explained in the next section.

3 Task and data description

The Hope Speech Content Identification in English, Tamil, and Malayalam language is organized by *EACL-2021* in a track on *Hope Speech Detection for Equality, Diversity, and Inclusion*. The objective of this task is to determine whether or not a comment contains a speech of hope. Every comment is labeled with either hope speech, not hope speech, and not in intended language.

The competition dataset was released in a phased manner. Initially, training and development datasets were released for each English, Tamil, and Malayalam corpus, resulting in six different data files. Every file had two fields; a comment and its label. In the given corpus of English, Tamil and Malayalam, the average comment length was one except for a few cases where it was more than one. The description of both training and development set for all three corpora is shown in Table 1. As shown in Table 1, the current system was trained on 22762, 16160, and 8564 samples and validated on 2843, 2018, and 1070 samples for English, Tamil, and Malayalam respectively. Later, the test dataset was released by organizers on which the final ranking of submitted models was released. The dataset details can also be found in (Chakravarthi, 2020; Chakravarthi and Muralidaran, 2021).

[2]The developed model code can be seen in the github repository: https://github.com/ankitmishra2232/Hope-Speech-Identification

Language	Hope speech		Not hope speech		Not in intended language		Total	
	Train	Dev	Train	Dev	Train	Dev	Train	Dev
English	1962	272	20778	2569	22	2	22762	2843
Tamil	6327	757	7872	998	1961	263	16160	2018
Malayalam	1668	190	6205	784	691	96	8564	1070

Table 1: Train and Dev datasets description

4 Methodology

The current paper proposed multi-label classification methods for the identification of Hope speech contents. Several conventional machine learning, deep learning, and hybrid learning approaches were employed to achieve the objective. A detailed description of all proposed methods is discussed in the subsection.

4.1 Data preprocessing

The dataset was preprocessed before feeding it to the machine learning models. The steps used for preprocessing were common for all three languages English, Tamil, and Malayalam. The Preprocessing was applied to the comment field of training and development data. Initially, Roman scripts present in texts were converted into lowercase. Then, all the punctuations, emoji, extra spaces, numbers, and stopwords were removed from the texts. The cleaned texts were then tokenized and encoded into the sequence of token indexes.

4.2 Classification models

The current paper employed several classification models for hope speech detection in YouTube comments. This section first explains the different conventional classifiers, followed by deep learning classifiers and finally hybrid classifiers used in the study.

4.2.1 Conventional machine learning classifier

Three traditional machine learning-based models were developed to categorize YouTube comments, including the Support Vector Machine (SVM), Logistic Regression (LR), and the Random Forest (RF). The input to these classifiers were Tf-idf vectors created from English, Tamil, and Malayalam comments. To acquire the vector, comments were first tokenized using the library *WhiteSpace Tokenizer*. The tokenized data were then stemmed using *Porter stemmer* library. Finally, the stemmed data were vectorized using a *Tf-idf vectorizer*. The models on the Tf-idf vector had very high training times.

4.2.2 Deep learning classifier

In the category of deep networks, the current study utilized convolutional neural network (CNN) and variants of recurrent neural networks namely long short term memory (LSTM) and bidirectional long short term memory (Bi-LSTM) in a single and multiple layers setting. To feed an equal length input to deep networks, the tokenized comments were first encoded and then padded with maximum comment length 10, 20, and 20 for English, Tamil, and Malayalam dataset respectively, because we checked the average words count for the datasets and used as maximum comment length.

The input to deep models was a one-hot vector where every word in a language was represented in its corresponding vocabulary dimensions. For example, in the English corpus vocabulary size was 20373, consequently, every word in English data was represented in a vector of 20373 dimensions (1×20373). The one-hot input representation was a high dimensional sparse vector, having a single'1'(that represented the index of the token), and all zeros. To convert it into a low dimensional dense valued vector, an embedding layer was used that represented every word in a 300 dimensional (1×300) dense vector. While representing one-hot vector into embedded dense vector several pre-trained weights from Word2Vec, GloVe, and random embeddings were used. The obtained embedded vectors were fed to the deep networks (such as single and multiple layers of CNN, LSTM, and Bi-LSTM) for further steps like contextual feature extraction followed by classification.

4.2.3 Hybrid Network

Further, several hybrid settings of deep neural networks were developed such as parallel CNN-CNN,

CNN-LSTM, CNN-Bi-LSTM, LSTM-LSTM, and so on. The architecture of the best two hybrid models is shown in Figure 1 and 2. The input to these networks was embedding vectors same as explained above in Section 4.2.2.

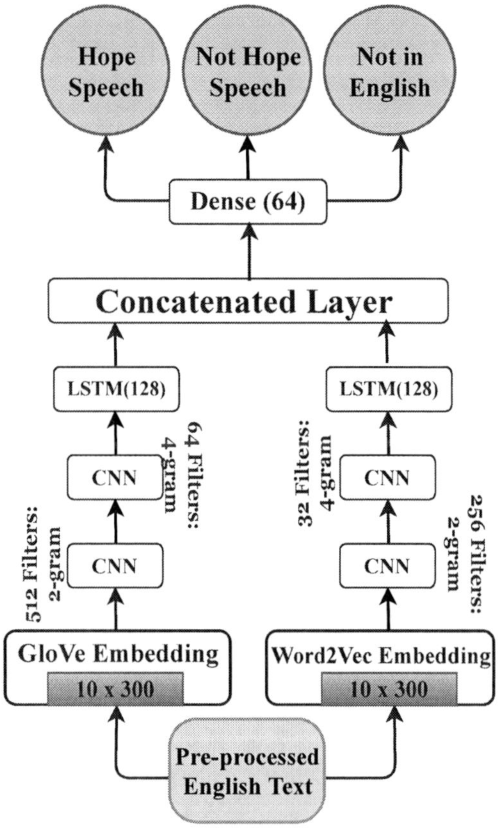

Figure 1: 2 Parallel CNN-Bi-LSTM model for English hope speech classification

The model shown in Figure 1 reported the best accuracy for the English dataset. As it is shown, the number of words fed from the pre-processed text was 10. Every word (having dimension 1×20373) was then represented in 300 dimensional embedded vector (1×300) using GloVe and Word2Vec embeddings. The obtained embedded vectors were fed to parallel 2 layered CNN and 1 layered LSTM model (2 parallel CNN-LSTM). The features (or output) extracted from LSTM layers were concatenated in a single vector. This vector was passed as input to a fully connected dense layer to classify every comment into three categories. The model was trained for 100 epochs with the "Adam" optimizer and "binary cross-entropy" loss function.

Alternatively, for Tamil and Malayalam datasets a three parallel Bi-LSTM model performed best

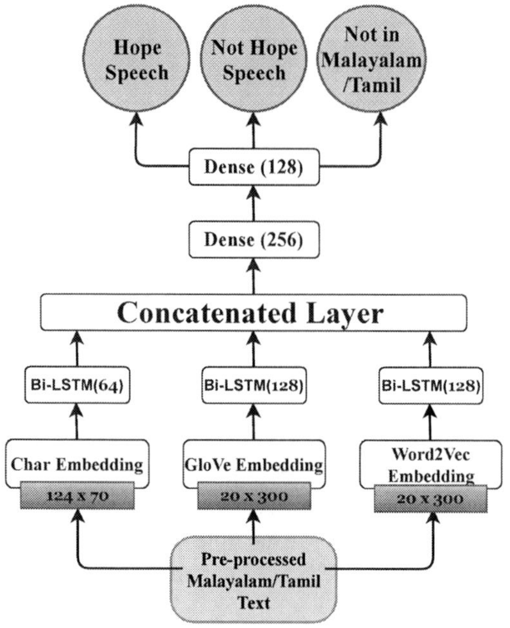

Figure 2: 3 Parallel Bi-LSTM model for Tamil and Malayalam hope speech classification

(as shown in Figure 2). The input to the first, second, and third Bi-LSTM was character embedding, word embedding, and word embedding respectively. From the corpus of Malayalam, a unique 124 characters were extracted. For every comment in the Malayalam set, a maximum of 70 characters were given as input to the model. To the second and third Bi-LSTM, the input was 300-dimensional word embeddings obtained from GloVe and Word2Vec. All three parallel embedding vectors were then fed to three parallel Bi-LSTM networks. The features extracted from Bi-LSTMs were concatenated and fed to the fully connected dense layer for classification. The model was trained for 100 epochs.

Similar steps were followed for Tamil hope speech identification except for a few differences that in Tamil corpus total unique characters were 218, total unique words were 32041, and training epochs were 150. In both Tamil and Malayalam cases, the optimizer was *Adam* and loss function was *binary-crossentropy*.

5 Results

As discussed above several classification models were built and experimented. We are reporting the results of the submitted models in the competition and a few other comparable models. All models were built in *Python* using libraries *Sklearn*, *Keras*,

Language	Type	Model	Embedding/Feature	Dev weighted F1
English	Conventional learning models	SVM	Tf-idf	0.85
		LR	Tf-idf	0.75
	Deep learning models	LSTM	GloVe	0.90
		Bi-LSTM	GloVe	0.90
		2 Layered CNN	Random	0.79
	Hybrid learning models	3 parallel LSTM	Glove, Word2Vec, Word2Vec	0.90
		2 parallel CNN-LSTM	**GloVe, Word2Vec**	**0.91**
		3 parallel CNN-LSTM	Word2Vec, Word2Vec, Word2Vec	0.88
		2 parallel LSTM-Bi-LSTM	Word2Vec, GloVe	0.90
Tamil	Conventional learning models	SVM	Tf-idf	0.48
		LR	Tf-idf	0.50
	Deep learning models	Bi-LSTM	Random	0.52
		CNN	Word2Vec	0.55
		2 layered CNN	Random	0.55
	Hybrid learning models	2 parallel LSTM	Word2Vec	0.50
		2 parallel CNN	Word2Vec	0.52
		3 parallel Bi-LSTM	**Word2Vec, Random**	**0.56**
Malayalam	Conventional learning models	SVM	Tf-idf	0.65
		LR	Tf-idf	0.72
	Deep learning models	CNN	Word2Vec	0.70
		LSTM	Word2Vec	0.75
		Bi-LSTM	Random	0.74
	Hybrid learning models	2 parallel LSTM	Word2Vec, Random	0.73
		2 parallel Bi-LSTM	Random, Random	0.77
		3 parallel CNN	Word2Vec, Random, Random	0.70
		3 parallel Bi-LSTM	**Word2Vec, Random, Random**	**0.78**

Table 2: Development dataset results of various models

Language	Model	Embedding/Features	Dev Weighted F1	Test Weighted F1	Ranking
English	2-Parallel CNN-LSTM	GloVe and Word2Vec	0.91	0.90	4
Tamil	3-Parallel Bi-LSTM	Word2Vec and Random	0.56	0.54	8
Malayalam	3-Parallel Bi-LSTM	Word2vec and Random	0.78	0.79	5

Table 3: Development and test dataset results of best performing submitted models

Pandas, *Numpy* an so on. The results reported here are for development data and test data. The metric used to evaluate the performance of a model was the weighted F1-score (or weighted F1). Table 2 shows the experimental results of various machine learning, deep learning, and hybrid learning models on the development dataset. For conventional classifiers SVM, and LR shown in Table 2, the feature used was Tf-idf vector whereas, for deep and hybrid models, features were embeddings.

In conventional models, for the English dataset, SVM reported weighted F1 0.85 which was higher than LR where weighted F1 was 0.75. The performance of the classification was even better for most of the deep and hybrid classifiers. As it is shown in Figure 2, LSTM and Bi-LSTM models with GloVe embedding reported 0.90 weighted F1, but at the same time, the performance of 2 layered CNN model with random embedding was very low as weighted F1 score was 0.79. The best-reported results were from the hybrid model *2-parallel CNN-LSTM* with GloVe and Word2Vec embeddings where weighted F1 was 0.91. The performance of *2-parallel LSTM-BiLSTM* and *3-parallel LSTM* was also comparable as it reported weighted F1 0.90. For the Tamil dataset, in conventional learning, the performance of LR (weighted F1 0.50) was better than SVM (weighted F1 0.48). The best performing models were 2-layered CNN and *3-parallel Bi-LSTM* with weighted F1 0.55 and 0.56 respectively. A similar pattern was observed for Malayalam data also. The best performing model for Malayalam set was *3 parallel Bi-LSTM* with weighted F1 0.78. Even, *2 parallel Bi-LSTM* with random embedding showed comparable results with weighted F1 0.77. The performance of SVM was reported least with a weighted F1 of 0.65.

The best performing models of English, Tamil, and Malayalam dataset was then validated with test dataset provided by organizers. The test dataset contained only a comment field, therefore, the predictions on test data for best models were submitted to the competition. Later, the organizer evaluated the submitted prediction label with the actual label of test data. The test dataset results are shown in Table 3. As it is reported in Table 3, on the English test dataset the weighted F1 was 0.90. For Tamil and Malayalam, the weighted F1 was 0.54 and 0.79 respectively. In the last column of Table 3, the final ranking of our models obtained in the competition for respective languages is shown.

As can be seen from Table 2 and 3, weighted F1 reported on development data and test data are almost equal. That verifies the authenticity of model training. The other observation is for the similar model *3-parallel Bi-LSTM* the classification accuracy of Malayalam hope speech was higher but for the Tamil dataset, it was only 0.54. That means to learn Tamil hope speech comment some other features and model can be investigated.

6 Conclusion

The current paper identified hope speech contents in YouTube comments using several machine learning, deep learning, and hybrid models. The task was proposed by *EACL 2021* for three different languages English, Tamil, and Malayalam. Every comment was categorized in one of three classes hope speech, not hope speech, and not in intended language. On the English dataset, the best performing model was *2-parallel CNN-LSTM* with GloVe and Word2Vec embeddings and it reported weighted F1 0.91 and 0.90 for development and test set respectively. Similarly, the best performing model of Tamil and Malayalam was *3-parallel Bi-LSTM*. For Tamil it reported weighted F1 0.56 and 0.54 on development and test dataset respectively. Similarly, for Malayalam, the reported weighted F1 was 0.78 and 0.79 on the development and test dataset.

References

Flor Miriam Plaza-del Arco, M Dolores Molina-González, L Alfonso Ureña-López, and M Teresa Martín-Valdivia. 2021. Comparing pre-trained language models for spanish hate speech detection. *Expert Systems with Applications*, 166:114120.

Mohit Bhardwaj, Md Shad Akhtar, Asif Ekbal, Amitava Das, and Tanmoy Chakraborty. 2020. Hostility detection dataset in hindi. *arXiv preprint arXiv:2011.03588*.

Bharathi Raja Chakravarthi. 2020. HopeEDI: A multilingual hope speech detection dataset for equality, diversity, and inclusion. In *Proceedings of the Third Workshop on Computational Modeling of People's Opinions, Personality, and Emotion's in Social Media*, pages 41–53, Barcelona, Spain (Online). Association for Computational Linguistics.

Bharathi Raja Chakravarthi and Vigneshwaran Muralidaran. 2021. Findings of the shared task on Hope Speech Detection for Equality, Diversity, and Inclusion. In *Proceedings of the First Workshop on Lan-*

guage Technology for Equality, Diversity and Inclusion. Association for Computational Linguistics.

Thomas Davidson, Dana Warmsley, Michael Macy, and Ingmar Weber. 2017. Automated hate speech detection and the problem of offensive language. *arXiv preprint arXiv:1703.04009*.

Jong Hyup Lee, Sun Ho Jung, and JaeHong Park. 2017. The role of entropy of review text sentiments on online wom and movie box office sales. *Electronic Commerce Research and Applications*, 22:42–52.

Alexander Pak and Patrick Paroubek. 2010. Twitter as a corpus for sentiment analysis and opinion mining. In *LREc*, volume 10, pages 1320–1326.

Georgios K Pitsilis, Heri Ramampiaro, and Helge Langseth. 2018. Effective hate-speech detection in twitter data using recurrent neural networks. *Applied Intelligence*, 48(12):4730–4742.

Sunil Saumya and Jyoti Prakash Singh. 2018. Detection of spam reviews: a sentiment analysis approach. *Csi Transactions on ICT*, 6(2):137–148.

Inna Vogel and Peter Jiang. 2019. Fake news detection with the new german dataset "germanfakenc". In *International Conference on Theory and Practice of Digital Libraries*, pages 288–295. Springer.

IRNLP_DAIICT@LT-EDI-EACL2021: Hope Speech detection in Code Mixed text using TF-IDF Char N-grams and MuRIL

Bhargav Dave
DA-IICT / Gandhinagar, India
bhargavdave1@gmail.com

Shripad Bhat
DA-IICT / Gandhinagar, India
shripadbhat30@gmail.com

Prasenjit Majumder
DA-IICT / Gandhinagar, India
prasenjit.majumder@gmail.com

Abstract

This paper presents the participation of the IRNLP_DAIICT team from Information Retrieval and Natural Language Processing lab at DA-IICT, India in LT-EDI@EACL2021 Hope Speech Detection task. The aim of this shared task is to identify hope speech from a code-mixed data-set of YouTube comments. The task is to classify comments into Hope Speech, Non Hope speech or Not in language, for three languages: English, Malayalam-English and Tamil-English. We use TF-IDF character n-grams and pretrained MuRIL embeddings for text representation and Logistic Regression and Linear SVM for classification. Our best approach achieved second, eighth and fifth rank with weighted F1 score of 0.92, 0.75 and 0.57 in English, Malayalam-English and Tamil-English on test dataset respectively. Our code is publicly available here[1].

1 Introduction

Hope can defined as a belief that the current situation would change for the better. It is vital for everyone since it helps in continuing our efforts even in difficult and unfavourable circumstances. It also encourages us to continuously improve our lives by thinking of a better future and take actions to achieve it.

In recent years social media has become one of the important aspect of our lives. People convey their opinions openly on social media on various topics. Understanding and analysing these opinions through Natural Language Processing techniques has been an active research area. Offensive content detection and classification on social media has been studied extensively. Hence, research should also focus on identifying positive online content that is encouraging and supportive. Thus identifying Hope speech in social media is an important task to gauge the opinion of people in tough times like COVID-19.

The goal of this shared task is to identify hope speech from a code-mixed dataset of comments of Dravidian Languages collected from YouTube. Shared task was introduced as three class classification of the YouTube comments into Hope Speech, Non Hope speech or Not in language, for three languages: English, Malayalam-English and Tamil-English. Shared task organizers define Hope speech as a text that offers support, reassurance, suggestions, inspiration and insight specifically in YouTube comments. The shared task focuses on hope speech for women in STEM, LGBTIQ individuals, racial minorities or people with disabilities in general for equality, diversity and inclusion (Chakravarthi and Muralidaran, 2021).

Our approaches consists of TF-IDF character n-grams and MuRIL embeddings for the text representation and Logistic Regression and Linear SVM for classification.

The remainder of this paper is organized as follows: the next section includes related work followed by Section 4 which describes the shared task dataset and Methods are presented in Section 4. Results and Analysis is given in final Section 5 and Section 6 present Conclusion.

2 Related Work

Social media content analysis is an active research area with tasks like Hate speech detection, Offensive language detection, etc. Some of the shared tasks organised recently for these are HASOC Track at FIRE[2] 2019, 2020 (Mandl et al., 2019, 2020) and OffensEval 2019, 2020 (Zampieri et al., 2019, 2020). Most popular methods of OffensE-

[1] https://github.com/bhargav25dave1996/IRNLP_DAIICT_LT-EDI-EACL2021

[2] http://fire.irsi.res.in

Proceedings of the First Workshop on Language Technology for Equality, Diversity and Inclusion, pages 114–117
April 19, 2021.

Label	English			Malayalam			Tamil		
	Train	Dev	Test	Train	Dev	Test	Train	Dev	Test
Not-Hope	20778	2569	2593	6205	784	776	7872	998	946
Hope Speech	1962	272	250	1668	190	194	6327	757	815
Not-in-language	22	2	3	691	96	101	1961	263	259
Total	22762	2843	2846	8564	1070	1071	16160	2018	2020

Table 1: Hope Speech Detection shared task Dataset Statistics

val (Zampieri et al., 2020) were pretrained embeddings like BERT (Devlin et al., 2019), ROBERTa (Liu et al., 2019) and ELMo (Peters et al., 2018). Best performing methods in HASOC (Mandl et al., 2020) Track use multilingual transformer based methods like XLM-ROBERTa, mBERT, etc and fine tune them for the task. TF-IDF along with Character n-grams and machine learning classifiers like Logistic Regression, SVM and XGboost also performed well and equivalent to deep learning classifiers in some of the tasks.

Hope speech detection shared task focuses on positive instead of negative comments/posts in social media. Hope speech has been to proven to be useful (Herrestad and Biong, 2010) for saving people from self harm and suicide. It has inspired people to demand rights for equality, diversity and inclusion (Chakravarthi, 2020).

3 Dataset

Hope Speech Detection shared task organizers provide datasets in three languages English, Malayalam-English and Tamil-English (Chakravarthi and Muralidaran, 2021). Dataset has been curated from Youtube comments that have been collected are pertaining to women in STEM, LGBTQ, COVID-19 and Black Lives Matters topics, using the YouTube Comment Scraper [3]. It contains 28451 comments in English, 20198 in Tamil and 10705 in Malayalam. Full statistic of dataset given in Table 1.

4 Methods

For all the YouTube comments we first preprocess the text and then create a text representation and finally classify the text using the machine learning classifiers. Figure 1 illustrates the set of steps used to classify the YouTube comments.

[3]https://github.com/philbot9/youtube-comment-scraper

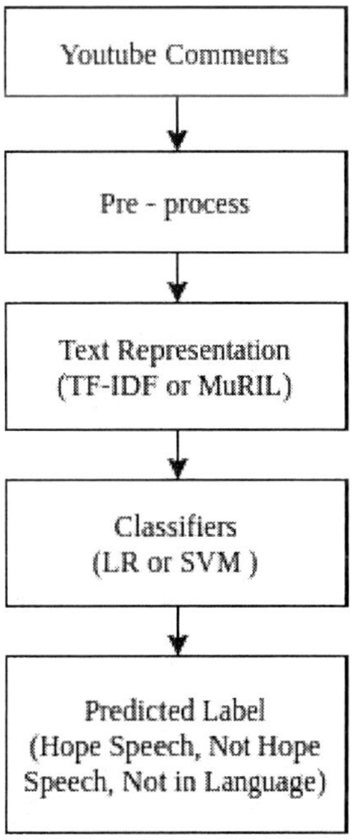

Figure 1: Steps involved in classification of Hope Speech

4.1 Pre-Processing

Since there is a lot of noise in the social media text we perform the following preprocessing operations. URL's, user mentions of the form @user, emojis, digits and punctuations is removed from the text. For English dataset, stopwords are removed and the text is lowercased.

4.2 Text representation and classifiers

Representation of the text is one of the fundamental tasks in Natural language processing. We explore two representation techniques: TF-IDF and MuRIL. TF-IDF is a very popular text representation technique which takes into account the frequency of the word in a given document and the number of documents in which a word is present. We employ Scikit-learn TF-IDF vectorizer API for obtaining the text representation. Instead of word based TF-IDF representation we make use of character n-grams based TF-IDF representation (TF-IDF (Char)) so as to effectively capture morphological variations of the words.

MuRIL[4] (Multilingual Representations for Indian Languages) is a transformer based language model trained on 17 Indian languages on self-supervised masked language modeling task. MuRIL training consists of translation and transliteration segment pairs in addition to the standard training used in Multilingual BERT. Pretrained MuRIL model is used to obtain the text representation in the form vectors of 768 dimension.

Logistic Regression (LR) and Linear SVM classifiers have been used to perform the classification of the text. The choice of the classifiers is based on the fact that they are simple, computationally inexpensive and interpretable. Scikit-learn API has been used to implement the classification task. So the four approaches we have used are TF-IDF (Char) + LR, TF-IDF(Char) + SVM, MuRIL + LR and MuRIL + SVM for each language.

5 Results and Analysis

The submission evaluation on the test data of all the three languages is shown in tables 2, 3, 4. It can be seen from the tables that our best method have been able to beat the baseline in all the three languages. Our methods achieve second, eighth and fifth rank in English, Malayalam and Tamil respectively. For English and Tamil language, TF-IDF (Char) + LR achieves the best results with weighted F1 score of 0.92 and 0.57 respectively. For the Malayalam language task, TF-IDF (Char) + SVM achieves the best weighted F1 score of 0.75.

Model	**W-Avg F1-score**
Baseline	0.90
TF-IDF (Char) + LR	**0.92**
TF-IDF (Char) + SVM	0.90
MuRIL + LR	0.87
MuRIL + SVM	0.87

Table 2: Results for the English on test dataset.

It can be observed that MuRIL is not performing good particularly in case of Tamil language. In all the languages TF-IDF character n-grams representation performed better than MuRIL. Although the training data for Tamil is higher and also balanced as compared to Malayalam, the weighted F1 score obtained for Malayalam is better than Tamil. Hence a larger dataset might not always give better results.

[4]https://tfhub.dev/google/MuRIL/1

Model	**W-Avg F1-score**
Baseline	0.73
TF-IDF (Char) + LR	0.72
TF-IDF(Char) + SVM	**0.75**
MuRIL + LR	0.61
MuRIL + SVM	0.61

Table 3: Results for the Malayalam on test dataset.

Model	W-Avg F1-score
Baseline	0.56
TF-IDF (Char) + LR	**0.57**
TF-IDF(Char) + SVM	0.56
MuRIL + LR	0.30
MuRIL + SVM	0.30

Table 4: Results for the Tamil on test dataset.

6 Conclusion and Future work

The details of our submission in Hope speech detection task have been presented in the paper. By exploring TF-IDF character n-grams and MuRIL to represent the text, we conclude that the former method is consistently performing better in all the three languages. The weighted F1 score for Tamil language is relatively lesser as compared to English and Malayalam which leads us to conclude that it is a difficult to identify in Hope speech in Tamil.

We have not explored deep learning based architectures like CNN, LSTM and Transformers for classification of Hope speech. These approaches could be a future direction for the researchers to improve the results.

Acknowledgments

We would like to thank the Hope Speech detection task organizers for giving us the opportunity to work on a new task. We also like to acknowledge the IRNLP lab at DAIICT, Gandhinagar for their contribution.

References

Bharathi Raja Chakravarthi. 2020. HopeEDI: A multilingual hope speech detection dataset for equality, diversity, and inclusion. In *Proceedings of the Third Workshop on Computational Modeling of People's*

Opinions, Personality, and Emotion's in Social Media, pages 41–53, Barcelona, Spain (Online). Association for Computational Linguistics.

Bharathi Raja Chakravarthi and Vigneshwaran Muralidaran. 2021. Findings of the shared task on Hope Speech Detection for Equality, Diversity, and Inclusion. In *Proceedings of the First Workshop on Language Technology for Equality, Diversity and Inclusion*. Association for Computational Linguistics.

Jacob Devlin, Ming-Wei Chang, Kenton Lee, and Kristina Toutanova. 2019. BERT: Pre-training of deep bidirectional transformers for language understanding. In *Proceedings of the 2019 Conference of the North American Chapter of the Association for Computational Linguistics: Human Language Technologies, Volume 1 (Long and Short Papers)*, pages 4171–4186, Minneapolis, Minnesota. Association for Computational Linguistics.

Henning Herrestad and Stian Biong. 2010. Relational hopes: A study of the lived experience of hope in some patients hospitalized for intentional self-harm. *International Journal of Qualitative Studies on Health and Well-being*, 5(1):4651. PMID: 20640026.

Yinhan Liu, Myle Ott, Naman Goyal, Jingfei Du, Mandar Joshi, Danqi Chen, Omer Levy, Mike Lewis, Luke Zettlemoyer, and Veselin Stoyanov. 2019. Roberta: A robustly optimized bert pretraining approach. *arXiv preprint arXiv:1907.11692*.

Thomas Mandl, Sandip Modha, Anand Kumar M, and Bharathi Raja Chakravarthi. 2020. Overview of the hasoc track at fire 2020: Hate speech and offensive language identification in tamil, malayalam, hindi, english and german. In *Forum for Information Retrieval Evaluation*, FIRE 2020, page 29–32, New York, NY, USA. Association for Computing Machinery.

Thomas Mandl, Sandip Modha, Prasenjit Majumder, Daksh Patel, Mohana Dave, Chintak Mandlia, and Aditya Patel. 2019. Overview of the hasoc track at fire 2019: Hate speech and offensive content identification in indo-european languages. In *Proceedings of the 11th Forum for Information Retrieval Evaluation*, FIRE '19, page 14–17, New York, NY, USA. Association for Computing Machinery.

Matthew Peters, Mark Neumann, Mohit Iyyer, Matt Gardner, Christopher Clark, Kenton Lee, and Luke Zettlemoyer. 2018. Deep contextualized word representations. In *Proceedings of the 2018 Conference of the North American Chapter of the Association for Computational Linguistics: Human Language Technologies, Volume 1 (Long Papers)*, pages 2227–2237, New Orleans, Louisiana. Association for Computational Linguistics.

Marcos Zampieri, Shervin Malmasi, Preslav Nakov, Sara Rosenthal, Noura Farra, and Ritesh Kumar. 2019. SemEval-2019 task 6: Identifying and categorizing offensive language in social media (OffensEval). In *Proceedings of the 13th International Workshop on Semantic Evaluation*, pages 75–86, Minneapolis, Minnesota, USA. Association for Computational Linguistics.

Marcos Zampieri, Preslav Nakov, Sara Rosenthal, Pepa Atanasova, Georgi Karadzhov, Hamdy Mubarak, Leon Derczynski, Zeses Pitenis, and Çağrı Çöltekin. 2020. SemEval-2020 task 12: Multilingual offensive language identification in social media (OffensEval 2020). In *Proceedings of the Fourteenth Workshop on Semantic Evaluation*, pages 1425–1447, Barcelona (online). International Committee for Computational Linguistics.

ZYJ@LT-EDI-EACL2021:XLM-RoBERTa-Based Model with Attention for Hope Speech Detection

Yingjia Zhao
Yunnan University/ Yunnan, P.R. China
zyj1309700118@gmail.com

Xin Tao
Yunnan University / Yunnan, P.R. China
taoxinwy@126.com

Abstract

Due to the development of modern computer technology and the increase in the number of online media users, we can see all kinds of posts and comments everywhere on the internet. Hope speech can not only inspire the creators but also make other viewers pleasant. It is necessary to effectively and automatically detect hope speech. This paper describes the approach of our team in the task of hope speech detection. We use the attention mechanism to adjust the weight of all the output layers of XLM-RoBERTa to make full use of the information extracted from each layer, and use the weighted sum of all the output layers to complete the classification task. And we use the Stratified-K-Fold method to enhance the training data set. We achieve a weighted average F1-score of 0.59, 0.84, and 0.92 for Tamil, Malayalam, and English language, ranked 3rd, 2nd, and 2nd.

1 Introduction

With the development of network media, people can express their opinions on the Internet at any time, among which there will be some hope speech. Hope speech will encourage people to stand firm in their beliefs and follow the path of their goals. At the same time, comments or posts containing hope speech can often contain factors such as Equality, Diversity, and Inclusion. They can also provide support, reassurance, suggestions, inspiration, and insight, etc., which can change people's emotions from negative to positive. The proportion of comments and posts on media platforms that contain hopeful statements can reflect the current emotional tendencies of online communities. As the proportion of words containing hope increases, the corresponding posts conveying negative emotions such as pessimism and despair will decrease, thus promoting social harmony. Because the network media platform needs to support multiple languages and faces users with different backgrounds, the multi-lingual, multi-modal, and non-standard writing style of online media posts makes it a very challenging task to effectively detect whether the comment or post belongs to the hope speech.

Our team participated the shared task on Hope Speech Detection for Equality, Diversity, and Inclusion at LT-EDI 2021- EACL 2021 (Chakravarthi, 2020; Chakravarthi and Muralidaran, 2021). The goal of this task is to identify whether a given comment contains hope speech or not. This is a comment/post level classification task. The task is divided into three sub-tasks based on three languages, namely English, Tamil, and Malayalam. Given a Youtube comment, the systems submitted by the participants should classify it into 'Hope speech', 'Not hope speech' and 'Not in intended language'.

In this task, we use XLM-RoBERTa as the base model to extract features and combine 12 layers of output with an embedding layer to do the classification task. In order to train the weight of each layer, we add an attention mechanism for the model. During the training, we process the training data through the Stratified-K-Fold method, each data set is trained to get the different weights, and finally, the best-predicted value is obtained through a voting mechanism. The rest of our paper is structured as follows. Section 2 describes the related work. Methods are described in Section 3. Experiments and results are described in Section 4. The conclusion is drawn in Section 5.

2 Related Work

While hope speech detection is a relatively new task, it can be categorized as a problem of sentiment analysis (Bakshi et al., 2016) and text classification. A great deal of work has been done by many researchers and practitioners from in-

Proceedings of the First Workshop on Language Technology for Equality, Diversity and Inclusion, pages 118–121
April 19, 2021.

dustry and academia. Turney (2002)proposed a simple unsupervised learning (Barlow, 1989) algorithm for classifying reviews as recommended or not recommended. Basiri et al. (2020)proposed an Attention-based Bidirectional CNN-RNN Deep Model (ABCDM) for polarity classification of long comments and short tweets, two independent bidirectional LSTM and GRU layers are used to extract past and future context by considering temporal information flow in both directions. Chen and Ke proposed a convolutional neural network-regional long short-term memory (CNN-RLSTM) that combines CNN and regional LSTM. At the sentence level (Kim and Hovy, 2004), the emotional information of the whole sentence is retained through CNN network, and through regional LSTM effectively distinguish between different target emotional polarity. Chen et al. proposed a multi-head attention-memory network (MNHMA) based on hierarchy for aspect-based sentiment analysis, which makes full use of the long-term semantic relationship of a given aspect term (Manandhar, 2014) in a sentence to reduce the loss of aspect information.

Wang et al. (2014) demonstrated the effectiveness of ensemble learning in sentiment analysis on ten publicly available datasets. Akhtar et al. (2017) proposed a cascade framework based on feature selection and classifier ensemble (Avidan, 2007). Particle swarm optimization algorithm is used for feature-based sentiment analysis. Because of the powerful performance of BERT (Devlin et al., 2018), it is natural to use it for sentiment analysis. Malhotra et al. proposed an efficacious transfer learning based ensemble model for sentiment analysis.

3 Methodology and Data

3.1 Data description

We make a statistic based on the data set provided by the organizer. We count the proportions of 'hope speech', 'not hope speech', and 'not in integrated language' in the training set and verification set. To make an intuitive observation, the statistical situation of three language datasets, English, Tamil, and Malayalam, are presented in one single table. As shown in Table 1.

3.2 XLM-RoBERTa with attention

In addition to the English dataset, this shared task also involves the training and classification of low-resource languages such as Tamil, and Malayalam.

	Label	Train	Dev
English	Hope speech	1960	272
	Not hope speech	20778	2569
	not-English	22	2
Malayalam	Hope speech	1668	190
	Not hope speech	6205	784
	not-Malayalam	691	96
Tamil	Hope speech	6327	757
	Not hope speech	7872	998
	not-Tamil	1961	263

Table 1: Train and Validation datasets description.

Therefore, XLM-RoBERTa, a pretraining enhancement model based on multiple languages, is undoubtedly the best choice. To further improve the performance of the model, we add a specific network structure based on XLM-RoBERTa. Since the output of each layer of XLM-RoBERTa contains different information, we combine the 12 layers of its output with the embedding layer to do the classification task. To adjust the weight of each layer, the attention mechanism is used to train the weight of each layer. Finally, the weighted sum of all layers is input into the classifier for the classification task, as shown in Figure 1.

4 Experiment and results

4.1 Data preprocessing

Since many words and symbols on social media are useless and sentence expression is not standardized enough, in order to extract useful features more effectively and reduce interference during training the model, we need to clean the text in the training data set with NLTK (Loper and Bird, 2002) tool. We perform the following preprocessing steps.

- **Remove Emoticons.** Text data contains a lot of emoticons. Emoticons increase the number of unknown words and reduce training effects. Emoticons are replaced by emotional words with their own meanings.
- **Convert Abbreviations.** All abbreviations are converted to complete parts. For English datasets, this helps the machine understand the meaning of words (e.g. "there's" becomes 'there' and 'are').
- **Remove Stop Word.** For English datasets, the stop words are meaningless words, such as'

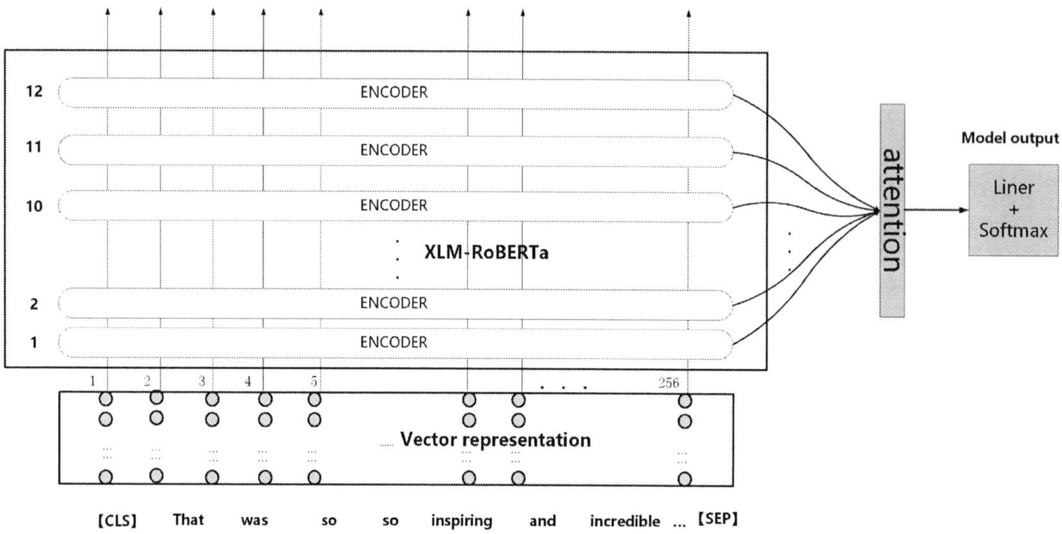

Figure 1: Schematic overview of the architecture of our model

is' /' our '/' the' /' in '/'at' etc. They don't add much meaning to the sentence. Single stop words are very frequent words. To reduce the number of vocabularies we have to deal with, and thus reduce the complexity of subsequent programs, we need to clear out stop words.

- **Stemming and Lemmatization.** For English datasets, to further simplify the textual data, we can standardize the different variations and inflections of words. Stemming extraction is the process of reducing a word to its stem or root. For example 'branching'/' branched '/' branches', can all be reduced to 'branch'. This helps reduce complexity while retaining the basic meaning of the word. For example, the suffixes 'ing' and 'ed'can be discarded;'ies' can be replaced by 'y' and so on. This may result in an incomplete word stem, but only as long as all forms of the word are reduced to the same stem. So they all have the same fundamental meaning.

4.2 Stratified-K-Fold method

Before training, we use the Stratified-K-fold method to process the dataset. The core of Stratified-K-Fold is to ensure stratified sampling. It needs to ensure that the ratio of all kinds of samples in test sets and training sets is the same as in the original data set, namely k-fold crossover segmentation. In the initial training set, each type of data is divided into k sub samples, one single subsample is reserved as the data of validation model, and the other k-1 samples are used for training. Finally, we get the final output from k results based on the voting (Onan et al., 2016) method.

maximum sequence length	learning rate
256	2e-5
Stratified-K-Fold number	**batch size**
5	4

Table 2: Details of the parameters

4.3 Experiment setting

In this experiment, XLM-RoBERTa-base pre-trained model is used. On the basis of the pre-training model, we add the attention mechanism to adjust the structure of the whole model. Then we began to train the model. The batch size is set to 4, the max sequence length is set to 256, the learning rate is set to 2e-5, and the Stratified-K-Fold number is set to 5. As shown in Table 2.

4.4 Results

The results submitted by teams are evaluated with a weighted average F1-score. According to the leaderboard provided by the organizer, our team's F1-score is 0.59, ranked 3rd place for the Tamil language. For the Malayalam language, our team's F1-score is 0.84 ranked 2nd place, and for the English language, our team's F1-score is 0.92 ranked 2nd place. As shown in Table 3.

	Best F1-score	Our Precision	Our Recall	Our F1-score	Rank
Tamil	0.61	0.59	0.59	**0.59**	3rd
Malayalam	0.85	0.84	0.84	**0.84**	2nd
English	0.93	0.92	0.93	**0.92**	2nd

Table 3

5 Conclusion

In this paper, we present our work in the task of hope speech detection for Tamil, Malayalam, and English language. Our team uses a model based on XLM-RoBERTa. This model uses an attention mechanism to adjust the weight of each output layer, makes full use of the information extracted from each layer to complete the classification task, and the Stratified-K-Fold method is used to enhance the training data. Finally, the model we submit achieves significant performance for all three languages. For future work, we will further optimize our model to achieve better results.

References

Md Shad Akhtar, Deepak Gupta, Asif Ekbal, and Pushpak Bhattacharyya. 2017. Feature selection and ensemble construction: A two-step method for aspect based sentiment analysis. *Knowledge-Based Systems*, 125:116–135.

Shai Avidan. 2007. Ensemble tracking. *IEEE transactions on pattern analysis and machine intelligence*, 29(2):261–271.

Rushlene Kaur Bakshi, Navneet Kaur, Ravneet Kaur, and Gurpreet Kaur. 2016. Opinion mining and sentiment analysis. In *2016 3rd international conference on computing for sustainable global development (INDIACom)*, pages 452–455. IEEE.

Horace B Barlow. 1989. Unsupervised learning. *Neural computation*, 1(3):295–311.

Mohammad Ehsan Basiri, Shahla Nemati, Moloud Abdar, Erik Cambria, and U Rajendra Acharya. 2020. Abcdm: An attention-based bidirectional cnn-rnn deep model for sentiment analysis. *Future Generation Computer Systems*, 115:279–294.

Bharathi Raja Chakravarthi. 2020. HopeEDI: A multilingual hope speech detection dataset for equality, diversity, and inclusion. In *Proceedings of the Third Workshop on Computational Modeling of People's Opinions, Personality, and Emotion's in Social Media*, pages 41–53, Barcelona, Spain (Online). Association for Computational Linguistics.

Bharathi Raja Chakravarthi and Vigneshwaran Muralidaran. 2021. Findings of the shared task on Hope Speech Detection for Equality, Diversity, and Inclusion. In *Proceedings of the First Workshop on Language Technology for Equality, Diversity and Inclusion*. Association for Computational Linguistics.

Ke Chen and Wende Ke. A hierarchical neural model for target-based sentiment analysis. *Concurrency and Computation: Practice and Experience*, page e6184.

Yuzhong Chen, Tianhao Zhuang, and Kun Guo. Memory network with hierarchical multi-head attention for aspect-based sentiment analysis. *Applied Intelligence*, pages 1–18.

Jacob Devlin, Ming-Wei Chang, Kenton Lee, and Kristina Toutanova. 2018. Bert: Pre-training of deep bidirectional transformers for language understanding. *arXiv preprint arXiv:1810.04805*.

Soo-Min Kim and Eduard Hovy. 2004. Determining the sentiment of opinions. In *COLING 2004: Proceedings of the 20th International Conference on Computational Linguistics*, pages 1367–1373.

Edward Loper and Steven Bird. 2002. Nltk: The natural language toolkit. *arXiv preprint cs/0205028*.

Shivani Malhotra, Vinay Kumar, and Alpana Agarwal. Bidirectional transfer learning model for sentiment analysis of natural language. *Journal of Ambient Intelligence and Humanized Computing*, pages 1–21.

Suresh Manandhar. 2014. Semeval-2014 task 4: aspect based sentiment analysis. In *Proceedings of the 8th international workshop on semantic evaluation (SemEval 2014)*.

Aytuğ Onan, Serdar Korukoğlu, and Hasan Bulut. 2016. A multiobjective weighted voting ensemble classifier based on differential evolution algorithm for text sentiment classification. *Expert Systems with Applications*, 62:1–16.

Peter D Turney. 2002. Thumbs up or thumbs down? semantic orientation applied to unsupervised classification of reviews. *arXiv preprint cs/0212032*.

Gang Wang, Jianshan Sun, Jian Ma, Kaiquan Xu, and Jibao Gu. 2014. Sentiment classification: The contribution of ensemble learning. *Decision support systems*, 57:77–93.

TEAM HUB@LT-EDI-EACL2021: Hope Speech Detection Based On Pre-trained Language Model

Bo Huang
School of Information Science
and Engineering Yunnan University,
Yunnan, P.R. China
hublucashb@gmail.com

Yang Bai
School of Information Science
and Engineering Yunnan University,
Yunnan, P.R. China
baiyang.top@gmail.com

Abstract

This article introduces the system description of TEAM _HUB team participating in LT-EDI 2021: Hope Speech Detection. This shared task is the first task related to the desired voice detection. The data set in the shared task consists of three different languages (English, Tamil, and Malayalam). The task type is text classification. Based on the analysis and understanding of the task description and data set, we designed a system based on a pre-trained language model to complete this shared task. In this system, we use methods and models that combine the XLM-RoBERTa pre-trained language model and the Tf-Idf algorithm. In the final result ranking announced by the task organizer, our system obtained F1 scores of 0.93, 0.84, 0.59 on the English dataset, Malayalam dataset, and Tamil dataset. Our submission results are ranked 1, 2, and 3 respectively.

1 Introduction and Background

According to relevant statistics, as of 2020, the number of people active in social media worldwide has reached 3.6 billion. Based on the analysis of the current growth rate, in the next 5 years, the total number of social media users will be 1.3 times the current number (Clement, 2020). The COVID-19 virus began to spread globally in 2019, and so far, more than 200 countries and regions have been affected by the epidemic to varying degrees. The number of fake news and negative comments circulating on online social media is 9 times the usual (Bhardwaj et al., 2020). In the past few years, eliminating abusive and hate speech in online social media comments has been widely used on various social media platforms. Most of these elimination systems are developed for languages with richer corpus resources, such as Chinese, Spanish, English, etc. (Malmasi and Zampieri, 2017a; Fortuna and Nunes, 2018; Chetty and Alathur, 2018; Pereira-Kohatsu et al., 2019). There is not much work on Hope Speech detection For example, Chakravarthi et al. developed a data set of hope speech to complete the recognition of Hope Speech in online social media (Chakravarthi, 2020).

The task goal proposed by the task organizer team of "Shared Task on Hope Speech Detection for Equality, Diversity and Inclusion" is to identify the content of posts related to *Hope speech*, *Not hope speech*, and *Not in intended language* from the dataset of hope speech obtained on YouTube (Chakravarthi, 2020; Chakravarthi and Muralidaran, 2021). So this sharing task is a comment/post level classification task. Also, this is the first task of identifying hopeful speeches for equality, diversity, and inclusiveness in a multilingual environment. The annotation data set we get contains three different languages (English, Malayalam, and Tamil).

In recent studies in the field of natural language processing(NLP), the pre-trained language model can achieve state-of-the-art results in many NLP tasks (Wang et al., 2019). Also, combined with the task description and the multilingual characteristics of the data set, in terms of model and method selection, we chose to use fine-tuned XLM-RoBERTa (Conneau et al., 2019) to complete our task. We have not done much work on data preprocessing. Our work focuses mainly on how to reduce the impact of multi-language and mixed code on the results. This is also a difficult problem that needs to be solved in this shared task. Therefore, in the method, we consider combining the semantic information of Term Frequency-Inverse Document Frequency (Tf-Idf) and XLM-RoBERTa. Then use Inception blocks (Szegedy et al., 2015) as the shared layer to learn the output information of Tf-Idf and XLM-RoBERTa. Then use this combined model to train on the training set of this task to get the

Proceedings of the First Workshop on Language Technology for Equality, Diversity and Inclusion, pages 122–127
April 19, 2021.

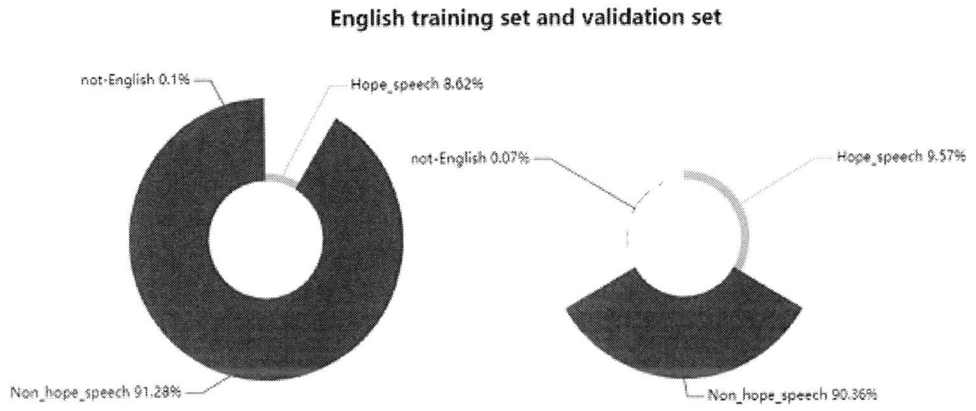

Figure 1: Labels distribution of English training set and validation set. In the training set, Non hope speech: 91.28%, Hope speech: 8.62%, Not English: 0.1%. In the validation set, Non hope speech: 90.36%, Hope speech: 9.57%, Not English: 0.07%.

trained weights. Finally, the trained weights are used to predict the result of the test set.

2 Related Work

So far, many organizations and teams have invested in the identification of negative content on social media platforms and have achieved some good results (Zampieri et al., 2020; Rangel et al., 2020; Chakravarthi et al., 2020; Malmasi and Zampieri, 2017b).

However, combined with our previous analysis, it is not difficult to know that just identifying negative content in social media is not complete. Because not only do we need to avoid negative information in our lives, we also need more positive and hopeful information (Chang, 2017). Some recent studies and reports have also revealed to us the importance of hope and the impact of hopelessness (Eslami et al., 2017; Hernandez and Overholser, 2020; Ranzadeh and Arsh Akmal, 2020). There is not much research and work on Hope Speech detection, but the recent research and results of Hope Speech detection by Palakodety et al. have revealed to us that Hope Speech detection has begun to attract the attention of the academic community (Palakodety et al., 2019).

Chakravarthi et al. used Support vector machine (SVM), Naive Bayesian (NB), k-nearest neighbors (KNN), Decision Tree (DT), Logistic Regression (LR), and other methods on the hope speech data set to get good results (Chakravarthi, 2020). Combine their work on the hope speech data set and the code-mixing in the data set in this task. We chose a pre-trained language model(XLM-RoBERTa) that is currently widely used in the field of natural language processing and fine-tuned it to complete the task.

3 Data And Methods

3.1 Data Description and Analysis

The task description shows us that the data used in the task comes from some comments and posts on YouTube. The data set contains three languages (English, Malayalam, and Tamil) training set and a validation set.

- **Hope_speech**: The comments express the praise of love, courage, interpersonal skills, beauty, perseverance, forgiveness, tolerance, future consciousness, and talent and wisdom. Comments that promote harmony, beauty, tolerance, and bring positive effects to people.
- **Non_Hope_speech**: The comments contain prejudices, attacks on individuals, anti-humanity, racial discrimination, and other content that cannot make readers feel hopeful.
- **Not_English, Not_Malayalam, Not_Tamil**: There are languages other than English, Malayalam, or Tamil in the data set of languages English, Malayalam, and Tamil. For example, there are comments posted in the language Tamil in the English data set.

Malayalam training set and validation set

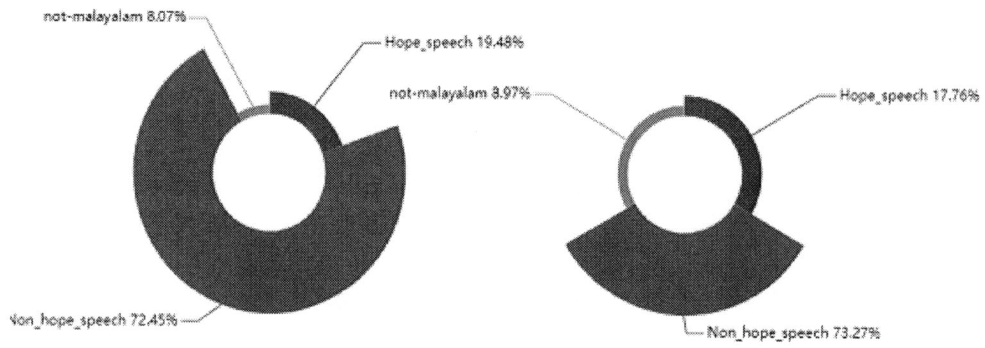

Figure 2: Labels distribution of Malayalam training set and validation set. In the training set, Non hope speech: 72.45%, Hope speech: 19.48%, Not Malayalam: 8.07%. In the validation set, Non hope speech: 73.27%, Hope speech: 17.76%, Not Malayalam: 8.97%.

On three different language data sets, the distribution probability of the number of labels on the training set and the validation set in each language data set is similar. Besides, in the three different language data sets, the data quantity distribution of the three different labels is very unbalanced. In particular, the number of the three labels Not_English (training set 0.1%, validation set 0.07%), Not_Malayalam (training set 8.07%, validation set 8.97%), Not_Tamil (training set 12.14%, validation set 13.03%) is very small in the English, Malayalam, and Tamil data sets. In the data sets of these three languages, the largest value of the labeling ratio in the data set of each language is the Non_Hope_speech label, which accounts for half of the total data volume, or much greater than half of the total data volume.

In addition to the above-mentioned feature of unbalanced data distribution for each label, the task data set also has a big feature that there is some code-mixing language data. Code-mixing language means that a post may be composed of two or more languages. Because users who use social media platforms have different cultural backgrounds and language habits, and posts on social media have no restrictions on grammar and text content structure, the result is a large number of code-mixing languages appearing on social media (Gupta et al., 2018). For us, in addition to data imbalance, code-mixing language is also one of the difficulties we have to face.

3.2 Methods

Based on our previous analysis of the task description and task data, combined with the characteristics of the pre-training language model, the pre-training language model we chose in this task is the XLM-RoBERTa model.

The structure of the XLM-RoBERTa pre-training language model can be seen as a combination of the XLM model and the RoBERTa model (Liu et al., 2019b). The structure of RoBERTa and BERT are all improvements from the Encoder part of the Transformer. Transformer has achieved good results on multiple tasks in the natural language field because of the addition of the Attention mechanism (Vaswani et al., 2017). Compared with Bert, RoBERTa deletes the task of predicting the next sentence in the pre-training stage, and also uses a new dynamic Masking mechanism. In terms of training data sets, XLM-RoBERTa uses a corpus of more than 100 different languages that is larger than the multilingual BERT. Therefore, XLM-RoBERTa's performance in the pre-training phase and certain downstream tasks is better than BERT. Besides, it is also superior to multilingual BERT in terms of cross-language functions.

To alleviate the undesirable effects of code-mixing on the results, we introduce Tf-Idf in our method. Use Tf-idf to weigh with the output of the last layer of XLM-RoBERTa to get a weighted output. Then input this weighted output and the output of the last layer of XLM-RoBERTa into the same Inception block. Use convolution kernels of

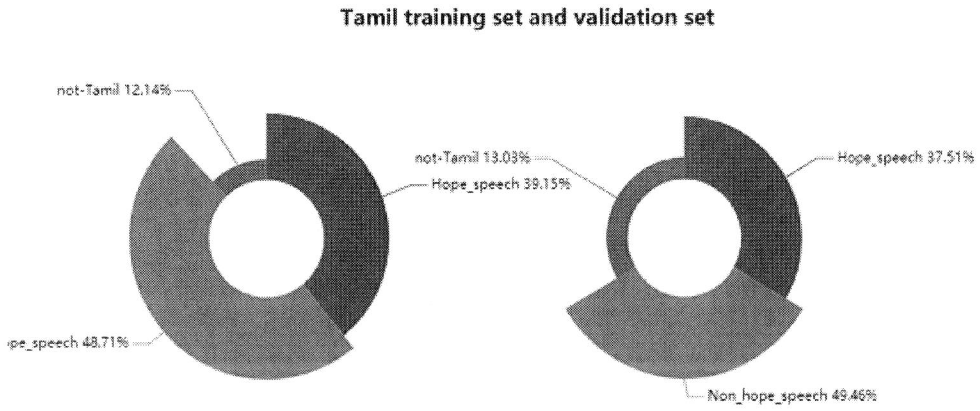

Figure 3: Labels distribution of Tamil training set and validation set. In the training set, Not hope speech: 48.71%, Hope speech: 39.15%, Not Tamil: 12.14%. In the validation set, Not hope speech: 49.46%, Hope speech: 37.51%, Not Tamil: 13.03%.

different sizes in the Inception block to capture semantic information of different lengths. So in this model, the inception block can be seen as a module with shared parameters. Use this module to learn the output of XLM-RoBERTa and the weighted semantic information of Tf-Idf. Finally, the output of the Inception module is obtained and input into the classifier to obtain the prediction result of the model. Compared with the sequence structure of LSTM, CNN can better identify the semantic information of a post on a social media platform. Because the order of some words in YouTube will be changed by various noises. At the same time, CNN structure will have better performance than serialized LSTM in training time. The structure of the model can be seen in Figure 4.

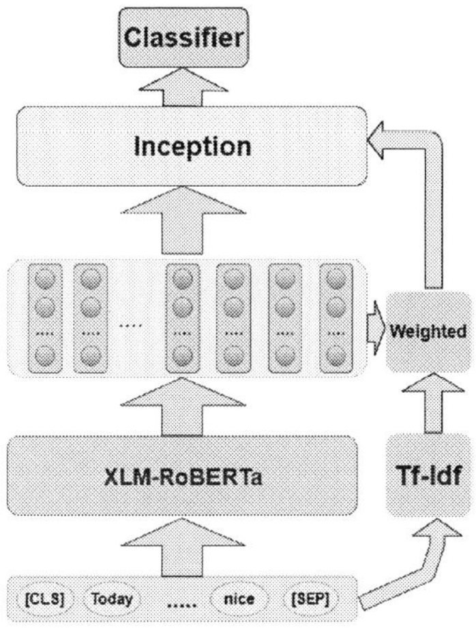

Figure 4: The model structure we used in this task.

4 Experiment and Results

4.1 Data Preprocessing

In terms of data preprocessing, our work is mainly focused on the corresponding Tf-Idf encoding from each language data set using the Tf-Idf algorithm. We merge the training set, and validation set of each language. Then use the Tf-Idf algorithm to get the Tf-Idf code of the sentence. Delete the Tf-Idf codes larger than the maximum sentence length, and perform zero-filling operations on the Tf-Idf codes smaller than the maximum sentence length. Finally, the processed Tf-Idf code is input into the model and combined with the output of XLM-RoBERTa.

4.2 Experiment setting

In the choice of the pre-training model XLM-RoBERTa, we use the XLM-RoBERTa-base pre-training language model composed of a 12-layer Encoder[1]. The structure of Inception we use is the solution implemented by Szegedy et. (Szegedy et al., 2015). Besides, because we are dealing with text data, the Conv1d convolution provided by Pytorch is used in the Inception block[2]. Combined with our previous analysis of the task and data, we choose CrossEntropyLoss in the loss function. We use Radam as the optimizer (Liu et al., 2019a). Because the data set category distribution of each

[1]https://huggingface.co/xlm-roberta-base/tree/main
[2]https://pytorch.org/

Language	F1 Score	Precision	Recall
English	0.93	0.93	0.93
Malayalam	0.85	0.85	0.85
Tamil	0.62	0.62	0.64

Table 1: The result of our model and method on the validation set provided by the task organizer.

Language	F1 Score	Precision	Recall
English	0.93	0.93	0.93
Malayalam	0.84	0.84	0.85
Tamil	0.59	0.61	0.61

Table 2: The results of our model and method on the test set. The score of the test set comes from the ranking list announced by the task organizer.

language is different, we set different hyperparameters for each language task. The parameters used in our experiments are all parameter combinations verified on the validation set.

- **English task**: The learning rate of XLM-RoBERTa is set to 3e-5, and the learning rate of the Inception block and linear classifier is set to 2e-4. The maximum sentence length is set to 65. Epoch and batch size are set to 5 and 32 respectively.
- **Malayalam task**: The learning rate of XLM-RoBERTa is set to 4e-5, and the learning rate of the Inception block and linear classifier is set to 1e-4. The maximum sentence length is set to 70. Epoch and batch size are set to 5 and 32 respectively.
- **Tamil task**: The learning rate of XLM-RoBERTa is set to 3e-5, and the learning rate of the Inception block and linear classifier is set to 1e-4. The maximum sentence length is set to 70. Epoch and batch size are set to 4 and 32 respectively.

4.3 Analysis of Results

The scores of each team on the test set announced by the task organizer team are ranked using weighted average F1-score. At the same time, the scores of the two evaluation indicators Precision and Recall are also announced.

Compare the contents of Table 1 and Table 2, the scores(F1 Score, Precision, Recall) of our model and method on the validation set are the same as those on the test set. By comparing the result score on the validation set with the score result on the test set, it is not difficult to find that there is a gap between the result score on the Tamil validation set and the result score on the test set. The scores of the validation set and the test set of the other two languages are very consistent. Among the three different languages, our model and method ranked first in the English task ranking, second in the Malayalam language task ranking, and third in the Tamil language task ranking.

5 Conclusion

In this task, our team used the XLM-RoBERTa model with cross-language capabilities as the basis and combined it with the Tf-Idf algorithm to complete this task. Our experimental results confirm the effectiveness of our method, and at the same time find the problem of our method and parameter settings on the Tamil language task data set. Our work in the data preprocessing part is not detailed enough. We ignore the influence of stop words, emoticons, and other special symbols on the results. This is a flaw in our work. In future work, we will make up for the shortcomings of our work in this task and improve our methods. Besides, we will continue to pay attention to the progress of related work on low-resource language communities, and the progress of hope speeches in the field of natural language processing.

References

Mohit Bhardwaj, Md Shad Akhtar, Asif Ekbal, Amitava Das, and Tanmoy Chakraborty. 2020. Hostility detection dataset in hindi. *arXiv preprint arXiv:2011.03588.*

Bharathi Raja Chakravarthi. 2020. HopeEDI: A multilingual hope speech detection dataset for equality, diversity, and inclusion. In *Proceedings of the Third Workshop on Computational Modeling of People's Opinions, Personality, and Emotion's in Social Media*, pages 41–53, Barcelona, Spain (Online). Association for Computational Linguistics.

Bharathi Raja Chakravarthi and Vigneshwaran Muralidaran. 2021. Findings of the shared task on Hope Speech Detection for Equality, Diversity, and Inclusion. In *Proceedings of the First Workshop on Language Technology for Equality, Diversity and Inclusion*. Association for Computational Linguistics.

BR Chakravarthi, R Priyadharshini, V Muralidaran, S Suryawanshi, N Jose, E Sherly, and JP McCrae. 2020. Overview of the track on sentiment analysis for dravidian languages in code-mixed text. In *Working Notes of the Forum for Information Retrieval*

Evaluation (FIRE 2020). CEUR Workshop Proceedings. In: CEUR-WS. org, Hyderabad, India.

Edward C Chang. 2017. Hope and hopelessness as predictors of suicide ideation in hungarian college students. *Death studies*, 41(7):455–460.

Naganna Chetty and Sreejith Alathur. 2018. Hate speech review in the context of online social networks. *Aggression and violent behavior*, 40:108–118.

Jessica Clement. 2020. Number of global social network users 2010-2023. *Retrieved April*, 30:2020.

Alexis Conneau, Kartikay Khandelwal, Naman Goyal, Vishrav Chaudhary, Guillaume Wenzek, Francisco Guzmán, Edouard Grave, Myle Ott, Luke Zettlemoyer, and Veselin Stoyanov. 2019. Unsupervised cross-lingual representation learning at scale. *arXiv preprint arXiv:1911.02116.*

Bahareh Eslami, Adrienne H Kovacs, Philip Moons, Kyomars Abbasi, and Jamie L Jackson. 2017. Hopelessness among adults with congenital heart disease: Cause for despair or hope? *International journal of cardiology*, 230:64–69.

Paula Fortuna and Sérgio Nunes. 2018. A survey on automatic detection of hate speech in text. *ACM Computing Surveys (CSUR)*, 51(4):1–30.

Deepak Gupta, Pabitra Lenka, Asif Ekbal, and Pushpak Bhattacharyya. 2018. Uncovering code-mixed challenges: A framework for linguistically driven question generation and neural based question answering. In *Proceedings of the 22nd Conference on Computational Natural Language Learning*, pages 119–130.

Silvia C Hernandez and James C Overholser. 2020. A systematic review of interventions for hope/hopelessness in older adults. *Clinical gerontologist*, pages 1–15.

Liyuan Liu, Haoming Jiang, Pengcheng He, Weizhu Chen, Xiaodong Liu, Jianfeng Gao, and Jiawei Han. 2019a. On the variance of the adaptive learning rate and beyond. *arXiv preprint arXiv:1908.03265.*

Yinhan Liu, Myle Ott, Naman Goyal, Jingfei Du, Mandar Joshi, Danqi Chen, Omer Levy, Mike Lewis, Luke Zettlemoyer, and Veselin Stoyanov. 2019b. Roberta: A robustly optimized bert pretraining approach. *arXiv preprint arXiv:1907.11692.*

Shervin Malmasi and Marcos Zampieri. 2017a. Detecting hate speech in social media. *arXiv preprint arXiv:1712.06427.*

Shervin Malmasi and Marcos Zampieri. 2017b. Detecting hate speech in social media. *arXiv preprint arXiv:1712.06427.*

Shriphani Palakodety, Ashiqur R KhudaBukhsh, and Jaime G Carbonell. 2019. Hope speech detection: A computational analysis of the voice of peace. *arXiv preprint arXiv:1909.12940.*

Juan Carlos Pereira-Kohatsu, Lara Quijano-Sánchez, Federico Liberatore, and Miguel Camacho-Collados. 2019. Detecting and monitoring hate speech in twitter. *Sensors*, 19(21):4654.

Francisco Rangel, Anastasia Giachanou, Bilal Ghanem, and Paolo Rosso. 2020. Overview of the 8th author profiling task at pan 2020: Profiling fake news spreaders on twitter. In *CLEF*.

Nematollah Ranzadeh and Shahnaz Arsh Akmal. 2020. The representation of thoughts of death in relation to hope and hopelessness in malakut. *Literary Text Research.*

Christian Szegedy, Wei Liu, Yangqing Jia, Pierre Sermanet, Scott Reed, Dragomir Anguelov, Dumitru Erhan, Vincent Vanhoucke, and Andrew Rabinovich. 2015. Going deeper with convolutions. In *Proceedings of the IEEE conference on computer vision and pattern recognition*, pages 1–9.

Ashish Vaswani, Noam Shazeer, Niki Parmar, Jakob Uszkoreit, Llion Jones, Aidan N Gomez, Lukasz Kaiser, and Illia Polosukhin. 2017. Attention is all you need. *arXiv preprint arXiv:1706.03762.*

Chenguang Wang, Mu Li, and Alexander J Smola. 2019. Language models with transformers. *arXiv preprint arXiv:1904.09408.*

Marcos Zampieri, Preslav Nakov, Sara Rosenthal, Pepa Atanasova, Georgi Karadzhov, Hamdy Mubarak, Leon Derczynski, Zeses Pitenis, and Çağrı Çöltekin. 2020. Semeval-2020 task 12: Multilingual offensive language identification in social media (offenseval 2020). *arXiv preprint arXiv:2006.07235.*

cs_english@LT-EDI-EACL2021: Hope Speech Detection Based On Fine-tuning ALBERT Model

Shi Chen
School of Information Science
and Engineering Yunnan University,
chen-s2020@139.com

Bing Kong
School of Information Science
and Engineering Yunnan University,
kongbing@ynu.edu.cn

Abstract

This paper mainly introduces the relevant content of the task "Hope Speech Detection for Equality, Diversity, and Inclusion at LT-EDI 2021-EACL 2021". A total of three language datasets were provided, and we chose the English dataset to complete this task. The specific task objective is to classify the given speech into 'Hope speech', 'Not Hope speech', and 'Not in intended language'. In terms of method, we use fine-tuned ALBERT and K fold cross-validation to accomplish this task. In the end, we achieved a good result in the rank list of the task result, and the final F1 score was 0.93, tying for first place. However, we will continue to try to improve methods to get better results in future work.

1 Introduction

As we all know, we are currently facing an incompletely harmonious and secure network environment. Nowadays, the number of Internet users is very large, especially the proportion of minors is steadily increasing, which shows how important it is to create a hopeful social media environment.

Such an environment that embodies equality, tolerance, and diversity can help people who are in depression, confusion, lack of identity and other difficulties gain hope. At the same time, it also brings a better online social experience to the entire user community on social media.

Currently, the detection and classification of social media speech are mostly biased towards offensive and controversial speech detection, but this task is hope speech detection. The difference is that the former uses detection of negative speech to eliminate the impact of offensive speech on the creation of a healthy network environment. The hope speech detection task focuses on detecting hopeful words to create a good network environment, rather than detecting and deleting negative comments to encourage people and deprive individuals of their freedom of speech (Chakravarthi, 2020). The data source of this task comes from YouTube comments. What we have to do is to divide it into three categories: 'Hope speech', 'Not hope speech' and 'Not in intended language'. And we used K-fold cross-validation and ALBERT model to complete the detection of hope speech.

2 Related Work

At present, there are many studies on offensive and discriminatory speech detection, but there are few studies on hope speech detection. Therefore, we have looked for many related social media speech detection studies that can help us complete this task as a reference.

Marzieh Mozafari et al. used the regularization method to adjust the input text in the detection of hate and discriminatory speech and used a fine-tuned BERT model (Mozafari et al., 2020). Polychronis Charitidis et al. used the most advanced deep learning architecture to detect hate speech, trained and evaluated it using annotated data sets, and proposed an overall learning architecture that combines the predictive capabilities of each classifier (Charitidis et al., 2019).

Based on BERT's pre-trained language model, Marzieh Mozafari et al. made new fine-tuning of transfer learning and discussed the effect of using BERT to detect hate speech in a social media environment (Mozafari et al., 2019). Shriphani Palakodety et al. performed the qualitative and quantitative analysis of this embedding space for a variety of languages, they used Active Learning to train set construction in the analysis of peaceful speech (Palakodety et al., 2019). Zewdie Mossie et al. used Word2Vec word embedding technology for feature extraction when conducting Vulnerable community identification, and compared the effects

Proceedings of the First Workshop on Language Technology for Equality, Diversity and Inclusion, pages 128–131
April 19, 2021.

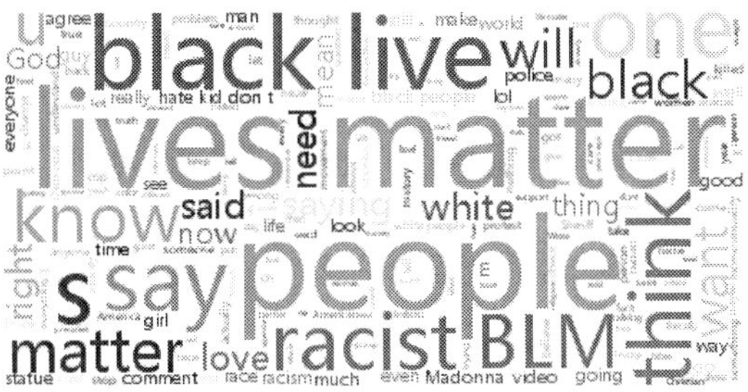

Figure 1: A word cloud image generated from the text marked with "Non hope speech" in the English training data set provided by the task organizer.

Figure 2: A word cloud image generated from the text marked with "Hope speech" in the English training data set provided by the task organizer.

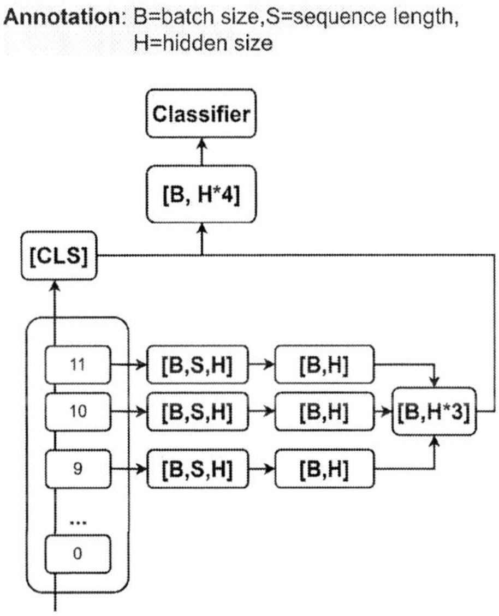

Figure 3: The fine-tuning strategies we use in English tasks. The output of layers 9-11 must be processed before being spliced with [CLS]. The processing method is to discard the first dimension data in the original data ([B, S, H] to [B, H]) to obtain a tensor output with the same shape as [CLS] (shape is [B, H]).

of classic classifiers with deep learning classifiers (Mossie and Wang, 2020). Shanita Biere et al. used natural language technology to detect hate speech on social media, using a convolutional neural network (CNN) (Biere et al., 2018).

Viktor Golem et al. tried different machine learning approaches, including traditional (shallow) machine learning models, deep learning models, and a combination of both for aggressive text detection(Golem et al., 2018). Jing MA et al. proposed a novel method that learns continuous representations of microblog events for identifying rumors. That model is based on recurrent neural networks (RNN) and that can capture the variation of contextual information of relevant posts over time (Ma et al., 2016). When discussing the detection of hate speech, Reynaldo Gil Pons et al. proposed an Attention-based Long Short-Term Memory Network, which is a model containing a bidirectional LSTM neural network (BILSTM)(De la Pena Saracén et al., 2018).

3 Data

The data sets we can use are the training set and validation set in three languages(Tamil, Malayalam, and English) provided by the task organizer team(Chakravarthi, 2020; Chakravarthi and Muralidaran, 2021). We only participate in the English task, so here we only analyze the English data set.

We use the official data set for visual analysis. We can observe that some words such as "live", "people", "black", "matter" "racist" in the English data set appear very frequently. The appearance of these words is very suitable for the theme of the mission we participated in. However, these words mostly express some negative information. And these data mainly come from social media platforms, on the other hand, they also reflect the current status quo on social media platforms. We visualize the text data of two different labels of "Non hope speech" and "Hope speech". Figures 1 and 2 show the results of text visualization.

There are three types of category labels that appear in the English data set. They are "Hope speech", "Non hope speech", "Not English". Through further analysis of the data set, most of the mark types in the English data are "Non hope speech" (around 90%). There is an imbalance of category labels in the data sets of the English data set.

4 Methods

4.1 K-fold cross-validation

K-fold cross-validation reduces variance by averaging the results of k different group training.

The specific steps are as follows: The first step is to randomly divide the original data into k parts without repeated sampling; The second step is to extract 1 copy as the test set, and the remaining k-1 copies are applied to the training set for model training; In the third step, repeat the second step k times, so that a model is obtained after training on each training set and used to test on the corresponding test set, calculate and save the evaluation index of the mode; The fourth step is to calculate the average of k groups of test results as an estimate of model accuracy, and as the performance index of the model under current k-fold cross-validation.

4.2 ALBERT Fine-tuning

The reason we choose the ALBERT fine-tuning program is that ALBERT's parameters are shared. Compared with BERT, ALBERT has fewer parameters, and the corresponding model training requires less time and memory. The advantage is that when the model is large, parameter sharing will be a strong regularization method for the model, and it is not easy to overfit.

The related work and conclusions of Sun and others on the fine-tuning of BERT have inspired us (Sun et al., 2019). We try to apply these conclusions to the ALBERT model. We chose to combine a portion of the output of the ALBERT encoder layer with [CLS] (the output shape is [batch_size, hidden_size]). We take the output of the encoder of the ALBERT model (layers 9-11) (the output shape is [batch_size, sequence_length, hidden_size]). Then take out the data of the 0th and 2nd dimensions of the output tensor of each layer of 9-11 layers to obtain three Tensors of the same shape (shape is [batch_size, hidden_size]). Next, the three tensors obtained in the previous step and the [CLS] output result of the ALBERT model are spliced together (the shape is [batch_size, hidden_size*4]). Finally, input the results of the previous step into the classifier.

5 Experiment and Results

5.1 Data Preprocessing

We combine the English data training set and the English data validation set provided by the task organizer team in one file. The purpose is to integrate the validation set provided by the task organizer into the k-fold cross-validation data set. Then perform 5-fold cross-validation data processing on this merged file to split the data into five data sets. Each data set contains a new training set and a new validation set.

Data	Precision	Recall	F1 Score
Test set	0.93	0.94	0.93
Validation set	0.94	0.95	0.94

Table 1: The resulting score of our model method on the test set and validation set. The test set result score comes from the result score published by the task organization team on the leaderboard. The resulting score on the verification set is the result score obtained by us using the official evaluation index and the verification set.

5.2 Experimental setting

For the English tasks, we set model training parameters as follows: epoch, batch size, maximum sequence length, and learning rate of the task are 5, 32, 60, and 3e-5, respectively. We combined the training set and validation set provided by the task manager into a new data set. Then performed k-fold cross-validation on it to get the result of the k-fold cross-validation vote. The voting method in the reasoning process is to take the average value of the probability value of k outputs as the final predicted output logical value. We choose the training language models of ALBERT-V2 version[1].

5.3 Analysis of Results

Hope Speech Detection for Equality, Diversity, and Inclusion at LT-EDI 2021-EACL 2021 task evaluation indicators adopt F1 score weighted average. In the results announced by the task organizer team, our English scores were tied for first place on the list. This result is due to the pre-trained language model in the Transformer structure. The main reason is that the pre-trained language model has been pre-trained on a large number of English data sets. The ALBERT model is based on the Transformer model (Lan et al., 2019). The Transformer model has great advantages in capturing global information (Vaswani et al., 2017).

[1]https://huggingface.co/albert-base-v2

Label	Precision	Recall	F1 Score	Count
Hope speech	0.74	0.50	0.60	250
Non hope speech	0.95	0.98	0.97	2593
Not English	0.00	0.00	0.00	3

Table 2: On the labeled test set data published by the task organizer team, we compare the predicted results with the real results.

6 Conclusion

For the English task in this competition, we use the last three layers of the ALBERT model output to fuse with the [CLS] output. Use K-fold cross-validation on the integrated method to obtain better results. Our test results for Youtube's hopeful speech are not bad. In the final result, Precision was 0.93, Recall was 0.94, F1 Score was 0.93, and the ranking was tied for first place. But in future work, we will try to improve our method and choose to try other models, hoping to achieve better results on such tasks.

References

Shanita Biere, Sandjai Bhulai, and Master Business Analytics. 2018. Hate speech detection using natural language processing techniques. *Master Business AnalyticsDepartment of Mathematics Faculty of Science.*

Bharathi Raja Chakravarthi. 2020. HopeEDI: A multilingual hope speech detection dataset for equality, diversity, and inclusion. In *Proceedings of the Third Workshop on Computational Modeling of People's Opinions, Personality, and Emotion's in Social Media*, pages 41–53, Barcelona, Spain (Online). Association for Computational Linguistics.

Bharathi Raja Chakravarthi and Vigneshwaran Muralidaran. 2021. Findings of the shared task on Hope Speech Detection for Equality, Diversity, and Inclusion. In *Proceedings of the First Workshop on Language Technology for Equality, Diversity and Inclusion*. Association for Computational Linguistics.

Polychronis Charitidis, Stavros Doropoulos, Stavros Vologiannidis, Ioannis Papastergiou, and Sophia Karakeva. 2019. Towards countering hate speech and personal attack in social media. *arXiv preprint arXiv:1912.04106.*

Viktor Golem, Mladen Karan, and Jan Šnajder. 2018. Combining shallow and deep learning for aggressive text detection. In *Proceedings of the First Workshop on Trolling, Aggression and Cyberbullying (TRAC-2018)*, pages 188–198.

Zhenzhong Lan, Mingda Chen, Sebastian Goodman, Kevin Gimpel, Piyush Sharma, and Radu Soricut. 2019. Albert: A lite bert for self-supervised learning of language representations. *arXiv preprint arXiv:1909.11942.*

Jing Ma, Wei Gao, Prasenjit Mitra, Sejeong Kwon, Bernard J Jansen, Kam-Fai Wong, and Meeyoung Cha. 2016. Detecting rumors from microblogs with recurrent neural networks.

Zewdie Mossie and Jenq-Haur Wang. 2020. Vulnerable community identification using hate speech detection on social media. *Information Processing & Management*, 57(3):102087.

Marzieh Mozafari, Reza Farahbakhsh, and Noel Crespi. 2019. A bert-based transfer learning approach for hate speech detection in online social media. In *International Conference on Complex Networks and Their Applications*, pages 928–940. Springer.

Marzieh Mozafari, Reza Farahbakhsh, and Noël Crespi. 2020. Hate speech detection and racial bias mitigation in social media based on bert model. *PloS one*, 15(8):e0237861.

Shriphani Palakodety, Ashiqur R KhudaBukhsh, and Jaime G Carbonell. 2019. Kashmir: A computational analysis of the voice of peace. *CoRR, abs/1909.12940.*

Gretel Liz De la Pena Sarracén, Reynaldo Gil Pons, Carlos Enrique Muniz Cuza, and Paolo Rosso. 2018. Hate speech detection using attention-based lstm. *EVALITA Evaluation of NLP and Speech Tools for Italian*, 12:235.

Chi Sun, Xipeng Qiu, Yige Xu, and Xuanjing Huang. 2019. How to fine-tune bert for text classification? In *China National Conference on Chinese Computational Linguistics*, pages 194–206. Springer.

Ashish Vaswani, Noam Shazeer, Niki Parmar, Jakob Uszkoreit, Llion Jones, Aidan N Gomez, Lukasz Kaiser, and Illia Polosukhin. 2017. Attention is all you need. *arXiv preprint arXiv:1706.03762.*

GCDH@LT-EDI-EACL2021: XLM-RoBERTa for Hope Speech Detection in English, Malayalam, and Tamil

Stefan Ziehe
Institute of Computer Science
University of Göttingen
stefan.ziehe@cs.uni-goettingen.de

Franziska Pannach
Göttingen Centre for Digital Humanites
University of Göttingen
franziska.pannach@uni-goettingen.de

Aravind Krishnan
Department of Electronics and Communication Engineering
College of Engineering, Trivandrum
aravindhp1999@gmail.com

Abstract

This paper describes approaches to identify Hope Speech in short, informal texts in English, Malayalam and Tamil using different machine learning techniques. We demonstrate that even very simple baseline algorithms perform reasonably well on this task if provided with enough training data. However, our best performing algorithm is a cross-lingual transfer learning approach in which we fine-tune XLM-RoBERTa.

1 Introduction

In recent years, the spread of negative comments and hatred through social media has created a focus on the detection of misinformation and hate speech in the NLP community.

On the other hand, Hope Speech detection is a relatively new task. It can be employed to identify the positive aspects of large collection of social media posts, e.g. detecting pro-peace voices during politically heated situations. These detection efforts can potentially counter-act the perceived majority of hatred, and be a means to prevent harsh measures such as the disabling of internet access (Palakodety et al., 2020).

The ability to identify and therefore foster these aspects of online communication is a step towards a more positive representation of the internet. The hypothesis is: if hate-speech can incite violence, Hope Speech can ease tensions. For the first time to our knowledge, a shared task has been announced to identify Hope Speech in a multi-lingual dataset of Youtube comments. (Chakravarthi and Muralidaran, 2021)

2 Data

The dataset consists of three different subsets. It contains 10,705 comments for Malayalam, of which 8,564 are assigned for training, 1,070 for validation, and 1,071 for testing. For Tamil, the organizers provided 20,198 comments, of which 16,160 were designated for training, 2,018 for validation, and a test set of 2,020 comments. The English data consists of 28,451 comments in total, 22,762 for training, 2,843 for development, and 2,846 for testing.

The organizers provided annotations for the classes *Hope Speech*, *non Hope Speech*, and *not-"target language"*, where "target language" is either Malayalam, Tamil, or English. Figure 1 illustrates how the different classes are represented in the data sets. Notably, we can observe that the Tamil data is more balanced, whereas the Malayalam and English data sets show an over-representation of non Hope Speech data. Furthermore, only 22 comments in the English training set are labelled "not-English", but 12 % of the comments in the Tamil training set are "not-Tamil", and 8 % of the Malayalam comments are "not-Malayalam".

Annotations for the Hope Speech class include utterances that convey a generally bright prospect to the future, are supportive, insightful, and promote values such as inclusiveness and equality, among others. Some of these concepts for the English training set are illustrated in figure 2. For a full description of the annotation process, see (Chakravarthi, 2020).

3 Baseline

Using scikit-learn (Pedregosa et al., 2011), we implemented two baseline algorithms for the task of

Proceedings of the First Workshop on Language Technology for Equality, Diversity and Inclusion, pages 132–135
April 19, 2021.

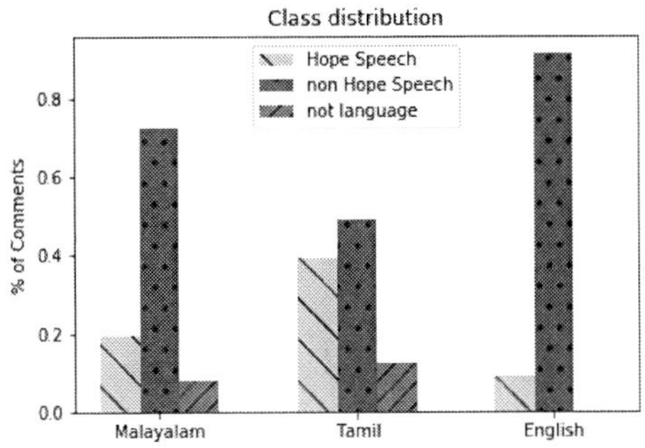

Figure 1: Comparison of Hope Speech to non Hope Speech data in the training sets

Figure 2: A selection of salient words that correspond with the Hope Speech label in the English training set.

Hope Speech detection, a Naive Bayes algorithm, and a Support Vector Machine. From the short texts, we first extracted a number of features including unigrams, bigrams, length and number of stopwords. Additionally, we assigned emotion scores for all three languages based on the NRC emotion lexicons (Mohammad et al., 2013). However, we found that solely relying on the textual data using a simple vectorizer based on tf-idf yielded better results.

As a first baseline, we implemented a Complement Naive Bayes model (Rennie et al., 2003). We iteratively found the best smoothing parameters $\alpha = 1.3$ for Malayalam, $\alpha = 10.5$ for Tamil and $\alpha = 1.4$ for English.

For the second baseline, we used an SVM with a degree of three and linear kernel. We found the best regularization parameters $c = 1.3$ for Malayalam, $c = 1.1$ for Tamil and $c = 1.4$ for English.

4 Transformer Model

Our main model is based on XLM-RoBERTa (Conneau et al., 2019), a pre-trained neural language model that uses the transformer architecture (more specifically, we use the `xlm-roberta-base` version from the huggingface transformers library (Wolf et al., 2020)). It is particularly useful for this task, because it is already pre-trained on 100 different languages, including Malayalam, Tamil and English.

We preprocess the provided datasets by tokenizing the comments using the pre-trained SentencePiece (Kudo and Richardson, 2018) tokenizer that belongs to XLM-RoBERTa. All comments are padded or truncated to a length of 128 tokens. XLM-RoBERTa is able to implicitly infer the language used in a text based on the tokens that it contains, which enables it to deal with code-switching. This also means that we can use batches that contain multiple languages at the same time during training.

The model is fine-tuned for hope speech detection on the combined training datasets for all three languages. In order to account for the different sizes of the datasets, Malayalam and Tamil samples are assigned sample weights of 2 and 3, respectively. We use a batch size of 64 and the Adam (Kingma and Ba, 2015) optimizer with a learning rate of $2 \cdot 10^{-5}$ for 4 epochs. We further employ decoupled weight decay (Loshchilov and Hutter, 2019) with a decay rate of 0.01 and shrinking learning rates for early transformer layers (Sun et al., 2019) with a decay rate of 0.95. Since the datasets only contain a small portion of all possible tokens, the token embeddings are deliberately not fine-tuned. Training takes place on an Nvidia GeForce RTX 2080 Ti in mixed precision mode and takes roughly 20 minutes.

5 Results

5.1 Baseline Results

Language	Precision	Recall	F1-Score
	SVM		
Malayalam	0.80	0.82	0.80
Tamil	0.61	0.61	0.60
English	0.80	0.82	0.80
	CNB		
Malayalam	0.78	0.76	0.77
Tamil	0.61	0.61	0.61
English	0.91	0.91	0.91

Table 1: Weighted Average Scores for SVM and Complement Naive Bayes on the development sets

We observe that even a simple algorithm such as Complement NB results in a high F1-Score of

0.91 for English. However, for Malayalam the SVM performs better with an F1-Score of 0.80. For Tamil, both baseline systems perform similarly with 0.60 (SVM) resp. 0.61 (CNB) F1-Score.

5.2 Results of the XLM-RoBERTa model

Class	Precision	Recall	F1-Score
	Malayalam		
HS	0.65	0.51	0.57
not HS	0.86	0.91	0.89
not ML	0.74	0.67	0.70
weighted avg	0.81	0.82	0.81
	Tamil		
HS	0.67	0.40	0.50
not HS	0.64	0.79	0.70
not Tamil	0.58	0.73	0.65
weighted avg	0.64	0.64	0.62
	English		
HS	0.63	0.57	0.60
not HS	0.95	0.96	0.96
not EN	0.00	0.00	0.00
weighted avg	0.92	0.92	0.92

Table 2: Results for the XLM-RoBERTa model by language and class (HS = Hope Speech) on the development sets

As seen in table 2, the fine-tuned XLM-RoBERTa model is an improvement over the baseline when applied to the development set. It performs strongest on English data, followed by Malayalam and Tamil, with F1-Scores of 0.92, 0.81 and 0.62 respectively.

Language	Precision	Recall	F1-Score
Malayalam	0.84	0.85	0.85
Tamil	0.59	0.59	0.58
English	0.93	0.93	0.93

Table 3: Official results for the XLM-RoBERTa model on the test set as provided by the task organizers

The official results on the test set (see table 3) place the model at first rank for English and Malayalam and fourth rank for Tamil in the competition.

5.3 Analysis

The improvements the fine-tuned XLM-RoBERTa model offers over the baseline models are not surprising, since large transformer models have a high capacity and are able to take the order of tokens into account. Differences between the languages are likely related to structural properties of the datasets, which is supported by the fact that the other competitors received similar results. In a similar way, imbalances in the datasets as described in section 2 can explain why the classifiers perform better on the *non Hope Speech* class than the other classes.

6 Conclusion

In this paper we presented several machine learning models trained for Hope Speech Detection in three different languages (Malayalam, Tamil and English). As baseline models we used SVM and Complement Naive Bayes classifiers for each language. The best results were achieved by a cross-lingual transfer learning approach in which we fine-tuned XLM-RoBERTa. In the competition, this model achieved the first rank for Malayalam and English and the fourth rank for Tamil. In conclusion, we provide a cross-lingual model that is both effective and relatively fast to train.

References

Bharathi Raja Chakravarthi. 2020. HopeEDI: A multilingual hope speech detection dataset for equality, diversity, and inclusion. In *Proceedings of the Third Workshop on Computational Modeling of People's Opinions, Personality, and Emotion's in Social Media*, pages 41–53, Barcelona, Spain (Online). Association for Computational Linguistics.

Bharathi Raja Chakravarthi and Vigneshwaran Muralidaran. 2021. Findings of the shared task on Hope Speech Detection for Equality, Diversity, and Inclusion. In *Proceedings of the First Workshop on Language Technology for Equality, Diversity and Inclusion*. Association for Computational Linguistics.

Alexis Conneau, Kartikay Khandelwal, Naman Goyal, Vishrav Chaudhary, Guillaume Wenzek, Francisco Guzmán, Edouard Grave, Myle Ott, Luke Zettlemoyer, and Veselin Stoyanov. 2019. Unsupervised cross-lingual representation learning at scale. *arXiv preprint arXiv:1911.02116*.

Diederik P. Kingma and Jimmy Ba. 2015. Adam: A method for stochastic optimization. In *3rd International Conference on Learning Representations, Conference Track Proceedings*.

Taku Kudo and John Richardson. 2018. SentencePiece: A simple and language independent subword tokenizer and detokenizer for neural text processing. In *Proceedings of the 2018 Conference on Empirical Methods in Natural Language Processing: System Demonstrations*, pages 66–71, Brussels, Belgium. Association for Computational Linguistics.

Ilya Loshchilov and Frank Hutter. 2019. Decoupled weight decay regularization. In *International Conference on Learning Representations*.

Saif Mohammad, Svetlana Kiritchenko, and Xiaodan Zhu. 2013. NRC-canada: Building the state-of-the-art in sentiment analysis of tweets. In *Second Joint Conference on Lexical and Computational Semantics (*SEM), Volume 2: Proceedings of the Seventh International Workshop on Semantic Evaluation (SemEval 2013)*, pages 321–327, Atlanta, Georgia, USA. Association for Computational Linguistics.

Shriphani Palakodety, Ashiqur R. KhudaBukhsh, and Jaime G. Carbonell. 2020. Hope speech detection: A computational analysis of the voice of peace. In *Proceedings of the 24th European Conference on Artificial Intelligence - ECAI 2020*, volume 325 of *Frontiers in Artificial Intelligence and Applications*, pages 1881–1889. IOS Press.

Fabian Pedregosa, Gaël Varoquaux, Alexandre Gramfort, Vincent Michel, Bertrand Thirion, Olivier Grisel, Mathieu Blondel, Peter Prettenhofer, Ron Weiss, Vincent Dubourg, Jake Vanderplas, Alexandre Passos, David Cournapeau, Matthieu Brucher, Matthieu Perrot, and Édouard Duchesnay. 2011. Scikit-learn: Machine learning in python. *Journal of Machine Learning Research*, 12(85):2825–2830.

Jason D Rennie, Lawrence Shih, Jaime Teevan, and David R Karger. 2003. Tackling the poor assumptions of naive bayes text classifiers. In *Proceedings of the 20th International Conference on Machine Learning (ICML-03)*, pages 616–623.

Chi Sun, Xipeng Qiu, Yige Xu, and Xuanjing Huang. 2019. How to fine-tune BERT for text classification? In *Chinese Computational Linguistics*, pages 194–206, Cham. Springer International Publishing.

Thomas Wolf, Lysandre Debut, Victor Sanh, Julien Chaumond, Clement Delangue, Anthony Moi, Pierric Cistac, Tim Rault, Rémi Louf, Morgan Funtowicz, Joe Davison, Sam Shleifer, Patrick von Platen, Clara Ma, Yacine Jernite, Julien Plu, Canwen Xu, Teven Le Scao, Sylvain Gugger, Mariama Drame, Quentin Lhoest, and Alexander M. Rush. 2020. Transformers: State-of-the-art natural language processing. In *Proceedings of the 2020 Conference on Empirical Methods in Natural Language Processing: System Demonstrations*, pages 38–45, Online. Association for Computational Linguistics.

TeamUNCC@LT-EDI-EACL2021: Hope Speech Detection using Transfer Learning with Transformers

Khyati Mahajan, Erfan Al-Hossami, and Samira Shaikh

Department of Computer Science
University of North Carolina at Charlotte
Charlotte, NC 28223
{kmahaja2, ealhossa, sshaikh2}@uncc.edu

Abstract

In this paper, we describe our approach towards the task of hope speech detection. We participated in Task 2: Hope Speech Detection for Equality, Diversity and Inclusion at LT-EDI-2021 @ EACL2021. The goal of this task is to predict the presence of hope speech, along with the presence of samples that do not belong to the same language in the dataset. We describe our approach to fine-tuning RoBERTa for Hope Speech detection in English and our approach to fine-tuning XLM-RoBERTa for Hope Speech detection in Tamil and Malayalam, two low resource Indic languages. We demonstrate the performance of our approach on classifying text into `hope-speech`, `non-hope` and `not-language`. Our approach ranked 1st in English ($F1 = 0.93$), 1st in Tamil ($F1 = 0.61$) and 3rd in Malayalam ($F1 = 0.83$). We make our code available on Github.[1]

1 Introduction

Hate speech and the need for its moderation on social media platforms has recently become the focus of research (Zhang and Luo, 2019; Das et al., 2020). The need for detection of hate speech is clear, and worthy of the efforts. However, detecting and removing hate speech, while providing important benefits to conversations online, should be supplemented by other efforts to improve human connection and communication. There is a clear need to find common themes in community and build bridges to reduce the recent wave of polarization which has gripped many social media platforms (Prasetya and Murata, 2020; Levy, 2020).

There has been extensive work including proposed tasks and datasets on hate speech detection online. There have been multiple *SemEval*[2] tasks to detect hate speech, including binary (2 classes, (Basile et al., 2019)), and multi-label (>2 classes with overlaps (Mollas et al., 2020)) annotations. Hate speech detection has also further been expanded to cover explainability for the approaches used by Mathew et al. (2020), who propose *HateXplain* in which the span of text constituting the hate speech must also be detected. However, hate speech is just one facet of human behavior, especially on social media (Chakravarthi et al., 2020; Mandl et al., 2020; Chakravarthi et al., 2021; Suryawanshi and Chakravarthi, 2021). There are equally interesting studies on prosocial behaviors online including solidarity (Herrera-Viedma et al., 2015; Santhanam et al., 2021 (in press) and altruism (Althoff et al., 2014), as well as hope speech.

The Hope Speech Detection for Equality, Diversity and Inclusion task at LT-EDI-2021 @ EACL2021 (Chakravarthi and Muralidaran, 2021) marks a step towards helping push for more positive, uplifting speech on social media. Exacerbated by the pandemic, and the subsequent need of communication to move to online communities, research in the detection of "hope speech", which promotes positive, uplifting discussion to build support, is an important step (Puranik et al., 2021; Ghanghor et al., 2021). Findings from this effort could have an overall positive effect in the real world.

The task mainly focuses on multilingual classification for identifying speech associated with promise, potential, support, reassurance, suggestions or inspiration provided to participants by their peers during periods of illness, stress, loneliness and depression (Snyder et al., 2005). In addition to being a multi-class problem, each language (English, Tamil and Malayalam) also had differing amounts of class imbalance. We describe our approach in detail in Section 2 and present our results in Section 3.

[1] https://tinyurl.com/teamuncc-hope
[2] https://semeval.github.io/

Proceedings of the First Workshop on Language Technology for Equality, Diversity and Inclusion, pages 136–142
April 19, 2021.

2 Method

RoBERTa is an improved BERT (Devlin et al., 2019) model by Facebook AI which achieves state-of-the-art results on several natural language understanding (NLU) tasks including GLUE (Wang et al., 2018) and SQuAD (Rajpurkar et al., 2016). RoBERTa is improved through training BERT for a longer duration on longer sequences, increasing the data quantity, removing the sentence prediction objective during pre-training, and changing the masking pattern applied during pre-training. With the aim of improving cross-lingual language understanding (XLU), XLM-RoBERTa was developed using a Transformer-based masked language model (MLM). XLM-RoBERTa was pre-trained using 2 terabytes of CommonCrawl data (Wenzek et al., 2020) containing one hundred languages. XLM-RoBERTa outperforms its multilingual MLMs mBERT (Devlin et al., 2019) and XLM (Lample and Conneau, 2019).

We thus do not propose a novel system, and instead rely on fine-tuning these two large transformers for the task of hope speech detection. We use the RoBERTa transformer (Liu et al., 2019) for English. We select XLM-RoBERTa (Conneau et al., 2020) for Tamil and Malayalam tasks due to its robustness and pre-training on low-resources languages including Tamil and Malayalam. For our implementation, we use the Simple Transformers[3] library which is built upon the transformers library by huggingface (Wolf et al., 2020). We use Adam (Kingma and Ba, 2014) as our optimizer. Our hyperparameters are presented in Table 1.

Hyperparameter	Value
epochs	6
bacth_size	8
α (English)	0.00002
α (Malayalam & Tamil)	0.00001
max_length	256
decay (L2)	0

Table 1: Hyperparameter values

3 Results

We present detailed results for each language below. We also compare with baselines provided in the original dataset paper (Chakravarthi, 2020), and include them in the results in Tables 2, 3, and 4. We report results to 2 significant digits, since the baseline provided by the task is also limited to 2 significant digits. We also provide the dataset distribution in these tables, in the "Support" column. We discuss our findings further in Section 4.

Evaluation for English. Table 2 overviews the results of detecting `hope-speech`, `non-hope`, and `not-english`. The baseline for English was weighted average $F1 = 0.90$ (Chakravarthi, 2020). Our approach scored a weighted average $F1 = 0.93$ on both the dev (N = 2843) and test (N = 2846) sets, achieving the 1st place in the task among 31 team submissions. We note the class imbalance between `hope-speech` ($N = 272$) and `non-hope` ($N = 2569$) denoted in the support column. While our approach does achieve high numbers overall, there is clearly room for improvement. Incorrectly labeled `non-hope` utterances (N = 59) tend to be fewer than incorrectly labeled `hope-speech` utterances (N = 118), hence the precision (0.69) is greater than the recall (0.53) on the test set.

Evaluation for Tamil. Table 3 overviews the results of detecting `hope-speech`, `non-hope`, and `not-tamil`. The baseline performance for Tamil was weighted average $F1$ = 0.56 (Chakravarthi, 2020). Our approach scored a weighted average $F1 = 0.61$ on the dev set (N = 2018) and a weighted average $F1 = 0.60$ on the test set (N = 2020) giving us the 1st place in the task as well against 30 team submissions. Similar to English, we observe higher precision (0.59) over recall (0.49) suggesting a tendency for false positives to be lower than false negatives.

Evaluation for Malayalam. Table 4 overviews the results of detecting `hope-speech`, `non-hope`, and `not-malayalam`. The baseline weighted F1 performance for Malayalam was $F1$ = 0.73 (Chakravarthi, 2020). At the time of submission, our submission scored weighted average $F1$ = 0.82 on the dev set (N = 1070) and weighted average $F1 = 0.83$ on the test set ($N = 1071$), ranking us 3rd for the task among 31 teams. The approach for Malayalam was incomplete - being trained only on 2 epochs instead of 6. After complete training ($epochs = 6$), our approach scores a weighted average $F1 = 0.87$ on the test set. We observe very little difference between precision and recall suggesting a balance between missed `hope-speech` and false alarm `hope-speech` utterances.

[3]https://simpletransformers.ai/

Class	Dev Set				Test Set				Baseline
	Support	Precision	Recall	F1	Support	Precision	Recall	F1	Test F1
Hope	272	0.69	0.55	**0.61**	250	0.69	0.53	**0.60**	0.42
Non-hope	2569	0.95	0.97	**0.96**	2593	0.95	0.98	**0.97**	0.95
Not-English	2	0.00	0.00	0.00	3	0.00	0.00	0.00	0.00
Accuracy	2843	-	-	**0.93**	2846	-	-	**0.94**	-
Macro	2843	0.55	0.51	**0.52**	2846	0.55	0.50	**0.52**	0.46
Weighted Avg	2843	0.93	0.93	**0.93**	2846	0.93	0.94	**0.93**	0.90

Table 2: Classification Results - English

Class	Dev Set				Test Set				Baseline
	Support	Precision	Recall	F1	Support	Precision	Recall	F1	Test F1
Hope	757	0.58	0.45	**0.51**	815	0.59	0.49	**0.54**	0.46
Non-hope	998	0.65	0.70	**0.67**	946	0.64	0.68	**0.66**	0.65
Not-Tamil	263	0.59	0.8	**0.68**	259	0.55	0.72	**0.63**	0.55
Accuracy	2018	-	-	**0.62**	2020	-	-	**0.61**	-
Macro	2018	0.61	0.65	**0.62**	2020	0.59	0.63	**0.61**	0.55
Weighted Avg	2018	0.62	0.62	**0.61**	2020	0.61	0.61	**0.60**	0.56

Table 3: Classification Results - Tamil

Class	Dev Set				Test Set				Baseline
	Support	Precision	Recall	F1	Support	Precision	Recall	F1	Test F1
Hope	190	0.69	0.61	**0.64**	194	0.70	0.72	**0.71**	0.36
Non-hope	784	0.89	0.91	**0.90**	776	0.91	0.91	**0.91**	0.86
Not-Malayalam	96	0.75	0.80	**0.77**	101	0.83	0.80	**0.81**	0.45
Accuracy	1070	-	-	**0.84**	1071	-	-	**0.87**	-
Macro	1070	0.78	0.77	**0.77**	1071	0.81	0.81	**0.81**	0.56
Weighted Avg	1070	0.84	0.84	**0.84**	1071	0.87	0.87	**0.87**	0.73

Table 4: Classification Results - Malayalam

3.1 Negative Results

Since there is class imbalance between the 3 classes (`non-hope` >> `hope-speech` >> `not-language`), we attempted to modify the class weights during our fine-tuning process weighing the minority classes more than the majority class. The class weights for `hope-speech` and `non-hope` for the English, Tamil, and Malayalam languages are computed using Equation 1 inspired by (King et al., 2001) and implemented by the scikit-learn library (Pedregosa et al., 2011). N represents the number of samples in the dataset and x is a class label.

$$weight_x = \frac{N}{(count(classes) \times count(x))} \quad (1)$$

To address the larger imbalance between the `not-language` and other classes, we manually assign weights for these classes, so that they weigh less than the `hope-speech` class. The `non-english` class was weighed as 1 and the `non-tamil` and `non-malayalam` classes were weighed as 0.5. In future work, these weights will be empirically chosen. However, we did not submit these as our final models since the performance on weighted average F1 was lower.

Results. The weighted average F1 using the class-weights approach described above were a bit lower than the results described in Tables 2, 3, and 4 across all languages. On the English dev set, we scored weighted average $F1$ = 0.92, with $F1$ = 0.60 for `hope-speech`, $F1$ = 0.95 for `non-hope`, and $F1$ = 0.00 for `non-english`. We note that all of the results are a bit lower than the

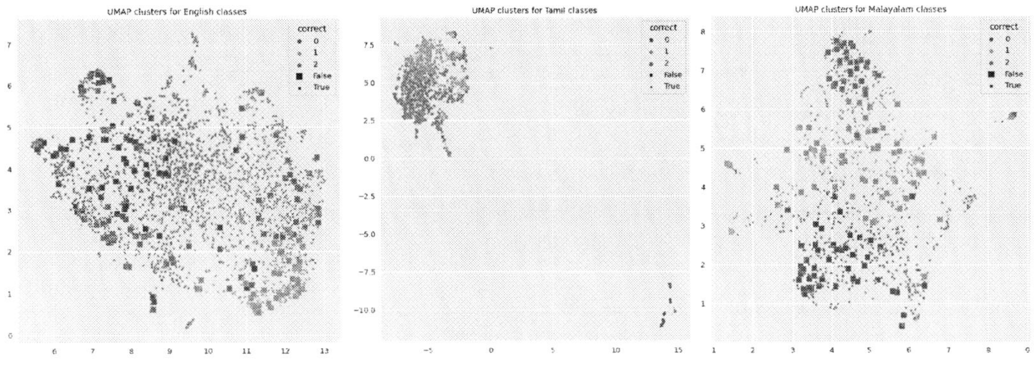

(a) English (b) Tamil (c) Malayalam

Figure 1: UMAP scatter plots visualizing clusters (color code) and prediction correctness (mark shape) using sentence transformers on the test set for an analytical evaluation of our approach.

our submission results. On the Tamil dev set, we scored weighted average $F1$ = 0.61, $F1$ = 0.57 for hope-speech, $F1$ = 0.65 for non-hope, and $F1$ = 0.60 for non-tamil. We note that all of the results are lower than the our original submission results with the exception of the hope-speech class. On the Malayalam dev set, we scored weighted average $F1$ = 0.84, $F1$ = 0.64 for hope-speech, $F1$ = 0.89 for non-hope, and $F1$ = 0.75 for non-malayalam. We note that all of the individual class results are slightly lower than the our submission results.

4 Qualitative Evaluation

In this section, we analytically go through sample records in the English test set to better understand the dataset, and to evaluate the strengths and weaknesses of our approach.

Analytical Evaluation. We use sentence-transformers (Reimers and Gurevych, 2019, 2020) to further evaluate our approach. Sentence transformers were created by utilizing word-level representation models such as BERT and RoBERTa for better downstream computational performance on sentence-level tasks, since utilizing word-level representations for tasks such as determining the similarity of 2 sentences takes much longer than computing sentence-level representations. We use the paraphrase-xlm-r-multilingual-v1 pretrained model to get our sentence embeddings, and then use K-means clustering using scikit-learn (Pedregosa et al., 2011) to cluster the test set into 3 clusters, the same number of classes as the classification task. We provide clustering results, showing cluster assignments of data samples and whether our classifiers labelled them correctly or not in Figure 1.

For English (Figure 1a), there are fewer misclassified samples, but most of them lie in cluster 1, shown on the bottom right of the UMAP scatter plot 1. This cluster, upon further observation, mostly consists of Youtube comments related to the Black Lives Matter (BLM) movement. We conclude that the our approach specifically struggles with correctly classifying such utterances, and elaborate with illustrative examples in the next section.

For Tamil (Figure 1b), we observe closely clustered data points, a property that is also reflected in our classification results as seen by the misclassified points (shown by square markers in the scatter plot). We see a similar trend as English in Malayalam (Figure 1c), however an observational analysis is not possible for Malayalam and Tamil since we do not speak the language, and wish not to rely on automatic translation systems for informal, code-mixed text (Chakravarthi, 2020).

Observations. In Table 5, we present a qualitative evaluation using select examples from the English test set. First, we examine misclassifications in the English test set and report on our observations. The model predicts 3 samples as non-hope when the ground-truth label is not-english. However upon examination, 2 of these 3 samples predominantly contain English words that seem to be non-hope sentences. We demonstrate one of the non-english sentences in the test set in the sixth row of Table 5). The third not-english sample contains a latin-alphabet utterance of a non-english sentence with some recognizable English words. Furthermore, upon

#	Sentence	Actual	Predicted	Cluster
1	Speak for yourself	**non-hope**	**non-hope**	**0**
2	What do you mean by the word sniped?	**non-hope**	**non-hope**	**0**
3	Everyone matters stop racism	**hope-speech**	**hope-speech**	**2**
4	Realize Black lives matter is designed to cause division. All lives matter is to state unity. We are in this together. The tactic of divide and conquer is ancient... But still works!	hope-speech	non-hope	1
5	It's one thing to ideally believe that all lives matter	non-hope	hope-speech	1
6	We have and they know we are Israelites the real jews and got jealous...	not-english	non-hope	2
7	Trying to end racism by supporting everyone equally. Blm mob	non-hope	hope-speech	2

Table 5: Illustrative examples of successful (bold) and failure cases of the TeamUNCC approach for English.

examining misclassifications of `non-hope` and `hope-speech`, we observe a trend that BLM related samples tend to compose quite a bit of our misclassified samples. Over 46 out of 177 samples seem to be BLM related. We observe that it can be ambiguous and tricky to determine whether it expresses hope or not. The ambiguity observation for some of the samples is inline with the findings of (Chakravarthi, 2020). In the fifth row, we note that the utterance expresses that all lives matter but the ground truth is `non-hope`. The fourth and seventh rows are similar, both utterances express support for equality but it also express negative sentiments towards the BLM movement; yet the ground truth labels for both these utterances are different. The first 3 rows showcase examples of where the classifications are correct. We observe that the model might have learned to look for linguistic markers such as questions and inquiries, and thus tended to label them as `non-hope`.

5 Conclusion

We found that fine-tuning RoBERTa (English) and XLM-RoBERTa (Tamil and Malayalam) for classification performed well. Providing class weights helped handle the data imbalance, leading to a balanced performance over the baselines. We submitted the results of our approach using the RoBERTa and XLM-RoBERTa models without class weights as our final submission for the Hope Speech Detection Task. Admittedly, our approach does not break new ground in terms of novelty of models or architecture; we instead rely upon fine-tuning pre-trained models. However, we present it as a first step in this direction, and aim to build on our success in future iterations. The Hope Speech Detection task was an important and necessary step towards promoting positive speech online. Our goal is to keep participating in the effort to detect and promote more positive speech online. Additionally, we hope to extend this task to COVID19 data, and work towards understanding community support during the pandemic.

References

Tim Althoff, Cristian Danescu-Niculescu-Mizil, and Dan Jurafsky. 2014. How to ask for a favor: A case study on the success of altruistic requests. In *Proceedings of the International AAAI Conference on Web and Social Media*, volume 8.

Valerio Basile, C. Bosco, E. Fersini, Debora Nozza, V. Patti, F. Pardo, P. Rosso, and M. Sanguinetti. 2019. Semeval-2019 task 5: Multilingual detection of hate speech against immigrants and women in twitter. In *SemEval@NAACL-HLT*.

Bharathi Raja Chakravarthi. 2020. HopeEDI: A multilingual hope speech detection dataset for equality, diversity, and inclusion. In *Proceedings of the Third Workshop on Computational Modeling of People's Opinions, Personality, and Emotion's in Social Media*, pages 41–53, Barcelona, Spain (Online). Association for Computational Linguistics.

Bharathi Raja Chakravarthi, M Anand Kumar, John Philip McCrae, Premjith B, Soman KP, and Thomas Mandl. 2020. Overview of the track on HASOC-Offensive Language Identification-DravidianCodeMix. In *Working Notes of the Forum for Information Retrieval Evaluation (FIRE 2020). CEUR Workshop Proceedings. In: CEUR-WS. org, Hyderabad, India.*

Bharathi Raja Chakravarthi and Vigneshwaran Muralidaran. 2021. Findings of the shared task on Hope Speech Detection for Equality, Diversity, and Inclusion. In *Proceedings of the First Workshop on Language Technology for Equality, Diversity and Inclusion*. Association for Computational Linguistics.

Bharathi Raja Chakravarthi, Ruba Priyadharshini, Navya Jose, Anand Kumar M, Thomas Mandl, Prasanna Kumar Kumaresan, Rahul Ponnusamy, Hariharan V, Elizabeth Sherly, and John Philip McCrae. 2021. Findings of the shared task on Offensive Language Identification in Tamil, Malayalam, and Kannada. In *Proceedings of the First Workshop on Speech and Language Technologies for Dravidian Languages*. Association for Computational Linguistics.

Alexis Conneau, Kartikay Khandelwal, Naman Goyal, Vishrav Chaudhary, Guillaume Wenzek, Francisco Guzmán, Édouard Grave, Myle Ott, Luke Zettlemoyer, and Veselin Stoyanov. 2020. Unsupervised cross-lingual representation learning at scale. In *Proceedings of the 58th Annual Meeting of the Association for Computational Linguistics*, pages 8440–8451.

Mithun Das, Binny Mathew, Punyajoy Saha, P. Goyal, and Animesh Mukherjee. 2020. Hate speech in online social media. *ACM SIGWEB Newsletter*, pages 1 – 8.

Jacob Devlin, Ming-Wei Chang, Kenton Lee, and Kristina Toutanova. 2019. Bert: Pre-training of deep bidirectional transformers for language understanding. In *Proceedings of the 2019 Conference of the North American Chapter of the Association for Computational Linguistics: Human Language Technologies, Volume 1 (Long and Short Papers)*, pages 4171–4186.

Nikhil Kumar Ghanghor, Rahul Ponnusamy, Prasanna Kumar Kumaresan, Ruba Priyadharshini, Sajeetha Thavareesan, and Bharathi Raja Chakravarthi. 2021. IIITK@LT-EDI-EACL2021: Hope Speech Detection for Equality, Diversity, and Inclusion in Tamil, Malayalam and English. In *Proceedings of the First Workshop on Language Technology for Equality, Diversity and Inclusion*, Online.

Enrique Herrera-Viedma, Juan Bernabe-Moreno, Carlos Porcel Gallego, and Maria de los Angeles Martinez Sanchez. 2015. Solidarity in social media: when users abandon their comfort zone-the charlie hebdo case. *ICONO 14, Revista de comunicación y tecnologías emergentes*, 13(2):6–22.

Gary King, Langche Zeng, et al. 2001. Logistic regression in rare events data. *Political Analysis*, 9(2):137–163.

Diederik P Kingma and Jimmy Ba. 2014. Adam: A method for stochastic optimization. *arXiv preprint arXiv:1412.6980*.

Guillaume Lample and Alexis Conneau. 2019. Cross-lingual language model pretraining. In *NeurIPS*.

Roee Levy. 2020. Social media, news consumption, and polarization: evidence from a field experiment. *News Consumption, and Polarization: Evidence from a Field Experiment (July 16, 2020)*.

Yinhan Liu, Myle Ott, Naman Goyal, Jingfei Du, Mandar Joshi, Danqi Chen, Omer Levy, Mike Lewis, Luke Zettlemoyer, and Veselin Stoyanov. 2019. Roberta: A robustly optimized bert pretraining approach. *arXiv preprint arXiv:1907.11692*.

Thomas Mandl, Sandip Modha, Anand Kumar M, and Bharathi Raja Chakravarthi. 2020. Overview of the HASOC Track at FIRE 2020: Hate Speech and Offensive Language Identification in Tamil, Malayalam, Hindi, English and German. In *Forum for Information Retrieval Evaluation*, FIRE 2020, page 29–32, New York, NY, USA. Association for Computing Machinery.

Binny Mathew, Punyajoy Saha, Seid Muhie Yimam, Chris Biemann, Pawan Goyal, and Animesh Mukherjee. 2020. Hatexplain: A benchmark dataset for explainable hate speech detection. *arXiv preprint arXiv:2012.10289*.

Ioannis Mollas, Zoe Chrysopoulou, Stamatis Karlos, and Grigorios Tsoumakas. 2020. Ethos: an online hate speech detection dataset. *arXiv preprint arXiv:2006.08328*.

F. Pedregosa, G. Varoquaux, A. Gramfort, V. Michel, B. Thirion, O. Grisel, M. Blondel, P. Prettenhofer, R. Weiss, V. Dubourg, J. Vanderplas, A. Passos, D. Cournapeau, M. Brucher, M. Perrot, and E. Duchesnay. 2011. Scikit-learn: Machine learning in Python. *Journal of Machine Learning Research*, 12:2825–2830.

H. Prasetya and T. Murata. 2020. A model of opinion and propagation structure polarization in social media. *Computational Social Networks*, 7:1–35.

Karthik Puranik, Adeep Hande, Ruba Priyadharshini, Sajeetha Thavareesan, and Bharathi Raja Chakravarthi. 2021. IIITT@LT-EDI-EACL2021-Hope Speech Detection: There is always hope in Transformers. In *Proceedings of the First Workshop on Language Technology for Equality, Diversity and Inclusion*. Association for Computational Linguistics.

Pranav Rajpurkar, Jian Zhang, Konstantin Lopyrev, and Percy Liang. 2016. Squad: 100,000+ questions for machine comprehension of text. In *Proceedings of the 2016 Conference on Empirical Methods in Natural Language Processing*, pages 2383–2392.

Nils Reimers and Iryna Gurevych. 2019. Sentence-bert: Sentence embeddings using siamese bert-networks. In *Proceedings of the 2019 Conference on Empirical Methods in Natural Language Processing*. Association for Computational Linguistics.

Nils Reimers and Iryna Gurevych. 2020. Making monolingual sentence embeddings multilingual using knowledge distillation. In *Proceedings of the 2020 Conference on Empirical Methods in Natural Language Processing*. Association for Computational Linguistics.

Sashank Santhanam, Vidhushini Srinivasan, Khyati Mahajan, and Samira Shaikh. 2021 (in press). Towards understanding how emojis express solidarity in crisis events. In *International Conference on Applied Human Factors and Ergonomics*. Springer.

CR Snyder, Kevin L Rand, and David R Sigmon. 2005. Hope theory: A member of the positive psychology.

Shardul Suryawanshi and Bharathi Raja Chakravarthi. 2021. Findings of the shared task on Troll Meme Classification in Tamil. In *Proceedings of the First Workshop on Speech and Language Technologies for Dravidian Languages*. Association for Computational Linguistics.

Alex Wang, Amanpreet Singh, Julian Michael, Felix Hill, Omer Levy, and Samuel Bowman. 2018. Glue: A multi-task benchmark and analysis platform for natural language understanding. In *Proceedings of the 2018 EMNLP Workshop BlackboxNLP: Analyzing and Interpreting Neural Networks for NLP*, pages 353–355.

Guillaume Wenzek, Marie-Anne Lachaux, Alexis Conneau, Vishrav Chaudhary, Francisco Guzmán, Armand Joulin, and Édouard Grave. 2020. Ccnet: Extracting high quality monolingual datasets from web crawl data. In *Proceedings of The 12th Language Resources and Evaluation Conference*, pages 4003–4012.

Thomas Wolf, Lysandre Debut, Victor Sanh, Julien Chaumond, Clement Delangue, Anthony Moi, Pierric Cistac, Tim Rault, Rémi Louf, Morgan Funtowicz, Joe Davison, Sam Shleifer, Patrick von Platen, Clara Ma, Yacine Jernite, Julien Plu, Canwen Xu, Teven Le Scao, Sylvain Gugger, Mariama Drame, Quentin Lhoest, and Alexander M. Rush. 2020. Transformers: State-of-the-art natural language processing. In *Proceedings of the 2020 Conference on Empirical Methods in Natural Language Processing: System Demonstrations*, pages 38–45, Online. Association for Computational Linguistics.

Z. Zhang and Lei Luo. 2019. Hate speech detection: A solved problem? the challenging case of long tail on twitter. *Semantic Web*, 10:925–945.

Autobots@LT-EDI-EACL2021: One World, One Family: Hope Speech Detection with BERT Transformer Model

Sunil Gundapu
Language Technologies Research Centre
KCIS, IIIT Hyderabad
Telangana, India
sunil.g@research.iiit.ac.in

Radhika Mamidi
Language Technologies Research Centre
KCIS, IIIT Hyderabad
Telangana, India
radhika.mamidi@iiit.ac.in

Abstract

The rapid rise of online social networks like YouTube, Facebook, Twitter allows people to express their views more widely online. However, at the same time, it can lead to an increase in conflict and hatred among consumers in the form of freedom of speech. Therefore, it is essential to take a positive strengthening method to research on encouraging, positive, helping, and supportive social media content. In this paper, we describe a Transformer-based BERT model for Hope speech detection for equality, diversity, and inclusion, submitted for LT-EDI-2021 Task 2. Our model achieves a weighted averaged f1-score of 0.93 on the test set.

1 Introduction

With the proliferation of the Internet, the number of marginalized people looking for help and online support has grown significantly worldwide[1]. Recently, social media networks (SMN), online blogs, and online support groups (OSG) have emerged as popular online support sources. These online support networks play an essential role in marginalized people, such as individuals belonging to LGBTQIA+ (Lesbian, Gay, Bisexual, Transgender, IntersexQueer/Questioning, and Asexual people) community, people with similar health problems or disabilities, and individuals who belong to racial and ethnic minorities. And some of the research studies (Ganda, 2014) have shown that SMNs and OSGs significantly influence people's self-identification and self-understanding. So it's necessary to detect the positive content from online sources.

In this paper, we discussed the identification of Hope Speech for Equality, Diversity, and Inclusion (EDI) from the YouTube comments. Hope can be defined as a state of mind that brings fortitude, support, and reassurance to life. Hope can also come from a motivational discussion about how people deal with difficult situations and cope with them. Hope speech has a positive impact on various aspects that harm people's lives. We describe the hope speech for our task as "social media comments that give inspiration, suggestions, insight, and support". We have done various experiments on the provided Hope Speech dataset for Equality, Diversity, and Inclusion problem using different state-of-the-art machine learning and deep learning models.

2 Shared Task Description

We are attempting this shared task for English language only. The LT-EDI-2021 Task 2 (Chakravarthi and Muralidaran, 2021) is as follows: Given a YouTube comment or post, the system should identify its class. We have three classes 'Hope speech', 'Not hope speech' and 'Other language.' We classify the comment into the 'Hope speech' category when it promotes hope, optimism, faith, support, reassurance, suggestions, or it offers EDI values. If a comment doesn't have attributes mentioned in the hope speech class, classify it into the 'Not hope speech' class. We categorize the comment into the 'Other language' class when the comment not in the English language. Table 1 shows few sample YouTube comments from HopeEDI.

3 Related Work

Over the past few years, various methods have been proposed to identify hate speech on social media platforms. Alrehili (2019) surveyed the different state of the art NLP approaches to detect hate speech in OSNs, and they say there has been significant research work so far on hate speech. Considering the research work on Hope Speech, much less has been done compared to Hate Speech. By choosing the YouTube comments, Severyn et al.

[1] https://www.statista.com/topics/2409/digital-health/

Proceedings of the First Workshop on Language Technology for Equality, Diversity and Inclusion, pages 143–148
April 19, 2021. ©2020 Association for Computational Linguistics

Example Comment	Label
These tiktoks radiate gay chaotic energy and i love it	Not Hope Speech
I feel so base for that guy! They treated him as if he wasn't a human just because of who he loved!	Hope Speech
CASA. LA. FEMMEnWesT. ViLLAGEn2008nNyc	Not English

Table 1: Example YouTube Comments

(2014) conducted a systematic study on opinion mining. For this work, the authors created a manually labeled 35K size YouTube comment dataset to model the polarity of comments based on the kernel models.

Recently, to support the Rohingyas refugees, Palakodety et al. (2019) analyze how the hope speech from the social media comments can be used to reduce tensions between India and Pakistan during the Puluma attack. In this work, the authors intend to find the hope speech in SMNs can reduce the strain and violence between two nations. The authors created a corpus of 921,235 English Youtube comments posted by 392,460 users to accomplish this work.

One of the notable research work for hope speech detection is HopeEDI (Chakravarthi, 2020) corpus creation. In this work, authors created a corpus from user-generated YouTube comments for English, Tamil, and Malayalam. Then they developed various machine learning models for benchmark results on the dataset.

4 Dataset Description

This paper used the corpus (HopeEDI) provided by the "Hope Speech Detection" organizers to train and tune the models. The HopeEDI for English dataset containing 28,451 samples, in that 2484 samples belongs to the 'Hope speech' class, 25,940 samples belong to the 'Not hope speech' class, and the remaining 27 samples belong to the 'Other language' class. Table 2 represents the annotated corpus distribution, and Figure 1 shows the number of comments for the class.

Labels(↓)	Train	Valid	Test
Not Hope Speech	20778	2569	2593
Hope Speech	1962	272	250
Other Language	22	2	3
Total	22762	2843	2846

Table 2: Dataset Statistics

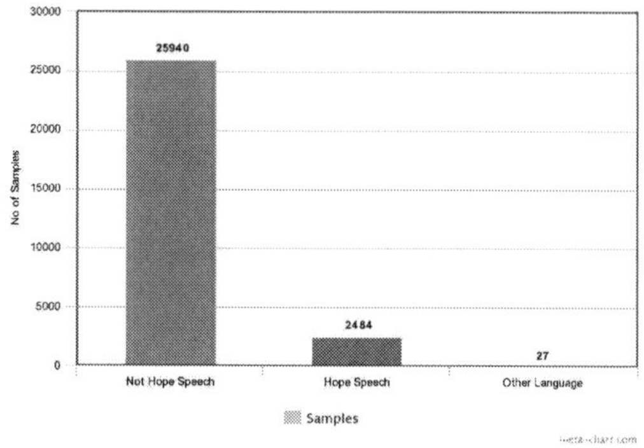

Figure 1: Distribution of samples per class

5 Proposed Approach

5.1 Data Preprocessing

Following pre-processing operations performed on the comments before feature engineering.

- All the comments in the dataset are converted to lowercase.
- Converted the online chatting abbreviations like 'ASAP', 'YOLO' into their original form by creating a slang words mapping dictionary.
- Expanded all contractions in the comments by writing regular expressions. For example, "they're" expanded into "they are", and "I'll" expand into "I will".
- In our problem, emojis play a crucial role, so we converted all the emojis into their respective keywords by using a python library called **demoji**[2].
- We removed all punctuation marks in the dataset.

5.2 Methodology

We started our experiments with various machine learning (ML) algorithms like Support Vector Machines (SVM), Logistic Regression (LR), Multi-Layer Perceptron (MLP), and XGBoost and deep

[2]https://pypi.org/project/demoji/

learning (DL) models like RNN (Recurrent Networks) and LSTMs (Long Short Term Memory) (Hochreiter and Schmidhuber, 1997) with various feature embeddings. However, Transformer based BERT model gave superior results to the above-mentioned techniques.

Our best hope speech detection model is ensembling of a pre-trained BERT and a rule based language identification model. The architecture of this ensemble model can be seen in Figure 2.

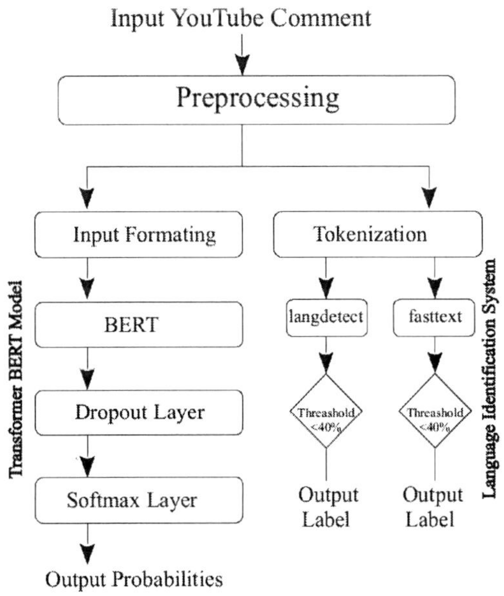

Figure 2: Ensembling Architecture

5.3 Transformer based BERT model

This section will describe the transformer based BERT model and then explain how we fine-tune this model to our problem.

5.3.1 Input Data Format

The input token sequence for the BERT model must be given in a certain format. Every input sequence must start with a [CLS] (classification token) token, and every sequence should be separated from other sequences by using a [SEP] (separation token) token. According to this BERT input data format, we added a [CLS] token to every input sequence and appended a [SEP] token after every sentence.

5.3.2 BERT Architecture

Bidirectional Encoder Representations from Transformers (BERT) (Devlin et al., 2019) is a "deep bidirectional" model designed to learn deep bidirectional representations from a large unsupervised text corpus. It reads the information from both the left and the right sides of input tokens during the training phase. In our ensembling architecture, we used the BERT base case model. The base model consists of 12 transformer blocks, 768 hidden blocks, 12 self-attention heads, and a total of 110 trainable parameters. And for better context learning BERT model uses the following two separate mechanisms:

1. **Masked Language Model (MLM):** In this mechanism, 15% of the tokens in the input sequence are masked out by replacing them with a [MASK] token. Then the complete sequence is fed to a deep bidirectional Transformer model. This model tries to estimate the actual value of the masked words based on the context of unmasked tokens in the input sequence.

2. **Next Sentence Prediction (NSP):** In this task, the model learns the relationship between input sequences to distinguish the two input sequences. BERT model takes pair of sequences as input and learns to predict whether the second sequence in the pair actually follows the first sequence or it is a random sequence.

Unlike traditional directional models, which reads the input sequence either from left to right or right to left, the BERT encoder attention mechanism processes the input sequence simultaneously, allowing all input tokens in the sequence to be processed in parallel. This feature enables the model to know the context of a token based on the tokens around it. We can see all the layers of BERT architecture in Figure 3. This pre-trained BERT model fine-tuned to our problem by adding a softmax classification layer on top of the BERT model output for the [CLS] token. Below is described how an input YouTube comment goes from the BERT model and gives an output class for the input.

- First, we preprocess the input sequence then arrange the sequence according to the input data format as described earlier.

- Then the preprocessed input fed to the BERT model. The BERT model generates sequence embeddings for all the tokens in the input sequence. But we consider the [CLS] token corresponding sequence embedding to detect hope speech.

- The sequence embedding corresponding to [CLS] token passed to a softmax classification layer to get each target class's output probabilities. The softmax layer uses a softmax activation function that calculates the probability for every possible output class given in (1). To avoid overfitting, added a dropout layer before the softmax layer with the dropout of 0.2.

$$Z = \frac{e^{z_i}}{\sum_{j=1}^{n} e^{z_j}} \quad (1)$$

In the above equation, where z is the sequence embedding, Z is a vector pf softmax probabilities, and the K in the number of target classes.

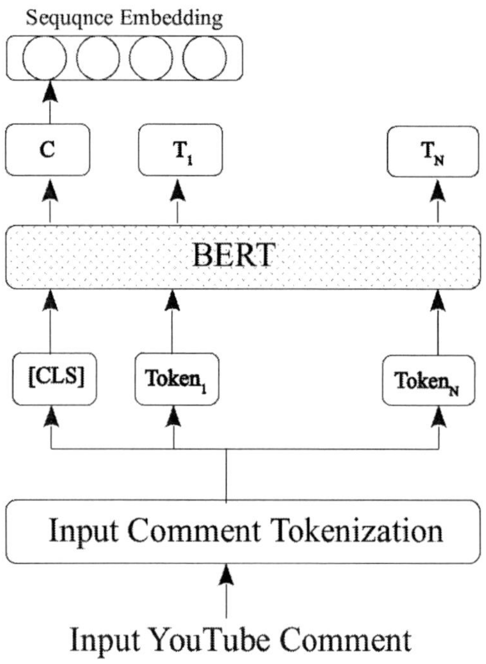

Figure 3: BERT Architecture

5.4 Rule based language identification model

If we examine our corpus, the 'Other language' class samples are very less (data skewing), so the statistical models are not predicting the 'Other language' samples at all. This is the main reason behind using the rule-based model in the architecture to identify those other than the English language comments. We use this model only to detect 'Other language' comments. This model identifies whether the given preprocessed comment from the English language is based on two python language identification libraries, **langdetect**[3], and **fasttext**[4]. Below explained how we identified the 'other language' class comments:

- Initially, we split the preprocessed input comment into meaningful tokens.
- Identify the language of each token in the input sequence using langdetect library. Then we calculate the percentage of English tokens in the input sequence. If the English tokens are less than 40%, then we consider that comment from the 'Other language' class—the same procedure used for the fasttext also.
- If the output of those two libraries is 'Other language,' then we predicted that the rule-based model's output is 'Other language'.

For other 'Hope speech' and 'Not hope speech' classes, we review the BERT model output only, but for the 'Other language' class, we consider the BERT and language identification model's output. And we added a constraint for only the 'Other language' class. At least any model, either BERT or Rule based model output, should be 'Other language' for the given input. If any input comment passes that constraint, we tagged a comment as 'Other language'.

6 Experiments and Results

To validate our approach, we conducted 3 experiments: Initially, we check the baseline model's (SVM, MLP, LR, XGBoost) results with n-gram level Term Frequency - Inverse Document Frequency (TF-IDF) vectors. Secondly, we trained the LSTM, RNN, and CNN models with pretrained Glove (Pennington et al., 2014) and FastText (Bojanowski et al., 2016) word embeddings. These models gave the better results than the baseline models but not at all contributing to the 'Other language' class whose training samples very less. Thirdly, we used the Transformer based BERT model with a rule based language identification model. This approach performed very well and gave the 0.93 wighted f1-score on test set. The rule based language identification model helped to identify the 'Other language' class samples. The

[3] https://pypi.org/project/langdetect/

[4] https://fasttext.cc/blog/2017/10/02/blog-post.html

Model	Validation Data			Test Data		
	Precision	Recall	F1-Score (weighted)	Precision	Recall	F1-Score (weighted)
SVM	0.91	0.90	0.91	0.88	0.87	0.87
LR	0.93	0.88	0.91	0.88	0.88	0.88
MLP	0.94	0.93	0.93	0.90	0.89	0.90
XGBoost	0.93	0.91	0.92	0.88	0.88	0.89
LSTM (with fasttext)	0.94	0.92	0.94	0.90	0.91	0.92
CNN (with fasttext)	0.95	0.91	0.94	0.91	0.92	0.92
RNN (with Glove)	0.93	0.92	0.93	0.91	0.89	0.90
BERT with LI	0.96	0.93	0.94	**0.93**	**0.93**	**0.93**

Table 3: Comparison between various model results

main motive of doing all these experiments is to assess how the proposed approach contributes to performance improvement.

We trained all our models using the training dataset and fine-tuned the model using the development. Evaluated the fine-tuned model by predicting the output labels for the unseen test set. Reported all the results in Table 3. SVM and LR performed very poorly on the test set. As already mentioned, the combination of BERT and the language recognition model has yielded better results than other approaches. And to calculate the model performance, we used the weighted average F1-score across all the classes.

As shown, Transformer based BERT model performed better than other ML and DL learning models for our hope speech detection problem. The supervised machine learning algorithms performed unsatisfactorily due to data imbalance problem. We tried to handle this class imbalance problem using Synthetic Minority Oversampling Technique (SMOTE) (Chawla et al., 2002), but it did not work well. Latterly, we used a rule-based language identification model to remove the non-intended language comments from our dataset. While observing the 'Other language' class comments, we find that some of the comments are wrongly tagged. The comment's actual content is in the English language, but the annotators tagged the comment as 'Other language'. And if we observe the word cloud of the 'Other language' class in Figure 4, we can only see English words only. We note that this is also a problem for not predicting 'Other language' comments.

To find the right set of hyper-parameters, we used the validation dataset. We implemented the ML algorithms using scikit-learn[5] and DL using

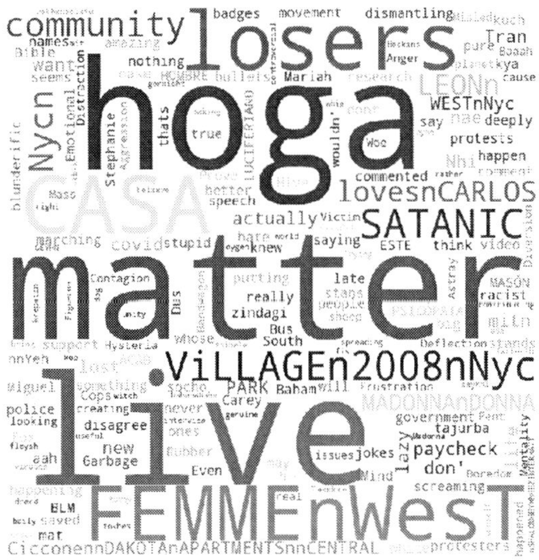

Figure 4: Word cloud of 'other language' class

Keras[6]. To implement BERT model used the HuggingFace[7], it's a PyTorch based transformer library. And all details of BERT model hyper-parameters are summarized in Table 4.

Hyper-parameters	Values
Model Type	BERT-Base
Learning Rate	23-5
Optimizer	Adam
Batch Size	16
Maximum Length	128
Epochs	10

Table 4: Hyper-parameters of BERT

[5]https://scikit-learn.org/stable/

[6]https://keras.io/

[7]https://huggingface.co/transformers/model_doc/bert.html

7 Conclusion

This paper described a transformer-based pretrained BERT model with a rule-based language identification system to detect hope speech in the YouTube comments. The BERT model helped for the better contextual representation of words in the comment, and the language identification model-assisted in detecting 'Other language' comments. In future work, we will handle the class imbalance problem efficiently by improving the dataset. And We will also explore with other transformer models like RoBERTa, XLNet, Albert, FLAIR, ELMo, etc., for a superior hope speech detection.

References

A. Alrehili. 2019. Automatic hate speech detection on social media: A brief survey. In *2019 IEEE/ACS 16th International Conference on Computer Systems and Applications (AICCSA)*, pages 1–6.

Piotr Bojanowski, Edouard Grave, Armand Joulin, and Tomas Mikolov. 2016. Enriching word vectors with subword information. *arXiv preprint arXiv:1607.04606*.

Bharathi Raja Chakravarthi. 2020. HopeEDI: A multilingual hope speech detection dataset for equality, diversity, and inclusion. In *Proceedings of the Third Workshop on Computational Modeling of People's Opinions, Personality, and Emotion's in Social Media*, pages 41–53, Barcelona, Spain (Online). Association for Computational Linguistics.

Bharathi Raja Chakravarthi and Vigneshwaran Muralidaran. 2021. Findings of the shared task on Hope Speech Detection for Equality, Diversity, and Inclusion. In *Proceedings of the First Workshop on Language Technology for Equality, Diversity and Inclusion*. Association for Computational Linguistics.

Nitesh Chawla, Kevin Bowyer, Lawrence Hall, and W. Kegelmeyer. 2002. Smote: Synthetic minority over-sampling technique. *J. Artif. Intell. Res. (JAIR)*, 16:321–357.

J. Devlin, Ming-Wei Chang, Kenton Lee, and Kristina Toutanova. 2019. Bert: Pre-training of deep bidirectional transformers for language understanding. In *NAACL-HLT*.

Madison Ganda. 2014. Social media and self: Influences on the formation of identity and understanding of self through social networking sites.

Sepp Hochreiter and Jürgen Schmidhuber. 1997. Long short-term memory. *Neural computation*, 9:1735–80.

Shriphani Palakodety, Ashiqur R. KhudaBukhsh, and Jaime G. Carbonell. 2019. Hope Speech Detection: A Computational Analysis of the Voice of Peace. *arXiv e-prints*, page arXiv:1909.12940.

Jeffrey Pennington, Richard Socher, and Christopher D. Manning. 2014. Glove: Global vectors for word representation. In *In EMNLP*.

A. Severyn, Alessandro Moschitti, O. Uryupina, Barbara Plank, and Katja Filippova. 2014. Opinion mining on youtube. In *ACL*.

Amrita@LT-EDI-EACL2021: Hope Speech Detection on Multilingual Text

Thara S, Ravi Teja T, Sai Rahul K
Amrita Vishwa Vidyapeetham,
Amritapuri, Kerala, India
thara@am.amrita.edu, ravitejatasubilli@gmail.com,
kothamasusairahul@gmail.com

Abstract

Analysis and deciphering code-mixed data is imperative in academia and industry, in a multilingual country like India, in order to solve problems apropos Natural Language Processing. This paper proposes a bidirectional long short-term memory (BiLSTM) with attention-based approach, in solving hope speech detection problem. Using this approach an F1-score of 0.73 (9 th rank) in Malayalam-English data set was achieved from a total of 31 teams who participated in the competition.

1 Introduction

Code-mixing may be defined as the phenomenon of mixing of elements of speech or text, from two or more languages, into a single utterance. Code-mixing is widely observed in social social-media platforms (Chakravarthi, 2020b). Code mixing imposes diverse challenges in Natural Language Processing (NLP) tasks like sentiment analysis (SA), named entity recognition (NER), and parts-of-speech (POS) tagging (Jose et al., 2020; Priyadharshini et al., 2020).

Nowadays, as more people lean on online communication platforms, it is incumbent on bloggers to stop the spread of negativity through online posts (Mandl et al., 2020; Chakravarthi et al., 2020, 2021). Studies have been carried out to surveil and cease the consumption of abusive comments on social-media platforms like You-tube and Twitter (Ghanghor et al., 2021a; Yasaswini et al., 2021; Hegde et al., 2021). Besides curbing dissemination of negativity, it is imperative for users online to endorse and promote positivity and hope (Chakravarthi and Muralidaran, 2021). As studies have shown that hope is an important factor in prevention of self-immolation and self-harm Snyder et al. (2002). Hope is generally attributed as assurance, encouragement, support, or motivation instilled in individuals by their peers or surroundings Chakravarthi (2020a); Puranik et al. (2021); Ghanghor et al. (2021b)

However, there is not much study done in understanding hope speech in the domain of code mixed communications. Hope Speech Detection for Equality, Diversity, and Inclusion-EACL 2021 is first such task [1] to detect hope speech in low resourced code-mixed languages like Malayalam-English, Tamil-English, Kannada-English.

2 Literature Survey

Since Hope Speech Detection for Equality, Diversity, and Inclusion-EACL 2021 is the first task in Hope Speech Detection, there is not much focus in this area. Most of the studies have been done in the NLP aspects of NER, SA and POS tagging on code mixed data.

In Sravani et al. (2018) the authors experimented with various word embedding techniques using 6 different classifiers and showed that Term Frequency and Inverse Document Frequency (TF-IDF) word embeddings yielded better results for NER task on English-Hindi code-mixed data.

In Thara and Poornachandran (2018) the authors discusses on the literature survey of code-mixed problems and datasets.

In Sasidhar et al. (2020) authors created a corpus of 12000 Hindi-English code mixed texts from various online communication platforms and annotated them as Happy, Sad and Anger based on the emotions. The authors achieved an accuracy of 83.21% using CNN-BiLSTM architecture.

In Sreelakshmi et al. (2020) the authors have

[1] https://competitions.codalab.org/competitions/27653

Proceedings of the First Workshop on Language Technology for Equality, Diversity and Inclusion, pages 149–156
April 19, 2021. ©2020 Association for Computational Linguistics

used Support Vector Machine (SVM)-Radial Basis Funcrion (RBF) classifier on features extracted using fastText for hate speech detection in Hindi-English code mixed corpus of 10000 texts which are equally divided into hate and non-hate classes. The authors obtained an accuracy of 0.75% using SVM-RBF algorithm.

In Liu et al. (2020) used an adversarial training with a pre-trained multilingual model XLM-R Conneau et al. (2020) on code-mixed Hindi-English data [2] and achieved an F1-score of 0.75 (1st rank) for SA.

3 Proposed Method

3.1 Data Description

Dataset consists of comments taken from YouTube[3] video comment section. Data set is classified into three classes namely Hope speech, Non-hope speech, not-Malayalam.

Hope speech: Comments having positive intentions, infused with inspiration provided by peers to an individual, promoting wellbeing, joy and happiness, comments promoting morals like equality, diversity and inclusion are labelled as Hope speech.

Non-hope speech:Comments that are biased and criticize without considering the outcome, and promote cultural, racially hatred interactions are classified as non-hope speech

Not-Malaylam: Comments that are not Malayalam or in Malayalam-English are categorized as not-Malayalam.

We merged the train and development data sets into a single data set. The merged data set is comprised of 9634 comments in total (Table 1), whereas the test data set (Table 2) has an aggregate of 1071 comments. 90 % of this merged data as were used as train data (Table 3) and 10 % as development data set (Table 4). Majority of the comments in the data set are labelled as non-hope speech, the data set as such is imbalanced

[2]https://competitions.codalab.org/competitions/20654

[3]https://www.youtube.com/

Class	Count	Percentage
Not-Malayalam	786	8.2 %
Hope speech	1860	19.3 %
Non-hope speech	6988	72.5 %
Total	9634	

Table 1: Total Data Statistics.

Class	Count	Percentage
Not-Malayalam	101	9.4 %
Hope speech	194	18.1 %
Non-hope speech	776	72.5 %
Total	1071	

Table 2: Test Data Statistics

Class	Count	Percentage
Not Malayalam	707	8.2 %
Hope speech	1674	19.3 %
Non-hope speech	6289	72.5 %
Total	8670	

Table 3: Train Data Statistics

Class	Count	Percentage
Not Malayalam	79	8.2 %
Hope speech	186	19.3 %
Non-hope speech	699	72.5 %
Total	964	

Table 4: Development Data Statistics

3.2 Data Preprocessing

Manual Cleaning: Data set contains 109159 comments/posts from YouTube video comment Section is comprised of abbreviations like: RSS (Rashtriya Swayamsevak Sangh), CAA (Citizenship Amendment Act), UAE (United Arab Emirates), ICMR (Indian Council of Medical Research), and usage of common internet slang like bro, sis, subs (subscriber) is widely observed throughout the data set. We manually expanded most of the abbreviation in train, development, and test data. We replaced commonly used internet slang like u (you), luv (love), vid (video), bro (brother), sis (sister), btw (by the way), rip (rest in peace) with the complete form of the word. We manually corrected misspelled English words. Numerical short-cuts like "3.5k" , "4 M" were rewritten in complete numerical form i.e. as "3500", "4000000". We desegmented words which have English prefix and Malayalam suffix like "machineil", "storyil", "collegeil" as "machine il", "story il","college il". Dates which are in numerical format like "29-12-2020" are rewritten as "December 29 2020". Symbols "&","+","%" are replaced with "and", "plus", "percentage".

Preprocessing: After manually cleaning the data, the following steps were used to preprocess the data.

Step 1: Remove emojis in the data and convert all words in Latin script into lower case

Step 2: Remove punctuation marks, @ from user mentions, # from hashtags.

Step 3: Replace characters and words which are occurring consecutively more than two times with a single occurrence.

3.3 Feature Extractions

Word2Vec and FastText algorithms were used for feature extractions

Word2Vec: Word2Vec (Mikolov et al., 2013) is a neural network based model which takes in text corpus as inputs, and yields word embeddings as output (a set of vectors). It is done using two different methods, one is Continuous-Bag-of Words (CBOW) and the other one is Skip-gram

In CBOW, initially every word in the vocabulary is given a random vector representation and the model is given a set of neighboring words, both from front and back of the word. The number of neighboring words is a hyperparameter, called as window size. The model is then asked to predict the present word. When training completes, the model outputs unique vector representation to each word in the vocabulary.

In Skip-gram method, just like with CBOW the model starts with a random vector representation for each word in the corpus. The model is then given a word and is asked to predict its surrounding neighbors, from the front and back of the word.

FastText : FastText, an extended version of Word2Vec is based on (Joulin et al., 2016; Bojanowski et al., 2017). FastText uses sub- word information to extract features. FastText first generates character n-grams for each word.
Example: 3-gram for word "bharat" would be < bh, har,ara, rat, at >. Unlike Word2Vec, FastText can handle Out-of-Vocabulary (OOV) words making use of the n-gram approach. OOV word vector representations can be obtained by adding the vector representations of sub words. Gensim implementation[4] were used for both FastText and Word2Vec.

3.4 Classification Model:

CNN: Studies have shown that CNN can be used in NLP. In (Kim, 2014), author shows that CNN with Word2Vec can attain remarkable results in sentence classification, with minimal hyperparameter training. The author has used seven different sets of data for this study. In (Zhang and Wallace, 2016) an extensive study on sensitivity of the model's performance for sentence classification was performed, based on model architecture and other hyperparameters.

In our experiments, we implemented a single layer 1-dimensional convolutional neural network (1D-CNN) with 256 kernels of size 1, followed by two feed-forward layers, where the first neural network has 256 units and the last one has 3 units, which is acting as the classification layer. A dropout is (Srivastava et al., 2014)used for regularization. The key-idea of dropout is to prevent units in the neural network (NN) from co-adapting too much, by randomly dropping units and their connection in the network during training.

[4] `https://pypi.org/project/gensim/`

Bi-LSTM: Long Short Term Memory networks(LSTM) (Hochreiter and Schmidhuber, 1997) are variants of RNN, designed to overcome the long term dependency problems in RNN. LSTMs address the long-term dependency problem by using an internal memory called cell state. LSTMs have the privilege to remove or add new information to this cell state by regulating a structure called gates.

We have implemented Bidirectional LSTM (BiLSTM) with attention mechanism. Bi-LSTM gives up representation of the input text from both directions, using two different LSTMs. Embeddings from Word2Vec and FastText are fed into the BiLSTM, the hidden states of BiLSTM layer are then fed into the attention layer which then gives a weighted context vector. The context vector is conveyed to a feed-forward layer having 3 units to classify the input.

4 Experiments and Results

We implemented all our models in tensorflow[5].

4.1 Experimental Methods

Word Embeddings: We experimented with embeddings of 100, 200, and 300 dimensions. We used Word2Vec and FastText (both Skip-gram and CBOW) embedding techniques, which yielded a best weighted F1-score.

Dropout and L2 regularization: We have considered a range of values between 0.0 and 1.0 for both dropout and regularization.

Optimizers: Adagrad, Adadelta, Adam, RMSprop, Stochastic Gradient Descent (SGD) were used as optimizers; the optimizer which resulted in a better F1-score was selected as the preferred optimizer.

Learning rate: We have considered a range of values between 10^{-5} to $10^{-}3$.

Epochs: Range of values between 30 and 100 with an interval of 10 were considered.

Data imbalance: The majority of the comments in the dataset belong to non-hope speech category. To address this data imbalance we experimented with up-sampling and data augmentation using back translation. We applied random up-sampling method to minority classes.

[5]https://www.tensorflow.org

4.2 Results

CNN with Word2Vec embeddings: Word embeddings from Word2Vec are feed into 1-D CNN; the results were evaluated using weighted F1-score. Various hyperparameters and word embeddings dimensions were experimented with. 1-D CNN with up-sampled data using Word2Vec embeddings (CNN_W2V_UP) obtained a weighted F1-score of 0.73 on development data set. 1-D CNN without any augmentation technique (CNN_W2V_NORM) obtained a weighted F1-score of 0.62 on development data set. 1-D CNN with data augmentation using back translation (CNN_W2V_AUG) obtained a weighted F1-score of 0.69 on development data set. See Table 5 and Figures: 2,3,4

Model	Dev_data	Test Data
CNN_W2V_NORM	0.62	0.62
CNN_W2V_AUG	0.69	0.68
CNN_W2V_UP	**0.73**	**0.75**

Table 5: **F1-score for development and test data.**CNN_W2V_UP: 1-D CNN with up-sampled data using Word2Vec embeddings, CNN_W2V_NORM: 1-D CNN without any augmentation technique using Word2Vec embeddings, CNN_W2V_AUG: 1-D CNN with data augmentation using back translation with Word2Vec embeddings.

CNN with FastText embeddings: Word embeddings from FastText are feed into 1-D CNN and we evaluated the results using weighted F1-score. We experimented with various hyperparameters and word embeddings dimensions. 1-D CNN with up-sampled data using FastText embeddings (CNN_ft_UP) obtained a weighted F1-score of 0.74 on development data set. 1-D CNN without any augmentation technique (CNN_ft_NORM) obtained a weighted F1-score of 0.70 on development data set. 1- D CNN with data augmentation using back translation (CNN_ft_AUG) obtained a weighted F1-score of 0.63 on development data set, see Table 6 and Figures: 5,6,7

Bi-LSTM with attention using FastText: Our initial experiments have shown that up-sampling yields better results compared to data augmentation using back translation, so we have used FastText as the feature extraction method and we used random up-sampling with attention based Bi-LSTM model. We obtained a weighted F1-score of 0.85 on the

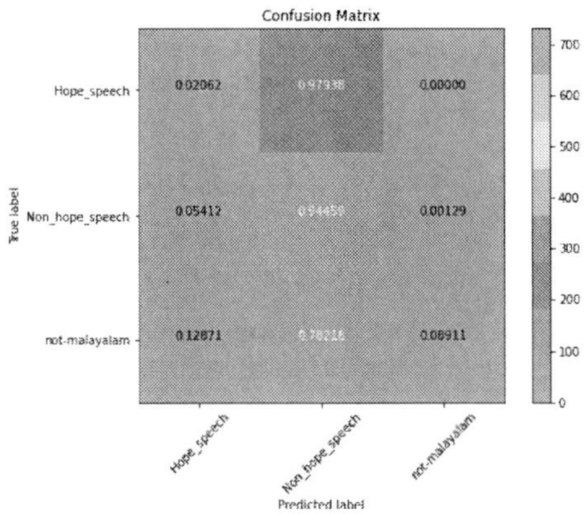

Figure 1: Confusion matrix for test data: 1-D CNN without any augmentation technique using Word2Vec embeddings.

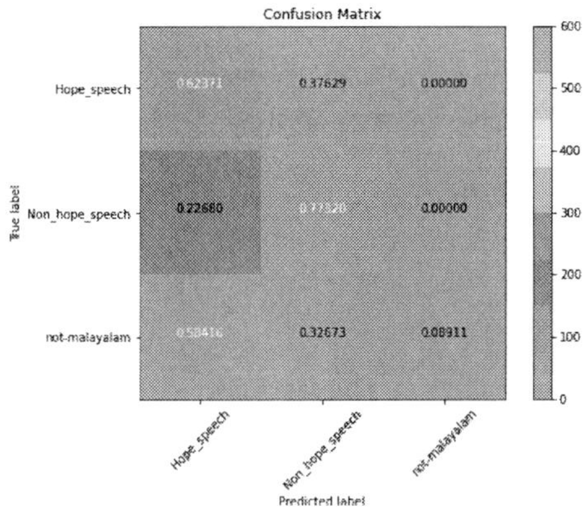

Figure 2: Confusion matrix for test data: 1-D CNN with data augmentation using back translation with Word2Vec embeddings.

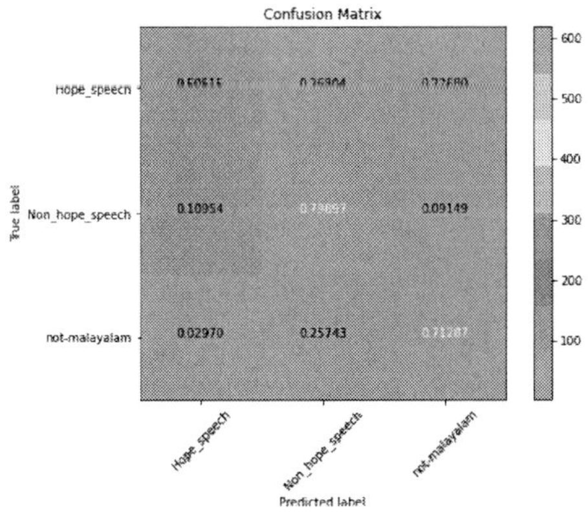

Figure 3: Confusion matrix for test data: 1-D CNN with up-sampled data using Word2Vec embeddings

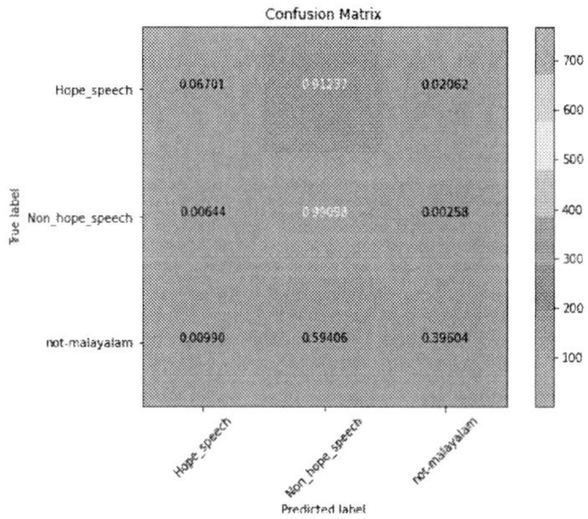

Figure 4: Confusion matrix for test data: 1-D CNN without any augmentation technique using FastText embeddings.

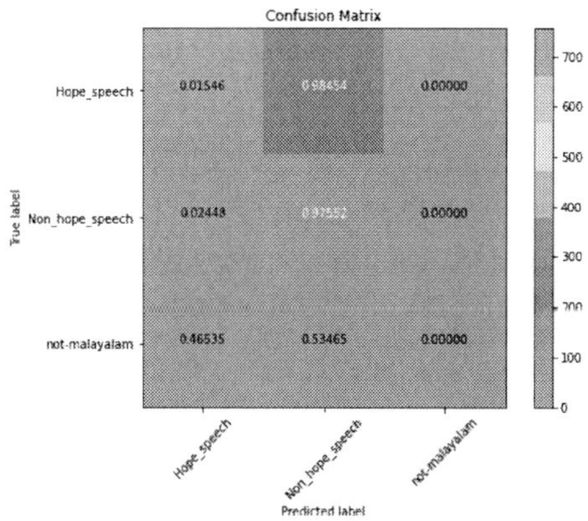

Figure 5: Confusion matrix for test data: 1-D CNN with data augmentation using back translation with FastText embeddings.

Model	Dev_data	Test Data
CNN_ft_AUG	0.63	0.62
CNN_ft_NORM	0.70	0.70
CNN_ft_UP	**0.74**	**0.76**

Table 6: **F1-score for development and test data**.CNN_ft_UP: 1-D CNN with up-sampled data using FastText embeddings, CNN_ft_NORM: 1-D CNN without any augmentation technique using FastText embeddings, CNN_ft_AUG: 1-D CNN with data augmentation using back translation with FastText embeddings.

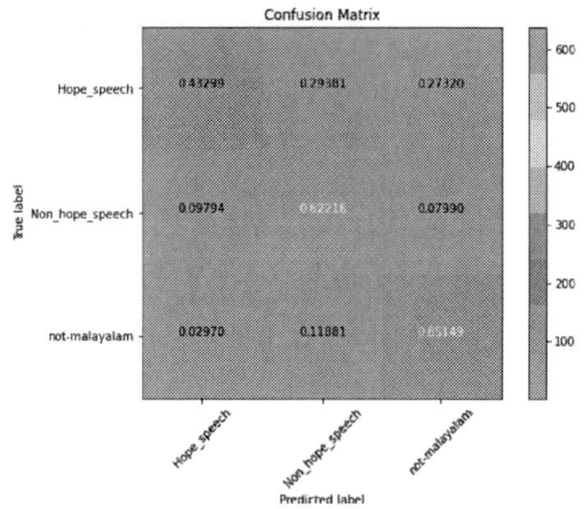

Figure 6: Confusion matrix for test data: 1-D CNN with up-sampled data using FastText embeddings.

development data set. We achieved an F1-score of 0.73 in the test data. As the F1-score for development data set of this model was the best compared to the rest of the models we submitted this model's results in the task. On the test data this model obtained an F1-score of 0.73, see Figure 8.

Model	Dev_data	Test Data
BiLSTM_ft_UP	0.85	0.73
CNN_W2V_UP	**0.73**	**0.75**
CNN_ft_UP	**0.74**	**0.76**

Table 7: **F1 score for development and test data**.CNN_W2V_UP: 1-D CNN with up-sampled data using Word2Vec embeddings,CNN_ft_UP: 1-D CNN without any augmentation technique using Word2Vec embeddings, Bi-LSTM_ft_UP: Bi-LSTM with up sampled data using FastText embeddings.

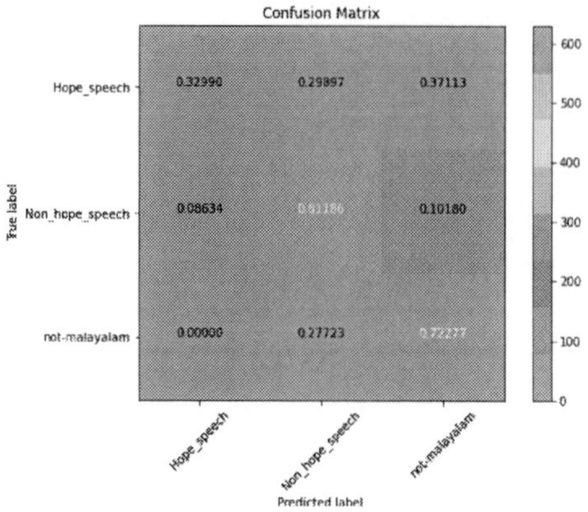

Figure 7: Confusion matrix for test data: Bi-LSTM with up-sampled data using FastText embeddings.

5 Conclusion

We evaluated the performance of our models on the test data using sklearn F1-score [6], we found that 1-D CNN on up-sampled data with both Word2Vec and FastText embeddings performed better than the Bi-LSTM model which we submitted for the task. However, Bi-LSTM performed relatively better on the development data set (see Table 7). We also observed that random up-sampling yielded better results compared to data augmentation with back translation method.

References

Piotr Bojanowski, Edouard Grave, Armand Joulin, and Tomas Mikolov. 2017. Enriching word vectors with subword information.

Bharathi Raja Chakravarthi. 2020a. HopeEDI: A multilingual hope speech detection dataset for equality, diversity, and inclusion. In *Proceedings of the Third Workshop on Computational Modeling of People's Opinions, Personality, and Emotion's in Social Media*, pages 41–53, Barcelona, Spain (Online). Association for Computational Linguistics.

Bharathi Raja Chakravarthi. 2020b. *Leveraging orthographic information to improve machine translation of under-resourced languages*. Ph.D. thesis, NUI Galway.

Bharathi Raja Chakravarthi, M Anand Kumar, John Philip McCrae, Premjith B, Soman KP, and Thomas Mandl. 2020. Overview of the track on HASOC-Offensive Language Identification-DravidianCodeMix. In *Working Notes of the Forum for Information Retrieval Evaluation (FIRE 2020)*.

[6] `https://pypi.org/project/scikit-learn/`

CEUR Workshop Proceedings. In: CEUR-WS. org, Hyderabad, India.

Bharathi Raja Chakravarthi and Vigneshwaran Muralidaran. 2021. Findings of the shared task on Hope Speech Detection for Equality, Diversity, and Inclusion. In *Proceedings of the First Workshop on Language Technology for Equality, Diversity and Inclusion*. Association for Computational Linguistics.

Bharathi Raja Chakravarthi, Ruba Priyadharshini, Navya Jose, Anand Kumar M, Thomas Mandl, Prasanna Kumar Kumaresan, Rahul Ponnusamy, Hariharan V, Elizabeth Sherly, and John Philip McCrae. 2021. Findings of the shared task on Offensive Language Identification in Tamil, Malayalam, and Kannada. In *Proceedings of the First Workshop on Speech and Language Technologies for Dravidian Languages*. Association for Computational Linguistics.

Alexis Conneau, Kartikay Khandelwal, Naman Goyal, Vishrav Chaudhary, Guillaume Wenzek, Francisco Guzmán, Edouard Grave, Myle Ott, Luke Zettlemoyer, and Veselin Stoyanov. 2020. Unsupervised cross-lingual representation learning at scale.

Nikhil Kumar Ghanghor, Parameswari Krishnamurthy, Sajeetha Thavareesan, Ruba Priyadharshini, and Bharathi Raja Chakravarthi. 2021a. IIITK@DravidianLangTech-EACL2021: Offensive Language Identification and Meme Classification in Tamil, Malayalam and Kannada. In *Proceedings of the First Workshop on Speech and Language Technologies for Dravidian Languages*, Online. Association for Computational Linguistics.

Nikhil Kumar Ghanghor, Rahul Ponnusamy, Prasanna Kumar Kumaresan, Ruba Priyadharshini, Sajeetha Thavareesan, and Bharathi Raja Chakravarthi. 2021b. IIITK@LT-EDI-EACL2021: Hope Speech Detection for Equality, Diversity, and Inclusion in Tamil, Malayalam and English. In *Proceedings of the First Workshop on Language Technology for Equality, Diversity and Inclusion*, Online.

Siddhanth U Hegde, Adeep Hande, Ruba Priyadharshini, Sajeetha Thavareesan, and Bharathi Raja Chakravarthi. 2021. UVCE-IIITT@DravidianLangTech-EACL2021: Tamil Troll Meme Classification: You need to Pay more Attention. In *Proceedings of the First Workshop on Speech and Language Technologies for Dravidian Languages*. Association for Computational Linguistics.

Sepp Hochreiter and Jürgen Schmidhuber. 1997. Long short-term memory. *Neural Comput.*, 9(8):1735–1780.

N. Jose, B. R. Chakravarthi, S. Suryawanshi, E. Sherly, and J. P. McCrae. 2020. A survey of current datasets for code-switching research. In *2020 6th International Conference on Advanced Computing and Communication Systems (ICACCS)*, pages 136–141.

Armand Joulin, Edouard Grave, Piotr Bojanowski, and Tomas Mikolov. 2016. Bag of tricks for efficient text classification.

Yoon Kim. 2014. Convolutional neural networks for sentence classification.

Jiaxiang Liu, Xuyi Chen, Shikun Feng, Shuohuan Wang, Xuan Ouyang, Yu Sun, Zhengjie Huang, and Weiyue Su. 2020. Kk2018 at SemEval-2020 task 9: Adversarial training for code-mixing sentiment classification. In *Proceedings of the Fourteenth Workshop on Semantic Evaluation*, pages 817–823, Barcelona (online). International Committee for Computational Linguistics.

Thomas Mandl, Sandip Modha, Anand Kumar M, and Bharathi Raja Chakravarthi. 2020. Overview of the HASOC Track at FIRE 2020: Hate Speech and Offensive Language Identification in Tamil, Malayalam, Hindi, English and German. In *Forum for Information Retrieval Evaluation*, FIRE 2020, page 29–32, New York, NY, USA. Association for Computing Machinery.

Tomas Mikolov, Kai Chen, Greg Corrado, and Jeffrey Dean. 2013. Efficient estimation of word representations in vector space.

Ruba Priyadharshini, Bharathi Raja Chakravarthi, Mani Vegupatti, and John P. McCrae. 2020. Named Entity Recognition for Code-Mixed Indian Corpus using Meta Embedding. In *2020 6th International Conference on Advanced Computing and Communication Systems (ICACCS)*, pages 68–72.

Karthik Puranik, Adeep Hande, Ruba Priyadharshini, Sajeetha Thavareesan, and Bharathi Raja Chakravarthi. 2021. IIITT@LT-EDI-EACL2021-Hope Speech Detection: There is always hope in Transformers. In *Proceedings of the First Workshop on Language Technology for Equality, Diversity and Inclusion*. Association for Computational Linguistics.

Turaga Sasidhar, Premjith B., and Soman Kp. 2020. Emotion detection in hinglish(hindi+english) code-mixed social media text. *Procedia Computer Science*, 171:1346–1352.

C. Snyder, Hal Shorey, Jennifer Cheavens, Kim Pulvers, Virgil III, and Cynthia Wiklund. 2002. Hope and academic success in college. *Journal of Educational Psychology*, 94:820–826.

Lolla Sravani, Atla Reddy, and Thara Sasidharan. 2018. A comparison study of word embedding for detecting named entities of code-mixed data in indian language. pages 2375–2381.

K. Sreelakshmi, Premjith B., and Soman Kp. 2020. Detection of hate speech text in hindi-english code-mixed data. *Procedia Computer Science*, 171:737–744.

Nitish Srivastava, Geoffrey Hinton, Alex Krizhevsky, Ilya Sutskever, and Ruslan Salakhutdinov. 2014. Dropout: A simple way to prevent neural networks from overfitting. *Journal of Machine Learning Research*, 15(56):1929–1958.

S Thara and Prabaharan Poornachandran. 2018. Code-mixing: A brief survey. In *2018 International Conference on Advances in Computing, Communications and Informatics (ICACCI)*, pages 2382–2388. IEEE.

Konthala Yasaswini, Karthik Puranik, Adeep Hande, Ruba Priyadharshini, Sajeetha Thavareesan, and Bharathi Raja Chakravarthi. 2021. IIITT@DravidianLangTech-EACL2021: Transfer Learning for Offensive Language Detection in Dravidian Languages. In *Proceedings of the First Workshop on Speech and Language Technologies for Dravidian Languages*. Association for Computational Linguistics.

Ye Zhang and Byron Wallace. 2016. A sensitivity analysis of (and practitioners' guide to) convolutional neural networks for sentence classification.

Hopeful_Men@LT-EDI-EACL2021: Hope Speech Detection Using Indic Transliteration and Transformers

Ishan Sanjeev Upadhyay*[1], **Nikhil E***[1], **Anshul Wadhawan**[2], and **Radhika Mamidi**[3]

[1,3]International Institute of Information Technology, Hyderabad
[2]Flipkart Private Limited
[1]{ishan.sanjeev, nikhil.e}@research.iiit.ac.in
[2]anshul.wadhwan@flipkart.com
[3]radhika.mamidi@iiit.ac.in

Abstract

This paper aims to describe the approach we used to detect hope speech in the HopeEDI dataset. We experimented with two approaches. In the first approach, we used contextual embeddings to train classifiers using logistic regression, random forest, SVM, and LSTM based models.The second approach involved using a majority voting ensemble of 11 models which were obtained by fine-tuning pre-trained transformer models (BERT, ALBERT, RoBERTa, IndicBERT) after adding an output layer. We found that the second approach was superior for English, Tamil and Malayalam. Our solution got a weighted F1 score of 0.93, 0.75 and 0.49 for English,Malayalam and Tamil respectively. Our solution ranked first in English, eighth in Malayalam and eleventh in Tamil.

1 Introduction

The spread of hate speech on social media is a problem that still exists today. While there have been attempts made at hate speech detection (Schmidt and Wiegand, 2017; Lee et al., 2018) to stop the spread of negativity, this form of censorship can also be misused to obstruct rights and freedom of speech. Furthermore, hate speech tends to spread faster than non-hate speech (Mathew et al., 2019).While there has been a growing amount of marginalized people looking for support online (Gowen et al., 2012; Wang and Jurgens, 2018), there has been a substantial amount of hate towards them too (Mondal et al., 2017). Therefore, detecting and promoting content that reduces hostility and increases hope is important. Hope speech detection can be seen as a rare positive mining task because hope speech constitutes a low percentage of overall content (Palakodety et al., 2020a). There has been work done on hope speech or help speech detection before that has used logistic regression and active learning techniques (Palakodety et al., 2020a,b). In our paper, we will be doing the hope speech detection task on the HopeEDI dataset (Chakravarthi, 2020; Chakravarthi and Muralidaran, 2021) which consists of user comments from Youtube in English, Tamil and Malayalam.

In this paper, we will first look at the task definition, followed by the methodology used. We will then look at the experiments and results followed by conclusion and future work.

*These authors contributed equally to this work.

2 Task Definition

The given problem is a comment level classification task for the identification of "hope speech" within YouTube comments, wherein they are to be classified as "Hope speech", "Not hope speech" and "Not in intended language". The data provided in the task was annotated at a per-comment basis wherein a comment could be composed of more than one sentence.

3 Methodology

This section talks about the methodology that we have used to solve the task. As shown in Figure 1, the pipeline involves preprocessing, language detection, transliteration (for Indian languages), and hope speech detection. These steps are described in this section.

3.1 Pre-processing Module

The preprocessing module involved the following:

- Removing special characters and excess whitespaces
- Removing emojis
- Make text lowercase.

Proceedings of the First Workshop on Language Technology for Equality, Diversity and Inclusion, pages 157–163
April 19, 2021.

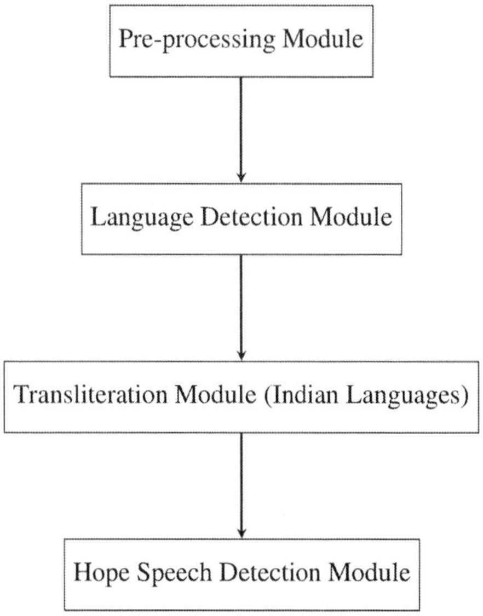

Figure 1: Methodology Pipeline

These steps were taken to make the text more uniform. Special characters like "@" and "#" were removed because they did not serve as good features for classification and language detection. Emojis were removed because they were sparsely used in the dataset.

3.2 Language Detection Module

The task involves classifying text into hope, not-hope and not-language. Language detection module marks the not-language sentences. We use Google's language detection library (Shuyo, 2010) to do this. The Tamil and Malayalam datasets are code-mixed. Inter-sentential,intra-sentential, tag code-mixing and code-mixing between Latin and native script is observed in the Tamil and Malayalam datasets. Google's language detection library does not work on such code-mixed data. Since the Tamil and Malayalam sentences involve code-mixed data, language detection can not be done on them using the Google language detection library. We observed that sentences that were marked as not-Tamil and not-Malayalam were mostly English sentences with some of them being Hindi and other languages. Hence, we adopted a heuristic where we marked sentences as not-Tamil or not-Malayalam if the sentences were detected to be in English or Hindi, other sentences were assumed to belong to the respective language.

3.3 Transliteration Module

After language detection, sentences that are classified to be in Tamil and Malayalam undergo transliteration. Tamil and Malayalam text have code-mixing between Latin and native script, hence transliteration is done to make the entire text in the native script. This step is also important because it makes the text closer to the kind of text IndicBert is trained on. Transliteration was done by using the indic-transliteration library .

3.4 Hope Speech Detection Module

After preprocessing and transliteration (for Indian languages), the text is sent to the hope speech detection module. The hope speech detection module is responsible for predicting if a text is hope speech or not hope speech. We have used the following for our experiment.

3.4.1 Models

Transformers (Vaswani et al., 2017) have performed well in various natural language processing (NLP) tasks. Unlike recurrent neural networks (RNN), transformers are non-sequential (ie. sentences are processed as a whole rather than word by word) and use self-attention at each input time step. Hence, they do not suffer from long dependency issues. Query, Key and Value are three different ways in which input vectors are used in the self-attention mechanism. The attention score for every input vector is calculated using a compatibility function which takes as input the query vector and all the keys. The final output is a weighted sum of values where the weights are the attention scores calculated by the compatibility function. We have used the following transformers in our experiment. We chose RoBERTa for our final model in English and ALBERT (IndicBERT) for Tamil and Malayalam.

BERT (Devlin et al., 2019) is based on the transformer architecture. Using its multi-layer encode module,It is able to jointly utilize both left and right contexts across all layers to pre-train its bidirectional representations. BERT is trained on two unsupervised prediction tasks, next sentence prediction and masked language modelling. We have fine tuned "bert-base-uncased" model on the dataset for one of our experiments.

RoBERTa (Liu et al., 2019) is a transformer architecture which is based on optimizations made to

https://github.com/sanskrit-coders/indic_transliteration

the BERT approach. It trains on more data and bigger batches, removes next sentence prediction objective that BERT used, trains on longer sequences and introduces dynamic masking (ie. mask tokens change during training epochs). RoBERTa outperforms BERT and XLNet on the GLUE benchmark. For the hope speech classification task in English, we fine-tuned the "roberta-base" model on the provided data. The roberta-base model is trained on 160 GB of English text from five different datasets.

ALBERT (Lan et al., 2020) is a transformer architecture based on BERT but with fewer parameters. There are two key changes made to ALBERT. The first is factorized embeddings parameterization, which decomposes the large vocabulary embedding matrix into smaller matrices. This makes it easier to grow hidden size without increasing the parameter size of vocabulary embeddings. This step leads to a reduction in parameters by 80% compared to BERT. The second is cross-layer parameter sharing, which prevents the parameters from increasing as the depth of the network increases. We fine-tuned the IndicBERT model for the hope speech classification task in Tamil and Malayalam. We used IndicBERT (Kakwani et al., 2020) which is a multilingual ALBERT model pre-trained on 12 major Indian languages. We also fine-tuned "albert-base-v2" model for our experiment in English.

LSTM Long Short-Term Memory (Hochreiter and Schmidhuber, 1997) networks seek to solve the short-term memory or vanishing gradient problem that RNNs face. They do so by having internal gates that regulate the flow of information. Information flows through a mechanism known as cell states. The cell can make decisions about what to store, what to forget and what the next hidden state should be. This is done through internal mechanisms called gates which contain sigmoid activations.

Random Forest Classifier Random forests (Breiman, 2001) use an ensemble of a large number of decision trees generally trained with the bagging method. These decision trees are created using random subsamples of the given dataset with replacement (bootstrap dataset) and a random subset of the features. New samples are classified by choosing the prediction made by most decision trees (majority voting).

Support Vector Machine Support vector machine (SVM) (Hearst, 1998) is a supervised learning method that can be used for classification or regression. We have used SVM for classification. The objective of the SVM classification algorithm is to find the hyper-plane that most accurately differentiates two classes that have been plotted on a f dimensional plane where f is the number of features.

Logistic Regression Logistic regression (McCullagh and Nelder, 1989)is a statistical model used for binary classification. It does so by using a logistic function to model the binary outcome. It can be extended for multiclass classification problems.

3.4.2 Ensemble Process

Ensembles can help make better predictions by reducing the spread of predictions. Hence, lowering variance and improving accuracy. We used a voting based ensemble method where we trained N models on N different training and validation data obtained by random shuffling. We then chose the majority voting as the merging technique to produce our final prediction y. In majority voting, the final prediction y is decided based on which prediction is made by the majority of the models . We made two ensembles, one each of 7 models and 11 models and chose the ensemble that gave the best weighted F1 score.

4 Experiments

Initially, the entire database is preprocessed to remove extra tab spaces, punctuations, emojis, mentions and links. In the case of Malayalam and Tamil, we also transliterate the entire database. Then we distributed our experimentation procedure into two different approaches. In the first approach, we fine-tune our pre-trained masked language models using the train and validation splits for the purpose of making them more suitable to the subsequent classification task. Thereafter, contextual embeddings for each sentence in the dataset are produced by calculating the average of the second to last hidden layer for every single token in the sentence. We then trained Logistic Regression, Random Forest, SVM and RNN-based classifier models using these embeddings. In the second approach, all the sentences are encoded into tokens using the respective tokenizers and then we add a linear layer on top of the pre-trained model layers after dropout. All the layers of the devised model are then trained such that the error is back propagated through the entire architecture and the pre-trained weights of the model are modified to reflect the new database. For both these approaches, we then calculated predictions for the test split and reported performance metrics. For English, we try out three different pre-trained models: "roberta-base", "bert-base-uncased", and "albert-base-v2" for both the approaches. For Tamil and Malayalam however, only the IndicBERT model is applicable for either approach.

Language	Database	Hope	Not Hope	Other Lang.
English	Train	1962	20778	22
	Dev	242	2569	2
Tamil	Train	6327	7872	1961
	Dev	757	998	263
Malayalam	Train	1668	6205	691
	Dev	190	784	96

Table 1: Data distribution by class

	English	Tamil	Malayalam
Training	22762	16160	2564
Development	2843	2018	1070
Test	2846	2020	1071
Total	28451	20198	10705

Table 2: Data distribution by language

4.1 Dataset

The HopeEDI dataset consists of Youtube comments marked as "hope", "not hope" and "other language" in three languages: English, Tamil and Malayalam. The distribution of hope, not hope and other language tag in the training and development datasets is shown in table 1. The ratio of hope to not hope is around 0.09 in English, 0.26 in Malayalam and 0.79 in Tamil. Table 2 shows the data distribution between training, development and test datasets. There are a total of 28,451 comments in English, 10,705 comments in Malayalam and 20,198 comments in Tamil. Data in Tamil and Telugu has code-mixing. In the English dataset, there are instances where English comments are annotated as not English. For example, "Fox News is pure Garbage!" is annotated as not English in the training set. This contributes some noise to the English dataset.

4.2 System Settings

In the first approach, we run the task of masked language modelling on our database for 4 epochs for each of the 5 model-database combinations. Afterwards, the sentence input token length is limited to 512 and the embeddings extracted by evaluation on the input sequences by the model are of length 768. The RNN based classifier is composed of an LSTM layer and two dense layers. In the second approach, the encoded sentences are in the form of a data loader class, containing the respective input IDs and attention masks, with a batch size of 16. These are then passed into a model that implements a dropout of 30% and the output from the final linear layer is used for classification.

4.3 Evaluation Metrics

We used F1 and weighted F1 scores for evaluating our model.

$$F1\ Score = 2 \times \frac{(precision \times recall)}{(precision + recall)}$$

Weighted F1 scores are calculated by taking the F1 scores for each label and then doing a weighted average by the number of true instances of each label.

$$weighted\ F1 = \frac{(F1_i \times y_i + F1_j \times y_j)}{(y_i + y_j)}$$

y_i and y_j are the number of true instances of class i and class j respectively and $F1_i$ and $F1_j$ are the F1 scores of class i and j respectively.

4.4 Results

Our experimentation involved two approaches. In the first approach, we used contextual embeddings (E) to train classifiers using logistic regression (LR), random forest (RF), SVM, and LSTM based models. In the second approach we used an ensemble of 11 models which were generated by finetuning (FT) pre-trained transformer models after adding an output layer. We used majority voting to get our final prediction. Results for both the approaches on our test split generated from the provided train and dev datasets are reported in Tables 3, 4 and 5 for English, Tamil and Malayalam respectively. We report the macro-averaged and weighted recall, precision and F1-score for each possible model-method combination. While the weighted F1 scores are more representative of how well a model performs, the disparity between the weighted and macro-averaged scores demonstrates how disproportionate a certain model's effectiveness is in predicting the different classes. For English, the second approach involving finetuning is the best performing one for each of the models tested, closely followed by the Logistic Regression and LSTM-based methods in the first approach. The roberta-base model seems to have a slight edge over the other two tested models. For Tamil and

Model	Method Used	Macro Precision	Weighted Precision	Macro Recall	Weighted Recall	Macro F1-Score	Weighted F1-Score
BERT	E + LR	0.778	0.911	0.656	0.924	0.695	0.913
	E + RF	0.834	0.902	0.526	0.916	0.528	0.881
	E + SVM	0.771	0.86	0.489	0.866	0.488	0.837
	E + LSTM	0.456	0.833	0.500	0.913	0.477	0.871
	FT	0.759	0.915	0.728	0.915	0.742	0.915
ALBERT	E + LR	0.703	0.881	0.538	0.912	0.549	0.883
	E + RF	0.832	0.900	0.506	0.914	0.491	0.874
	E + SVM	0.456	0.833	0.500	0.913	0.477	0.871
	E + LSTM	0.657	0.878	0.571	0.905	0.591	0.887
	FT	0.755	0.916	0.705	0.924	0.725	0.919
RoBERTa	E + LR	0.794	0.914	0.657	0.926	0.700	0.915
	E + RF	0.840	0.905	0.535	0.917	0.544	0.885
	E + SVM	0.821	0.899	0.517	0.915	0.512	0.878
	E + LSTM	0.791	0.918	0.693	0.928	0.729	0.921
	FT	0.753	0.915	0.748	0.922	0.745	**0.923**

Table 3: Metrics for English language

Model	Method Used	Macro Precision	Weighted Precision	Macro Recall	Weighted Recall	Macro F1-Score	Weighted F1-Score
Indic -BERT	E + LR	0.473	0.482	0.484	0.520	0.441	0.464
	E + RF	0.511	0.516	0.506	0.544	0.458	0.482
	E + SVM	0.278	0.309	0.500	0.556	0.357	0.397
	E + LSTM	0.591	0.587	0.501	0.557	0.364	0.403
	FT	0.635	0.637	0.627	0.636	0.623	**0.629**

Table 4: Metrics for Tamil language

Model	Method Used	Macro Precision	Weighted Precision	Macro Recall	Weighted Recall	Macro F1-Score	Weighted F1-Score
Indic -BERT	E + LR	0.645	0.729	0.501	0.790	0.447	0.699
	E + RF	0.395	0.623	0.499	0.788	0.440	0.696
	E + SVM	0.386	0.610	0.492	0.777	0.433	0.683
	E + LSTM	0.367	0.579	0.471	0.745	0.413	0.652
	FT	0.776	0.842	0.743	0.842	0.756	**0.837**

Table 5: Metrics for Malayalam language

Malayalam, the second approach is still the best performer, but by a greater margin.

5 Conclusion and Future Work

In this paper, we presented our approach for hope speech detection in English, Tamil, and Malayalam on the HopeEDI dataset. We used two approaches. The first approach involved using contextual embeddings to train various classifiers. The second approach involved using a majority voting ensemble of 11 models which were obtained by fine-tuning pre-trained transformer models. The second approach using the roberta-base model was the best performing model for English, giving a weighted F1 score of 0.93. The second approach using IndicBERT model gave the best performance for Tamil and Malayalam, giving a weighted F1 score of 0.75 for Malayalam and 0.49 for Tamil. In the future, we plan to fine-tune transformers pre-trained on code mixed data. Data augmentation methods like synonym replacement and random insertion could be used to fine-tune the model on more data.

References

Leo Breiman. 2001. Random forests. *Mach. Learn.*, 45(1):5–32.

Bharathi Raja Chakravarthi. 2020. HopeEDI: A multilingual hope speech detection dataset for equality, diversity, and inclusion. In *Proceedings of the Third Workshop on Computational Modeling of People's Opinions, Personality, and Emotion's in Social Media*, pages 41–53, Barcelona, Spain (Online). Association for Computational Linguistics.

Bharathi Raja Chakravarthi and Vigneshwaran Muralidaran. 2021. Findings of the shared task on Hope Speech Detection for Equality, Diversity, and Inclusion. In *Proceedings of the First Workshop on Language Technology for Equality, Diversity and Inclusion*. Association for Computational Linguistics.

Jacob Devlin, Ming-Wei Chang, Kenton Lee, and Kristina Toutanova. 2019. BERT: Pre-training of deep bidirectional transformers for language understanding. In *Proceedings of the 2019 Conference of the North American Chapter of the Association for Computational Linguistics: Human Language Technologies, Volume 1 (Long and Short Papers)*, pages 4171–4186, Minneapolis, Minnesota. Association for Computational Linguistics.

Kris Gowen, Matthew Deschaine, Darcy Gruttadara, and Dana Markey. 2012. Young adults with mental health conditions and social networking websites: Seeking tools to build community. *Psychiatric Rehabilitation Journal*, 35(3):245–250.

Marti A. Hearst. 1998. Support vector machines. *IEEE Intelligent Systems*, 13(4):18–28.

Sepp Hochreiter and Jürgen Schmidhuber. 1997. Long short-term memory. *Neural Computation*, 9(8):1735–1780.

Divyanshu Kakwani, Anoop Kunchukuttan, Satish Golla, Gokul N.C., Avik Bhattacharyya, Mitesh M. Khapra, and Pratyush Kumar. 2020. IndicNLPSuite: Monolingual corpora, evaluation benchmarks and pre-trained multilingual language models for Indian languages. In *Findings of the Association for Computational Linguistics: EMNLP 2020*, pages 4948–4961, Online. Association for Computational Linguistics.

Zhenzhong Lan, Mingda Chen, Sebastian Goodman, Kevin Gimpel, Piyush Sharma, and Radu Soricut. 2020. Albert: A lite bert for self-supervised learning of language representations.

Younghun Lee, Seunghyun Yoon, and Kyomin Jung. 2018. Comparative studies of detecting abusive language on Twitter. In *Proceedings of the 2nd Workshop on Abusive Language Online (ALW2)*, pages 101–106, Brussels, Belgium. Association for Computational Linguistics.

Yinhan Liu, Myle Ott, Naman Goyal, Jingfei Du, Mandar Joshi, Danqi Chen, Omer Levy, Mike Lewis, Luke Zettlemoyer, and Veselin Stoyanov. 2019. Roberta: A robustly optimized bert pretraining approach.

Binny Mathew, Ritam Dutt, Pawan Goyal, and Animesh Mukherjee. 2019. Spread of hate speech in online social media. In *Proceedings of the 10th ACM Conference on Web Science*, WebSci '19, page 173–182, New York, NY, USA. Association for Computing Machinery.

P. McCullagh and J.A. Nelder. 1989. *Generalized Linear Models, Second Edition*. Chapman and Hall/CRC Monographs on Statistics and Applied Probability Series. Chapman & Hall.

Mainack Mondal, Leandro Araújo Silva, and Fabrício Benevenuto. 2017. A measurement study of hate speech in social media. In *Proceedings of the 28th ACM Conference on Hypertext and Social Media*, HT '17, page 85–94, New York, NY, USA. Association for Computing Machinery.

Shriphani Palakodety, Ashiqur R. KhudaBukhsh, and Jaime G. Carbonell. 2020a. Hope speech detection: A computational analysis of the voice of peace.

Shriphani Palakodety, Ashiqur R. KhudaBukhsh, Jaime G. Carbonell, Shriphani Palakodety, Ashiqur R. KhudaBukhsh, and Jaime G. Carbonell. 2020b. Voice for the voiceless: Active sampling to detect comments supporting the rohingyas. *Proceedings of the AAAI Conference on Artificial Intelligence*, 34(01):454–462.

Anna Schmidt and Michael Wiegand. 2017. A survey on hate speech detection using natural language processing. In *Proceedings of the Fifth International Workshop on Natural Language Processing for Social Media*, pages 1–10, Valencia, Spain. Association for Computational Linguistics.

Nakatani Shuyo. 2010. Language detection library for java.

Ashish Vaswani, Noam Shazeer, Niki Parmar, Jakob Uszkoreit, Llion Jones, Aidan N. Gomez, Lukasz Kaiser, and Illia Polosukhin. 2017. Attention is all you need.

Zijian Wang and David Jurgens. 2018. It's going to be okay: Measuring access to support in online communities. In *Proceedings of the 2018 Conference on Empirical Methods in Natural Language Processing*, pages 33–45, Brussels, Belgium. Association for Computational Linguistics.

Hopeful NLP@LT-EDI-EACL2021: Finding Hope in YouTube Comment Section

Vasudev Awatramani
Dept. of Computer Science and Engineering
Maharaja Agrasen Institute of Technology
New Delhi
vasudev.w13@gmail.com

Abstract

The proliferation of Hate Speech and misinformation in social media is fast becoming a menace to society. In compliment, the dissemination of hate-diffusing, promising and anti-oppressive messages become a unique alternative. Unfortunately, due to its complex nature as well as the relatively limited manifestation in comparison to hostile and neutral content, the identification of Hope Speech becomes a challenge. This work revolves around the detection of Hope Speech in Youtube comments, for the *Shared Task on Hope Speech Detection for Equality, Diversity, and Inclusion* (Chakravarthi and Muralidaran, 2021). We achieve an f-score of 0.93, ranking 1st on the leaderboard for English comments.

1 Introduction

With the rampant adoption of social media, problems like hostile speech detection have caught extensive attention in Natural Language Processing (NLP) research (Chakravarthi et al., 2020; Mandl et al., 2020; Chakravarthi et al., 2021; Suryawanshi and Chakravarthi, 2021). However, there has been little work on the identification of text that promotes positivity and social well-being. As social media becomes predominant in the daily lives of people, it is crucial, not only to protect users from hateful and discriminative content but also encourage communication that triggers optimism and hope. Such expression in a narrow sense may be referred to as Hope Speech and its identification in the digital space as Hope Speech Detection (Puranik et al., 2021; Ghanghor et al., 2021). However, such a task is further challenging as the definition is highly subjective and evolving. Neutral or Positive content with no indication of hostility is not necessarily a sufficient determinant. Advocacy of ideas that promote social well-being, ethics, equality, inclusion, tolerance, diversity, a fair representation of minorities, or either the appreciation or motivation for an individual or a group, are a few indicators of Hope Speech. Moreover, criticism of oppressive or malicious elements of society may also fall under such a category. Furthermore, one does not need to express such beliefs with the present but may incorporate past or future developments.

2 Related Work

Hope Speech Detection is a nascent research task by (Palakodety et al., 2020). The authors proposed automatic identification of positive web content that may diffuse hostility on social media platforms due to political tensions around the *2019 Pulwama Terror Attack*[1]. The authors mined a multilingual (Hindi and English) corpus by scrapping comments from Youtube videos related to the crisis. The authors developed a comprehensive system that took statistical NLP features: n-grams, along with temporal sentiment scores. The system also employed language identification using polyglot FastText (Bojanowski et al., 2017), to achieve an F1-score of 78.51 and 95.48 AUC. However, the work differs from HopeEDI (Chakravarthi, 2020) as it focuses on alleviation of tension and violence and ignores other aspects of hope.

The study focuses on HopeEDI dataset as part of the *Shared Task on Hope Speech Detection for Equality, Diversity, and Inclusion*. We compare our experimental outcomes with the results with (Chakravarthi, 2020) as the baseline. Chakravarthi (2020) employed TFIdf: token frequency-inverse document frequency along with classifiers such as Multinomial Naive Bayes, K-nearest neighbours, Support Vector Machine, Decision Tree and Logistic Regression. Decision tree delivered the highest F-Score for English and Malayalam while Tamil performed well with Logistic Regression. A more thorough comparison occurs in Section 4.

Proceedings of the First Workshop on Language Technology for Equality, Diversity and Inclusion, pages 164–167
April 19, 2021.

3 Experiments

The HopeEDI dataset consists of 3 languages: English, Tamil and Malayalam. The task can be addressed as a sequence classification problem with 3 class: Hope Speech, Not Hope Speech and Not belonging to the given language. Weighted F1 score is employed as an evaluation metric over the 3 languages separately. Moreover, Tamil and Malayalam consist of text samples in romanized and native scripts. This section describes the experiments conducted for the task and states their outcomes over the validation set.

3.1 Transfer Learning

Customarily, models involving NLP Tasks were trained after random initialization of the network parameters. In Transfer Learning, a neural network is fine-tuned on a particular task after being pre-trained on a general task enabling a given neural network to converge faster and lesser amount of data. Originally, transfer learning has been mainly linked with the fine-tuning of deep learning models trained on the ImageNet dataset(Deng et al., 2009). Recently, the field of NLP has witnessed the emergence of various transfer learning techniques and architectures which considerably improved upon the state-of-the-art on a wide array of NLP tasks. Transfer learning can be employed for applications where there is a lack of availability of sufficient training data. The target dataset should ideally be related to the priorly trained dataset for effective learning. This nature of training is generally attributed as Semi-Supervised training where the network is first trained as a language model on a comprehensive dataset followed by supervised training on a labelled training dataset.

We evaluate such models for the task of hostility-diffusing speech detection, trained over a batch size of 128 over 4 epochs. For English, we experiment with BERT(Devlin et al., 2019) and RoBERTa(Liu et al., 2019).

Model	F1-Score
BERT-base-cased	0.9230
BERT-large-cased	0.9253
RoBERTa-base	0.9313
RoBERTa-large	0.9261

Table 1: Weighted F1 score over English Validation Set

3.2 Paraphrasing is not always Adversarial

Adversarial perturbations attempt to fool models by feeding deceptive input. In general, when a data sample is perturbed, they appear to maintain the same fidelity for humans but manage to get the confuse model prediction. The model mispredicts the target for the perturbed sample as opposed to predicting correctly in the original scenario.

Paraphrasing(Lei et al., 2019) is one such attack that preserves both semantic meaning and syntactically validity as well as transforms text into suitable replacements. However, we apply an earlier variation of sentence-level paraphrasing(Mallinson et al., 2017) as a means for language-targetted data augmentation.

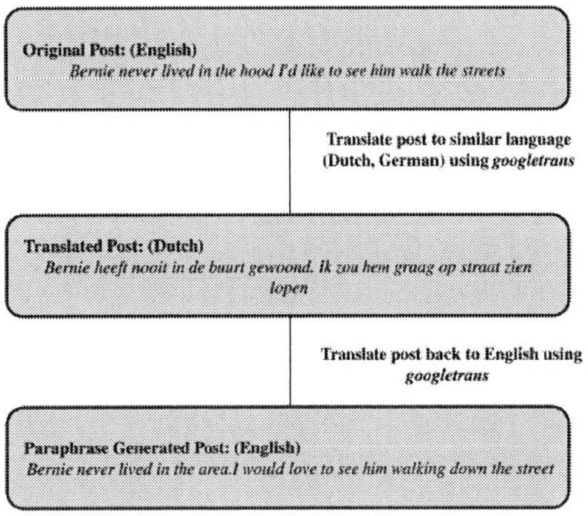

Figure 1: Paraphrase Generation

In this approach, we consider Dutch as the translating language. Both English and Dutch fall under the West Germanic hierarchy of Proto-Germanic languages, with English being Anglo-Frisian and Dutch being Netherlandic-German. Therefore, by choosing a similar language, the generated paraphrases do not lose much semantic meaning but add variability for effective data augmentation. It may noted, this approach cannot be extended to other languages in the task such as Malayalam and Tamil, because translation method (googletrans) employed cannot handle romanized and transliterated text effectively.

Approach	F1-Score
BERT + Paraphrasing Aug.	0.90
RoBERTa + Paraphrasing Aug.	0.90

Table 2: Weighted F1 score over Test Sets using Paraphrasing Data Augmentation

4 Results

Following are described results of the task evaluated over the test set. Our system ranked 1st overall with F1-Score of 0.93 for English, and 4th for Malayalam with 0.78 F-Score.

Model	F1-Score
Baseline (Chakravarthi, 2020)	0.90
roBERTa-base	0.90
BERT-large-cased	0.88

Table 3: Weighted F1 score over English Test Set

Model	F1-Score
Baseline (Chakravarthi, 2020)	0.73
mBERT-cased	0.81
XLM-RobERTa-Large	0.81

Table 4: Weighted F1 score over Malayalam Test Set

5 Conclusion

In this work, we present a simple means of Hope Speech Identification using Pre-trained transformers and Paraphrasing Generation for Data Augmentation. Our future work shall concentrate on interpretability, specifically answering questions like what makes a text an instance of Hope Speech. Moreover, we will attempt to couple more modalities with text, such as audio recording and images or even video clips that collectively promote hope speech.

References

Piotr Bojanowski, Edouard Grave, Armand Joulin, and Tomas Mikolov. 2017. Enriching word vectors with subword information. *Transactions of the Association for Computational Linguistics*, 5(0):135–146.

Bharathi Raja Chakravarthi. 2020. HopeEDI: A multilingual hope speech detection dataset for equality, diversity, and inclusion. In *Proceedings of the Third Workshop on Computational Modeling of People's Opinions, Personality, and Emotion's in Social Media*, pages 41–53, Barcelona, Spain (Online). Association for Computational Linguistics.

Bharathi Raja Chakravarthi, M Anand Kumar, John Philip McCrae, Premjith B, Soman KP, and Thomas Mandl. 2020. Overview of the track on HASOC-Offensive Language Identification-DravidianCodeMix. In *Working Notes of the Forum for Information Retrieval Evaluation (FIRE 2020). CEUR Workshop Proceedings. In: CEUR-WS. org, Hyderabad, India.*

Bharathi Raja Chakravarthi and Vigneshwaran Muralidaran. 2021. Findings of the shared task on Hope Speech Detection for Equality, Diversity, and Inclusion. In *Proceedings of the First Workshop on Language Technology for Equality, Diversity and Inclusion*. Association for Computational Linguistics.

Bharathi Raja Chakravarthi, Ruba Priyadharshini, Navya Jose, Anand Kumar M, Thomas Mandl, Prasanna Kumar Kumaresan, Rahul Ponnusamy, Hariharan V, Elizabeth Sherly, and John Philip McCrae. 2021. Findings of the shared task on Offensive Language Identification in Tamil, Malayalam, and Kannada. In *Proceedings of the First Workshop on Speech and Language Technologies for Dravidian Languages*. Association for Computational Linguistics.

J. Deng, W. Dong, R. Socher, L. Li, Kai Li, and Li Fei-Fei. 2009. Imagenet: A large-scale hierarchical image database. In *2009 IEEE Conference on Computer Vision and Pattern Recognition*, pages 248–255.

Jacob Devlin, Ming-Wei Chang, Kenton Lee, and Kristina Toutanova. 2019. BERT: Pre-training of deep bidirectional transformers for language understanding. In *Proceedings of the 2019 Conference of the North American Chapter of the Association for Computational Linguistics: Human Language Technologies, Volume 1 (Long and Short Papers)*, pages 4171–4186, Minneapolis, Minnesota. Association for Computational Linguistics.

Nikhil Kumar Ghanghor, Rahul Ponnusamy, Prasanna Kumar Kumaresan, Ruba Priyadharshini, Sajeetha Thavareesan, and Bharathi Raja Chakravarthi. 2021. IIITK@LT-EDI-EACL2021: Hope Speech Detection for Equality, Diversity, and Inclusion in Tamil, Malayalam and English. In *Proceedings of the First Workshop on Language Technology for Equality, Diversity and Inclusion*, Online.

Qi Lei, Lingfei Wu, Pin-Yu Chen, Alex Dimakis, Inderjit S. Dhillon, and Michael J Witbrock. 2019. Discrete adversarial attacks and submodular optimization with applications to text classification. In *Proceedings of Machine Learning and Systems*, volume 1, pages 146–165.

Yinhan Liu, Myle Ott, Naman Goyal, Jingfei Du, Mandar Joshi, Danqi Chen, Omer Levy, Mike Lewis, Luke Zettlemoyer, and Veselin Stoyanov. 2019. Roberta: A robustly optimized bert pretraining approach.

Jonathan Mallinson, Rico Sennrich, and Mirella Lapata. 2017. Paraphrasing revisited with neural machine translation. In *Proceedings of the 15th Conference of the European Chapter of the Association for Computational Linguistics: Volume 1, Long Papers*, pages 881–893, Valencia, Spain. Association for Computational Linguistics.

Thomas Mandl, Sandip Modha, Anand Kumar M, and Bharathi Raja Chakravarthi. 2020. Overview of the HASOC Track at FIRE 2020: Hate Speech and Offensive Language Identification in Tamil, Malayalam, Hindi, English and German. In *Forum for Information Retrieval Evaluation*, FIRE 2020, page 29–32, New York, NY, USA. Association for Computing Machinery.

Shriphani Palakodety, Ashiqur R. KhudaBukhsh, and Jaime G. Carbonell. 2020. Hope speech detection: A computational analysis of the voice of peace. In *ECAI 2020 - 24th European Conference on Artificial Intelligence, 29 August-8 September 2020, Santiago de Compostela, Spain, August 29 - September 8, 2020 - Including 10th Conference on Prestigious Applications of Artificial Intelligence (PAIS 2020)*, volume 325 of *Frontiers in Artificial Intelligence and Applications*, pages 1881–1889. IOS Press.

Karthik Puranik, Adeep Hande, Ruba Priyadharshini, Sajeetha Thavareesan, and Bharathi Raja Chakravarthi. 2021. IIITT@LT-EDI-EACL2021-Hope Speech Detection: There is always hope in Transformers. In *Proceedings of the First Workshop on Language Technology for Equality, Diversity and Inclusion*. Association for Computational Linguistics.

Shardul Suryawanshi and Bharathi Raja Chakravarthi. 2021. Findings of the shared task on Troll Meme Classification in Tamil. In *Proceedings of the First Workshop on Speech and Language Technologies for Dravidian Languages*. Association for Computational Linguistics.

NLP-CUET@LT-EDI-EACL2021: Multilingual Code-Mixed Hope Speech Detection using Cross-lingual Representation Learner

Eftekhar Hossain*, Omar Sharif† and Mohammed Moshiul Hoque†
†Department of Computer Science and Engineering
*Department of Electronics and Telecommunication Engineering
Chittagong University of Engineering and Technology, Bangladesh
{eftekhar.hossain, omar.sharif, moshiul_240}@cuet.ac.bd

Abstract

In recent years, several systems have been developed to regulate the spread of negativity and eliminate aggressive, offensive or abusive contents from the online platforms. Nevertheless, a limited number of researches carried out to identify positive, encouraging and supportive contents. In this work, our goal is to identify whether a social media post/comment contains hope speech or not. We propose three distinct models to identify hope speech in English, Tamil and Malayalam language to serve this purpose. To attain this goal, we employed various machine learning (support vector machine, logistic regression, ensemble), deep learning (convolutional neural network + long short term memory) and transformer (m-BERT, Indic-BERT, XLNet, XLM-Roberta) based methods. Results indicate that XLM-Roberta outdoes all other techniques by gaining a weighted f_1-score of 0.93, 0.60 and 0.85 respectively for English, Tamil and Malayalam language. Our team has achieved 1st, 2nd and 1st rank in these three tasks respectively.

1 Introduction

Nowadays, online and social media platforms have enormous influence and impact on people's societal life. When people undergo a challenging or unfavourable time, they start to find emotional support from their friends, relatives or even virtual platforms to overwhelm this situation. Due to Covid-19 pandemic, various online forums have become a popular medium of seeking help, suggestion or support. Thus, researchers are trying to develop a computational model that can find positive and supportive social media information. In general, the hope speech contains words of inspiration, promise and suggestions. Chakravarthi (2020) considered those words as hope speech that offer suggestions, reassurance, support, insight and inspiration. Hope speech can be beneficial to save individuals who wish to harm themselves or even attempt to suicide. Such speech inspires people during the period of depression, loneliness and stress with the words of promise, suggestions and support (Herrestad and Biong, 2010). The major concern of this research is to originate a computational model on top of this dataset to identify hope speech from the social media posts/comments. Lack of resources on hope speech research, scarcity of training corpora and multilingual code-mixing are the key concerns to develop such models.

Machine learning (ML), and deep learning (DL) based techniques can be utilized to address the problem of hope speech detection. In recent years, transformers have gained immense popularity due to its ability to handle the dependencies between input and output with both attention and recurrence. Consequently, many NLP tasks have accomplished using the transformer-based model to obtain the state-of-the-art performance (Chen et al., 2021). The principal contributions in this research as listed below:

- Develop a model with cross-lingual contextual word embeddings (i.e. transformers) to identify the hope speech considering the code-mixed data for English, Tamil and Malayalam languages.
- Investigated the superiority of various ML, DL and transformer-based techniques with detail experimentation.

The rest of the paper organized as follows: works related to hope speech detection discussed in Section 2. Task and dataset are described in detail in Section 3. Section 4 explains the various techniques used to develop the model for performing the assigned task. Experimental

Proceedings of the First Workshop on Language Technology for Equality, Diversity and Inclusion, pages 168–174
April 19, 2021.

findings and error analysis of the models are introduced in Section 5.

2 Related Work

With the substantial growth of the Internet and online contents, several methods have been developed to identify, classify and stop the expansion of negativity such as hate speech detection (Mandl et al., 2020; Chakravarthi et al., 2020), hostility detection (Sharif et al., 2021), aggressive language identification (Kumar et al., 2020), and flagging abusive contents (Akiwowo et al., 2020). However, very few researchers have put their focus on the other side that is hope speech detection. A little work has conducted till to date in this research avenue of NLP. Palakodety et al. (2019a) analyzed how hope speech can be utilized to mitigate tension between two rival (Pakistan and India) countries. Supporting texts regarding Rohingya community culled from social media in Hindi and English languages (Palakodety et al., 2019b). However, details of the dataset such as inter-annotator agreement, diversity of annotators were not clearly described. Chakravarthi (2020) developed a multilingual code-mixed hope speech dataset for Equality, Diversity and Inclusion (HopeEDI) in English, Tamil and Malayalam language. Data collected from social media like Facebook, YouTube in trending topics, i.e. COVID-19, LGBTIQ issues, and India-China war. Their models achieved the highest weighted f_1 score of 0.90, 0.56, 0.70 with a decision tree, naive Bayes, logistic regression techniques for English, Tamil and Malayalam languages.

3 Task and Dataset Descriptions

In this shared task, we have to perform multi-class classification where we aim to identify whether a given comment contains hope speech or not. Our system goal is to classify a post/comment into one of the three predefined classes: hope speech (HS), not hope speech (NHS) and not intended language (NIL). The shared task organizers (Chakravarthi and Muralidaran, 2021) developed a hope speech corpus in multilingual code-mixed setup. A total of 28541 (for English), 20198 (for Tamil) and 10705 (for Malayalam) texts are available in the corpus. This corpus partitioned into three independent sets: train, validation and test. Initially, the model is developed on top of the train set, and model hyperparameters are tuned based on the validation set's performance. Finally, the model evaluated on the unseen instances of the test set. Table 1 shows detail statistics of train, validation and test set for each class.

Further investigation on the training set revealed that the training set is highly imbalanced where several documents in 'not intended language' class are much lower than 'hope speech' and 'not hope speech' classes. The average number of words in 'not intended language' is approximately four words for Tamil and Malayalam languages. The model generalization capability on unseen data might degrade due to the lower number of examples on these classes. Detail analysis of the training set presented in table 2.

4 Methodology

This section provides a brief discussion of the schemes and techniques employed to address the task (Section 3). Initially, different feature extraction techniques are exploited with machine learning, and deep learning approaches for a baseline evaluation. Moreover, we also applied transformers to obtain a better outcome. Figure 1 shows the abstract process of hope speech detection. Architectures and parameters of different approaches are described in the following subsections.

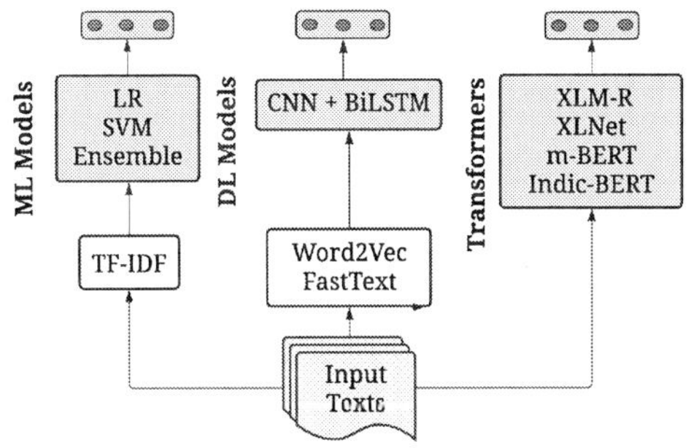

Figure 1: Abstract process of hope speech detection

4.1 Feature Extraction Techniques

ML and DL based techniques are incapable of processing strings or plain text from the raw forms. Thus, extracting of appropriate or relevant features is a prerequisite to train ML and DL based systems. We utilize TF-IDF (Tokunaga and Makoto, 1994), and FastText (Bojanowski et al., 2016) techniques for extracting features from the texts.

	English			Tamil			Malayalam		
	HS	**NHS**	**NIL**	**HS**	**NHS**	**NIL**	**HS**	**NHS**	**NIL**
Train	1962	20778	22	6327	7872	1961	1668	6205	691
Valid	272	2569	2	757	998	263	190	784	96
Test	250	2593	3	815	946	259	194	776	101

Table 1: Number of instances in train, validation and test sets for each language. Here HS, NHS and NIL indicates hope speech, not hope speech and not intended language respectively.

Language	Classes	Total words	Unique words	Max. length (words)	Avg. words (per text)
English	HS	49210	4811	197	25.08
	NHS	317854	19740	191	15.29
	NIL	325	239	47	14.77
Tamil	HS	56000	17274	193	8.85
	NHS	76302	23977	176	9.69
	NIL	7309	2093	48	3.72
Malayalam	HS	25144	11827	96	15.07
	NHS	60313	24607	95	9.72
	NIL	2644	1040	35	3.82

Table 2: Training set statistics for each language. Here HS, NHS and NIL indicates hope speech, not hope speech and not intended language respectively.

TF-IDF: TF-IDF is a measure that calculates the relevancy of a word to a document in a collection of documents. We calculate the TF-IDF value of unigram features for all the languages. During the calculation minimum and maximum document frequency value set at 1.

Word Embedding: Embedding features can capture the semantic meaning of a word. To get embeddings features for all the languages, we used Keras embedding layer with embedding size 100. During the training phase, Keras tries to find the optimal values of the embedding layer's weight matrix by doing simple matrix multiplication and thus create a mapping of each unique words into a vector of real numbers. We utilize the full vocabulary of the corpus and choose maximum input text length 100, 50, and 80 respectively for English, Tamil, and Malayalam data.

FastText: To alleviate the problem of out of vocabulary words in keras embeddings, we use FastText embedding. Instead of learning vectors directly for words, FastText represents each word as n-gram of characters. Therefore even if a word was not encountered during training, it could be split into n-gram to get its embedding. Pre-trained (Grave et al., 2018) embedding vectors are used to accomplish the tasks of each language. We retain the default embedding dimension 300 for FastText embedding.

4.2 ML Baselines

To address the problem, we investigate the performance of three traditional ML approaches, including logistic regression (LR), support vector machine (SVM) and Ensemble. Scikit-learn library is employed for the implementation of these models. TF-IDF features are used to train all the ML methods for three languages.

LR: LR is constructed by using 'lbfgs' solver along with 'l2' penalty. The regularization parameter C settled to 2, 5, and 1 respectively for English, Tamil, and Malayalam data.

SVM: For SVM, 'linear' kernel is utilized with C value of 10, 1 and 0.5 respectively for English, Tamil, and Malayalam language.

Ensemble: To perform classification task ensemble approach has proven superior compared to individual models outcome (Roy et al., 2018). We employ decision tree (DT) and random forest (RF) classifiers along with SVM and LR to develop an ensemble method. For RF, 100 'n_estimators' is chosen while 'gini' criterion used for both DT and RF. On the other hand, previously mentioned parameters have retained in LR and SVM. The majority voting technique is utilized to get the prediction from the ensemble approach.

4.3 DL Baselines

A deep learning-based approach is applied with word embedding features to address the task. The model is developed in TensorFlow backend by using Keras library. The combination of convolutional neural network (CNN) and bidirectional long short term memory (BiLSTM) has achieved an outstanding result in many NLP tasks (Sharif et al., 2020). In this approach, we employ one BiLSTM layer on top of a convolution layer. Initially embedding features are feed to the CNN layer consisting of 128 filters. Following this, to choose appropriate features, a max-pooling is applied with window size 5. The resultant vector is then passed into the BiLSTM layer. In order to capture long term dependencies, 100 bidirectional cells are used in this layer. To mitigate the chance of overfitting BiLSTM layer dropout technique is utilized with a dropout rate of 0.2. Afterwards, the concatenated output of the BiLSTM layer transferred into a softmax layer for the prediction.

4.4 Transformers

We employed four pre-trained transformer models such as multilingual bidirectional encoder representations from transformers (m-BERT), Indic-BERT, XLNet, and XLM-Roberta (XLM-R) and fine-tuned them on the dataset with varying hyperparameters. For fine-tuning, maximum text length settled to 50 for Tamil and 100 for Malayalam and English. The models are fetched from Huggingface[1] transformers library and implemented using Ktrain (Maiya, 2020) package.

m-BERT: m-BERT (Devlin et al., 2018) is pre-trained on a large corpus of multilingual data. To accomplish our purpose, we employed 'bert-base-multilingual-cased' model and fine-tuned it on our dataset with batch size 12.

Indic-BERT: Indic-BERT (Kakwani et al., 2020) is a multilingual model pre-trained specifically on 12 major Indian languages. It has fewer parameters than other multi-lingual models (i.e. m-BERT, XLM-R). Nevertheless, it outperforms other transformers on various task (Kulkarni et al., 2021). The model is fine-tuned with the batch size of 8.

XLNet: XLNet (Yang et al., 2019) is an auto-regressive language model which utilizes the recurrence to output the joint probability of a sequence of words. It combines transformer mechanism with slight modification in language modelling approach. For the implementation 'xlnet-base-cased' model is used and for all the languages we choose batch size 12 for fine-tuning.

XLM-Roberta: XLM-R (Conneau et al., 2019) is referred as cross lingual representation learner. It is a multi-lingual transformer-based model pre-trained with more that 100 languages and achieves the state-of-the-art performance on cross-lingual NLP tasks. We used 'xlm-Roberta-base' model and select a batch size of 4 to fine-tuned it on our datasets.

All transformer models are fine-tuned using Ktrain 'fit_onecycle' method, trained for 30 epochs with a learning rate of $2e^{-5}$. The early stopping technique is employed to avoid the overfitting problem.

5 Results and Analysis

This section presents a comprehensive performance analysis of various machine learning, deep learning and transformer models for three languages (English, Tamil and Malayalam). Weighted f_1 score uses to determine the excellence of the models. In some cases, other evaluation metrics like precision and recall also considered. Table 3 presents the evaluation results of all models on the test set. It observed that ensemble achieved the highest f_1-score of 0.905 and 0.573 respectively for English and Tamil data in ML models. On the other hand, maximum f_1 score of 0.813 is obtained by SVM for the Malayalam language. For all the languages, LR also performed quite similar to SVM but failed to beat other models.

In deep learning, the combination of CNN and BiLSTM experiments with two different embedding features (i.e. Keras embedding and FastText). Both models obtained the highest f_1-score of around 0.90 for English while achieved approximately 0.79 for Malayalam dataset. However, the combination of CNN-BiLSTM model with FastText embedding features shows 1% rise in f_1-score (from 0.54 to 0.55) for Tamil language.

[1] https://huggingface.co/transformers/

Method	Classifiers	English			Tamil			Malayalam		
		P	R	F	P	R	F	P	R	F
ML	LR	0.914	0.869	0.886	0.569	0.563	0.562	0.815	0.798	0.804
	SVM	0.915	0.877	0.892	0.582	0.574	0.564	0.820	0.809	0.813
	Ensemble	0.904	0.920	0.905	0.584	0.584	0.573	0.80	0.811	0.794
DL	C + L (KE)	0.906	0.892	0.899	0.569	0.559	0.540	0.806	0.796	0.791
	C + L (FT)	0.898	0.899	0.898	0.565	0.557	0.548	0.789	0.788	0.786
Trans	m-BERT	0.928	0.927	0.928	0.588	0.591	0.588	0.808	0.823	0.804
	Indic-BERT	0.913	0.920	0.910	0.593	0.592	0.578	0.839	0.842	0.840
	Xlnet	0.931	0.929	0.930	0.558	0.560	0.558	0.779	0.797	0.781
	XLM-R	**0.931**	**0.931**	**0.931**	**0.610**	**0.609**	**0.602**	**0.859**	**0.852**	**0.854**

Table 3: Performance comparison of different models on test set where P, R, F denotes precision, recall and weighted f_1-score. Here, C+L means the combination of CNN and BiLSTM method and KE and FT represents Keras and FastText embeddings.

On the other hand, Transformer based models showed remarkable performance for all three languages. In English data, m-BERT, XLNet, and XLM-R got the highest f_1-score of approximately 0.93. However, considering both the precision and recall values, only XLM-R outperformed the other models. For the Tamil language, f_1-score of around 0.56 and 0.58 respectively obtained by XLNet and Indic-BERT. A slight rise of 1% in f_1-score (0.588) is noticed for m-BERT but it cannot beat XLM-R performance (f_1 score = 0.602). In case of Malayalam data, Indic-BERT (f_1 score = 0.84) shows an increase of 4% to 6% than the f_1-score obtained by m-BERT (0.804) and XLNet (0.781). Nevertheless, it failed to reach the outcome of XLM-R (f_1 score = 0.854), which outdoes all the models.

The results show that **XLM-R** outperformed ML, DL, and other transformer-based models for all three languages. The ability of cross-lingual understanding at different linguistic levels might be the reason for this superior performance of XLM-R.

5.1 Error Analysis

It is evident from the Table 3 that XLM-R is the best performing model to detect hope speech for English, Tamil and Malayalam languages. A detail error analysis is carried out using the confusion matrix to investigate more insights concerning the individual class performance (Figure 2). From the Figure 2(a), it is noticed that among 250 HS instances, 93 are misclassified as NHS. However, the model ultimately failed to detect any of the not-English data and incorrectly classified them as NHS. Similarly, 81 (out of 815) HS and 76 (out of 946) NHS are misclassified as a not-Tamil class in the Tamil language. However, the misclassification rate is comparatively low for nT class. Figure 2(c) shows that the model correctly classified 143 HS (out of 194) instances. Moreover, it wrongly classified 47 samples (as NHS) and 4 samples (as nM). Likewise, among 101 instances of NM, the model misclassified 20 texts while correctly identifying 81 instances. On the other hand, the NHS class received 668 correct classification out of 756 instances, and only misclassified 88 instances as other classes.

We noticed that the model mostly gets confused with HS and NHS class in all languages from the error analysis. The possible reason is that there may be plenty of code-mixed words common in both classes. Thus the system could not apprehend the inherent meaning of the sentences. The high-class imbalance may be another likely reason why the model gives the most priority to the not hope speech class and therefore incorrectly classified hope speech as not hope speech. Increasing the number of instances in the NHS class may mitigate the chance of excessive misclassification.

6 Conclusion

This paper describes and analyses the several ML, DL, and transformer-based methods that we have adopted to participate in the hope speech detection shared task at EACL 2021. Employing TF-IDF, embedding features initially, we performed experiments with ML (LR, SVM, ensemble) and DL (CNN+BiLSTM) approaches. The outcome shows that the ensemble technique achieved

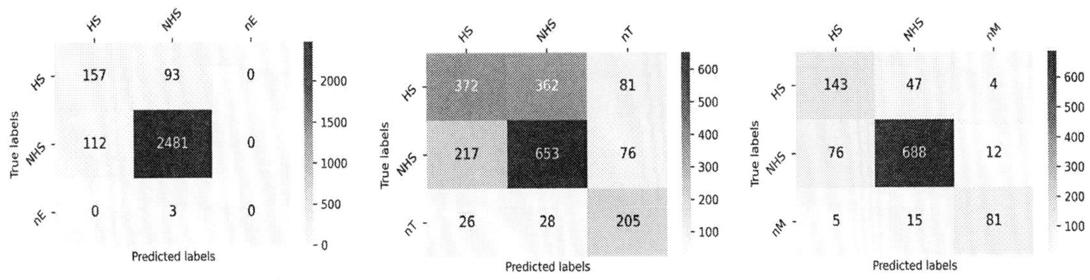

(a) (b) (c)

Figure 2: Confusion matrix of XLM-R technique for (a) English, (b) Tamil and (c) Malayalam languages.

higher performance compared to other ML/DL models. Further, transformer-based techniques are employed to improve the overall performance. The XML-R model outperformed all the models' performance by achieving the highest weighted f_1-score of 0.931, 0.854, and 0.602 respectively for English, Tamil Malayalam language. In the future, contextualized embeddings (such as ELMO, FLAIR) and transformers ensemble might explore to investigate the system's performance.

References

Seyi Akiwowo, Bertie Vidgen, Vinodkumar Prabhakaran, and Zeerak Waseem, editors. 2020. *Proceedings of the Fourth Workshop on Online Abuse and Harms*. Association for Computational Linguistics, Online.

Piotr Bojanowski, Edouard Grave, Armand Joulin, and Tomás Mikolov. 2016. Enriching word vectors with subword information. *CoRR*, abs/1607.04606.

Bharathi Raja Chakravarthi. 2020. HopeEDI: A multilingual hope speech detection dataset for equality, diversity, and inclusion. In *Proceedings of the Third Workshop on Computational Modeling of People's Opinions, Personality, and Emotion's in Social Media*, pages 41–53, Barcelona, Spain (Online). Association for Computational Linguistics.

Bharathi Raja Chakravarthi, M Anand Kumar, John Philip McCrae, Premjith B, Soman KP, and Thomas Mandl. 2020. Overview of the track on HASOC-Offensive Language Identification-DravidianCodeMix. In *Working Notes of the Forum for Information Retrieval Evaluation (FIRE 2020). CEUR Workshop Proceedings. In: CEUR-WS. org, Hyderabad, India.*

Bharathi Raja Chakravarthi and Vigneshwaran Muralidaran. 2021. Findings of the shared task on Hope Speech Detection for Equality, Diversity, and Inclusion. In *Proceedings of the First Workshop on Language Technology for Equality, Diversity and Inclusion*. Association for Computational Linguistics.

Ben Chen, Bin Chen, Dehong Gao, Qijin Chen, Chengfu Huo, Xiaonan Meng, Weijun Ren, and Yang Zhou. 2021. Transformer-based language model fine-tuning methods for covid-19 fake news detection.

Alexis Conneau, Kartikay Khandelwal, Naman Goyal, Vishrav Chaudhary, Guillaume Wenzek, Francisco Guzmán, Edouard Grave, Myle Ott, Luke Zettlemoyer, and Veselin Stoyanov. 2019. Unsupervised cross-lingual representation learning at scale. *CoRR*, abs/1911.02116.

Jacob Devlin, Ming-Wei Chang, Kenton Lee, and Kristina Toutanova. 2018. BERT: pre-training of deep bidirectional transformers for language understanding. *CoRR*, abs/1810.04805.

Edouard Grave, Piotr Bojanowski, Prakhar Gupta, Armand Joulin, and Tomás Mikolov. 2018. Learning word vectors for 157 languages. *CoRR*, abs/1802.06893.

Henning Herrestad and Stian Biong. 2010. Relational hopes: A study of the lived experience of hope in some patients hospitalized for intentional self-harm. *International journal of qualitative studies on health and well-being*, 5(1):4651.

Divyanshu Kakwani, Anoop Kunchukuttan, Satish Golla, Gokul N.C., Avik Bhattacharyya, Mitesh M. Khapra, and Pratyush Kumar. 2020. IndicNLPSuite: Monolingual corpora, evaluation benchmarks and pre-trained multilingual language models for Indian languages. In *Findings of the Association for Computational Linguistics: EMNLP 2020*, pages 4948–4961, Online. Association for Computational Linguistics.

Atharva Kulkarni, Meet Mandhane, Manali Likhitkar, Gayatri Kshirsagar, Jayashree Jagdale, and Raviraj Joshi. 2021. Experimental evaluation of deep learning models for marathi text classification.

Ritesh Kumar, Atul Kr. Ojha, Bornini Lahiri, Marcos Zampieri, Shervin Malmasi, Vanessa Murdock, and Daniel Kadar, editors. 2020. *Proceedings of the Second Workshop on Trolling, Aggression and Cyberbullying*. European Language Resources Association (ELRA), Marseille, France.

Arun S. Maiya. 2020. ktrain: A low-code library for augmented machine learning.

Thomas Mandl, Sandip Modha, Anand Kumar M, and Bharathi Raja Chakravarthi. 2020. Overview of the HASOC Track at FIRE 2020: Hate Speech and Offensive Language Identification in Tamil, Malayalam, Hindi, English and German. In *Forum for Information Retrieval Evaluation*, FIRE 2020, page 29–32, New York, NY, USA. Association for Computing Machinery.

Shriphani Palakodety, Ashiqur R. KhudaBukhsh, and Jaime G. Carbonell. 2019a. Kashmir: A computational analysis of the voice of peace. *CoRR*, abs/1909.12940.

Shriphani Palakodety, Ashiqur R. KhudaBukhsh, and Jaime G. Carbonell. 2019b. Voice for the voiceless: Active sampling to detect comments supporting the rohingyas. *CoRR*, abs/1910.03206.

Arjun Roy, Prashant Kapil, Kingshuk Basak, and Asif Ekbal. 2018. An ensemble approach for aggression identification in English and Hindi text. In *Proceedings of the First Workshop on Trolling, Aggression and Cyberbullying (TRAC-2018)*, pages 66–73, Santa Fe, New Mexico, USA. Association for Computational Linguistics.

Omar Sharif, Eftekhar Hossain, and Mohammed Moshiul Hoque. 2020. Techtexc: Classification of technical texts using convolution and bidirectional long short term memory network.

Omar Sharif, Eftekhar Hossain, and Mohammed Moshiul Hoque. 2021. Combating hostility: Covid-19 fake news and hostile post detection in social media.

Takenobu Tokunaga and Iwayama Makoto. 1994. Text categorization based on weighted inverse document frequency. In *Special Interest Groups and Information Process Society of Japan (SIG-IPSJ*. Citeseer.

Zhilin Yang, Zihang Dai, Yiming Yang, Jaime G. Carbonell, Ruslan Salakhutdinov, and Quoc V. Le. 2019. Xlnet: Generalized autoregressive pretraining for language understanding. *CoRR*, abs/1906.08237.

Simon @ DravidianLangTech-EACL2021: Detecting Hope Speech with BERT

Qinyu Que
School of Information Science and Engineering,
Yunnan University, Yunnan, P.R. China
1309487642@qq.com

Abstract

In today's society, the rapid development of communication technology allows us to communicate with people from different parts of the world. In the process of communication, each person treats others differently. Some people are used to using offensive and sarcastic language to express their views. These words cause pain to others and make people feel down. Some people are used to sharing happiness with others and encouraging others. Such people bring joy and hope to others through their words. On social media platforms, these two kinds of language are all over the place. If people want to make the online world a better place, they will have to deal with both. So identifying offensive language and hope language is an essential task. There have been many assignments about offensive language. Shared Task on Hope Speech Detection for Equality, Diversity, and Inclusion at LT-EDI 2021-EACL 2021 uses another unique perspective – to identify the language of Hope to make contributions to society. The XLM-Roberta model is an excellent multilingual model. Our team used a fine-tuned XLM-Roberta model to accomplish this task.

1 Introduction

Social media is a way to bring people from different regions closer together. Different people have different cultural backgrounds and different world views. This allows people to have a fierce clash of ideas on social platforms. In these interactions, the way people treat each other is very different. Hate speech offensive speech and offensive speech are not recommended (Chakravarthi et al., 2020; Mandl et al., 2020; Chakravarthi et al., 2021; Suryawanshi and Chakravarthi, 2021). So we also do a lot of work to avoid this, for example, we have a lot of competitions to identify offensive content(GermEval[1], IberLEF[2]). And we welcome those who use the language of hope to encourage people to get back on their feet and renew their strength in the face of hardship. To this end, Shared Task on Hope Speech Detection for Equality, Diversity, and Inclusion at LT-EDI 2021-EACL 2021 was organized by the event organizers. Hope Speech can help people find ways to realize their dreams(Blasius and Phelan, 1997; Chang, 1998; Youssef and Luthans, 2007; Cover, 2013; Snyder et al., 1991). People can learn and master these techniques to make their lives better. Hope Speech is seen by medical personnel as vital to people's recovery. Hope speech makes the whole social environment more optimistic. Therefore, it is very necessary to detect hope speech. The second paragraph of the paper introduces the work done by scholars in relevant fields, the third paragraph introduces the detailed content of tasks, the fourth paragraph introduces the details of data and the methods of processing data, the fifth paragraph introduces the model used by our team, the sixth paragraph introduces the details and results of experiments, and finally the conclusion we have reached.

2 Related Work

Some works have been done on the classification of hope speech. (Puranik et al., 2021; Ghanghor et al., 2021) analyze the evolving international crisis via a substantial corpus constructed using comments on YouTube videos. As well as detecting offensive content, Hope speech can be classified as a useful tool in its own field. Mathur et al. (Mathur et al., 2018) used transfer learning to complete the task of classifying offensive content of tweets in hot data sets. Their team used a convolutional neural network to pre-train English tweets and then re-train

[1] https://projects.fzai.h-da.de/iggsa/germeval/
[2] http://hitz.eus/sepln2019/?q=node/21

Proceedings of the First Workshop on Language Technology for Equality, Diversity and Inclusion, pages 175–179
April 19, 2021.

Indo-English tweets. Kamble and Joshi (Kamble and Joshi, 2018) used three classical deep learning models to complete the classification of English-Hindi tweets. By comparing these three classical deep learning models, they found that the use of specific embedding can improve the representation of the target group, and thus improve the score of F1. Santosh and Aravind (Santosh and Aravind, 2019) used different LSTM(Mathur et al., 2018) models to classify hate speech, one is the sub-word level LSTM model and the other is the hierarchical LSTM model based on phonetic location words. Waseem et al.(Waseem and Hovy, 2016) found the influence of different extra language features combined with N-gram characters on classification tasks.

3 Task Details

Shared task on Hope Speech Detection for Equality, Diversity, and Inclusion at LT-EDI 2021-EACL 2021 gives the participants three languages to choose from. The three languages are English, Tamil and, Malayalam. The event organizer provides us with a training data set and a test data set. Through the data set, we find that this is a tripartite task. Our group believes that a lot of work has already been done on the task of classifying English. So our team chose a Tamil sub-task and a Malayalam sub-task.

4 Date Details and Data Preprocessing

4.1 Date Description

In each subtask, the data set contains three tags:

- Hope speech: This tag indicates that the comment is Hope speech.
- Not hope speech: This tag indicates that a comment is Not hope speech.
- Not in intended language: This tag indicates that is not the language used by the subtask.

We can see that the label classification is very clear. The details of the data set are showed in Table 1 and Table 2.

Label	Train set	validation set
Non hope speech	72.45%	73.27%
Hope speech	19.48%	17.76%
Not Malayalam	8.07%	8.97%

Table 1: Label distribution of Malayalam language subtask

Label	Train set	validation set
Non hope speech	48.71%	49.46%
Hope speech	39.15%	37.51%
Not Tamil	12.14%	13.03%

Table 2: Label distribution of Tamil language subtask

4.2 Data Preparation

The data sets we used were collected from YouTube (Chakravarthi, 2020; Chakravarthi and Muralidaran, 2021). Before training the dataset, we first clean up the dataset. The cleaned data set is more standardized, and we remove miscellaneous words and symbols, reducing the amount of training. The main work of data set cleaning is as follows:

- Deleting the emoticons
- Replacing emojis with words, such as words 'crying' instead of a crying face emoji, and words 'panda' instead of a panda emoji.
- Deleting the URL
- Deleting punctuation marks

5 Model Description

In a recent categorization task competition, many teams using the fine-tuned BERT(Devlin et al., 2019) model did well. Our team used XLM-Roberta(Conneau et al., 2020) as a preprocessing model in the experiment. The XLM-Roberta model is a multilingual processing model trained on processing text in 100 different languages. This fits nicely with the shared task of handling multilingual text. Compared with the BERT model, the XLM-Roberta model has improved various performances. This is due to the increased training volume of the XLM-Roberta model, whose training datasets are several orders of magnitude larger than the Wiki-100 corpus used to train its predecessor. Based on the XLM-Roberta model, we used two fine-tuning methods to accomplish this task. The two approaches are shown in Figures 1 and 2.

5.1 Method 1

Firstly, the pooler output of XLM-Roberta (P_O) of XLM-Roberta model is obtained through XLM-Roberta model. Second, input the output of the last three hidden layers of the XLM-Roberta model

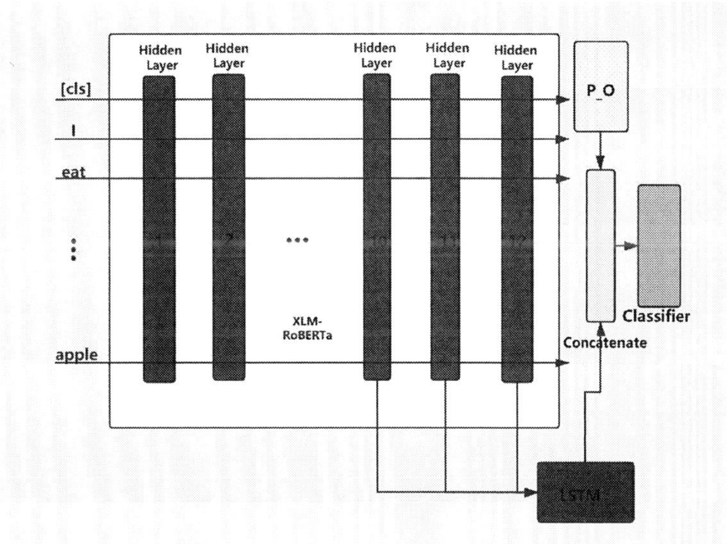

Figure 1: Method 1

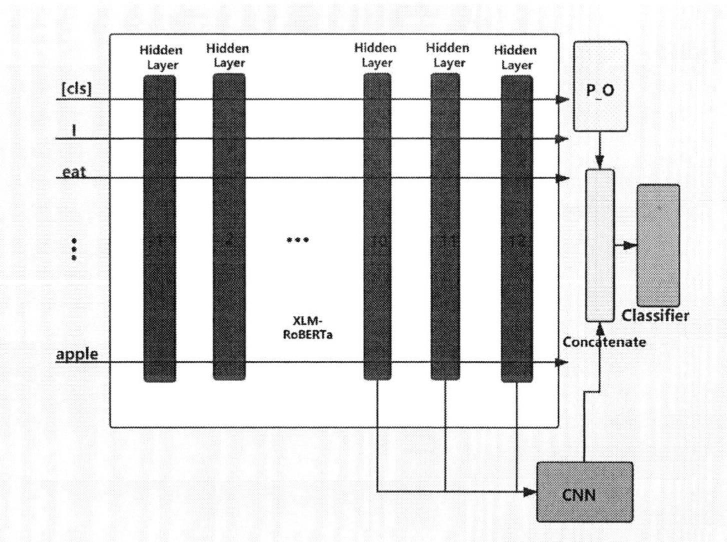

Figure 2: Method 2

Hyper-parameter	Value
dropout	0.5
learning rate	1e-5
epoch	8
per gpu train batch size	32
gradient accumulation steps	8

Table 3: The hyper-parameters

into the LSTM model. Finally, the output obtained from the LSTM model is connected with P_O and put into the classifier.

5.2 Method 2

Firstly, the Pooler output of XLM-Roberta (P_O) of the XLM-Roberta model is obtained through the XLM-Roberta model. The second step is to input the output of the last three hidden layers of the XLM-Roberta model into the CNN(Simonyan and Zisserman, 2014) model. Finally, the output obtained from the CNN model is connected with P_O and put into the classifier.

6 Experiment and Results

In the experimental process, the same hyper-parameter is used in the two methods. Table 3 is the details of the hyper-parameter we used. The training set and validation set used by our team were derived from the training set provided by the event organization after separation using hierarchical K-fold cross-validation. Method 1 performed better on the validation set, so we submitted the results of Method 1. In the Tamil language sub-task, our final F1-score In the official test set is 0.49. In the Malayalam language sub-task, our final F1-score In the official test set is 0.49.

7 Conclusion

This article describes the models and results used by the Simon team in the hope speech classification task. Our results are not good in the leaderboard, which may have something to do with the imbalance of the data set. In the future, we will continue to improve our model to get better results.

References

Mark Blasius and Shane Phelan. 1997. *We are everywhere: A historical sourcebook of gay and lesbian politics*. Psychology Press.

Bharathi Raja Chakravarthi. 2020. HopeEDI: A multilingual hope speech detection dataset for equality, diversity, and inclusion. In *Proceedings of the Third Workshop on Computational Modeling of People's Opinions, Personality, and Emotion's in Social Media*, pages 41–53, Barcelona, Spain (Online). Association for Computational Linguistics.

Bharathi Raja Chakravarthi, M Anand Kumar, John Philip McCrae, Premjith B, Soman KP, and Thomas Mandl. 2020. Overview of the track on HASOC-Offensive Language Identification-DravidianCodeMix. In *Working Notes of the Forum for Information Retrieval Evaluation (FIRE 2020). CEUR Workshop Proceedings. In: CEUR-WS. org, Hyderabad, India*.

Bharathi Raja Chakravarthi and Vigneshwaran Muralidaran. 2021. Findings of the shared task on Hope Speech Detection for Equality, Diversity, and Inclusion. In *Proceedings of the First Workshop on Language Technology for Equality, Diversity and Inclusion*. Association for Computational Linguistics.

Bharathi Raja Chakravarthi, Ruba Priyadharshini, Navya Jose, Anand Kumar M, Thomas Mandl, Prasanna Kumar Kumaresan, Rahul Ponnusamy, Hariharan V, Elizabeth Sherly, and John Philip McCrae. 2021. Findings of the shared task on Offensive Language Identification in Tamil, Malayalam, and Kannada. In *Proceedings of the First Workshop on Speech and Language Technologies for Dravidian Languages*. Association for Computational Linguistics.

Edward C Chang. 1998. Hope, problem-solving ability, and coping in a college student population: Some implications for theory and practice. *Journal of clinical psychology*, 54(7):953–962.

Alexis Conneau, Kartikay Khandelwal, Naman Goyal, Vishrav Chaudhary, and Veselin Stoyanov. 2020. Unsupervised cross-lingual representation learning at scale. In *Proceedings of the 58th Annual Meeting of the Association for Computational Linguistics*.

Rob Cover. 2013. Queer youth resilience: Critiquing the discourse of hope and hopelessness in lgbt suicide representation. *M/C Journal*, 16(5).

Jacob Devlin, Ming-Wei Chang, Kenton Lee, and Kristina Toutanova. 2019. BERT: Pre-training of deep bidirectional transformers for language understanding. In *Proceedings of the 2019 Conference of the North American Chapter of the Association for Computational Linguistics: Human Language Technologies, Volume 1 (Long and Short Papers)*, pages 4171–4186, Minneapolis, Minnesota. Association for Computational Linguistics.

Nikhil Kumar Ghanghor, Rahul Ponnusamy, Prasanna Kumar Kumaresan, Ruba Priyadharshini, Sajeetha Thavareesan, and Bharathi Raja Chakravarthi. 2021. IIITK@LT-EDI-EACL2021: Hope Speech Detection for Equality, Diversity, and

Inclusion in Tamil, Malayalam and English. In *Proceedings of the First Workshop on Language Technology for Equality, Diversity and Inclusion*, Online.

Satyajit Kamble and Aditya Joshi. 2018. Hate speech detection from code-mixed hindi-english tweets using deep learning models. *arXiv preprint arXiv:1811.05145*.

Thomas Mandl, Sandip Modha, Anand Kumar M, and Bharathi Raja Chakravarthi. 2020. Overview of the HASOC Track at FIRE 2020: Hate Speech and Offensive Language Identification in Tamil, Malayalam, Hindi, English and German. In *Forum for Information Retrieval Evaluation*, FIRE 2020, page 29–32, New York, NY, USA. Association for Computing Machinery.

Puneet Mathur, Rajiv Shah, Ramit Sawhney, and Debanjan Mahata. 2018. Detecting offensive tweets in hindi-english code-switched language. In *Proceedings of the Sixth International Workshop on Natural Language Processing for Social Media*, pages 18–26.

Karthik Puranik, Adeep Hande, Ruba Priyadharshini, Sajeetha Thavareesan, and Bharathi Raja Chakravarthi. 2021. IIITT@LT-EDI-EACL2021-Hope Speech Detection: There is always hope in Transformers. In *Proceedings of the First Workshop on Language Technology for Equality, Diversity and Inclusion*. Association for Computational Linguistics.

TYSS Santosh and KVS Aravind. 2019. Hate speech detection in hindi-english code-mixed social media text. In *Proceedings of the ACM India Joint International Conference on Data Science and Management of Data*, pages 310–313.

Karen Simonyan and Andrew Zisserman. 2014. Very deep convolutional networks for large-scale image recognition. *Computer Science*.

Charles R Snyder, Cheri Harris, John R Anderson, Sharon A Holleran, Lori M Irving, Sandra T Sigmon, Lauren Yoshinobu, June Gibb, Charyle Langelle, and Pat Harney. 1991. The will and the ways: development and validation of an individual-differences measure of hope. *Journal of personality and social psychology*, 60(4):570.

Shardul Suryawanshi and Bharathi Raja Chakravarthi. 2021. Findings of the shared task on Troll Meme Classification in Tamil. In *Proceedings of the First Workshop on Speech and Language Technologies for Dravidian Languages*. Association for Computational Linguistics.

Zeerak Waseem and Dirk Hovy. 2016. Hateful symbols or hateful people? predictive features for hate speech detection on twitter. In *Proceedings of the NAACL student research workshop*, pages 88–93.

Carolyn M Youssef and Fred Luthans. 2007. Positive organizational behavior in the workplace: The impact of hope, optimism, and resilience. *Journal of management*, 33(5):774–800.

MUCS@LT-EDI-EACL2021:CoHope-Hope Speech Detection for Equality, Diversity, and Inclusion in Code-Mixed Texts

F. Balouchzahi, B. K. Aparna, H. L. Shashirekha
Department of Computer Science,
Mangalore University
frs_b@yahoo.com, aparnabk14@gmail.com, hlsrekha@gmail.com

Abstract

This paper describes the models submitted by the team MUCS for "Hope Speech Detection for Equality, Diversity, and Inclusion-EACL 2021" shared task that aims at classifying a comment / post in English and code-mixed texts in two language pairs, namely, Tamil-English (Ta-En) and Malayalam-English (Ma-En) into one of the three predefined categories, namely, "Hope_speech", "Non_hope_speech", and "other_languages". Three models namely, CoHope-ML, CoHope-NN, and CoHope-TL based on Ensemble of classifiers, Keras Neural Network (NN) and BiLSTM with Conv1d model respectively are proposed for the shared task. CoHope-ML, CoHope-NN models are trained on a feature set comprised of char sequences extracted from sentences combined with words for Ma-En and Ta-En code-mixed texts and a combination of word and char ngrams along with syntactic word ngrams for English text. CoHope-TL model consists of three major parts: training tokenizer, BERT Language Model (LM) training and then using pre-trained BERT LM as weights in BiLSTM-Conv1d model. Out of three proposed models, CoHope-ML model (best among our models) obtained 1st, 2nd, and 3rd ranks with weighted F1-scores of 0.85, 0.92, and 0.59 for Ma-En, English and Ta-En texts respectively.

1 Introduction

The recent wave of using social media especially during the outbreak of Covid-19 has increasingly affected the amount of user-generated data and text over the internet that has provided immense opportunities in automated text analysis and Computational Linguistics (Bohra et al., 2018). Most of tools and systems to analyze social media texts are designed to handle them in their native script. However, social media texts are often code-mixed, i.e., written in Roman script mixing English words rather than in the native script of language due to difficulty in using tools provided to pen the comments in native script (Jose et al., 2020; Priyadharshini et al., 2020) . Further, users may prefer using Roman scripts even though the language has its own standardized written form and script (Sitaram and Black, 2016). The analysis of Romanized and code-mixed texts is more challenging task compared to analysis of texts in native scripts because of the inconsistent Romanization conventions and non-standard grammars in code-mixed texts (Riyadh and Kondrak, 2019).

Hope speech detection is defined as analysis and detection of inspirational talk and comments/posts with positive vibes, etc. against people with not straight desires such as Lesbian, Gay, and Transgender or positive suggestion for Covid-19 guidelines, etc. (Chakravarthi, 2020). Even though a couple of studies and workshops are focused on analyzing code-mixed texts in tasks such as Sentiments Analysis (SA) and Offensive Language Identification (OLI) it has been rarely experimented on Hope Speech Detection even in native scripts. In this direction, the "Hope Speech Detection for Equality, Diversity, and Inclusion"[1] shared task aims at classifying a comment/post in English and code-mixed texts in two language pairs, namely, Tamil-English (Ta-En) and Malayalam-English (Ma-En) into one of the three predefined categories, namely, "Hope_speech", "Non_hope_speech", and "other_languages". The details of the datasets provided by organizers are given in (Chakravarthi, 2020).

In this paper, we, team MUCS describe the three models CoHope-ML, CoHope-NN and CoHope-TL submitted for "Hope Speech Detection for Equality, Diversity, and Inclusion" shared task. The char sequences extracted from sentences com-

[1] https://sites.google.com/view/lt-edi-2021

Proceedings of the First Workshop on Language Technology for Equality, Diversity and Inclusion, pages 180–187
April 19, 2021. ©2020 Association for Computational Linguistics

bined with words in the sentences are used to train CoHope-ML and CoHope-NN models for code-mixed Ma-En and Ta-En texts whereas a combination of char and word ngrams along with syntactic ngrams are used to train the same models for English texts. CoHope-TL model is comprised of three major steps: (i) training tokenizer, (ii) training BERT LM using raw texts from Dakshina Dataset[2] [5], for Ma-En and Ta-En code mixed texts and pre-trained BERT LM from Kaggle[3] for English, and (iii) transferring obtained weights and building BiLSTM-Conv1d model.

The rest of paper is organized as follows: while Section 2 describes the recent literature on code-mixed text processing, Section 3 focuses on the description of the models submitted to the shared task followed by experiments and results in Section 4. Conclusion and future plans are included in Section 5.

2 Related Work

Researchers have developed a vast range of datasets, tools and models for Text Classification (TC). However, comparatively very less work has been done on the classification of code-mixed texts and the available literature focus on SA and OLI tasks for several languages pairs. Hope Speech detection is a new challenge that has been explored rarely. Some of recent studies on TC tasks for code-mixed texts are given below:

(Chakravarthi et al., 2020b) presents an overview of OLI shared task on code-mixed texts in Dravidian languages[4] consisting of two subtasks A and B to classify a given text into "offensive" or "not-offensive" categories. While Subtask A is to classify code-mixed Ma-En YouTube comments, SubTask B is to classify Romanized Malayalam and Romanized Tamil texts from YouTube or Twitter comments. Datasets used in this shared tasks are described in (Chakravarthi et al., 2020c) and (Chakravarthi et al., 2020a). Two models based on different configurations of LSTM proposed by (Renjit and Idicula, 2020) for the OLI shared task obtained a weighted F1-score of 0.53 for Romanized Malayalam text in Subtask B. A Universal LM has been trained for Ma-En code-mixed texts from Wikipedia articles in native script combined with translated and transliterated versions by (Arora, 2020). The authors transferred the obtained LM to TC model from fastai library to classify code-mixed texts in Ma-En and obtained 0.91, 0.74 weighted F1-score for Subtask A and Romanized Malayalam text of Subtask B respectively.

"Sentiment Analysis of Dravidian Languages in Code-Mixed Text"[5] which focuses on SA of code-mixed texts in Ta-En and Ma-En language pairs (Chakravarthi et al., 2020d) is another shared task on Dravidian languages. Datasets described in (Chakravarthi et al., 2020c) and (Chakravarthi et al., 2020a) are used in this shared task and they include five categories, namely, "Positive", "Negative", "Unknown_state", "Mixed-Feelings", and "Other_languages" for each language pairs. The overall results of this shared task reported in leaderboard illustrates that XLM-Roberta model proposed by (Sun and Zhou, 2020) with a weighted F1-score of 0.65 and 0.74 for Ta-En and Ma-En language pairs respectively obtained first rank for both subtasks. The proposed XLM-Roberta model uses extracted output of Convolution Neural Networks (CNN) which enables it to utilize the semantic information from texts. Another XLM-Roberta model proposed by (Ou and Li, 2020) ensembles pre-trained multi-language models and K-folding method to classify code-mixed texts. The proposed model with 0.63 and 0.74 weighted F1-score obtained third and first ranks on Ta-En and Ma-En language pairs respectively.

3 Methodology

The proposed models are described in terms of feature engineering to extract the required features followed by description of the classifiers.

3.1 Feature Engineering

Framework of the proposed methodology for CoHope-ML and CoHope-NN consists of a step of preprocessing the train and test data followed by feature engineering module to extract features and use them to train and test the models.

Preprocessing steps includes converting emojis to corresponding text (using emoji library[6]), removing punctuations, words of length less than 2, unwanted characters (such as !()-[];:'" ¡¿./?$=% +@*_ ', etc.) and converting text to lowercase.

Feature engineering module uses everygrams[7]

[2]https://github.com/google-research-datasets/dakshina

[3]https://www.kaggle.com/christofhenkel/pytorchpretrainedbert

[4]https://competitions.codalab.org/competitions/25295#learn_the_details

[5]https://dravidian-codemix.github.io/2020/index.html

[6]https://pypi.org/project/emoji/

[7]https://www.kite.com/python/docs/nltk.everygrams

Input text	Extracted features
"yuvanvera level ya." (in Ta-En)	yu, uv, va, an, n_, _v, ve, er, ra, a_, _l, le, ev, ve, el, l_, _y, ya, yuv, uva,van, an_, _ve, ver, era, ra_, _le, lev, eve, vel, el_, _ya, yuva, uvan, van_, _ver, vera, era_, _lev, leve, evel, vel_, yuvan, uvan_, _vera, vera_, _leve, level, evel_, yuvan_, _vera_, _level, level_,yuvanvera, level, ya

Table 1: Examples of input text and extracted features for code-mixed texts

function from NLTK library to extract char sequences of length 3 to 6 from texts along with tokenized words for Ma-En and Ta-En language pairs as features. For English texts SNgramExtractor[8] library is used to extract syntactic ngrams of length 2 to 3 (Sidorov et al., 2013) (Posadas-Durán et al., 2015) in addition to traditional char ngrams of length 3 to 5 and word ngrams of length 1 to 3 as features. The extracted features are represented as TFIDF vectors for further processing. Tables 1 and 2 give samples of input texts and features extracted from the corresponding texts.

3.2 Models Description

The proposed models are described below:

3.2.1 CoHope-ML

There are various notions of ensemble learning such as bagging, stacking, etc. Due to simplicity and efficiency of bagging method, CoHope-ML model is developed as a hard voting classifier based on bagging by ensembling three sklearn[9] classifiers, Logistic Regression (LR), eXtreme Gradient Boosting (XGB) (Chen and Guestrin, 2016) and Multi-Layer Perceptron (MLP)[10]. Idea behind ensembling simple classifiers as estimators is to build a robust classifier utilizing the strength of each classifier. Parameters used for each estimator are given in Table 3. CoHope-ML model is trained on TFIDF vectors obtained in feature engineering module. The framework of CoHope-ML is shown in Figure 1.

[8]https://pypi.org/project/SNgramExtractor/

[9]https://scikit-learn.org/stable/

[10]https://scikit-learn.org/stable/modules/neural_networks_supervised.html

Input text	Extracted features
"Economic news have little effect on financial markets." (in English)	Economic, news, have, little, effect, on, financial, markets., Economic news, news have, have little, little effect, effect on, on financial, financial markets., Economic news have, news have little, have little effect, little effect on, effect on financial, on financial markets., _Ec, Eco, con, ono, nom, omi, mic, ic_, _ne, new, ews, ws_, _ha, hav, ave, ve_, _li, lit, itt, ttl, tle, le_, _ef, eff, ffe, fec, ect, ct_, _on, on_, _fi, fin, ina, nan, anc, nci, cia, ial, al_, _ma, mar, ark, rke, ket, ets, ts., s._, _Eco, Econ, cono, onom, nomi, omic, mic_, _new, news, ews_, _hav, have, ave_, _lit, litt, ittl, ttle, tle_, _eff, effe, ffec, fect, ect_, _on_, _fin, fina, inan, nanc, anci, ncia, cial, ial_, _mar, mark, arke, rket, kets, ets., ts._, _Econ, Econo, conom, onomi, nomic, omic_, _news, news_, _have, have_, _litt, littl, ittle, ttle_, _effe, effec, ffect, fect_, _fina, finan, inanc, nanci, ancia, ncial, cial_, _mark, marke, arket, rkets, kets., ets._, news_Economic, have_news, effect_little, have_effect, effect_on, markets_financial, on_markets, have_, effect_on_markets, on_markets_financial

Table 2: Examples of input text and extracted features for English texts

Estimators	Parameters
XGB	max_depth=20, n_estimators=80, learning_rate=0.1, colsample_bytree=.7, gamma=.01, reg_alpha=4, objective='multi: softmax'
MLP	hidden_layer_sizes= (150,100,50), max_iter=300,activation = 'relu', solver='adam', random_state=1
LR	Default parameters

Table 3: Parameters for estimators in CoHope-ML

3.2.2 CoHope-NN

The framework of CoHope-NN model is shown in Figure 2. It makes use of a Keras[11] dense Neural Network (NN) architecture adopted from

```
https://www.kaggle.com/ismu94/
tf-idf-deep-neural-net
```

CoHope-NN model is trained for 40 epochs with a batch size of 128 on TFIDF vectors obtained from feature engineering module.

3.2.3 CoHope-TL

Based on TL, CoHope-TL adopts the architecture described in

```
https://huggingface.co/blog/
how-to-train
```

to train Tokenizers and LMs using transformers for Ta-En and Ma-En language pairs. Tokenizer and LM for English are publicly available at:

```
https://www.kaggle.
com/christofhenkel/
torch-bert-weights
```

The steps involved in designing CoHope model are described below:

Training Tokenizer: Romanized text from Dakshina dataset (Roark et al., 2020) combined with code-mixed texts from (Chakravarthi et al., 2020c) and (Chakravarthi et al., 2020a) are preprocessed and used to train a byte-level Byte-pair encoding tokenizer[12] with a vocab size of 52000 words and min frequency of 2 (separately for each language pairs Ma-En and Ta-En). The resulting tokenizer is later used in training BERT LM.

Training BERT LM: BERT LM is trained using the trained tokenizer and raw texts used in previous step and transformers library[13] with following configurations:

- vocab_size=52_000
- max_position_embeddings=514
- num_attention_heads=12
- num_hidden_layers=6
- type_vocab_size=1

[11]https://keras.io/

[12]https://huggingface.co/transformers/tokenizer_summary.html

[13]https://pypi.org/project/transformers/

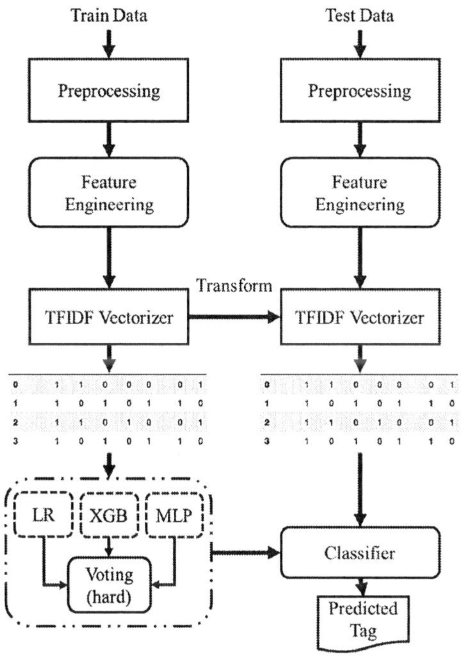

Figure 1: Framework of CoHope-ML model

The resulting LM is in turn trained for Ta-En and Ma-En language pairs separately and the weights are transferred for the construction of the classifier.

Model Construction: a BiLSTM-Conv1D architecture which is a BiLSTM model over convolutional layers with :

- Kernel size of 3
- Filter = 32
- MaxPooling1D with pool size of 2
- Length of words sequences = 250 with padding for short sentences

is used to train CoHope-TL model for 50 epochs with a batch size of 126. Table 4 gives summary of the layers in BiLSTM-Conv1D model and the frame work of CoHope-TL is shown in Figure 3.

4 Experimental Results

4.1 Datasets

Datasets used in this study include unannotated Romanized text from Dakshina (Roark et al., 2020) combined with texts from (Chakravarthi et al., 2020c), (Chakravarthi et al., 2020a) and annotated datasets provided by organizers which are

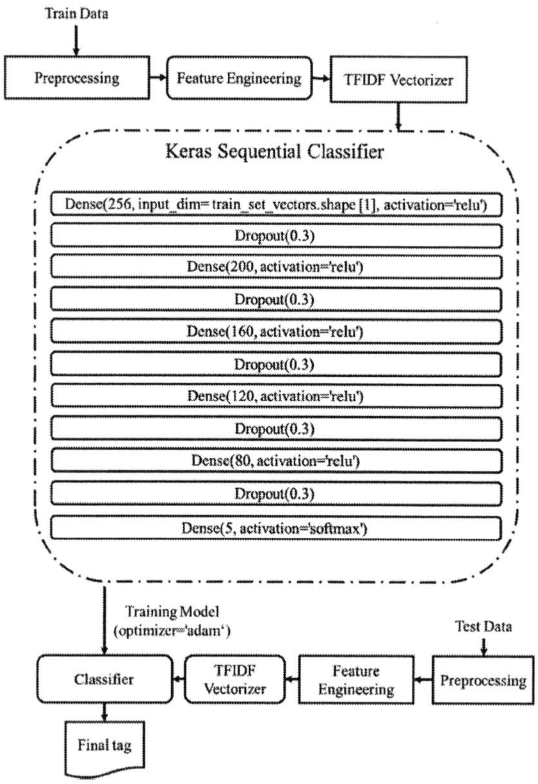

Figure 2: Framework of CoHope-NN model

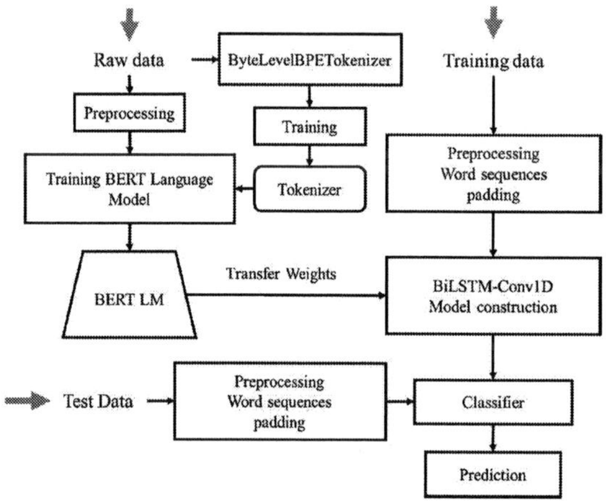

Figure 3: Framework of CoHope-TL

Layer(Type)	Output shape	
	Ta-En and Ma-EN	English
Embedding	(None,250,768)	(None,250,1024)
Conv1D	(None, 250, 32)	(None, 250, 32)
MaxPooling1D	(None, 125, 32)	(None, 125, 32)
Bidirectional	(None, 600)	(None, 600)
Dense	(None, 3)	(None, 3)

Table 4: Layers in BiLSTM-Conv1D

Set	LP	NO	HS	OL
Train	Ma-En	6205	1668	691
	Ta-En	7872	6327	1961
	English	20778	1962	22
Dev.	Ma-En	784	190	96
	Ta-En	998	757	263
	English	2569	272	2
Test	Ma-En	776	194	101
	Ta-En	946	815	259
	English	2593	250	3

Table 5: Label distribution over annotated datasets

described in (Chakravarthi, 2020). Statistics of the Tamil-English[14] (TaCo) and Malayalam-English[15] (MaCo) code-mixed raw texts are shown in Figure 4. It can be observed that MaCo code-mixed texts are noticeably less than TaCo code-mixed texts.

Annotated datasets include two code-mixed datasets Ta-En and Ma-En along with English datasets. Texts in the datasets for each Language Pairs (LP) are distributed in three categories namely, "Hope_speech (HS)", "Non_hope_speech (NO)", and "other_languages (OL)". Statistics of labels distribution in train, development (Dev.) and test sets and given in Table 5. It can be observed that as Ma-En code-mixed texts include significant number of samples in Malayalam native script and English text includes more samples, the proposed models are expected to perform better for Ma-En code-mixed texts and English texts compared to Ta-En code-mixed texts.

4.1.1 Results

Out of three proposed models, the results reported by organizers in leaderboard obtained 1st, 2nd, and 3rd ranks for Ma-En, English and Ta-En texts respectively for CoHope-ML model (best among our models). Comparison of weighted scores of all the

	P	R	F1	Rank
LP	CoHope-ML			
Ma-En	0.85	0.85	0.85	1
Ta-En	0.59	0.59	0.59	3
English	0.92	0.93	0.92	2
	CoHope-NN			
Ma-En	0.83	0.83	0.83	
Ta-En	0.57	0.57	0.56	
English	0.91	0.92	0.91	
	CoHope-TL			
Ma-En	0.79	0.76	0.77	
Ta-En	0.55	0.54	0.54	
English	0.90	0.90	0.90	

Table 6: Results of the proposed models

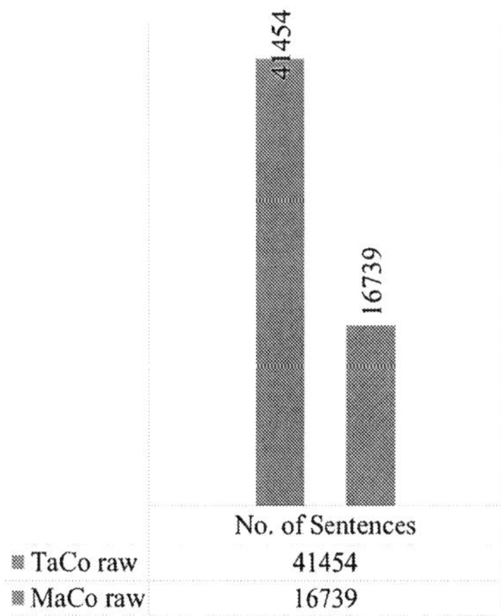

Figure 4: Statistics of raw texts

models proposed by MUCS is shown in Table 6. As it is illustrated in Table 6, both CoHope-ML and CoHope-NN models utilizing char sequences, traditional n-grams and syntactic ngrams features outperformed the CoHope-TL model. The results also illustrate that models performed better for texts with more native scripts.

The Confusion Matrix (CM) for Ma-En, Ta-En, and English texts using CoHope-ML model are shown in Figures 5, 6 and 7 respectively. The confusion matrices illustrates that CoHope-ML model rarely gets confused between other languages and the intended language in Malayalam and English since both datasets are having significant number of samples in native scripts.

5 Conclusion and Future Work

In this paper we, team MUCS, present the description of three proposed models for the task of "Hope Speech Detection for Equality, Diversity,

[14]TaCo: texts from combination of Tamil-English with Romanized Tamil (Dakshina) datasets

[15]MaCo: texts from combination of Malayalam-English with Romanized Malayalam (Dakshina) datasets

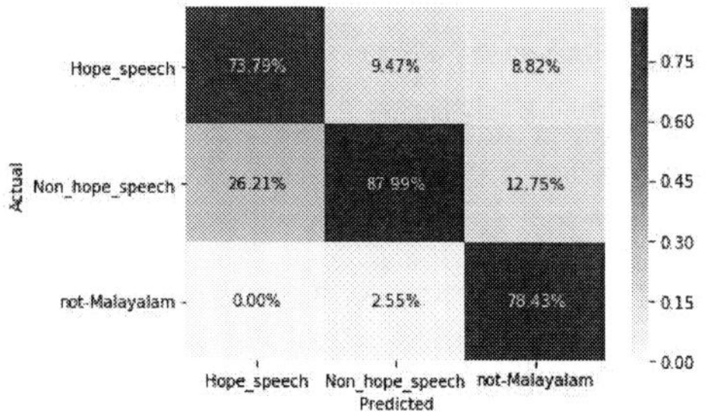

Figure 5: CM for Ma-En texts using CoHope-ML model

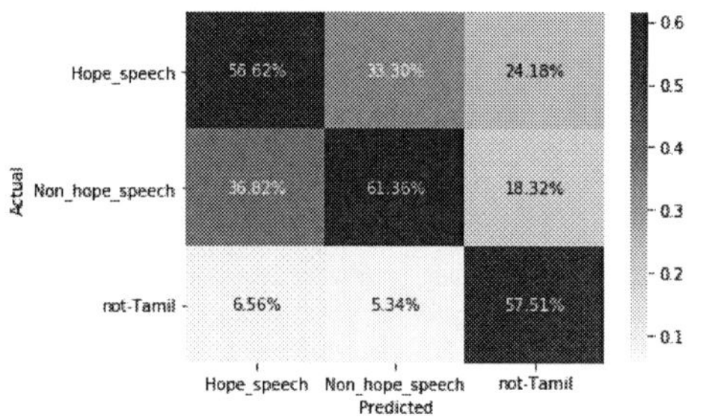

Figure 6: CM for Ta-En texts using CoHope-ML model

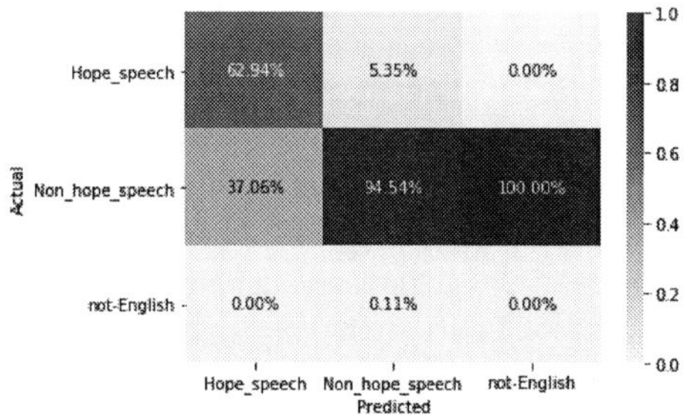

Figure 7: CM for English texts using CoHope-ML model

and Inclusion-EACL 2021". Proposed models includes a ML voting classifier - CoHope-ML, a DL NN model - CoHope-NN and a TL based model - CoHope-TL. The first two models are trained on a combination of char sequences and words for Ta-En and Ma-En code-mixed texts and combination of traditional char and word ngrams with syntactic word ngrams for English. CoHope-TL model utilizes BERT LM as weights in a BiLSTM-Conv1D architecture. Out of three proposed models, CoHope-ML model (best among our models) obtained weighted F1-scores of 0.85, 0.92 and 0.59 and 1, 2, 3 ranks for Malayalam-English, English, and Tamil-English texts. As future work, we planned to explore syntactic ngrams features for code-mixed texts and improve CoHope-NN architecture by experimenting on different NN layers and configurations. We also would like to compare different approaches based on TL for code-mixed texts from low resource languages.

References

Gaurav Arora. 2020. Gauravarora@ HASOC-Dravidian-CodeMix-FIRE2020: Pre-training ULM-FiT on Synthetically Generated Code-Mixed Data for Hate Speech Detection. *arXiv preprint arXiv:2010.02094*.

Aditya Bohra, Deepanshu Vijay, Vinay Singh, Syed Sarfaraz Akhtar, and Manish Shrivastava. 2018. A dataset of Hindi-English code-mixed social media text for hate speech detection. In *Proceedings of the second workshop on computational modeling of people's opinions, personality, and emotions in social media*, pages 36–41.

Bharathi Raja Chakravarthi. 2020. HopeEDI: A multilingual hope speech detection dataset for equality, diversity, and inclusion. In *Proceedings of the Third Workshop on Computational Modeling of People's Opinions, Personality, and Emotion's in Social Media*, pages 41–53, Barcelona, Spain (Online). Association for Computational Linguistics.

Bharathi Raja Chakravarthi, Navya Jose, Shardul Suryawanshi, Elizabeth Sherly, and John Philip McCrae. 2020a. A sentiment analysis dataset for code-mixed Malayalam-English. In *Proceedings of the 1st Joint Workshop on Spoken Language Technologies for Under-resourced languages (SLTU) and Collaboration and Computing for Under-Resourced Languages (CCURL)*, pages 177–184, Marseille, France. European Language Resources association.

Bharathi Raja Chakravarthi, M Anand Kumar, John Philip McCrae, Premjith B, Soman KP, and Thomas Mandl. 2020b. Overview of the track on HASOC-Offensive Language Identification-

DravidianCodeMix. In *Working Notes of the Forum for Information Retrieval Evaluation (FIRE 2020). CEUR Workshop Proceedings. In: CEUR-WS. org, Hyderabad, India.*

Bharathi Raja Chakravarthi, Vigneshwaran Muralidaran, Ruba Priyadharshini, and John Philip McCrae. 2020c. Corpus creation for sentiment analysis in code-mixed Tamil-English text. In *Proceedings of the 1st Joint Workshop on Spoken Language Technologies for Under-resourced languages (SLTU) and Collaboration and Computing for Under-Resourced Languages (CCURL)*, pages 202–210, Marseille, France. European Language Resources association.

Bharathi Raja Chakravarthi, Ruba Priyadharshini, Vigneshwaran Muralidaran, Shardul Suryawanshi, Navya Jose, Elizabeth Sherly, and John P. McCrae. 2020d. Overview of the Track on Sentiment Analysis for Dravidian Languages in Code-Mixed Text. In *Forum for Information Retrieval Evaluation*, FIRE 2020, page 21–24, New York, NY, USA. Association for Computing Machinery.

Tianqi Chen and Carlos Guestrin. 2016. Xgboost: A scalable tree boosting system. In *Proceedings of the 22nd acm sigkdd international conference on knowledge discovery and data mining*, pages 785–794.

Navya Jose, Bharathi Raja Chakravarthi, Shardul Suryawanshi, Elizabeth Sherly, and John P. McCrae. 2020. A Survey of Current Datasets for Code-Switching Research. In *2020 6th International Conference on Advanced Computing and Communication Systems (ICACCS)*, pages 136–141.

X. Ou and H. Li. 2020. YNU@Dravidian-CodeMix-FIRE2020: XLM-RoBERTa for Multi-language Sentiment Analysis. In *Forum for Information Retrieval Evaluation*. CEUR Workshop Proceedings.

Juan-Pablo Posadas-Durán, Ilia Markov, Helena Gómez-Adorno, Grigori Sidorov, Ildar Batyrshin, Alexander Gelbukh, and Obdulia Pichardo-Lagunas. 2015. Syntactic n-grams as features for the author profiling task.

Ruba Priyadharshini, Bharathi Raja Chakravarthi, Mani Vegupatti, and John P. McCrae. 2020. Named Entity Recognition for Code-Mixed Indian Corpus using Meta Embedding. In *2020 6th International Conference on Advanced Computing and Communication Systems (ICACCS)*, pages 68–72.

Sara Renjit and Sumam Mary Idicula. 2020. CUSATNLP@ HASOC-Dravidian-CodeMix-FIRE2020: Identifying Offensive Language from ManglishTweets. *arXiv preprint arXiv:2010.08756.*

Rashed Rubby Riyadh and Grzegorz Kondrak. 2019. Joint approach to deromanization of code-mixed texts. In *Proceedings of the Sixth Workshop on NLP for Similar Languages, Varieties and Dialects*, pages 26–34.

Brian Roark, Lawrence Wolf-Sonkin, Christo Kirov, Sabrina J Mielke, Cibu Johny, Isin Demirsahin, and Keith Hall. 2020. Processing South Asian languages written in the Latin script: the Dakshina dataset. *arXiv preprint arXiv:2007.01176.*

Grigori Sidorov, Francisco Velasquez, Efstathios Stamatatos, Alexander Gelbukh, and Liliana Chanona-Hernández. 2013. Syntactic dependency-based n-grams: More evidence of usefulness in classification. In *International Conference on Intelligent Text Processing and Computational Linguistics*, pages 13–24. Springer.

Sunayana Sitaram and Alan W Black. 2016. Speech synthesis of code-mixed text. In *Proceedings of the Tenth International Conference on Language Resources and Evaluation (LREC'16)*, pages 3422–3428.

R. Sun and X. Zhou. 2020. SRJ @ Dravidian-CodeMix-FIRE2020:Automatic Classification and Identification Sentiment in Code-mixed Text. In *Forum for Information Retrieval Evaluation*. CEUR Workshop Proceedings.

Spartans@LT-EDI-EACL2021: Inclusive Speech Detection using Pretrained Language Models

Megha Sharma *
Amazon
meghshar@amazon.com

Gaurav Arora *
Jio Haptik
gaurav@haptik.ai

Abstract

We describe our system that ranked first in Hope Speech Detection (HSD) shared task and fourth in Offensive Language Identification (OLI) shared task, both in Tamil language. The goal of HSD and OLI is to identify if a code-mixed comment or post contains hope speech or offensive content respectively. Our work extends that of (Arora, 2020a) as we use their strategy to synthetically generate code-mixed data for training a transformer-based model RoBERTa and use it in an ensemble along with their pre-trained ULMFiT.

1 Introduction

Language has the ability to build relationships and forge connections but it is equally liable for creating barriers and impacting someone's sense of belonging. The language used on the internet has an impact on people across the globe. It is important to build language technology which makes everyone feel valued and included. We make contributions to this field by competing in two shared tasks:

1. Hope Speech Detection (HSD) at First Workshop on Language Technology for Equality, Diversity, Inclusion[1] (LT-EDI-2021)

2. Offensive Language Identification (OLI) in Dravidian Languages at First Workshop on Speech and Language Technologies for Dravidian Languages[2] (DravidianLangTech-2021)

Hope is considered significant for the well-being, recuperation and restoration of human life by health professionals. Hope speech reflects the belief that one can discover pathways to one's desired objectives and become motivated to utilize those pathways (Snyder et al., 1991; Chang, 1998). The goal of HSD task is to identify whether a YouTube comment contains hope speech or not. The datasets are available in English, code-mixed Tamil-English and Malayalam-English. OLI task intends to identify offensive language content in datasets comprising of comments/posts in code-mixed Tamil-English, Malayalam-English and Kannada-English which are collected from social media. Both datasets have been annotated at a comment level wherein a comment could comprise of more than one sentence but on average it has a single sentence.

Our work is an extension of the work done in (Arora, 2020a) as we use their synthetic code-mixed dataset for Tamil and ULMFiT model trained on that dataset. We pre-train a transformer based model RoBERTa (Liu et al., 2019) from scratch on code-mixed data and build an ensemble using ULMFiT and RoBERTa to achieve:

- Weighted F1 score of 0.61 for Tamil HSD and Rank 1 amongst 30 participating teams

- Weighted F1 score of 0.75 for Tamil OLI and Rank 4 amongst 30 participating teams

We review some related work from literature before explaining the details of our approach and the results. All experiments described in the paper can be reproduced using the source code available on GitHub[3].

2 Related Work

As noted on the LT-EDI 2021's website[4], this is the first shared task on HSD. Some work has been previously done for HSD (Palakodety et al., 2019),

*equal contribution
[1]https://sites.google.com/view/lt-edi-2021/home
[2]https://dravidianlangtech.github.io/2021/
[3]https://github.com/goru001/nlp-for-tanglish
[4]https://sites.google.com/view/lt-edi-2021

Proceedings of the First Workshop on Language Technology for Equality, Diversity and Inclusion, pages 188–192
April 19, 2021.

Metric	Offensive Language Identification			Hope Speech Detection		
Number of classes	6			3		
	Train	Valid	Test	Train	Valid	Test
Dataset size	35139	4388	4392	16160	2018	2021
%age of examples containing only Roman characters	80.4%	81%	81.2%	83.9%	83.8%	84.8%
min. no. of examples in a class	454	65	-	1961	263	-
max. no. of examples in a class	25425	3193	-	7872	998	-
avg. no. of examples in a class	5856.5	731.33	-	5386.67	672.67	-
min no. of tokens in an example	1	2	1	1	1	2
max no. of tokens in an example	183	93	138	204	159	187
avg no. of tokens in an example	12.04	12.03	11.89	9.57	9.97	11.07
median no. of tokens in an example	9	9	9	7	7	8

Table 1: Dataset statistics for OLI and HSD tasks

Model Architecture	Perplexity	Vocab size
RoBERTa	8.4	10000
ULMFiT	37.50	8000

Table 2: Validation set perplexity of RoBERTa and ULMFiT

but we are not aware of any work for HSD in Tamil language. OLI has been an area of active research in both academia and industry for the past two decades. Recent work has been done for OLI in Dravidian languages in HASOC task at FIRE (Mandl et al., 2020). HASOC task, which attracted over 40 research groups, consisted of building Hate Speech and Offensive Language identification systems by using datasets prepared by extracting comments/posts from YouTube and Twitter. In this paper, we build classification models for HSD and OLI using Transfer Learning, details of which have been explained in Section 3.

3 Methodology

In this section we look at classification datasets, discuss details of RoBERTa and ULMFiT models and the classifiers which are trained on top of these language models.

3.1 Dataset

Dataset for RoBERTa pre-training. We use synthetically generated code-mixed data for Tamil[5] prepared in (Arora, 2020a) to pretrain RoBERTa from scratch. The dataset is a collection of Tamil sentences written in Latin script. It was prepared by transliterating Tamil Wikipedia articles using Indic-Trans[6] library.

Classification datasets. Table 1 shows statistics of datasets of both tasks. We observe that the statistics are fairly consistent across train, valid and test sets. Classification dataset for HSD (Chakravarthi, 2020) has 3 classes whereas that in OLI has 6 classes. Both the classification datasets have significant class imbalance depicting real-world scenarios. Additionally, they contain code-mixed comments/posts in both Latin and native scripts, making the tasks challenging.

3.2 Modeling Details

We take a two-step approach to the problem by pre-training ULMFiT (Howard and Ruder, 2018) and RoBERTa (Liu et al., 2019) models on synthetically generated code-mixed language followed by an ensemble of two classifiers which are trained on top of ULMFiT and RoBERTa language models respectively.

3.2.1 ULMFiT Model

We use pre-trained ULMFiT model for code-mixed Tamil similar to the one used in (Arora, 2020b). Its embedding size is 400, number of hidden activations per layer are 1152 and the number of layers are 3. Two linear blocks with batch normalization and dropout have been added as custom head for the classifier with rectified linear unit activations for the intermediate layer and a softmax activation

[5]Pre-training dataset can be downloaded from https://github.com/goru001/nlp-for-tanglish

[6]https://github.com/libindic/indic-trans

Dropout Multiplicity	Batch Size	Epochs	Learning Rate	Adam Beta1	Adam Beta2	Adam Epsilon	LR Scheduler Type
0.1	8	3	5e-05	0.9	0.999	1e-08	LINEAR

Table 3: RoBERTa Classification Model Hyperparams for OLI

Model	Precision	Recall	F1 Score	Accuracy
Baseline KNN	0.62	0.72	0.65	0.72
ULMFit	0.73	0.78	0.73	0.78
RoBERTa	0.74	0.77	0.75	0.77
Ensemble	**0.75**	**0.79**	**0.76**	**0.79**

Table 4: Validation set results for OLI

Model	Precision	Recall	F1 Score	Accuracy
Baseline KNN Model	0.53	0.53	0.53	0.53
ULMFit	0.63	0.63	0.63	0.63

Table 5: Validation set results for HSD

at the last layer.

3.2.2 RoBERTa Model

RoBERTa model builds on BERT (Devlin et al., 2019) and modifies BERT's key hyperparameters, removes the next-sentence pre-training objective and trains with much larger mini-batches and learning rates. RoBERTa has the same architecture as BERT but it uses a different pre-training scheme and tokenizes text using Byte-Pair Encoding (Sennrich et al., 2016). We use implementation of RoBERTa in Huggingface's Transformers library[7] to pre-train the model from scratch. We train it for 7 epochs using a learning rate of 5e-5 and a dropout of 0.1 for attention and hidden layers. Table 2 compares perplexity of our pre-trained RoBERTa model with that of ULMFiT model which is also trained on the same code-mixed data.

3.3 Classification data pre-processing

We pre-process the classification datasets of both tasks by transforming comments in native script into Latin script using Indic-Trans library. This step is required because both of our pre-trained language models, ULMFiT and RoBERTa, are trained on code-mixed data in Latin script. We also perform other basic pre-processing steps like lowercasing and removing @username mentions. We did not apply other pre-processing steps such as stop words removal or removal of words that are too short since both of our pre-trained language models are trained on complete sentences and we wanted the model to figure out on its own if stop/short words are important for classification or not.

4 Experiment and Results

In this section we discuss details and results of our baseline model, classification models and ensemble strategy.

4.1 Experiment Details

4.1.1 OLI Task

Baseline Model. Our baseline uses KNN classifier on embeddings generated using code-mixed ULMFiT model from iNLTK[8] (Arora, 2020b). We set k=5 for all our experiments with uniform weighting on neighbors.

Ensemble. Our final model is a weighted ensemble of two classifiers where their weights sum to 1. Training of classifiers happens in two steps. First we fine-tune our language model on the downstream task of OLI and then train a classifier on the fine-tuned language model. Table 3 contains details of hyperparameters of the first classifier which is trained on our pre-trained RoBERTa. We train the second classifier using fine-tuned ULMFiT language model which is available in iNLTK. We experiment with different weights of classifiers in the ensemble. Best results on the validation set are obtained by setting a weight of 0.5 for both classifiers. Figure 1 shows the variation of weighted F1 score

[7] https://huggingface.co/transformers/model_doc/roberta.html

[8] https://github.com/goru001/inltk

Offensive Language Identifiation				Hope Speech Detection			
Precision	**Recall**	**F1 Score**	**Rank**	**Precision**	**Recall**	**F1 Score**	**Rank**
0.74	0.78	0.75	4/30	0.62	0.62	0.61	1/30

Table 6: Test set results for OLI task and HSD task

by changing weights of RoBERTa based classifier.

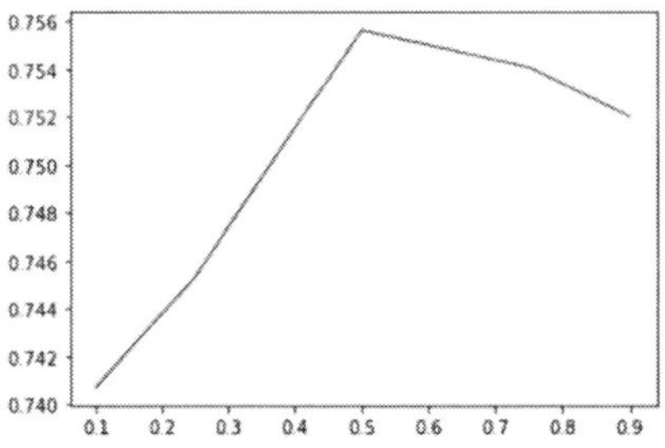

Figure 1: Change in Tamil OLI validation set F1 score on y-axis with change in RoBERTa weight shown on x-axis

4.1.2 HSD Task

We use a similar approach as that used for OLI task. Baseline model is built using the KNN algorithm and the final model is a classifier trained on a fine-tuned ULMFiT language model. Due to time and resource constraints, we weren't able to train RoBERTa based classifier.

4.2 Results

In both tasks weighted averaged Precision, weighted averaged Recall and weighted averaged F-Score are used as evaluation and ranking criteria. We participated in sub-task for Tamil and got Rank 4 in OLI task and Rank 1 in HSD task (Chakravarthi and Muralidaran, 2021). Table 4 shows the performance of different models on the validation set of former task. Best F1 score of 0.76 is obtained by using the ensemble of classifiers trained on RoBERTa and ULMFiT model which are pre-trained on code-mixed data. Table 5 contains results of models on the validation set of the latter task. We obtain an F1 score of 0.63 with ULMFiT based classifier. Results on the test-set for both the tasks have been shown in Table 6.

5 Conclusion and Future Work

In this paper we present RoBERTa language model for code-mixed Tamil which we pre-trained from scratch. Using transfer learning we fine-tune RoBERTa and ULMFiT language models on downstream tasks of OLI and HSD. We got Rank 4 in the former task using an ensemble of classifiers trained on RoBERTa and ULMFiT and Rank 1 in the latter task using classifier based on ULMFiT. In future research we will explore other transformer architectures like BERT (Devlin et al., 2018), T5 (Raffel et al., 2020), XLM (Conneau et al., 2019). We will work on improving code-mixed data generation strategies. We plan to create a dataset using a combination of native Tamil sentences, their transliterations and translations in English.

Acknowledgments

We would like to thank our teams at Amazon and Jio Haptik for motivating us to participate in these shared tasks. Please note that this work is not a by-product of any formal collaboration with Amazon and Jio Haptik. We participated in these tasks out of personal interests and in our own time.

References

Gaurav Arora. 2020a. Gauravarora@hasoc-dravidian-codemix-fire2020: Pre-training ulmfit on synthetically generated code-mixed data for hate speech detection.

Gaurav Arora. 2020b. iNLTK: Natural language toolkit for indic languages. In *Proceedings of Second Workshop for NLP Open Source Software (NLP-OSS)*, pages 66–71, Online. Association for Computational Linguistics.

Bharathi Raja Chakravarthi. 2020. HopeEDI: A multilingual hope speech detection dataset for equality, diversity, and inclusion. In *Proceedings of the Third Workshop on Computational Modeling of People's Opinions, Personality, and Emotion's in Social Media*, pages 41–53, Barcelona, Spain (Online). Association for Computational Linguistics.

Bharathi Raja Chakravarthi and Vigneshwaran Muralidaran. 2021. Findings of the shared task on Hope Speech Detection for Equality, Diversity, and Inclusion. In *Proceedings of the First Workshop on Language Technology for Equality, Diversity and Inclusion*. Association for Computational Linguistics.

E. C. Chang. 1998. Hope, problem-solving ability, and coping in a college student population: some implications for theory and practice. *J Clin Psychol*, 54(7):953–962.

Alexis Conneau, Kartikay Khandelwal, Naman Goyal, Vishrav Chaudhary, Guillaume Wenzek, Francisco Guzmán, Edouard Grave, Myle Ott, Luke Zettlemoyer, and Veselin Stoyanov. 2019. Unsupervised cross-lingual representation learning at scale. *arXiv preprint arXiv:1911.02116*.

Jacob Devlin, Ming-Wei Chang, Kenton Lee, and Kristina Toutanova. 2018. BERT: pre-training of deep bidirectional transformers for language understanding. *CoRR*, abs/1810.04805.

Jacob Devlin, Ming-Wei Chang, Kenton Lee, and Kristina Toutanova. 2019. Bert: Pre-training of deep bidirectional transformers for language understanding.

Jeremy Howard and Sebastian Ruder. 2018. Fine-tuned language models for text classification. *CoRR*, abs/1801.06146.

Yinhan Liu, Myle Ott, Naman Goyal, Jingfei Du, Mandar Joshi, Danqi Chen, Omer Levy, Mike Lewis, Luke Zettlemoyer, and Veselin Stoyanov. 2019. Roberta: A robustly optimized bert pretraining approach.

Thomas Mandl, Sandip Modha, Anand Kumar M, and Bharathi Raja Chakravarthi. 2020. Overview of the hasoc track at fire 2020: Hate speech and offensive language identification in tamil, malayalam, hindi, english and german. In *Forum for Information Retrieval Evaluation*, FIRE 2020, page 29–32, New York, NY, USA. Association for Computing Machinery.

Shriphani Palakodety, Ashiqur R. KhudaBukhsh, and Jaime G. Carbonell. 2019. Kashmir: A computational analysis of the voice of peace. *CoRR*, abs/1909.12940.

Colin Raffel, Noam Shazeer, Adam Roberts, Katherine Lee, Sharan Narang, Michael Matena, Yanqi Zhou, Wei Li, and Peter J. Liu. 2020. Exploring the limits of transfer learning with a unified text-to-text transformer.

Rico Sennrich, Barry Haddow, and Alexandra Birch. 2016. Neural machine translation of rare words with subword units. In *Proceedings of the 54th Annual Meeting of the Association for Computational Linguistics (Volume 1: Long Papers)*, pages 1715–1725, Berlin, Germany. Association for Computational Linguistics.

C. R. Snyder, C. Harris, J. R. Anderson, S. A. Holleran, L. M. Irving, S. T. Sigmon, L. Yoshinobu, J. Gibb, C. Langelle, and P. Harney. 1991. The will and the ways: development and validation of an individual-differences measure of hope. *J Pers Soc Psychol*, 60(4):570–585.

CFILT IIT Bombay@LT-EDI-EACL2021: Hope Speech Detection for Equality, Diversity, and Inclusion using Multilingual Representation from Transformers

Pankaj Singh, Prince Kumar and Pushpak Bhattacharyya
Indian Institute of Technology Bombay
Mumbai, India
pankajsingh7@iitb.ac.in, {princekumar, pb}@cse.iitb.ac.in

Abstract

With the internet becoming part and parcel of our lives, engagement in social media has increased a lot. Identifying and eliminating offensive content from social media has become of utmost priority to prevent any kind of violence. However, detecting encouraging, supportive and positive content is equally important to prevent misuse of censorship targeted to attack freedom of speech. This paper presents our system for the shared task Hope Speech Detection for Equality, Diversity, and Inclusion at LT-EDI, EACL 2021. The data for this shared task is provided in English, Tamil, and Malayalam which was collected from YouTube comments. It is a multiclass classification problem where each data instance is categorized into one of the three classes: 'Hope speech', 'Not hope speech', and 'Not in intended language'. We propose a system that employs multilingual transformer models to obtain the representation of text and classifies it into one of the three classes. We explored the use of multilingual models trained specifically for Indian languages along with generic multilingual models. Our system was ranked 2nd for English, 2^{n}d for Malayalam, and 7th for the Tamil language in the final leader board published by organizers and obtained a weighted F1-score of 0.92, 0.84, 0.55 respectively on the hidden test dataset used for the competition. We have made our system publicly available at GitHub.

1 Introduction

The prominence of web-based media is expanding quickly because it is being used to create and share content, even by those who are ignorant of online media. Several web platforms allow users to add textual feedback on non-textual content, such as images, photos, animations, etc. With millions of videos posted by its users and billions of comments on all these videos, YouTube is undoubtedly the most famous of them.

Online social media comments/posts have been examined to identify and avoid the propagation of negativity using strategies such as detecting abusive language detection (Lee et al., 2018) and hate speech (Schmidt and Wiegand, 2017). There is a lot of work that is being done to remove the negativity from the web but Hope speech detection focuses to spread positivity by detecting content that is encouraging, positive, and supportive.

When it comes to hope speech detection there has not been much work done but recently the NLP community has started showing interest in this area. In a work by Palakodety et al. (2019), they have analyzed YouTube comments and performed the task of hope speech detection to identify hostility-diffusing content. Here the authors have not taken other aspects like equality, diversity, and inclusion into account.

Chakravarthi et al. (2020) did work in Indian languages where they manually annotated the YouTube comments for Tamil and Malayalam languages for performing sentiment analysis. In a similar work, Chakravarthi (2020) released the dataset consisting of YouTube comments with hope and not-hope speech annotation.

Hate speech is a well-researched area related to Hope speech. According to the survey done by Schmidt and Wiegand (2017), automatic hate detection was needed due to a large number of people using the net and the massive scale with which the web is growing. Zhang and Luo (2018) used deep neural networks for the task and they were able to outperform the best performing method by up to 5 percentage points in macro-average F1-score.

Multilingual BERT (Pires et al., 2019) is a variant of BERT (Devlin et al., 2019) that has been heavily used by the NLP community. Pires et al. (2019) in their work showed that multilingual rep-

Proceedings of the First Workshop on Language Technology for Equality, Diversity and Inclusion, pages 193–196
April 19, 2021. ©2020 Association for Computational Linguistics

resentation by multilingual BERT handles cross linguality without being explicitly trained for it. It also handles transfer across scripts and to code-switching fairly well. Conneau et al. (2020) proposed another variant of the BERT model called XLM-RoBERTa by pre-training multilingual models at scale. There have been various attempts to tackle problems related to Indian languages by training transformer models specifically for Indian languages. Indic BERT (Kakwani et al., 2020) and MuRIL (`https://tfhub.dev/google/MuRIL/1`) are two such transformer-based language models.

We plan to tackle the Hope speech discovery for the English, Tamil, and Malayalam language by obtaining representation from multilingual transformer models. Tamil and Malayalam are Dravidian languages locally spoken in the states of Tamil Nadu and Kerala respectively on Indian territory. For a country like India, where people speak many languages, code-mixing is fairly common (Barman et al., 2014; Bali et al., 2014; Gupta et al., 2018). The dataset for this task is code-mixed such as tag, inter-sentential, and intra-sentential (Chakravarthi, 2020).

The shared task was launched as a part of the first workshop on Language Technology for Equality, Diversity, Inclusion (LT-EDI-EACL-2021) (Chakravarthi and Muralidaran, 2021). It was conducted for English, Tamil, and Malayalam language categories. The task was to classify a given piece of text scraped from YouTube comments into one of the three possible categories. These three possible categories or labels were:

- Label 1: Hope Speech
- Label 2: Not hope speech
- Label 3: Not in intended language

The rest of the paper is paper is organized as follows. In Section 2, we provide the dataset details and statistics. Section 3 consists of our system description and architecture details. In Section 4, we describe our experimental setups and report our results. We conclude this paper in Section 5 and briefly discuss our future plans for tackling this problem.

2 Dataset

The organizers of LT-EDI 2021 have provided the dataset for training, validation, and testing of the systems for the shared tasks. The dataset consists of pairs of text and their corresponding label. Training and validation sets were provided with labels for developing the systems for the given shared task and a test set was supplied without ground truth labels for a fair evaluation and publishing final results and team ranking among participants.However, the labels for test data were also made available once competition concluded and final results were declared. However, the labels for test data were also made available once the competition concluded and the final results were declared. The dataset was unevenly distributed across three possible classes for all three languages. Table 1 shows the class distribution of the dataset for English, Tamil, and Malayalam.

Language	Label 1	Label 2	Label 3
English	20,778	1962	22
Tamil	7,872	6,327	1,961
Malayalam	6,205	1,668	691

Table 1: Distribution of training data samples across three classes

3 System Description

The core deep learning model of our system consists of BERT-based transformer model in a multilingual setting. We did not perform any kind of pre-processing of the text data to avoid computational overhead at run time and to evaluate efficacy of multilingual transformers on raw text. We obtained a pooled 768-dimensional vector representation for the entire raw text of each instance. This vector is then fed to a softmax layer which gives the probability distribution of the sentence being from given three possible classes. This setup of trained end-to-end with cross-entropy loss function and F1-score as an evaluation metric.

4 Experiments and Results

We have experimented with various multilingual transformer-based models that were trained on multiple languages together. Multilingual models pretrained specifically for Indian languages were also employed for the given shared tasks.

4.1 Experimental Setups

We report the performances of our system for the four multilingual transformer models. These four models are multilingual BERT, XLM-RoBERTa,

Language	mBERT	XLM-RoBERTa	IndicBERT	MuRIL
English	0.925	**0.928**	0.918	0.918
Tamil	0.570	**0.582**	0.547	0.567
Malayalam	0.850	**0.860**	0.835	0.823

Table 2: Performance (Weighted F1-score) of our system on test set for various multilingual transformer models

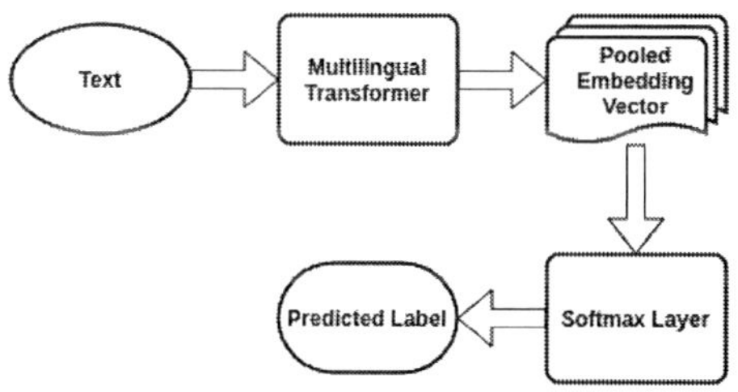

Figure 1: Architectural flowgraph of the our system

IndicBERT, and MuRIL. Among these fours, the last two models were pre-trained specifically for Indian languages. IndicBERT is an ALBERT based model that was pre-trained on 12 major Indian languages and MuRIL (Multilingual Representations for Indian Languages) is a BERT-based model pre-trained on 17 Indian languages and their transliterated counterparts.

After extensive experimentation, we finalized hyper-parameters which worked well for all four transformer models. To have a fair comparison between all models, it was also important to not have a large variation in hyper-parameters and training methodology since all the models have a common base transformer architecture as BERT. Following hyper-parameters were finally used to train the system in all four experimental setups:

- **Loss function:** Cross-Entropy
- **Optimizer:** Adam
- **Maximum token length:** 70
- **Epochs:** 20
- **Batch size:** 64
- **Learning rate:** 0.00002

4.2 Results

In this section, we present our results on the test set for the four experimental setups discussed above. In line with shared task organizers, we also used weighted F1-score as an evaluation metric.

In Table 2, the performance of our system using above mentioned four transformer model as the base is reported. This performance is on the test set. XLM-RoBERTa was the best performing multilingual model for all the three language categories. Multilingual models trained specifically for Indian languages performed at par if not better than generic multilingual models. Among the three language categories, all of our systems achieved the best scores for English and worst scores for Tamil. The high F1-score for the English language category can be attributed to the heavily skewed distribution of the dataset samples across three classes. Since Label 1 was very dominant, it increased the weighted F1-score for the English language.

We submitted our best performing system to the competition and obtained encouraging results. In the final leader board published by organizers, our team was placed at 2nd, 2nd, and 7th rank for English, Malayalam, and Tamil language categories. After extensive experimentation and hyper-parameter tuning we were able to improve our scores published on the competition leader-board for Tamil and Malayalam languages.

5 Conclusion and Future Work

In this paper, we have described our system submitted for the shared task in Hope Speech detection and reported its performance. We have extensively experimented with the possibility of employing multilingual models for given tasks. We report the performance of four different multilingual models which include transformer models specifically trained for Indian languages. Our experiments showed that transformer models pre-trained on a smaller set of languages have the potential to perform at par or better than models trained on hundreds of languages.

In the future, we plan to introduce some linguistic-based features and combined them with multilingual transformer representation to improve the overall effectiveness of the system. We also plan to systematically study the effect of abolishing the 'Not in intended language' class from the dataset as it opens up the opportunity to have a single system or deep learning model for all three languages.

Acknowledgments

We thank the entire organizing team of LT-EDI 2021- EACL 2021 for providing us the platform and opportunity to work on such a problem of potentially high social impact.

References

Kalika Bali, Jatin Sharma, Monojit Choudhury, and Yogarshi Vyas. 2014. "i am borrowing ya mixing?" an analysis of english-hindi code mixing in facebook. In *Proceedings of the First Workshop on Computational Approaches to Code Switching*, pages 116–126.

Utsab Barman, Joachim Wagner, Grzegorz Chrupała, and Jennifer Foster. 2014. DCU-UVT: Word-level language classification with code-mixed data. In *Proceedings of the First Workshop on Computational Approaches to Code Switching*, pages 127–132, Doha, Qatar. Association for Computational Linguistics.

Bharathi Raja Chakravarthi. 2020. HopeEDI: A multilingual hope speech detection dataset for equality, diversity, and inclusion. In *Proceedings of the Third Workshop on Computational Modeling of People's Opinions, Personality, and Emotion's in Social Media*, pages 41–53, Barcelona, Spain (Online). Association for Computational Linguistics.

Bharathi Raja Chakravarthi, Navya Jose, Shardul Suryawanshi, Elizabeth Sherly, and John Philip McCrae. 2020. A sentiment analysis dataset for code-mixed Malayalam-English. In *Proceedings of the 1st Joint Workshop on Spoken Language Technologies for Under-resourced languages (SLTU) and Collaboration and Computing for Under-Resourced Languages (CCURL)*, pages 177–184, Marseille, France. European Language Resources association.

Bharathi Raja Chakravarthi and Vigneshwaran Muralidaran. 2021. Findings of the shared task on Hope Speech Detection for Equality, Diversity, and Inclusion. In *Proceedings of the First Workshop on Language Technology for Equality, Diversity and Inclusion*. Association for Computational Linguistics.

Alexis Conneau, Kartikay Khandelwal, Naman Goyal, Vishrav Chaudhary, Guillaume Wenzek, Francisco Guzmán, Edouard Grave, Myle Ott, Luke Zettlemoyer, and Veselin Stoyanov. 2020. Unsupervised cross-lingual representation learning at scale. In *Proceedings of the 58th Annual Meeting of the Association for Computational Linguistics*, pages 8440–8451, Online. Association for Computational Linguistics.

Jacob Devlin, Ming-Wei Chang, Kenton Lee, and Kristina Toutanova. 2019. BERT: Pre-training of deep bidirectional transformers for language understanding. In *Proceedings of the 2019 Conference of the North American Chapter of the Association for Computational Linguistics: Human Language Technologies, Volume 1 (Long and Short Papers)*, pages 4171–4186, Minneapolis, Minnesota. Association for Computational Linguistics.

Deepak Gupta, Pabitra Lenka, Asif Ekbal, and Pushpak Bhattacharyya. 2018. Uncovering code-mixed challenges: A framework for linguistically driven question generation and neural based question answering. In *Proceedings of the 22nd Conference on Computational Natural Language Learning*, pages 119–130.

Divyanshu Kakwani, Anoop Kunchukuttan, Satish Golla, Gokul N.C., Avik Bhattacharyya, Mitesh M. Khapra, and Pratyush Kumar. 2020. IndicNLPSuite: Monolingual corpora, evaluation benchmarks and pre-trained multilingual language models for Indian languages. In *Findings of the Association for Computational Linguistics: EMNLP 2020*, pages 4948–4961, Online. Association for Computational Linguistics.

Younghun Lee, Seunghyun Yoon, and Kyomin Jung. 2018. Comparative studies of detecting abusive language on twitter. In *Proceedings of the 2nd Workshop on Abusive Language Online (ALW2)*, pages 101–106, Brussels, Belgium. Association for Computational Linguistics.

Shriphani Palakodety, Ashiqur R. KhudaBukhsh, and Jaime G. Carbonell. 2019. Kashmir: A computational analysis of the voice of peace. *CoRR*, abs/1909.12940.

Telmo Pires, Eva Schlinger, and Dan Garrette. 2019. How multilingual is multilingual BERT? In *Proceedings of the 57th Annual Meeting of the Association for Computational Linguistics*, pages 4996–5001, Florence, Italy. Association for Computational Linguistics.

Anna Schmidt and Michael Wiegand. 2017. A survey on hate speech detection using natural language processing. In *Proceedings of the Fifth International Workshop on Natural Language Processing for Social Media*, pages 1–10, Valencia, Spain. Association for Computational Linguistics.

Ziqi Zhang and Lei Luo. 2018. Hate speech detection: A solved problem? the challenging case of long tail on twitter. *CoRR*, abs/1803.03662.

IIITK@LT-EDI-EACL2021: Hope Speech Detection for Equality, Diversity, and Inclusion in Tamil , Malayalam and English

Nikhil Kumar Ghanghor [1], **Rahul Ponnusamy** [2], **Prasanna Kumar Kumaresan** [2]
Ruba Priyadharshini [3] **Sajeetha Thavareesan** [4] **Bharathi Raja Chakravarthi** [5]
[1] Indian Institute of Information Technology Kottayam
[2]Indian Institute of Information Technology and Management Kerala
[3] ULTRA Arts and Science College, Madurai, India, [4]Eastern University, Sri Lanka
[5] National University of Ireland Galway
nkghanghor18bcs@iiitkottayam.ac.in

Abstract

This paper describes the IIITK's team submissions to the hope speech detection for equality, diversity and inclusion in Dravidian languages shared task organized by LT-EDI 2021 workshop@EACL 2021. We have used the transformer-based pretrained models along with the customized versions of those models with custom loss functions. Our best configurations for the shared tasks achieve weighted F1 scores of 0.60 for Tamil, 0.83 for Malayalam, and 0.93 for English. We have secured ranks of 4, 3, 2 in Tamil, Malayalam and English respectively. We have open-sourced our code implementations for all the models across both the tasks on GitHub [1].

1 Introduction

According to Wikipedia hope is being defined as *an optimistic state of mind that is based on the expectation of outcomes with respect to events and circumstances in one's life or the world at large.* The hope speech detection shared task [2] organized by LT-EDI aimed to detect hope speeches in the given corpus for English, Tamil, and Malayalam (Chakravarthi and Muralidaran, 2021). The data set has been gathered from some social media remarks. We participated in this task given a social media remarks in hope speech, frameworks need to characterize if a post is hope speech or not.

Tamil (ISO 639-3: tam) and Malayalam (ISO 639-3: tam) belong to same family. Tamil was the first to be listed as a classical language of India, one of 22 scheduled languages in the Constitution of India, also official language of Tamil Nadu, Puducherry, Singapore and Sri Lanka and is one of the world's longest-surviving classical languages (Norman, 1977; Stein, 1977; Hart III, 2015). The oldest epigraphic documents discovered date from about the 6th century BC on pottery, rock edicts and hero blocks. Over 55 percent of the epigraphic inscriptions discovered by the Archaeological Survey of India (about 55,000) are in the Tamil language (Maloney, 1970; Abraham, 2003). A Tamil prayer book in ancient Tamil script called Thambiran Vanakkam was written by Portuguese Christian missionaries in 1578, thereby rendering Tamil the first Indian language to be printed and published (Balachandran, 2005). Malayalam split from Tamil during 16th century by Thunchaththu Ramanujan Ezhuthachan until then it was west coast dialect of Tamil (Menon, 1938; Steever, 1998).

Over time various methodologies are being proposed by the researchers throughout the Natural Language Processing (NLP) community for building better textual analysis systems. Solving the text classification problem has been improvised throughout by building better architectures and better representation techniques for texts. The community has also benefitted by borrowing the ideas from other domains like computer vision and incorporating those in these systems which have given promising results. Initially, the models used to deal with the Bag Of Words (BOW) representations, then came the ideas of lemmatization and stemming, which helped in improving the representation techniques further. Then around the early 2010s word embeddings were proposed by (Mikolov et al., 2013).

The NLP domain has also observed many architectural innovations which have further pushed the performances to give state of the art (SOTA) results. Some of them are the LSTMs (Hochreiter and Schmidhuber, 1997), BiLSTMs (Ghaeini et al., 2018), GRUs (Chung et al., 2014) and then the mighty transformers (Vaswani et al., 2017). The introduction of transformers changed the entire land-

[1]https://github.com/nikhil6041/HopeSpeechDetection

[2]https://competitions.codalab.org/competitions/27653

Proceedings of the First Workshop on Language Technology for Equality, Diversity and Inclusion, pages 197–203
April 19, 2021. ©2020 Association for Computational Linguistics

scape, and the models built upon the transformer architecture are consistently pushing the results on the GLUE (Wang et al., 2019) benchmarks. There have been instances where the researchers have tried to incorporate the architectural innovations from different domains to NLP. In this paper, we have tried several architectures built upon the transformer architecture and have fine-tuned them on our task, details of which are being discussed in the later sections of the paper.

2 Related Work

Hope speech detection is a relatively new field and an active area of research in the NLP domain. With the rise of the Internet and the social media platforms, people from various places around the globe are now connected through these platforms which have given them a common place to express their views. These views can often be specifically targeted to a particular person or community that can convey either of a positive, neutral or negative emotion to the concerned person or community. This makes it an important aspect to have systems that can automatically classify these content and filter out the ones having a negative impact on the society. In other words, this also means that we have systems that explicitly detect positive content and help it stay in the social good system. As defined earlier, hope speech can also be considered a piece of text conveying a positive sentiment to the reader of it. One of the first works on hope speech detection is done by Chakravarthi (2020a), Puranik et al. (2021), and Palakodety et al. (2020) . Palakodety et al. (2020) used the polyglot word embeddings to have clusters of texts that conveys similar sentiments and obtained promising results. Hope speech detection can also be considered as the opposite task of hate speech detection.

There has been a significant amount of work done for the hate speech detection task (Mandl et al., 2020; Chakravarthi et al., 2020c; Yasaswini et al., 2021; Ghanghor et al., 2021; Hegde et al., 2021). It has even been a part of several conferences like SemEval [3] as challenges. However, these conferences mainly focused on datasets which were constructed for resource abundant languages. However, in the mid-2020s several competitions have been organized which centred around these under-resourced languages. To build a system that performs well on under-resourced languages like Dravidian languages, several researchers have developed systems that have given noticeable results on these tasks (Hande et al., 2020; Chakravarthi, 2020b; Chakravarthi et al., 2020d,b,a). HASOC-Dravidian-CodeMix-FIRE2020 participants used traditional ml methods like Naive Bayes Classifier, Support Vector Machines (SVMs) and Random Forest along with the pretrained transformers models like XLM-Roberta (XLMR) (Conneau et al., 2020) and BERT (Devlin et al., 2019) for the offensive content identification in code-mixed datasets (Tamil-English and Malayalam-English). (Arora, 2020) at HASOC-Dravidian-CodeMix-FIRE2020 used ULMFit (Howard and Ruder, 2018) to pretrain on a synthetically generated code-mixed dataset and then fine-tuned it to the downstream tasks of text classification.

3 Dataset Description

Distribution	Tamil	Malayalam	English
Train	16,160	8,564	22,762
Dev	2,018	1,070	2,843
Test	2,020	1,071	2,846

Table 1: Hope Speech EDI Dataset

The competition organizers have provided us with datasets (Chakravarthi, 2020a) for three different languages Tamil, Malayalam and English. Across each dataset we had three different classes Hope_Speech, Non_Hope_Speech and not_**lang** where **lang** can be either of Tamil, Malayalam or English depending upon the dataset we are dealing with. The train, dev and test set distributions of the dataset are as shown in the table 1.

4 Methodology

The analysis of the nature of texts has been one of the central tasks in NLP. Textual analysis can be defined as a separation of the texts into different classes based upon the underlying meaning they convey (Priyadharshini et al., 2020). The NLP domain has observed many advancements for solving the textual analysis problem. However, it remains an unsolved problem because of the linguistic diversity worldwide and the difficulties in expressing texts to a suitable format for feeding it into the textual analysis systems (Jose et al., 2020). Over time, various methods have been proposed for representation of texts, ranging from Bag of Words, TF-IDF to word embeddings. The word embeddings

[3] https://semeval.github.io/

were introduced with the Word2Vec model, which gives a vectorized representation for a word. After the introduction of the Word2Vec word embedding model, different word embedding techniques have been proposed throughout the NLP domain such as Glove (Pennington et al., 2014), Doc2Vec (Le and Mikolov, 2014), Fasttext (Bojanowski et al., 2017). Using these different kinds of word representations, various different models have been proposed for solving the textual analysis problem. These models consisted of the primitive machine learning models like Naive Bayes (NB), Logistic Regression (LR), Multinomial Naive Bayes (MNB), Support Vector Machines (SVMs). Apart from these models, various models based upon neural networks were also being used such as LSTMs, Bidirectional LSTMs, GRUs. However, the current State Of The Art (SOTA) models are based upon the transformer architecture. There are numerous models built upon the transformer architecture which were being trained on large corpora of texts and are available for fine-tuning to different downstream tasks like textual classification, question answering. These models based upon the transformer architecture uses their tokenizers for the conversion of texts into embeddings which are based upon their own vocabularies. One major problem faced with these models built upon the transformer architecture is that they are only available for high resourced languages like English, German, and Chinese. To use these models for under-resourced languages, the researchers came up with the idea of cross-lingual transfer learning, which means training a model on a high resourced language and then fine-tuning it on a downstream task. A separate benchmark known as XNLI (Conneau et al., 2018) was being made to evaluate the model's performances across multiple languages.

The competition organizers have used the SVMs, MNBs , Decision Trees and other machine learning models as the baseline models for the given datasets. So, we went with using the models built upon the transformer architecture while approaching the problem. We have used the hugging face [4] transformers library for our implementations and used the original versions of the models as well as their customized versions with different loss functions. We have used multilingual-cased BERT (mBERT-cased), XLM-Roberta (XLMR), IndicBERT (Kakwani et al., 2020) , BERT-base-cased (BERT-cased) and BERT-base-uncased (BERT-uncased) models for our implementations. Pertaining to the large size of mBERT-cased and XLMR models we have used their customized versions as well by freezing the original model and stacking a fully connected layer of 512 neurons with a final layer having the same number of neurons as the number of our output classes. With this customized versions, we have used two different loss functions the Negative Log Likelihood (NLL) loss function with class weights, and the Sadice (Li et al., 2020) Loss function both of which were used to handle the data imbalance in the datasets. A pictorial representation of our customized architecture can be seen in the figure 1. Out of all the models mentioned above, mBERT-cased, XLMR, and IndicBERT are multilingual models, and BERT-cased and BERT-uncased models are monolingual models.

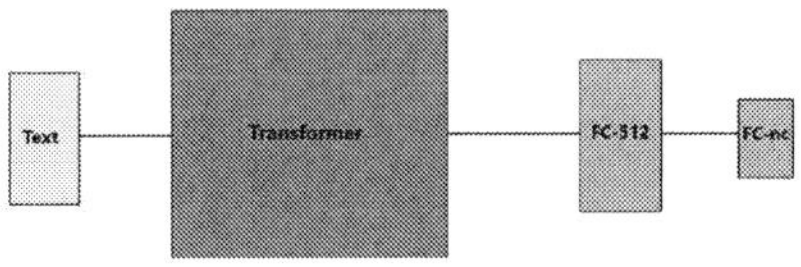

Figure 1: **Custom architecture :** We defined our custom architecture apart from the original transformer models as being built upon the transformer models as the base unit. The output attention heads from the transformer layers are further connected to a 512 neuron fully connected (FC) layer which is finally connected to another fully connected layer having number of neurons same as the number of classes denoted by nc

5 Results and Discussion

We have tried several different combinations of models discussed in the section 4 across the datasets of each language and have reported our results on the development set and the test set in the Table 2 and Table 3 respectively. The results are being reported in terms of weighted F1 scores as it was the evaluation measure being used by the competition organizers. We have used mBERT-cased, XLMR and IndicBERT as our models common across all the three datasets.

The original versions of these models as well as their customized versions, were also being used for finetuning purposes over the datasets. Attributing to the huge model size of mBERT-cased and

[4] https://huggingface.co/transformers/

Model	Tamil	Malayalam	English
mBERT-cased	0.62	0.84	0.93
Custom mBERT-cased with NLL loss and Class weights	0.52	0.63	0.87
Custom mBERT-cased with Sadice Loss	0.50	0.65	0.84
XLMR	0.62	0.83	0.93
Custom XLMR with NLL loss and Class weights	0.33	0.62	0.86
Custom XLMR with Sadice Loss	0.33	0.62	0.86
IndicBERT	0.59	0.82	0.92
BERT-cased	-	-	0.92
BERT-uncased	-	-	0.92

Table 2: Experiments with development dataset (in terms of weighted F1 scores)

Model	Tamil	Malayalam	English
mBERT-cased	**0.60**	**0.83**	**0.93**
Custom mBERT-cased with NLL loss and Class weights	0.50	0.65	0.87
Custom mBERT-cased with Sadice Loss	0.50	0.64	0.85
XLMR	0.59	0.59	**0.93**
Custom XLMR with NLL loss and Class weights	0.30	0.61	0.87
Custom XLMR with Sadice Loss	0.30	0.62	0.87
IndicBERT	0.55	0.72	0.92
BERT-cased	-	-	**0.93**
BERT-uncased	-	-	0.92

Table 3: Experiments with test dataset (in terms of weighted F1 scores)

XLMR we have also tried out their customized versions with the NLL loss and Sadice loss functions. Since the IndicBERT model is comparatively smaller than the other models, its original version was only being considered. Apart from these multilingual models two different monolingual models for the English dataset were also considered. Out of all the models, the original versions outperformed the customized versions of the models.

For the Tamil dataset XLMR, mBERT-cased and IndicBERT gave similar results on the development dataset. However, mBERT-cased gave comparatively better performances than XLMR and IndicBERT on the test dataset. For the Malayalam dataset, XLMR, mBERT-cased and IndicBERT had almost equivalent performances on the development dataset, but mBERT-cased gave much better results on the test set. Surprisingly, XLMR performed even worse than the IndicBERT model on the test set for Malayalam. For the English dataset, apart from the XLMR, IndicBERT, mBERT-cased the BERT-cased and BERT-uncased versions were also being tried and almost each model performed equivalently on the development dataset as well as the test datasets. The superior performance of mBERT over the other two models can be attributed to the training strategy of mBERT. It employs zero-shot cross-lingual model transfer, in which task-specific annotations in one language are used to fine-tune the model for evaluation in another language. A brief explaination of the multilingual nature of mBERT is being discussed in (Pires et al., 2019). On the other hand XLMR although being trained over much more data and having the same training strategy as (Liu et al., 2019) was expected to perform better across the multilingual tasks but it hasn't. We hypothesize the reason behind the degradation in it's performance can be attributed to the code-mixed nature of our dataset in hand. Since the XLMR model was being trained over the CommonCrawl data it could be possible that the data being utilised for the pretraining had very fewer instances of code-mixed data which thus leads to an overall inferior performance as compared to other models. The customized versions of these models were expected to address the skewness of the dataset but failed to do so. When inspecting these model's performances the reason for this performance degradation turned out to be the freezening of the base layers of the transformer models. The performance of these custom models can be further improved by having unfreezed layers which can further increase the performance of these models and can be considered for the future works on this task.

6 Conclusion

We have presented the IIITK team's approach for the hope speech detection shared task organized by DravidianLangTech. Our approach consisted of using the existing pretrained models and finetuning their original as well as the custom versions on the datasets. Out of all the models, the mBERT-cased model gave the best results for the Tamil and Malayalam datasets as 0.60 and 0.83 weighted F1 scores. For the English dataset, mBERT-cased and BERT-cased gave exactly similar results of 0.93 weighted F1 scores.

References

Shinu A Abraham. 2003. Chera, Chola, Pandya: Using archaeological evidence to identify the Tamil kingdoms of early historic South India. *Asian Perspectives*, pages 207–223.

Gaurav Arora. 2020. Gauravarora@hasoc-dravidian-codemix-fire2020: Pre-training ulmfit on synthetically generated code-mixed data for hate speech detection.

R Balachandran. 2005. Pioneers of tamil literature: Transition to modernity. *Indian Literature*, 49(2 (226):179–184.

Piotr Bojanowski, Edouard Grave, Armand Joulin, and Tomas Mikolov. 2017. Enriching word vectors with subword information.

Bharathi Raja Chakravarthi. 2020a. HopeEDI: A multilingual hope speech detection dataset for equality, diversity, and inclusion. In *Proceedings of the Third Workshop on Computational Modeling of People's Opinions, Personality, and Emotion's in Social Media*, pages 41–53, Barcelona, Spain (Online). Association for Computational Linguistics.

Bharathi Raja Chakravarthi. 2020b. *Leveraging orthographic information to improve machine translation of under-resourced languages*. Ph.D. thesis, NUI Galway.

Bharathi Raja Chakravarthi, Navya Jose, Shardul Suryawanshi, Elizabeth Sherly, and John Philip McCrae. 2020a. A sentiment analysis dataset for code-mixed Malayalam-English. In *Proceedings of the 1st Joint Workshop on Spoken Language Technologies for Under-resourced languages (SLTU) and Collaboration and Computing for Under-Resourced Languages (CCURL)*, pages 177–184, Marseille, France. European Language Resources association.

Bharathi Raja Chakravarthi and Vigneshwaran Muralidaran. 2021. Findings of the shared task on Hope Speech Detection for Equality, Diversity, and Inclusion. In *Proceedings of the First Workshop on Language Technology for Equality, Diversity and Inclusion*. Association for Computational Linguistics.

Bharathi Raja Chakravarthi, Vigneshwaran Muralidaran, Ruba Priyadharshini, and John Philip McCrae. 2020b. Corpus creation for sentiment analysis in code-mixed Tamil-English text. In *Proceedings of the 1st Joint Workshop on Spoken Language Technologies for Under-resourced languages (SLTU) and Collaboration and Computing for Under-Resourced Languages (CCURL)*, pages 202–210, Marseille, France. European Language Resources association.

Bharathi Raja Chakravarthi, Ruba Priyadharshini, Vigneshwaran Muralidaran, Shardul Suryawanshi, Navya Jose, Elizabeth Sherly, and John P. McCrae. 2020c. Overview of the Track on Sentiment Analysis for Dravidian Languages in Code-Mixed Text. In *Forum for Information Retrieval Evaluation*, FIRE 2020, page 21–24, New York, NY, USA. Association for Computing Machinery.

Bharathi Raja Chakravarthi, Navaneethan Rajasekaran, Mihael Arcan, Kevin McGuinness, Noel E. O'Connor, and John P. McCrae. 2020d. Bilingual lexicon induction across orthographically-distinct under-resourced Dravidian languages. In *Proceedings of the 7th Workshop on NLP for Similar Languages, Varieties and Dialects*, pages 57–69, Barcelona, Spain (Online). International Committee on Computational Linguistics (ICCL).

Junyoung Chung, Caglar Gulcehre, KyungHyun Cho, and Yoshua Bengio. 2014. Empirical evaluation of gated recurrent neural networks on sequence modeling.

Alexis Conneau, Kartikay Khandelwal, Naman Goyal, Vishrav Chaudhary, Guillaume Wenzek, Francisco Guzmán, Edouard Grave, Myle Ott, Luke Zettlemoyer, and Veselin Stoyanov. 2020. Unsupervised cross-lingual representation learning at scale.

Alexis Conneau, Guillaume Lample, Ruty Rinott, Adina Williams, Samuel R. Bowman, Holger Schwenk, and Veselin Stoyanov. 2018. Xnli: Evaluating cross-lingual sentence representations.

Jacob Devlin, Ming-Wei Chang, Kenton Lee, and Kristina Toutanova. 2019. Bert: Pre-training of deep bidirectional transformers for language understanding.

Reza Ghaeini, Sadid A. Hasan, Vivek Datla, Joey Liu, Kathy Lee, Ashequl Qadir, Yuan Ling, Aaditya Prakash, Xiaoli Z. Fern, and Oladimeji Farri. 2018. Dr-bilstm: Dependent reading bidirectional lstm for natural language inference. Cite arxiv:1802.05577Comment: 18 pages, Accepted as a long paper at NAACL HLT 2018.

Nikhil Kumar Ghanghor, Parameswari Krishnamurthy, Sajeetha Thavareesan, Ruba Priyadharshini, and Bharathi Raja Chakravarthi. 2021. IIITK@DravidianLangTech-EACL2021: Offensive Language Identification and Meme Classification in Tamil, Malayalam and Kannada. In *Proceedings of the First Workshop on Speech and Language Technologies for Dravidian Languages*, Online. Association for Computational Linguistics.

Adeep Hande, Ruba Priyadharshini, and Bharathi Raja Chakravarthi. 2020. KanCMD: Kannada CodeMixed dataset for sentiment analysis and offensive language detection. In *Proceedings of the Third Workshop on Computational Modeling of People's Opinions, Personality, and Emotion's in Social Media*, pages 54–63, Barcelona, Spain (Online). Association for Computational Linguistics.

George L Hart III. 2015. *Poets of the Tamil anthologies: Ancient poems of love and war.* Princeton University Press.

Siddhanth U Hegde, Adeep Hande, Ruba Priyadharshini, Sajeetha Thavareesan, and Bharathi Raja Chakravarthi. 2021. UVCE-IIITT@DravidianLangTech-EACL2021: Tamil Troll Meme Classification: You need to Pay more Attention. In *Proceedings of the First Workshop on Speech and Language Technologies for Dravidian Languages*. Association for Computational Linguistics.

Sepp Hochreiter and Jürgen Schmidhuber. 1997. Long short-term memory. *Neural computation*, 9(8):1735–1780.

Jeremy Howard and Sebastian Ruder. 2018. Universal language model fine-tuning for text classification.

Navya Jose, Bharathi Raja Chakravarthi, Shardul Suryawanshi, Elizabeth Sherly, and John P. McCrae. 2020. A Survey of Current Datasets for Code-Switching Research. In *2020 6th International Conference on Advanced Computing and Communication Systems (ICACCS)*, pages 136–141.

Divyanshu Kakwani, Anoop Kunchukuttan, Satish Golla, Gokul N.C., Avik Bhattacharyya, Mitesh M. Khapra, and Pratyush Kumar. 2020. IndicNLPSuite: Monolingual Corpora, Evaluation Benchmarks and Pre-trained Multilingual Language Models for Indian Languages. In *Findings of EMNLP*.

Quoc V. Le and Tomas Mikolov. 2014. Distributed representations of sentences and documents.

Xiaoya Li, Xiaofei Sun, Yuxian Meng, Junjun Liang, Fei Wu, and Jiwei Li. 2020. Dice loss for data-imbalanced nlp tasks.

Yinhan Liu, Myle Ott, Naman Goyal, Jingfei Du, Mandar Joshi, Danqi Chen, Omer Levy, Mike Lewis, Luke Zettlemoyer, and Veselin Stoyanov. 2019. Roberta: A robustly optimized bert pretraining approach.

Clarence Maloney. 1970. The beginnings of civilization in South India. *The Journal of Asian Studies*, pages 603–616.

Thomas Mandl, Sandip Modha, Anand Kumar M, and Bharathi Raja Chakravarthi. 2020. Overview of the HASOC Track at FIRE 2020: Hate Speech and Offensive Language Identification in Tamil, Malayalam, Hindi, English and German. In *Forum for Information Retrieval Evaluation*, FIRE 2020, page 29–32, New York, NY, USA. Association for Computing Machinery.

Chelnat Achyuta Menon. 1938. *Ezuttaccan and his age.* Ph.D. thesis, SOAS University of London.

Tomas Mikolov, Kai Chen, Greg Corrado, and Jeffrey Dean. 2013. Efficient estimation of word representations in vector space.

KR Norman. 1977. The Poems of Ancient Tamil: Their Milieu and Their Sanskrit Counterparts.

Shriphani Palakodety, Ashiqur R. KhudaBukhsh, and Jaime G. Carbonell. 2020. Hope speech detection: A computational analysis of the voice of peace.

Jeffrey Pennington, Richard Socher, and Christopher Manning. 2014. Glove: Global vectors for word representation. In *Proceedings of the 2014 Conference on Empirical Methods in Natural Language Processing (EMNLP)*, pages 1532–1543, Doha, Qatar. Association for Computational Linguistics.

Telmo Pires, Eva Schlinger, and Dan Garrette. 2019. How multilingual is multilingual bert?

Ruba Priyadharshini, Bharathi Raja Chakravarthi, Mani Vegupatti, and John P. McCrae. 2020. Named Entity Recognition for Code-Mixed Indian Corpus using Meta Embedding. In *2020 6th International Conference on Advanced Computing and Communication Systems (ICACCS)*, pages 68–72.

Karthik Puranik, Adeep Hande, Ruba Priyadharshini, Sajeetha Thavareesan, and Bharathi Raja Chakravarthi. 2021. IIITT@LT-EDI-EACL2021-Hope Speech Detection: There is always hope in Transformers. In *Proceedings of the First Workshop on Language Technology for Equality, Diversity and Inclusion*. Association for Computational Linguistics.

Sanford B Steever. 1998. Introduction to the Dravidian languages. *The Dravidian languages*, 1:39.

Burton Stein. 1977. Circulation and the historical geography of Tamil country. *The journal of Asian studies*, 37(1):7–26.

Ashish Vaswani, Noam Shazeer, Niki Parmar, Jakob Uszkoreit, Llion Jones, Aidan N. Gomez, Lukasz Kaiser, and Illia Polosukhin. 2017. Attention is all you need.

Alex Wang, Amanpreet Singh, Julian Michael, Felix Hill, Omer Levy, and Samuel R. Bowman. 2019. Glue: A multi-task benchmark and analysis platform for natural language understanding.

Konthala Yasaswini, Karthik Puranik, Adeep Hande, Ruba Priyadharshini, Sajeetha Thavareesan, and Bharathi Raja Chakravarthi. 2021. IIITT@DravidianLangTech-EACL2021: Transfer Learning for Offensive Language Detection in Dravidian Languages. In *Proceedings of the First Workshop on Speech and Language Technologies for Dravidian Languages*. Association for Computational Linguistics.

Association for Computational Linguistics
209 N. Eighth Street
Stroudsburg, Pennsylvania 18360

ISBN 978-1-7138-2970-6

CURRAN ASSOCIATES INC.
proceedings.com